PRAISE FOR *THE STARDAY STORY*

"The story of Starday, Nashville maverick of the fifties and sixties, is told well in this book for which Nathan Gibson was fortunate to have the help of Starday's glory years' president, the late Don Pierce. At a time of turmoil in Nashville, Pierce found ways to record and market a diversity of gritty music that's stood the test of time: rockabilly, gospel, bluegrass, honky-tonk, old-time, historic country, and more. Pierce's own comments and insights mix enthusiasm and business acumen in unique ways that make for fascinating reading."

—**Neil V. Rosenberg,** professor emeritus of folklore at Memorial University of Newfoundland and coauthor of *Bluegrass Odyssey: A Documentary in Pictures and Words, 1966–86*

"Starday is arguably the greatest maverick country music label of the 1950s–60s. Despite minimal investments in sessions and infrastructure, Starday produced lasting classics by George Jones, the Stanley Brothers, Cowboy Copas, Minnie Pearl, the Country Gentlemen, Ola Belle Reed, Charlie Monroe, Red Sovine, the Blue Sky Boys, Buzz Busby, Harry Choates, Johnny Bond, Carl Story, Jim & Jesse, the Stoneman Family, the Lewis Family, and many more, from celebrities to obscurities. Nate Gibson illuminates Starday's beginnings, growth, successes, failures, and demise, offering rare insights into country music and the industry it built over half a century ago."

—**Dick Spottswood,** author of *Banjo on the Mountain: Wade Mainer's First Hundred Years* and producer and online host of *The Dick Spottswood Show,* www.bluegrasscountry.org

"Based on a close collaboration between Starday founder Don Pierce and musician/scholar Nathan Gibson, *The Starday Story* is more than a company history; it's also the story of a man who believed in American grassroots music—from honky tonk to southern gospel to bluegrass—and tirelessly worked from 1953 until 1970 to build one of the largest, broadest-based, and most artistically successful post–World War II independent record companies."

—**Kip Lornell,** editor, with Tracy E. W. Laird, of *Shreveport Sounds in Black and White*

"In *The Starday Story*, Nate Gibson, musician, scholar, and sprightly writer, assembles a wealth of facts and photos and establishes the record label as a productive locus for an investigation of the relations between art and commerce and the connections among the varieties of American country music."

—**Henry Glassie,** professor emeritus of folklore at Indiana University and author of fourteen books, including *The Spirit of Folk Art, Passing the Time in Ballymenone,* and *The Stars of Ballymenone*

American Made Music Series
Advisory Board

David Evans, General Editor

Barry Jean Ancelet

Edward A. Berlin

Joyce J. Bolden

Rob Bowman

Susan C. Cook

Curtis Ellison

William Ferris

John Edward Hasse

Kip Lornell

Bill Malone

Eddie S. Meadows

Manuel H. Peña

David Sanjek

Wayne D. Shirley

Robert Walser

THE  STORY

THE HOUSE THAT COUNTRY MUSIC BUILT

by Nathan D. Gibson with Don Pierce

University Press of Mississippi / Jackson

www.upress.state.ms.us

The University Press of Mississippi is a member of
the Association of American University Presses.

The Starday logo has been provided courtesy of
Moe Lytle and © Gusto Records, Inc. Neither Moe Lytle
nor any of his employees—that he is aware of—have had
any input into this book, and he has not read the book.
He has only skimmed through a rough copy and, therefore,
does not endorse or give any permissions other than the
use of the logo. The book appears to end prior to Moe Lytle
purchasing Starday in 1973. The only thing pertaining to
Gusto Records after 1973 is a partial listing of the Starday
product that we have available now.

Copyright © 2011 by University Press of Mississippi
All rights reserved
Manufactured in the United States of America

First printing 2011

∞

Library of Congress Cataloging-in-Publication Data

Gibson, Nathan D.
The Starday story : the house that country music built /
by Nathan D. Gibson ; with Don Pierce.
p. cm. — (American made music series)
Includes bibliographical references and index.
ISBN 978-1-60473-830-8 (cloth : alk. paper) —
ISBN 978-1-60473-831-5 (ebook) 1. Starday Records, Inc.
2. Sound recording industry. 3. Country music—History
and criticism. I. Pierce, Don, 1915–2005. II. Title.
ML3792.S72G53 2011
782.421642—dc22   2010024269

British Library Cataloging-in-Publication Data available

CONTENTS

vii		FOREWORD
xi		INTRODUCTION
3	1	YOU ALL COME
24	2	ROCK IT
49	3	DON'T STOP THE MUSIC
79	4	RANK STRANGER
107	5	SUNNY TENNESSEE
129	6	GIDDY-UP GO
152	7	A SATISFIED MIND
171		NOTES
173		RECOMMENDED LISTENING
177		RECORD LISTING
249		BIBLIOGRAPHY
257		INDEX

FOREWORD

Country music and Starday Records were a labor of love for me from 1946 to 1970. I salute Nate Gibson and the publishers of this book for making the story available to country music fans.

I put up $330.00 to form the Starday Company with my friend Pappy Daily in 1953 and I was made president of the corporation. We never borrowed a dime. I am indebted to Pappy Daily for providing my opportunity and for his contribution in getting Starday Records started.

The story really starts when I associated with Bill McCall and 4 Star Records of Los Angeles in 1946. I was a stockholder and learned a lot about country music as it was our main endeavor. We had considerable success with T. Texas Tyler, the Maddox Bros. and Rose, Webb Pierce, Hank Locklin, and others. Working coast to coast in my car with record distributors, country music deejays, juke box operators, record dealers, artists, and songwriters was an education that I brought to Starday. The early successes of "Y'all Come" by Arlie Duff and "Why Baby Why" by George Jones established the label.

The association with Mercury Records of Chicago in 1957 enabled me to move Starday from Los Angeles to Nashville. It was in Nashville that Starday became a force in country music.

Working with Nate Gibson brought back so many memories. Nate is dedicated and he tirelessly examined all the Starday material that I had kept down through the years. He journeyed repeatedly to Nashville to interview all the people who were associated with Starday. He made many friends in Nashville, a city that I deeply appreciate. The ex-employees and musicians and songwriters were glad to be interviewed and help get the story told.

Starday records continue to be available from Starday-Gusto Records, 1900 Elm Hill Pike, Nashville, TN 37203.

It's very sad that Tommy Hill, who produced most of the music in the Starday Studios, passed away in 2003 and was not available for Nate Gibson to work with. Tommy was a great part of the Starday success and a dear friend. I'm also indebted to the late Martin Haerle of Stuttgart, Germany, plus Suzanne Mathis who had so much to do with the colorful Starday LP jackets. Chuck Chellman, Charlie Dick, Joan Proctor, John Rumble, "Hoss" Linneman, D. Kilpatrick, and Ralph Emery also contributed to Starday and to this story.

Don Pierce in his office lined with Starday LPs, November 1962 (Courtesy of Don Pierce)

It is gratifying that Starday achieved a respected position in the country music industry and achieved recognition internationally. I had wonderful, dedicated people to work with. The employees, the writers, the artists, the deejays, the distributors, the studio technicians, and the recognition by the music industry trade papers, the *Billboard, Cash Box, Music City News* and others who covered the country music industry. All this plus the never ending support from my family.

I regret my dear friends Cowboy Copas, Red Sovine, Tommy Hill, the Willis Brothers, Johnny Bond, and so many others are no longer with us, but their friendship and contribution will never be forgotten.

To maintain my dedication to country music and to provide recognition to people whose contributions merited Hall of Fame recognition, I started the Golden Eagle Master Achievement Awards that are presented each year in Nashville at the annual banquet of the Reunion of Professional Entertainers. Since 1990 these awards have gone to Webb Pierce, Faron Young, Ray Price, Porter Wagoner, Bill Anderson, Patsy Cline, Johnny Bond, and Conway Twitty, all of whom have since made it to the Hall of Fame. I'd like to think my award focused attention on their careers and helped them to get lasting recognition. I have also given awards to Cowboy Copas, Jean Shepard, Sonny

James, Carl Smith, Ferlin Husky, Tommy Hill, D. Kilpatrick, Pappy Daily, Joe Allison, Hawkshaw Hawkins, Tom Perryman, Roy Clark, Ralph Emery, and Jimmy Dean because I believe these people are deserving of special recognition.[Smith was inducted into the Country Music Hall of Fame in 2003, Roy Clark in 2009, and both Dean and Husky in 2010.]

I would like Starday to be remembered as a factor during a most difficult period for country record sales. Due to the new and overwhelming popularity of Elvis Presley and the advent of rock and roll, it was a difficult time for a country music record label to prosper. I'm proud Starday was able to do so.

Starday helped with the formation of the Country Music Association and I served on the board for several years. I also contributed to the building of the Country Music Hall of Fame building in Nashville. The tradition must be preserved. Country music will always be a part of our American culture and I'm glad I was able to make a contribution with Starday Records, truly, "The House That Country Music Built."

—DON PIERCE

INTRODUCTION

The Starday story is the tale of one of, if not *the*, most important independent labels in country music history—an empire based on East Texas honky-tonk, rockabilly, bluegrass, western swing, cowboy trios, old-time stringband music, Cajun ditties, jug bands, gospel quartets, square dance jigs, cornball comedians, polkas, and almost anything else that has, at one time or another, fallen under the mighty umbrella of "country music." Among industry professionals, the story is legendary. Among performers, the catalogue is textbook. Among record collectors, Starday can be an obsession. Yet beyond these insider circles, the Starday story has largely remained cloaked in mystery and obscurity. With the assistance of Starday president and co-founder Don Pierce, as well as dozens of Starday artists, employees, and family members, this shall finally end.

Shortly after I embarked upon this project, several friends and colleagues inquired as to how I wound up writing a book about Starday Records. I assume that many readers might be pondering the same question, and so I will do my best to explain. Several years ago, while attending Emerson College in Boston, Massachusetts, I met a professor named Rex Trailer. I soon discovered that he had played host to a country and western–themed children's television show for more than twenty years throughout New England called *Boomtown*. I further discovered that he had performed with Gene Autry and Bill Haley in the early 1950s and had recorded some mighty fine tunes on his own (my band later covered his 1956 ABC-Paramount recording of "Hoofbeats"). As I studied poetry and songwriting, Rex became my professor, mentor, senior advisor, and close friend. In 2001 we wrote and recorded a rockabilly-flavored country album entitled *Nate Gibson & the Gashouse Gang* and sang our playful compositions about TV remotes and the joys of Necco wafers.

It was while crafting those tunes that we discovered another 1950s country and western–themed children's television star living just two hours away. Kenny Roberts, known as both "The King of the Yodelers" and "The Jumping Cowboy," was a prolific recording artist who had four Top 20 country hits on the Coral label prior to 1951 (including "I Never See Maggie Alone," which reached number nine in *Billboard*'s pop charts as well)! Both Rex and Kenny had played music with Bill Haley during Haley's early cowboy days and each were members of the Massachusetts Country Music Hall of Fame. They knew all about each other from having watched their TV shows—although, surprisingly, the two cowboys had never met. Rex and I invited Kenny to one of our recording sessions and we were thrilled with Kenny's enthusiastic response.

Months prior to the session, I found a copy of Kenny's Starday album *Indian Love Call* (SLP 336). I bought it and was mesmerized. It was Suzanne Mathis's album art that first attracted me. It was so bright and campy. Then I listened to Kenny's awe-inspiring yodels. I began looking for and buying more Starday Records. Then more. And more. After I heard Kenny's stories about getting on the label and recording in Nashville with the Willis Brothers, I wanted to know more. Kenny then directed me to Howard Vokes, "Pennsylvania's King of Country Music," who also recorded an album for Starday. Howard kindly answered my many questions and also put me in touch with the talented Rose Lee Maphis. After an informative discussion regarding her Starday recordings with husband Joe, Rose Lee gave me the phone number of . . . Don Pierce. Wow, Don Pierce! I was excited to talk with and meet the man behind the label and couldn't believe he was so accessible. It was almost too easy. As I later discovered, directly across the street from Johnny Cash's House of Cash in Hendersonville was a giant sign for an office building that included several names, one of which was Don F. Pierce. Anybody could have found him.

I first called Don from Boston and told him that I was interested in his label and that I had some questions. He told me to get on a plane and come down to Nashville, and I did as I was told. We met at Don's office and talked for hours about Starday and country music in general and I was amazed by his personal stories and vast knowledge of the industry. As I looked around his office I saw several golf trophies, numerous framed articles on the Starday label, a giant cartoon sketch of Don (a long-ago Christmas gift from his Starday employees) and a plaque that read *"Billboard's* Country Music Man of the Year—1959." And here I was sitting with this legendary octogenarian who, leaning back in his office chair with his feet propped up on his desk and a cigar in hand, was spouting out vivid details of events that happened fifty and sixty years ago. I couldn't believe these stories had never been published. (I also couldn't believe that Don excused himself from our meeting so he could finish eighteen holes of golf before it got too dark!)

Don told me about starting the careers of George Jones, Roger Miller, Willie Nelson, Dottie West, Jimmy Dean, and many others. He remembered how Starday revived the careers of Cowboy Copas, Red Sovine, Johnny Bond, Moon Mullican, and more. He created the largest bluegrass catalog in the world. He told me about the early days of rockabilly and rivaling Sun Records. He spoke of marketing innovations, taking country music overseas and most importantly, preserving traditional country music when nobody else would.

I still wanted to know more and couldn't fathom how Starday, the leading independent country music label during the "Country Music Boom Years," had never had a single book dedicated to the subject. Don said that he would like to see one. I expressed to Don that I had just graduated with a Fine Arts degree in writing, literature, and publishing, and that I also shared his passion for country music. During my following trip to Nashville, in July 2003, we inked a deal to tell the story together. And that, my friends, is how *The Starday Story—The House That Country Music Built* came to be.

In the years that followed I regularly traveled back and forth between Boston and Nashville. Don shared with me his entire Rolodex and I instantly obtained access to countless musicians and industry professionals linked to Starday. I dedicated my life to researching the label and uncovering as many of the stories as possible, which proved to be one of the most difficult, yet enjoyable, endeavors in my life. There was always the intense pressure to "Hurry up and do it now while there are still people around who will enjoy it," but also the constant and even greater pressure to "Take your time and do it right." Sadly, several individuals who had dedicated their time and energy to this project passed away and are unable to celebrate in the finished work. Then, on April 3, 2005, I was saddened beyond words by the news that my collaborator and good friend Don Pierce, 89 years of age, had also passed on.

I received my last letter from Don just two weeks before his death. He was excited about the book and I dearly wish he could have seen the finished product. It is, however, somewhat comforting to know that Don knew his legacy would be remembered and retold. He was an incredible man and, as you will soon understand, his stories need to be preserved. I'm honored to be able to share these stories with the masses, and I'm hopeful that both Don Pierce and the Starday label will receive more credit for their massively important roles in country music history.

There are far too many people to thank everyone who has helped throughout the process, though a few people deserve special recognition. First I shall thank Andrew Brown, for without his generosity, continued support, and wisdom, this book would not be in your hands. I must also thank Suzanne Mathis both for designing such wonderful Starday album art and for her creative contributions and consultation for this book cover. Also deserving of my gratitude are Carmen Mitchell and Ruth White, both incredibly helpful to me, as a first-time author, with their invaluable publishing and legal advice. Dawn Oberg of the Country Music Hall of Fame was an immense help to me throughout my various stages of research and is deserving of much praise and gratitude. Country music fanatics Bob Ford and Darwin Lee Hill were also very generous in sharing their vast music collections and wisdom with me. Further, a sincere thank you is bestowed to Allan Turner and the *Hillbilly Researcher* for making their discography research (the Dixie custom series and the Starday singles #101–376) available for reprinting. Several other key contributors to the record listings published here are noted as such. I thank those within the Department of Folklore and Ethnomusicology at Indiana University for their acceptance and support of my ongoing country music research. (I had no idea at the time that sitting in a basement with Orangie Ray Hubbard, listening to our favorite records, or backing up Glenn Barber at a rockabilly festival could be considered ethnographic research.) I thank Dr. Jason Jackson for his guidance during indexing. I must also extend my sincere gratitude to Craig Gill and the good folks at the University Press of Mississippi. Andrew Brown, Dick Spottswood, and Neil V. Rosenberg, each offered valuable critiques of the early manuscript, and their contributions are much appreciated. A very special thanks to Will Rigby, my copy editor, are also in order. In addition, Don and Lari Pierce, Suzanne Mathis, Joan Proctor, and Jerri Smith were all so generous in welcoming a weary traveler into their homes over the years.

I also would like to take this opportunity to thank my family and friends for their ongoing support. Over the last few years my father and I had a healthy competition to see who would finish writing our books first. While I was researching the Starday saga, my father kept busy editing a collection of his "wisdom-discoveries," as he calls them, from his more than fifty years in the ministry. I may have lost this particular battle (see *Beyond the Orthodox Box: Thoughts of a Free Mind and Liberated Spirit* by F. Donald Gibson), though the competition was certainly a healthy motivator. I now take great pride in having both books next to each other on the same shelf. My mother, Julie, and brother, Adam, have been equally supportive and encouraging throughout this often stressful process. Renee Payot and Moseley are also due *immense* thanks for their day-to-day dealings with me in my more often than not sleep-deprived state. Enough kind words could not be said. I further extend my thanks to all current and former band members (Nate Gibson & the Gashouse Gang) for their continued willingness to learn and perform song after song from the Starday catalogue. I also appreciate my many similarly project-oriented friends who continually motivate me to keep writing and creating, no matter the day's circumstances: Tim Barney, Idan Ben-Arieh, Fred Chao, Chris Cugini, Pat Duggan, Emily Gabrian, Amma Ghartey-Tagoe, Aman Gill, Tobias Hathorn, Al Hawkes, Rob Lowe, Garet McIntyre, Sean Mencher, Peter Meulenbrook, Barry Neely, Travis Quam, Tom Umberger, and countless others. Thank you!

Many Starday artists and employees donated their time to making sure this story was told, and told accurately, and I am deeply indebted to them. Sadly, personal interviews with several important Starday personnel remain absent. Starday engineer Tommy Hill passed away just before I seriously undertook this project. Gospel legend Roy "Pop" Lewis passed away at age 98, just days after my initial request for an interview. Buck Owens had expressed an interest in this project as well, informing his manager, "Oh yeah, I've got some great Don Pierce stories to tell this guy," but passed on just days before our interview was to take place. I would have loved to share their stories within this Starday context, though it simply was not to be. In addition, numerous artists have come forth in the last year or so to share their stories. While I am always excited to talk with anybody about Starday, especially artists who recorded for Starday, I am unfortunately unable to include everybody's story. In this introduction to the label, there simply isn't enough space to cover every angle. I do, however, want to thank even those artists who generously offered their time but were not featured in this book. Their accounts greatly aided my understanding of the label's history and my hope is that future Starday projects will develop and those stories will be afforded their just due. And to Rudy Grayzell, I can't thank you enough for your help and continued phone calls along the way. And lastly (seriously), this project would have been absolutely impossible were it not for the hundreds of good people within the eBay community who were eager to see this project come to fruition and who sold me their Starday stuff for cheap. I am eternally grateful for the opportunity to share with you now the completed work. Thank you!

So this is it. This is their story. The people who made Starday Records. The artists and behind-the-scenes people. The innovative business tactics of an independent powerhouse record label. The struggle to keep traditional country music alive in one of country music's most turbulent times. The fight against rock 'n' roll. The efforts to preserve America's roots music. The resistance to the Nashville Sound. Bluegrass. Gospel and sacred. The honky-tonk. The rockabilly. Western swing and cowboy westerns. The old-timey and old-timers. Anything and everything Americana. It is the struggle to make music that you actually enjoy and still make money. And it is the preservation of a label that ultimately preserved our nation's musical heritage.

It should be noted that this book is not in any way meant to be the complete everything-that-ever-happened-at-Starday story, as that would surely encompass hundreds of volumes. Nor is this meant to be a guide for record collectors with dead wax pressing numbers and a listing of all the obscure records, one-offs, and label misprints. It is not a sessionography of every single studio session for every artist. And it is not the George Jones story or the Stanley Brothers story or the Roger Miller story. Those stories have already been told in depth several times before. Likewise, it is not heavily concentrated on any one particular aspect of the label. Because this story has never been published in book form, and because several versions of this story have been rehashed rather inaccurately, let this book serve as your guide and

Don Pierce and Nathan Gibson at Shawnee Waters in 2003. Photo by Lari Pierce. (Courtesy of Nathan Gibson)

introduction to one of the most important and innovative independent music labels of the twentieth century.

As you peruse the book, enjoy the dozens of unpublished behind-the-scenes photographs from Don's personal collection. Over the years Don had collected hundreds of photographs from the Starday studio sessions and social gatherings and it was such a thrill to pick through them and choose the very best for this book. In addition, a good number of these photos have been plucked from my personal inventory of country music promotional photographs. Special credit and thanks are due to the specific artists who donated photographs from their private collections as noted. In particular, I would like to thank Bud Daily, son of Harold "Pappy" Daily, and the daughters of Jack Starns, Joyce Kelley and Darlena Blackwell, for the generous sharing of their stories and family images.

From the firsthand experiences of Don Pierce, as well as many of the artists and industry professionals, this truly is *The Starday Story: The House That Country Music Built*. We thank you for your continued support of traditional country music.

Country Musically,
NATHAN GIBSON

THE STARDAY STORY

★ ★ ★

1

YOU ALL COME

Lefty Frizzell's boyish good looks and quirky, swooping vocal style won him the hearts of millions of fans across the United States. By the end of 1951 he had appeared on the Grand Ole Opry and the Louisiana Hayride, had four songs in *Billboard*'s Top 10 charts simultaneously, and had just completed a nationwide tour with country music superstar Hank Williams. His #1 successes included "If You've Got the Money, I've Got the Time," "I Want To Be With You Always," "I Love You a Thousand Ways," "Always Late," "Give Me More, More, More (of Your Kisses)," as well as several other top chart entries. Frizzell certainly had talent. He also possessed charm. He had a Gibson J-200 guitar customized by Paul Bigsby and by 1951 had attained a celebrity status enjoyed by few other country music performers.

By 1952 Frizzell had his own Cadillac. He also had a tour bus. He even had his own private plane. He had millions of adoring fans waiting for him to play their dancehall or auditorium and he also had women. The man who made Frizzell's dream that reality, promoting him through the biggest boom of his career, was his manager and promoter Burl Houston Starns Jr., better known in country music circles as Jack Starns Jr. (the spelling of Starns has varied depending on the publication or family member, but on Starday legal documents and contracts the preferred spelling was Starns).

Frizzell and Starns's relationship began in January 1950 when Frizzell was booked at Neva's Club in Beaumont, Texas. The club owner was Starns's wife, Neva Starns Dupree, who maintained the adjacent café, cooked the food, booked the nightclub talent, and also managed a majority of the acts who played the club (via Neva's Managing and Booking Agency). Neva, an experienced manager of East Texas nightclubs, purchased the café on Port Arthur Road that previously had been owned by western swingster Cliff Bruner. She had just begun booking hillbilly talent when Frizzell arrived in town.

Frizzell at this time was still gaining national popularity, but had recently become frustrated and dissatisfied with his existing management team of Jim Beck and Art Satherley, who kept 66 percent of his total earnings. When Jack

Lefty Frizzell in the Starnses's living room (Courtesy of Joyce Kelley and Darlena Blackwell)

Starns learned of Frizzell's unfortunate situation, he thought he could be a better managerial fit for Lefty. Having become increasingly familiar with the ins and outs of the music business through Neva's management operation, he then set out to convince Frizzell. Beaumont radio station KTRM disc jockey Boyd Whitney is said to have introduced the two.

Starns followed Frizzell and his band for the next week, catering to their every need. If a band member didn't show up, Starns would find another. If a club lacked a sound system, Starns would get one. Starns bought the entire band new duds as an advance against show royalties and also picked up their hotel tab for the week. He promised to promote Frizzell to the fullest extent and even offered to "take care of" the whole Beck and Satherley contract fiasco. All Frizzell would have to do is split his earnings with Starns 50/50. Those earnings included royalties from Lefty's Columbia recordings, royalties from cover versions by other artists, royalties from sheet music sales, and money made from personal appearances as well as any radio, TV, and movie spots. After a week of deliberation, Frizzell accepted the offer. After all, getting 50 percent of his total earnings was a lot better than 33 percent. The deal became official on January 26, 1950.

Early in the relationship, change proved positive. Starns assisted Frizzell in both the bus and plane acquisitions. He secured multiple show dates on the Louisiana Hayride and the Grand Ole Opry and, along with Neva, even bought a second club, the Reo Palm Isle in Longview, Texas, to give Frizzell and his band another home base. Further, when Uncle Sam acquired the services of three of Frizzell's bandmates, including his brother, Starns went out and auditioned Blackie Crawford and his Tune Toppers to fill the vacancies.

Unfortunately, the relationship soured not long after. Frizzell became agitated with Starns's zig-zag booking of back and forth shows in Louisiana, Chicago, Dallas, California, Arkansas, and so on. Despite the success, Frizzell had grown weary and tired from the excessive traveling. Soon, all he desired was a break at home with his pregnant wife, Alice, and his daughter. By October 1951 Frizzell was ready to give up the touring, the drinking, and the womanizing. He wanted it to end, but knew he could not return to Beaumont until his contract ended. Sometime in mid-October, Frizzell asked Alice to fetch the contract, which had been in Starns's control since it had been signed, so that he could inform her as to when he would be home next. It was then that Frizzell discovered a clause at the end of his contract giving Starns the option for, "His services in a similar capacity for two years, the term of which option is to immediately follow the term of this contract."[1]

Frizzell went to his grave adamantly swearing that Starns added the clause after the contract had been signed, but after a heated debate with Starns, decided to finish the last year of the contract and hoped he could somehow get out of the next two years. Frustrated with touring the Canadian provinces in the winter of 1951, however, Frizzell threatened to cancel his remaining shows. Starns then threatened to put him behind bars. The tour was completed as scheduled but when Lefty returned, Starns served him papers suing for $25,500. The claim:

> That prior to January 26, 1951, the defendant had attempted to engage in the writing and publishing of songs for profit, as well as that of a musician

Jack Starns, ca. 1940s (Courtesy of Joyce Kelley and Darlena Blackwell)

presenting and singing such songs at various places of entertainment where he might procure employment; that nevertheless the said defendant had not acquired sufficient publicity and reputation whereby he was able, with profit to himself, to follow such composing, selling and producing of said music, nor the vending of his services as a musician and entertainer.[2]

Backing his statement was a copy of the contract signed by Frizzell and a copy of the letter notifying Frizzell that he would be exercising his option for the following two years. The $25,500 was made up of money Starns would have made if Frizzell had not cancelled twenty shows in Ohio due to a sore throat plus two royalty checks, one each from Columbia and Frizzell's publisher, Hill and Range.

Frizzell then countersued for $50,000, claiming that Starns never properly "took care of" the Beck and Satherley contract. If the claim could be proven, Starns's contract with Frizzell would have been bogus and Frizzell would be due the $50,000 Starns had already collected from the deal. Starns and his lawyers then amended their claim so that it included an extra $13,000 in royalties (accrued from January to June) as well as half of Frizzell's estimated income for the next two years, bringing their total claim to over $100,000. A court date was set for June 1952, though Frizzell and Starns settled just before their scheduled court date. The exact settlement was never disclosed, though Lefty's wife Alice remembered, "Lefty had paid out over $25,000" just to get

Starns out of his life and that after all was said and done, "he didn't have a dime left."[3]

Thus, the seeds were planted, not only for a great country song, but also for the beginning of a legendary country music label.

Despite the legal troubles and the separation with Frizzell, life remained fairly luxurious for Jack "Stickpen" Starns, as he came to be known in Texas. During the previous two and a half years he had gained valuable experience as both a manager and a promoter. He learned a few legal tricks along the way and he had made valuable connections with musicians, club owners and promoters throughout the country. He retained Frizzell's backing band, now called Blackie Crawford and his Western Cherokees, and most importantly, Starns had money. Why not form a record label? The only thing Starns lacked was a partner who really knew about the country music industry. He had hoped to find someone who could recognize market trends and who would know what was selling at the time. He had also hoped to find someone with access to talented artists interested in recording for a new label. Enter Harold Westcott "Pappy" Daily of Houston, Texas.

How "Pappy" Daily and Jack Starns became business partners is still something of a mystery, though Starns was surely aware of Daily's established jukebox operations. Daily got his start in the music business as a South Coast Amusement Company jukebox operator and distributor in the early 1930s. Initially he was servicing "one-armed bandit" gambling machines as well as jukeboxes, but soon found the jukebox business far more profitable. By 1935, *Billboard* magazine reported that Daily was the largest operator of music in Texas. In 1946 he opened his own record store in Houston, Daily's Record Ranch, and featured local artists on the Saturday morning jamborees broadcast from within the store. He then became a key distributor for Decca and MGM, in addition to servicing other major labels such as Brunswick, Capitol, RCA, and even Frizzell's Columbia. In addition, Daily also distributed many independent labels such as Blue Bonnet and 4 Star.

Perhaps most important of all these was 4 Star Records, owned by Bill McCall and based in Pasadena, California. Daily had inked a deal with McCall to make him 4 Star's Texas distributor; in exchange for their business, Daily would round up local talent, record them at his own expense, and send the masters to 4 Star. Though he never received money from 4 Star for his scouting services, he was grateful for the opportunity to help a new artist get started. If Daily heard a song he liked, not only could he help the artist wax a recorded version, he also would convince 4 Star to press it, and then stock the song on jukeboxes throughout Texas. Daily became a one-man hit-making machine. According to Daily's son Bud Daily, it was because of this generosity and sincere love for country music that country music star Hank

Pappy Daily arriving in San Antonio, ca. 1959 (Courtesy of Bud Daily)

Locklin first dubbed him "Pappy." As he continued to assist more and more artists, the name stuck. Starday artist James O'Gwynn further explained to Martin Hawkins in 1976, "[Pappy] is one of the greatest men in the country business. He has been just like a father to us, and all the musicians around Houston think the world of him."[4]

Among those early Texas artists Daily helped and sent to 4 Star were Locklin, Jerry Jericho, R. D. Hendon, Eddie Noack, and Webb Pierce. As far as 4 Star was concerned, they could not find a better distributor. Not only did Daily record and produce the artists, he even bought enough of the pressings to guarantee 4 Star would at least break even. Daily later recalled, "I felt that everybody should have an opportunity and I started out with that in mind, rather than making money. Of course, you've got to make money to be successful, but I did it from the standpoint of trying to give as many people the opportunity they wanted."[5]

Yet, while Bill McCall's pockets got bigger, not once did he offer Daily any form of compensation. According to Don Pierce, then vice president of 4 Star,

McCall never even gave Daily a discount on the records he purchased. Pierce recalls, "Pappy didn't ask for anything. He was happy to promote and sell the records. And I think he enjoyed helping these young guys get a start in the business. But it wasn't long before he realized that Bill McCall was taking total advantage of him." They severed their relationship in 1952, roughly the same time Starns settled his case with Frizzell.

Thus, Starns, an artist manager with pockets jingling and a reputation as a stern businessman, set out to meet Daily, the lovable record producer and music distributor ready to start making money for himself. It seemed only natural that the two would find each other and form their own record label. As Bud Daily recalls, "Jack was a promoter. He did shows and so forth. He thought a record company would be a wise step. So he came over and saw Dad and talked him into it. Dad was reluctant even though he'd had some success producing Webb Pierce."[6]

As reluctant as Daily might have been at first, the two eventually agreed to form a label. Starns, after all, had a plan. In a letter he wrote to *Country Song Roundup* in October 1952, Starns said: "A good recording company is first, good songs are next, a good artist that is willing to work and cooperate is next, then you go from there."[7] He already had several cooperative artists lined up with good songs in mind. All he needed now was a good recording company. Daily was convinced and on June 20, 1953, *Billboard* announced the formation of a new record label: Starday Records—the "Star" originating from Starns's last name, the "Day" from Daily's.

The first groups signed to the new label were those who had already performed at Neva's Café and who were managed by Neva Starns. Like Daily, who had gained a reputation as a second parent to many of his young artists, Neva was supportive and loved by the acts she managed. Though she was never formally a Starday "owner," many of the early Starday contracts and press releases listed her as such. (In some cases contracts simply listed Jack Starns Jr. as the sole owner of Starday.) Jack and Neva worked closely together in those early months to make Starday successful in Beaumont, despite their vastly different managing styles. Joyce Kelley, daughter of Jack and Neva and unofficial Starday employee, remembers: "[Neva] was one of the truest, loveliest ladies you'll ever meet. I couldn't live long enough to become as nice as she was. She wouldn't have known how to spank you even if she could. She would never even raise her voice. Kinda different from Daddy. I would never ever say anything to my Daddy in my whole life except, 'Yes sir.' 'No sir.' We all did it. It's not that we thought he would hurt us, but we never wanted to try him."

The most significant act immediately signed to the new label was thirty-year-old Robert Lawrence (sometimes listed as Larry) "Blackie" Crawford and his band, the Western Cherokees. Not only did the band write and record their

Neva Starns (Courtesy of Joyce Kelley and Darlena Blackwell)

own songs (Crawford also co-wrote Frizzell's signature cut "Always Late"), they also backed the majority of the early Starday artists on their recordings. Crawford, a bandleader, guitarist, and vocalist, was associated with Bob Manning and his Riders of the Silver Sage in the late 1940s. By 1950 that band evolved into the Sons of Texas, then led by Crawford, and was based out of Dallas. The boys then became Frizzell's backing band and renamed themselves the Tune Toppers in early 1951 but later that year changed their name to the Western Cherokees.

After the split with Frizzell, Neva Starns organized a recording contract with Coral Records where they recorded two sessions. In December 1951 the boys returned to Beaumont after a brief stint in Oklahoma City, and became the resident band at the Starnses's Palm Isle nitery three nights a week. When they were signed to Starday in May 1953, the group consisted of Crawford on vocals and lead guitar, Robert Shivers on solo fiddle and vocals, Glendle "Pee Wee" Wharton on fiddle (Wharton left the group shortly after the first Starday session), Bob Heppler on second fiddle and vocals, Bobby Black on steel guitar, Milburn "Burney" Annett on piano and vocals, Luther Nallie on rhythm guitar, tenor banjo, and occasionally lead guitar, Blackie's brother Bud Crawford on bass, and Jimmy Dennis on drums. As was the case with most western swing bands, membership changed frequently. During their Starday tenure other known musicians included Sinton "Corlue" Bordelon on steel guitar, Freddie Frank on guitar and vocals, Herman McCoy on lead guitar, Jimmy Biggar on steel guitar, and the Hayes Brothers—Joe "Red"

Blackie Crawford's first publicity photo for Starday (Courtesy of Nathan Gibson)

Hayes on fiddle, Kenneth "Little Red" Hayes also on fiddle, and Leon Hayes on upright bass.

The very first Starday recordings were made at Bill Holford's ACA Recording Studios in Houston, Texas. The first eight 78 masters (101, 102, 103, and 104) were cut at ACA on May 21, 1953, and the 45 masters were cut on May 27. It is likely that they were all released in either late June or early July. The first Starday release was credited to Mary Jo Chelette, a thirteen-year-old songstress from Port Arthur, Texas.

Mary Jo Chelette promoting both her and Starday's first single, "Cat Fishing" (Courtesy of Nathan Gibson)

Though Chelette often performed with her two sisters as the Chelette Sisters, her first and Starday's first release was a solo effort about the perils of being a young girl titled "Gee, It's Tough To Be Thirteen" (101). The sad lament was paired with a more upbeat toe-tapper in "Cat Fishing," though neither side took with the masses. Chelette went on to record several more songs for Starday including her answer record "Son of Mexican Joe" (answer to Jim Reeves's hit "Mexican Joe") paired with "You Can Be the One" (an answer to Hank Locklin's hit "Let Me Be the One") (112).

The second Starday release (102) featured Crawford himself singing "Mariuch (Mootie-Ooch)," a swinging western novelty tune sung in a noticeably strained Italian dialect. The flipside was a flashy instrumental, "Cherokee Steel Guitar," featuring twin guitar and twin fiddle parts. The next release (103) was a catchy solo effort by the Cherokees' own fiddler, Bob Heppler. "I Don't Like It" was a well-rehearsed gem in the western swing genre, though apparently the disc jockeys either didn't like it or they just didn't hear it.

The fourth release, however, was that special song—the hit. It had an instantly recognizable refrain and is among country music's most beloved standards. Arlie Duff, who would quickly become known as "The Singing Schoolteacher," recalls in his autobiography: "On the way to Beaumont I stopped off at Neva's Café to coffee up. I could hear a country band playing in the back. Neva said Blackie Crawford and the Western Cherokees were rehearsing. She asked me if I had ever done any singing. Said I had done some gospel singing with my dad and sister. Then she asked if I had written any songs. I said, 'No. Wait a minute, yes. I did write one.' 'What's it called?' '"You All Come."' 'You mind doing it with the band?' I went back, shook hands with old Blackie and the boys, huddled and a song was born."[8]

Roughly two weeks later Jack and Neva took Duff to Holford's ACA Recording studio where they were joined by Daily. As Duff tore into his rip-roaring, top-of-his-lungs, top-of-his-vocal-range country call, both Starns and Daily knew they were capturing a hit. With a melody lifted directly from the old children's folk song "She'll Be Coming 'Round the Mountain," "You All Come" was both catchy and oddly familiar. The flipside, "Poor Ole Teacher" (104), was written on the spot. As Duff recalled to researcher Andrew Brown: "We got through with 'You All Come,' and they said, 'Well, what else you got?' I said, 'I don't have anything . . . I thought you'd have something.' [Laughter] I said, 'Where's the piano . . . let me sit down a few minutes, and I'll have one.' So I wrote 'Poor Ole Teacher' . . . [It took] about five minutes, probably. The idea was . . . it was what was actually happening to me. The school board, you know, it was politics, a lot of it. A group got in and fired half the teachers. I was one of 'em they fired. Then they hired me back, then fired me again. Then hired me back again. And they gave me a $100 raise very time they hired me back. [Laughter] 'About that time, the school board met, and wham, he's gone again.' That was a line in the song."

Once the record was released, Neva took over as Duff's manager and began to book the singer across Texas, Oklahoma, and Louisiana. The gigs began to pile up and the radio plugs kept coming. Soon, Duff was receiving billing alongside such stars as Jimmy Heap, Minnie Pearl, Hank Locklin, and Red Foley (who would later serve as best man at his wedding). So much traveling was required that Duff hired Jack and Neva's son, Bill Starnes, who was then

Arlie Duff sporting his Warren, TX, basketball coach letter jacket, ca. 1954 (Courtesy of Nathan Gibson)

managing Ferlin Husky as well, to drive Duff's Cadillac between shows. Yet Duff, who was both a high school teacher and basketball coach, was not quite prepared for a musician's life on the road. "My first booking was Magnolia Gardens, just south [actually east] of Houston. Leading a rather sheltered life, I just wasn't ready for my next encounter," Duff recalled. "Fleshy ladies with tight roll cigarettes hanging from their lips, a baby in one hand and a bottle of suds in the other. I hurried back to the motel as soon as it was over, read a few verses from a Gideon, and my face began to clear up."9

Duff, knowing that many country hits were based on old country phrases, wrote "You All Come" after hearing his grandmother say it seventeen times on the way to school one day. In a fit of inspiration, he wrote the song in twenty minutes. He auditioned it at Neva's Café six months later. He recorded it two weeks after that. And on December 5, 1953, Duff entered the *Billboard* charts.

While this momentum was building, Starns and Daily realized just how little they knew about running a record label. The Starns duo knew how to book and promote the artists, and Daily knew how to scout talent and produce a good record. Unfortunately, nobody knew how to get their records played on radio stations or sold in stores on a national level. Around this time Daily received a phone call from his California friend, Don Pierce. Like Daily, Pierce was frustrated with McCall and 4 Star and was looking for a new label where he could put his knowledge of the music industry to use.

Pierce, who changed his name from Picht after an onslaught of mispronunciations, was born October 10, 1915, and grew up in Seattle, Washington. After completing a BA in economics at the University of Washington, a brief career as an insurance salesman, and a three-year stint in the army, Pierce found himself in California in 1946. While searching for employment, Pierce responded to an ad about a record operation in Los Angeles. Dick Nelson, who had started the Gilt-Edge label, was offering an opportunity with a new record label he started along with recording engineer Cliff McDonald, called 4 Star Records. They had already scored a few hits with T. Texas Tyler, but had recently fallen on hard times. In order to make money and keep recording, McDonald offered Pierce a half interest share in his All-Star Artist Bureau. With the eagerness of another hit on the way and also getting a start in the potentially lucrative music industry, Pierce accepted the offer and promptly cashed in his $5,000 in war bonds.

Unfortunately for Pierce, McDonald began recording veteran pop bands such as Ted Fio Rito and Ray Herbeck as well as jazz bands such as Slim Gaillard and Charles "Baron" Mingus. Though the artists were popular and well established, the recordings never made any money for the label, and therefore neither Pierce nor McDonald ever received any royalties from Nelson. Finances continued to get worse, when along came a mining engineer named Bill McCall. McCall owned and operated the milling plant which made the raw material 4 Star records were pressed from and became quite wealthy in the process. To help Nelson out of certain doom, McCall paid him $5,000 for his 50 percent share of 4 Star. Pierce remembers that McCall was also somehow able to talk McDonald out of 5 percent of his stock. This left Pierce stranded as a minority stockholder in a sinking company. All Pierce could do was to continue promoting and selling records in the hope of finding another hit and recouping at least a fragment of his investment.

Though his relationship with McCall was strained, to say the least, Pierce acknowledges that McCall was the man who taught him about the record business. While under McCall's tutelage, Pierce was responsible for the office administration work, national sales and promotion as well as a large portion of the recording (Pierce produced T. Texas Tyler's 1948 classic "Deck of Cards," which reached the #2 spot on *Billboard*'s country charts, as well as "Philadelphia Lawyer" by the Maddox Brothers and Rose). It was the responsibility of Pierce to travel from coast to coast establishing relationships with disc jockeys, jukebox operators and distributors; during one of these road trips, Pierce met Daily in Houston. The two became fast friends. As Pierce recalled to Colin Escott, "I would always go to Houston and work with him [Daily] down there because he had been so fantastic at not only finding talent, but recording them. He'd send in the tapes, order a thousand copies of the record, then go out and promote and sell the record. How often do you find a distributor that will do that?"[10]

During his time at 4 Star, Pierce also learned the importance of music publishing. Pierce and McCall had been stocking up on publishing rights to the songs they were releasing, but for a long time had no connection with BMI or ASCAP. They had simply wanted to control the songs to ensure they would still get royalties if somebody else covered their song and scored a huge hit. It seemed to Pierce that because he was driving coast to coast and getting airplay on as many radio stations as possible, 4 Star should be making money from his efforts. After some resistance from McCall, the two registered with BMI and when their first statement came in with a check for over $2,000, they knew they had to have more copyrights.

As the company began to turn a profit, Pierce jumped at the opportunity to get out. McCall, however, would not make it easy. According to Pierce, "I finally got him to agree at his lawyer's office to buy my stock or to pay me a bonus of $10,000. He agreed to pay $15,000 and acquire my shares. But when it came time to consummate the agreement, he said, 'No, I'm not gonna buy the stock.'" The two went back and forth until, eventually, they found themselves in a courtroom. Pierce called McCall's lawyer to the stand to testify under oath against McCall, which he did, and it seemed as though Pierce was finally free. Again McCall agreed to buy him out, but before any money exchanged hands, again McCall backed out.

To the rescue came Syd Nathan, owner of the mighty independent King Records. As Pierce remembers, "The first time I came to Cincinnati, that old nearly blind Jewish gentleman invited me to his house, fed me on pheasant and cold beer, and somehow seemed to like me." The two became good friends and, when Pierce learned that McCall was about to strike a deal with Nathan and King Records to handle all of 4 Star's promotions, Pierce phoned Nathan. Pierce says: "I phoned him [Nathan] and told him what Bill was trying to do to me. He said, 'I'll send Jack Kelly, my vice president out there,' and Jack Kelly told Bill, 'We will not take on your line and distribute it until you complete your deal . . . and you've taken care of Don.' I'll never forget it. It's great to have friends like Syd Nathan."

McCall and Pierce finally parted ways in March or April 1953. "Bill finally did get me down to $12,000, and paid me over a period of three years, so that gives you some idea of what I went through with him. He took me to the cleaners big time," adds Pierce. (It also provides an idea of what the Maddox Brothers and Rose, T. Texas Tyler, Webb Pierce, Patsy Cline, or any other 4

Star artists might have dealt with in their business with McCall.) Despite the aggravation, Don Pierce was a free man.

After a few months of unsuccessful job hunting in Los Angeles, Pierce, by now both a husband and a father, was growing desperate. He attempted to create a country label with Lew Chudd of Imperial Records, though Chudd had just gotten rid of one business partner and was not looking for another. Pierce recalls: "It was along about August of 1953 that I picked up the *Billboard* and saw some record reviews on a label called Starday. I called the *Billboard* in Hollywood and I said, 'Who is operating that country label?' 'Why, Pappy Daily is operating that.' Pappy is a friend of mine, and I called him. He said, 'Yeah, we started a label with Jack Starns who is separated now from Lefty Frizzell. What are you doing?' 'Well, I left Bill McCall.' 'I'm glad to hear that. You just get on the next airplane and come down here right away.'"

Pierce took his orders from Daily and caught the first plane headed south. Once in Houston, Pierce got acquainted with Starns and the three men founded the Starday Recording and Publishing Company. The publishing company, Starrite, and subsequent BMI affiliation was significant because the first four Starday releases (including the first pressings of "You All Come") failed to reference any publishing information on the label. This would have made collecting airplay royalties next to impossible. Each man contributed $333 to the cause and each man owned one-third of the Starday pie. Starns became the designated talent scout. Daily was in charge of record production. Pierce, who would be the only full-time employee, was designated as the Starday president and returned to California to set up the corporation.

As promising as things appeared, the corporation becoming official and a hit song on the charts, nobody made any money from Starday during the first fourteen months of operation. Every penny made was put back into the company for more record releases, production costs, office fees, etc. Starns still made money from his nightclubs and Daily made money through his distributorship. In order for Pierce to draw an immediate paycheck he set up his own rhythm and blues label, Hollywood Records.

Shortly after returning to California, Pierce became acquainted with John Dolphin, one of Los Angeles's R&B moguls. Dolphin owned Dolphin's of Hollywood, among the most prominent record stores in Los Angeles, and ran radio broadcasts by Hunter Hancock and Dick "Huggie Boy" Hugg from the store. He had also started his own record label, Dolphin's of Hollywood, which later became Recorded In Hollywood, and began releasing records in 1948. By 1953 Dolphin had released several successful recordings by Linda Hayes, Percy Mayfield, Little Caesar, Pee Wee Crayton, and Red Callender, but had recently encountered economic hardship and could no longer afford to operate the label. Pierce took over the label in 1953 and changed the name to Hollywood Records, while Dolphin continued to produce the recording sessions. Pierce remembers being approached by Dolphin with the business opportunity. "He [Dolphin] had a hit with Linda Hayes and Linda and her husband were screaming about royalties and one thing or another and he made some kind of a deal to settle up with 'em. And now they want to record again. He says, 'Don she's just coming off a hit and you have the chance to make the next record on her. So go to Capitol and make this record.' I did and I paid for it and it was a successful record." According to Pierce, Hayes's "Take Me Back" (Hollywood 1003) sold over 150,000 copies.

Pierce adds, "We made two or three other sessions with Linda, didn't do much with 'em, and I turned her over to Buck Ram. Buck worked with her for a while, but the outcome of that, was Linda's daughter was the lead soloist for the Platters and so she brought her daughter and the Platters over to Buck and he brought them to Mercury. So it started with John Dolphin and Linda Hayes and it ended up with Mercury and the Platters. There's a lot of crazy things working in the music business. So I missed the big stuff. I missed the Platters."

Despite the missed opportunity, the Hollywood label did score several other successes. Dolphin introduced Pierce to Jack Lauderdale of Swingtime Records and helped Pierce acquire various Christmas masters. Though initially leased, Pierce later bought perennial favorites such as "Lonesome Christmas" by Lowell Fulson, "Merry Christmas Baby" by Charles Brown and several other holiday masters. Pierce remembers, "I was absolutely amazed at the number of records we sold on that stuff. Must have been 50,000 or 60,000. I must have sold them every year for ten or fifteen years." The Hollywood label released several other R&B and blues successes, including the first long-play release of Ray Charles's Swingtime recordings. Pierce continued to run the label, separate from Starday, until his retirement from the music business.

Perhaps the most important "gift" Dolphin gave to Pierce was a free office for Starday and Hollywood Records at 2528 West Pico Boulevard, Los Angeles. Pierce relates, "My associate, John, got me this place for nothing to open up Starday and operate out there. He had paid a lease, was no longer paying on it, but had some time left on it and so we had a place to stay." When that time ran out, Pierce struck a deal with Charley Washburn of Coast Record Company which enabled Starday to keep the office space, rent-free, as long as Coast's pressing plant could press the Starday releases. Pierce then hired Murray "Jack" Frost, another disgruntled ex–4 Star employee, for $80 a week. Frost helped with the administrative duties and ran the Starday office while Pierce was on the road.

Just as the Starday Recording Company got set up, "You All Come" began to catch on. In November 1953 Daily placed a $500 full-page ad in *Billboard* to get the word out. Within weeks the song was steadily rising, eventually peaking at the #7 C&W position. The job of setting up a distributorship became much easier. "I could get on the phone, pick the ones I wanted, and tell them, 'Look, we've got a full-page ad coming out. We're on the charts with the record. My line is available," adds Pierce. "I want you to sell my product. You made money with me at 4 Star and I want you to be my distributor for Starday.'" Within weeks Pierce had set up a nationwide network of thirty-one distributors.

Pierce then decided to further "shop" the new hit. Pierce remembers, "There was a place called Melrose Pub. We'd have lunch there a lot and Decca Studios was right next door. So the Mills Brothers would be hanging around there, sometimes you'd see Satchmo [Louis Armstrong], this guy and that guy. And some of 'em would come in and they had a little corner down there in the café where it was off from the others. They would come out of the Paramount Studios or the Decca Studios and eat in there." It was during one of these casual lunches that he slipped his friend Sonny Burke of Decca Records a copy of Duff's hit. Burke placed the record into a stack of records he had agreed to play for their top artist. When Bing Crosby first heard the song, he loved it and pulled it from the stack. Rumor has it that Crosby actually recorded "You All Come" during one of his breaks while filming *White Christmas*. Apparently the Cass County Boys cut everything except Crosby's vocals and in between a set change Crosby rode his bike from the set to the studio to cut the vocals, Santa Claus costume and all.

The Crosby recording sold over 400,000 copies and not only solidified Starday as an up-and-coming independent record label, but also established Starrite as a hit-making publishing house. To thank Crosby, Starday sent him a pair of blue and gold custom boots that read "Y'all" down one boot and "Come" down the other. (The original single listed the song title as "You All Come," but after Crosby's cover, Starrite sheet music was printed listing the song as "You All Come" with "Y'all Come" below in parenthesis. From that point on, most cover artists chose the "Y'all Come" spelling.) To thank Starday, Crosby sang his new song on the Bob Hope show and recorded a transcription for the newly founded radio program *Houston Jamboree* in Houston, where "Y'all Come" became the theme song.

The popularity of the song continued to grow. Within months, several cover versions were released by "Little" Jimmy Dickens, Johnny Hicks, Jimmie Osborne, Grandpa Jones, and others. Perhaps nobody was more surprised by the song's success than the band members who backed Duff on the original recording. In an interview with Andrew Brown, steel guitarist Bobby Black admitted to being dumbfounded. According to Black, "Arlie was a likeable guy, kind of a clown. It was hard to believe he was a teacher. We didn't look down on him, but he had the most insignificant songs that we were going over, I felt.

I thought, 'Man, why are we doing these tunes? They're so corny.' We were always looking for something more swinging to play, so I felt like we had to lower ourselves to play these. I remember somebody, maybe Blackie, saying, 'Aw, play really corny on this stuff,' so I did, of course." After it became a hit, Black continues, "Oh, I couldn't believe it. I remember when we recorded it, I thought it was the corniest thing. It was almost a joke to me. As it turned out, naturally, that was the thing that made the most noise."[11]

Indeed, noise was made. Arlie Duff was awarded a BMI songwriter's award for the Most Popular Song of 1953. The song later attained country music standard status after successful recordings by Bill Monroe (who used it as the closing theme song to his shows), Bobby Bare, Patti Page, Faron Young, Jeanette Hicks, Bobby Vinton, Minnie Pearl, Glen Campbell, Buck Owens, Porter Wagoner, "Cousin" Herb Henson, Joe Maphis, the Sunshine Boys, the Lonesome Pine Fiddlers, the Willis Brothers, and countless others.

The tremendous success of Duff's spirited yelp provided enough money for Starday to record and promote several new artists without ever having to borrow a dime—something Pierce remained fiercely proud of. The money also afforded Starns the opportunity to purchase a tape recorder, a mixer, and a couple microphones which he promptly set up in his living room. There, on Voth Road in Beaumont, is where Starday would record several memorable tracks between late 1953 to mid-1954. As George Jones described in his autobiography, "The 'studio' was actually Jack's living room, where he had tacked cardboard egg cartons on the walls to absorb sound. There was one microphone for the singer and all of the musicians. . . . There was a single light bulb in the center of the room and one 'engineer,' a guy who turned the recording machine on and off."[12] The so-called engineer, usually Starns's son Bill, would be sitting in one room and would signal to the band to start playing by turning the light off and then on again. Though Jack Starns's knowledge of acoustics and recording was extremely limited, Starday recorded the majority of their early recordings between this studio and ACA Studio in Houston until Daily heavily invested in Bill Quinn's Gold Star Recording Studio several months later.

The second batch of artists signed to Starday included local Beaumont artist Patsy Elshire and Houston country singer and television personality "Cowboy" Bill Potter. Elshire was another girl country crooner and began her recording career at age thirteen with Slim Watts and His All-Stars (Watts later recorded two sides for Starday). She remembers: "Every day at noon my mother would pick me up from school and take me to KTRM so I could do the noon radio show. That's where Slim worked as a disc jockey, and the Big Bopper too. I'd get out of lunch just a little bit early 'cause the school knew what was going on and I would go out there and sing. Bill Monroe's daughter, Melissa Monroe, had just released a record called 'Guilty Tears' and she and

I at that time sounded so much alike that when I sang it with a band people called the radio station and wondered if I was Melissa Monroe. They said, 'No, that's Patsy Elshire.'"

By the time Starday signed Elshire on July 1, 1953, she was sixteen years old and was performing with Blackie Crawford and the Western Cherokees. Due to the fact that Elshire and Chelette both shared the same band, manager, and even a record (Starday 123 features a pair of answer tunes, one by each), the two often toured and performed together, along with the other Starday acts. Elshire recalls: "I was about the same age as she [Chelette] and her two sisters. She was real sweet and real pretty. They always dressed in white western outfits and she had beautiful red hair and I was a little bit jealous of her. Well, I mean, there were three of them and only one of me. But we would play in Houston on Saturday night at the Palladium and we would do the Houston Jamboree. That Neva Starns was a go-getter. She liked to book us shows and she was like a second mom to me. Neva would always check me over before I would go on stage and she would give me these little pep talks. She would do all her people that way."

The aforementioned Houston Hometown Jamboree was a variety show created by Jack and Neva Starns to showcase both Starday and other local talent each weekend. The show, which took place at the City Auditorium in Houston, opened on March 13, 1954, and Bing Crosby's "Y'all Come" transcription aired welcoming the fans. Opening night of the "Free-For-All Hillbilly Music Fest" included headliners Arlie Duff, Jimmy Dennis, Billy Jo Moore, Patsy Elshire, Sonny Burns, George Jones, Blackie Crawford and the Western Cherokees, and the Starday Melodymakers. Locals who performed were the Chelette Sisters of Port Arthur, Carl Bradley of Port Neches, and the Duff Trio of Nederland. Hank Locklin, Tommy Sands, Jerry Jericho, Laura Lee McBride, Smokey Stover, and Bob Heppler rounded out the night of entertainment, which also included a half-hour gospel segment.

Booking the Jamboree talent became the responsibility of Jack and Neva Starns, as well as disc jockeys Biff Collie, who later recorded for Starday, and "Tater" Pete Hunter. The show, broadcast live on KNUZ radio and TV, also boasted a talent contest which, if won six weeks in a row, awarded the winner a Starday recording contract. The Western Cherokees became the house band, though by mid-1954 the Western Cherokees had split into two factions. According to band member Freddie Frank: "I went along with the Western Cherokees as an extra singer and extra fiddle player. 'Red' and 'Little Red' Hayes, [steel guitarist] Jimmy Biggar... they split up the band sometime. See, they'd book it as the Starday band but if they got two good bookings, they'd take Arlie Duff and part of 'em and go one way, and a bunch of them would go to Oklahoma or somewhere else. They had a whole bunch of musicians

Sonny Burns and his Fender Telecaster (Courtesy of Andrew Brown)

that hung around there [in Beaumont] and played. . . . It was just like a domino game. You shuffled the musicians and you'd draw a hand, you know, and see who was going to play. So 'Red' and 'Little Red' would go someplace; me, Jimmy Biggar, and [pianist] Burney Annett would go somewhere else."

Blackie Crawford led one of the Western Cherokee groups, but by the summer of 1954 he had left the band and was replaced as bandleader by Tommy Hill (who would play a major role at Starday in the coming years). Another faction of the band maintained status as the house band at the Houston Hometown Jamboree and was led by Elshire's "lover" and one of Starday's newest acquisitions. Elshire clarifies, "Well, he wasn't really my lover, I was just in love with him. He had no idea. But I loved that man dearly. We all did. He was tall, dark, and handsome and boy, could he sing!" That man was Houston's own Clyde "Sonny" Burns Jr.

Burns was a charismatic showman from Galveston, Texas, and was already well known throughout the Houston music scene by the time he signed with

Starday toward the end of 1953. He got his start playing guitar on Sleepy Bob Everson's KLEE radio show, *Corn's A-Poppin'*, around 1949 and by 1953 was the host of his own radio show and television show on KNUZ, Houston. With the increased exposure, Burns became Starday's first marketable "star." Though his first release showed great promise, it was his second record (118) and the first released version of Eddie Noack's "Too Hot To Handle," that solidified Burns's "star" status. Despite cover versions by Gene O'Quin, Jimmie Skinner, Frankie Miller (years later), and several others, Burns's regional hit outsold them all. Noack recalled to Bill Millar in a 1976 interview: "I hadn't seen him [Burns] in a long time but he called me and said, 'I gotta cut a session for Starday but I don't have enough musicians.' He had him a fiddler named Eddie Caldwell and I took over what band I had which was myself, I played rhythm, Joe Brewer (steel), Theron Poteet (piano), and Buck Henson (bass). Sonny sang and played lead." The tune, which has since been recorded by several other Starday artists, was recorded at Holford's ACA Studios. Noack added, "I'd originally written and recorded the song for Gold Star, with Link Davis on fiddle, but Bill Quinn had never put it out. Quinn waited until Sonny had a hit with it and then leased my version to TNT."[13]

Burns followed the success of "Too Hot" with several other up-tempo boppers, such as the rollicking "Another Woman Looking For A Man" (152) and the Johnny-Cash-meets-Eddie-Noack "A Real Cool Cat" (209). But it was the ballads that established Burns's reputation as a crooner in his early days. Among his classic Starday recordings are weepers such as "Powder and Paint" (118), "A Place For Girls Like You" (131, also a Top 10 hit for Faron Young and the second big hit for Starrite publishing), "Waltzing With Sin" (152), and "Six Feet of Earth" (189).

As his popularity continued to climb in 1954, Daily thought it would be best if Burns recorded a few duets with the label's newest recording artist, George Jones. As Daily recalled to Martin Hawkins, "Sonny Burns was a fine, fine singer. His recordings sold well too, consistently. We always had advance orders on them. He outsold George Jones by a mile. In fact, when we had them duet on a couple of discs, it was to help George's career, not Sonny's."[14] And help George Jones's career it did.

2

ROCK IT

The immediate success enjoyed by Starday was rare for an independent label, especially one devoted entirely to country music. At the onset of World War II, the American Federation of Musicians declared a nationwide recording ban, claiming that jukeboxes and radio airplay cut into a musician's potential salary and that the recording companies should contribute to a fund to pay unemployed musicians. The ban began on August 1, 1942, and carried into November 1944, when Columbia and Victor reached an agreement with the musician's union (Decca struck their deal with the AFM in September 1943). Although the recording ban ended, the recording industry's production remained limited throughout the war. The use of shellac, the brittle material used in the making of both phonograph records and bombshells, was initially frozen by the United States government but was later made available in limited quantities.

In preparation of the ban, major labels had been warned to stock up on their shellac supplies. In an attempt to maximize profit, the more popular big band and pop catalogs comprised the majority of releases, drastically reducing both the country and "race" records. When the ban was lifted, numerous independent labels formed, eager to cash in on the surplus of unrecorded talent. In addition, several independent studios and pressing plants were popping up as well, thus making the record business far more accessible to average businessmen than it had been prior to 1941. According to Pierce, most of the new labels primarily focused on the more lucrative rhythm and blues market, while the country and western musicians remained a largely ignored minority. As Pierce recalls, "There was just a much bigger market [in R&B] than in country. Just think, in those days the rhythm and blues businesses are all independents. Majors didn't do much with it. You had Imperial. You had Modern. You had Specialty. You had Atlantic. You had Chess. Those guys are selling tons of records, way more than the country music buyer. Five to one. So it sustained about ten successful independent labels. But 4 Star and Starday were about the only ones that were country."

Though there were other successful independents recording country music, most of them relied heavily on rhythm and blues as well. Sam Phillips's Sun Records started just prior to Starday and quickly scored hits in the rhythm and blues market, yet it took over three years before the Sun name would appear on any *Billboard* country charts. Even Syd Nathan's King label, which started out primarily as a country label, was by 1954 relying on rhythm and blues tarts by Billy Ward and the Dominoes, the Ink Spots, and others.

Starday chose to be different from the others and to release only country material (it should be noted that Pierce's Hollywood R&B label was operated independently from Starday, with no input or investment from either Daily or Starns), though it still shared one significant commonality with the other successful independents. Like Herb Abramson, who started Atlantic Records, Herman Lubinsky, who started Savoy, Ike and Ben Berman of Apollo, and Pierce's friend John Dolphin of Recorded In Hollywood, Pappy Daily ran a record store. According to researcher Charlie Gillett, "Most independent record firms started through a combination of accident, coincidence, and opportunism, often by people who owned record shops or a chain of jukeboxes, who saw that the audience wanted certain kinds of music that existing companies didn't know about or disdained dealing with."[1]

Daily's association with the record store and jukebox business, as well as his admiration for country music, certainly gave him an advantage. Even so, connections and knowledge of the industry will only take someone so far. As Starns proudly proclaimed, "A good recording company is first, good songs are next." Starday already had "You All Come," but Starns said "*songs.*" An even bigger hit lay just around the corner. Pierce recalls: "I was returning from one of my trips across the state of Texas and I stopped at Midland. Red Hayes was there. Red had done a lot of the fiddle work on the recordings that we made in Houston. He said, 'I have a song that I want you to hear.' He sang it for me, and it was terrific. It was 'A Satisfied Mind.' Red said, 'You can have the song for Starday, but I want to make the first record on it.' I said, 'That's agreed.' So I called Pappy and Red went down and made the first record on it. The records got circulated to radio stations, including KWTO in Springfield, Missouri, home of the Ozark Jubilee, where Jean Shepard heard it, and where Red Foley heard it, and where Porter Wagoner heard it. They all recorded it, and they all had a hit, and it established Porter Wagoner's career."

The tune is credited to both Joe "Red" Hayes and Jack Rhodes, though according to steel guitar player Al Petty, Freddie Frank, and Kenneth "Little Red" Hayes, the co-author's younger brother, Rhodes contributed nothing to the song. Rhodes was the step-brother of famed songwriter and soon-to-be Starday recording artist Leon Payne, though Rhodes himself was not known primarily as a songwriter. Instead, Rhodes was an entertainer, operating a band

Publicity photo for Joe "Red" Hayes, "The man with the Satisfied Mind" (Courtesy of Nathan Gibson)

called the Lone Star Buddies (sometimes called Jack Rhodes' Ramblers), and a businessman, operating the Trail 80 Courts motel in Mineola, Texas. The motel, which also hosted a small recording studio, became a haven for local songwriters hoping to get their songs published and recorded. Among other talents, Rhodes possessed a keen ear for good songs and he would often edit, pitch, and promote the songs he liked to various labels. In return for his efforts and connections, he would receive a percentage of the writer's credit. Such was the case with Hayes's "A Satisfied Mind" (164), with publishing revenues generated by cover versions catapulting both Rhodes and Starday on the fast track to success. According to Hayes himself, "The song came from my mother. Everything in the song are things I heard her say over the years. I put a lot of thought into the song before I came up with the title. One day my father-in-law asked me who I thought the richest man in the world was, and I mentioned some names. He said, 'You're wrong, it is the man with a satisfied mind.'"[2]

Pierce tells: "Porter probably sold 150–160,000 and Shepard probably did about 110,000 and Red Foley and his daughter probably did 110,000. They could see that song was dynamite and they all jumped on it at once. All three of 'em came out in one week. But two of 'em, Red and Porter, had earlier recording dates. Jean made an understanding with them that she couldn't get her recording out until, I think it was, six weeks later when she would go from Springfield out to Los Angeles to record for Capitol and she would do it then and they would all release 'em at the same time. They did and they all hit the charts. I just love that song."

Wagoner's version entered the *Billboard* charts in May 1955 and reached the #1 spot, while Red and Betty Foley's rendition hit #3 and Shepard's interpretation climbed up to #4, all within a few weeks of each other. But the song's success did not stop there. The tune, one of the most instantly recognizable country standards, was later covered by numerous music legends including Ella Fitzgerald, Bob Dylan, the Byrds, Mahalia Jackson, Ian and Sylvia, Johnny Cash, Faron Young, Lucinda Williams, Jonathan Richman, Roberta Sherwood, Marty Stuart, Lindsey Buckingham, Glen Campbell, Bobby Hebb, Frank Ifield, the Blue Sky Boys, Jeff Buckley, Roy Acuff, Pat Boone, Loretta Lynn, Red Sovine, Oak Ridge Boys, Hugo and Luigi, and countless others.

Thus the song collected a significant sum of money from BMI, which became increasingly important in keeping Starday afloat. This much-needed income was largely thanks to a second recording ban put into effect by the musician's union on January 1, 1948. At that time, the union took exception to the growing number of disc jockeys playing records, which resulted in no compensation to the artist. The Taft-Hartley Labor Act of 1946 had made it illegal to force radio stations to hire union musicians, which was a boon to radio stations, and ushered in the disc jockey (whereas before they would have had live bands). This issue was resolved with a much bigger emphasis placed on BMI/ASCAP affiliation, and radio stations paying them to play records. Pierce elaborates, "So that ["A Satisfied Mind"] was just a real lucky break for us, and it enabled me to go into New York and sit down and talk with BMI and tell them that we were now demanding a guarantee. They agreed to guarantee us $12,000 a year for the performing rights on the Starday catalog. So when I saw Pappy, it was agreed that both Pappy and I could draw a salary for the first time out of Starday, using the BMI money."

Initially it seems strange that Pierce and Daily would not share the BMI money with Starns, though they were not without reason. Jack Starns wanted out. Starns and Pierce clashed from the very onset of Starday and the two simply could not work through their differences. Pierce shares his side: "Jack didn't like me at all, because I was running Starday as a record company, and Jack felt that Starday should be a vehicle for him to manage his artists and to promote the artists' personal appearances. So there was a legitimate conflict of interest. Jack would record Roy Drusky in Dallas without saying anything to us at all, and we would have to follow through and get a contract with him after the session had been made, and pay for the session. The same thing happened again. His interests were diametrically opposed to our needs."

Pierce further elaborated on their differences to Colin Escott: "Jack would say, 'I need to get a release on this or that artist, and we need to have records by such-and-such a time because we're going to be traveling up to Arkansas.' I said, 'Well, that hasn't got anything to do with the record company.' We had our releases scheduled for the next month and all of a sudden he would demand that something else be done that had nothing to do with the record company, something to assist him in booking and promoting. One time he had [Houston bandleader] R. D. Hendon, and when he couldn't get a release date from me, he just went to Plastic Products in Memphis, says, 'Press up some records,' gave it a release number, and took off. You can't run a record company that way. He grew to dislike me a lot."[3]

The dislike grew stronger, and when "A Satisfied Mind" broke open in mid-1955, Starns jumped at his chance to leave the label and make a few dollars in the process. Pierce explains: "He said to Pappy, 'Who the hell is that guy to tell me what to do? I started Lefty, and we started Starday and *let* him be the president, and now he's telling me what to do?' He says, 'I will sell my stock to you, Pappy, for $8,000, but I won't sell anything to Don Pierce.' Well, Pappy bought the stock and then called me. And I said, 'Well Pappy, of course I want to buy half of it.' 'Well, you certainly deserve to be able to buy half of it, for what you're doing with the label.' So Pappy and I owned the company, and we were each drawing a salary. I think I drew $600 a month while Pappy drew $400, because I had to spend all my time on the business and Pappy spent his time recording in the studio. And then what he was doing as a distributor he would have been doing anyway."

Around the time that Jack Starns broke off his relationship with Starday, he and Neva were divorced and went their separate ways. Neva moved to Springfield, Missouri, later that year and became a road manager for both Patsy Elshire and Jean Shepard, among others. She later remarried and moved to Longview, Texas, where she succumbed to kidney failure at the age of 52. Jack Starns Jr. married Jimmie Evelyn Fregia in 1955 and quickly faded from the music business. According to Joyce Kelley, "Daddy got fed up with the music business and the whole genre of it. After he and my mother divorced he went into the mobile home business and said, 'I've had enough of these hillbillies!' He went into two or three businesses and stayed in Texas, though he spent a brief time in Lake Charles, LA. He later started his King of the Road company in El Paso and had 11 mobile home dealerships throughout Louisiana and Texas." Though the elder Starns chose to get out of the music business altogether, his son Bill Starnes remained and went on to manage George Jones, Tammy Wynette, Ray Price, and David Allen Coe, among others.

A short while later Pierce and Daily stumbled upon yet another source of income. Pierce explains: "Another fortunate development for me was Mr. Ralph Peer. Mr. Peer was one of the original icons of the country music business, having represented RCA in the field, traveling through the South, and discovering Jimmie Rodgers, the Carter Family, and others. I got acquainted with him because I was doing some business with Southern Music [Peer's company], and he was aware of what I was doing by reading about me in the *Billboard* and *Cash Box* magazines. He was still very interested in the country music industry. One day he called up and it was really strange. He said, 'Don, I'd like for you to come out to my place and have lunch with me.' He had a place at 9000 Sunset, a very expensive part of Hollywood. A butler answered the door and brought me in. Mr. Peer was a redheaded person from Kansas City. He was a giant music publisher and the first one really to have his own branch offices throughout the world. He was a connoisseur of art, and owned Southern Music and Peer International. We visited and he said, 'I know you're up to your ears in country music; that's what got me started. I'm naturally interested in it. You travel all over and that's what I used to do.

"He said, 'I want to do some business with you. I'd like for you to be a kind of scout or an associate of some kind.' I said, 'Mr. Peer, I'm your competitor. I'm a music publisher too. I don't know what you have in mind or how this could be done.' He said, 'You have your publishing. I will make a deal with you where my companies will handle the worldwide rights to your songs outside of the U. S. and Canada. And if there's any sheet music that comes out of your songs, I will do the sheet music and all of those auxiliary things that you're not in a position to do.' I said, 'I'll call Pappy Daily and I'm sure we can do that.' He said, 'Don, I know you're not making much money. I'll let you have a draw of $100 a week.' 'That's wonderful,' I said, 'But I don't know whether I will create enough income for you on that basis.' He says, 'Don't worry about that.' It wasn't long before we had 'Y'all Come' and 'A Satisfied Mind,' and he sold about 22,000 piano copies [sheet music for piano] on each, and he had the worldwide rights to them. He was quite happy with the arrangement and he told me, 'Whenever you're in New York, I want you to come to our offices.' Mr. Peer didn't have an office in New York! He said it depressed him to go to the Brill Building and see those people sitting around doing nothing, while Don Pierce is out in his car running all over the country. So he'd pick me up in New York and drive me around Manhattan in his car and we would visit. He was an absolutely

George Jones at his first Starday photo shoot, ca. 1955 (Courtesy of Nathan Gibson)

delightful fellow. I rank him up with Pappy Daily and Syd Nathan as the three angels in the business for Don Pierce."

With a little more revenue coming in, a few more hits in the catalog, and fewer people sharing money, Starday was slowly becoming a lucrative endeavor. The Starrite publishing catalog continued to grow and major labels were now looking to Starday for their next big hits. But perhaps the biggest surprise for Pierce and Daily was the looming success of Starns's protégé, George Glenn Jones, who was signed to a recording contract several months prior to Starns's exit from the label.

Jones recalls: "I went into the Marine Corp in '51 and they heard about me in '52, just before I went in the service, and they got in touch with my kinfolks, my mother, and they got my mailing address at the Marine Corps in San Diego and sent me a letter. He [Starns] told me to look him up when I got home and so I definitely got a hold of him when I got out because that was really all I wanted to do, sing and make music. So he took me to Houston to Pappy Daily's office and him and Pappy Daily put me in the studio [Starns's living room] right away with egg crates all over the wall and 18 wheelers, you could hear 'em going down the highway, and we did our first sessions."

That was Daily's first encounter with Jones, regarded by many as country music's greatest vocalist. Growing up in a very musical family in Saratoga, Texas, about forty miles from Beaumont, Jones often sang with his siblings, both at home and at church every Sunday. His family moved to Beaumont when he was seven years old and he received his first guitar at the age of nine. Shortly thereafter, Jones began playing the streets of Beaumont for spare change and quickly realized that his brand of singing and entertainment was earning him more money than many grown men. Thus, Jones was quick to trade in his singing-in-church-every-Sunday ways for a singing-in-the-honky-tonks-every-Saturday-night lifestyle. To complement the nightly gigs, he also began playing music on radio stations KTXJ in Jasper and later on KRIC in Beaumont. At the age of sixteen he was taken in by the regionally popular husband-and-wife duo Eddie and Pearl and continued playing the nightclub circuit. Two years later Jones married a wealthy woman whose parents bought him a new guitar. The marriage fell apart the following year but Jones kept the guitar and used it to entertain his fellow marines.

Upon his return to Texas, Daily finally got to hear what Starns had gotten so excited about, though he wasn't initially impressed. As Daily recalled, "I never will forget when George came to me. He had a burning desire to imitate Lefty Frizzell. I got him off of that kick and then he sang like Roy Acuff. And I said, 'George, can you sing like George Jones?' And he says, 'Yessir.' And I said, 'Well, let me hear you.' And he did. I was so sold on George that I stuck with him when a lot of other people wanted to give up on him. And course my faith was justified."[4]

Jones often jokes about his first disc, "No Money In This Deal," as a prophetic song about his Starday contract, and he later recalled the recording experience in his autobiography. Jones wrote, "When anybody gets nervous they rely on their reflexes, and I was no exception. I simply did what I was doing all along, singing like my musical influences—Hank Williams, Roy Acuff and Lefty Frizzell. . . . I was so naïve that I actually didn't realize that Pappy and Jack were trying to find someone with a different sound, his own sound. And so, inside that makeshift studio, I searched for the voice of George Jones. That was probably the birthplace of my own style."[5]

Jones' first record (130) was released in March 1954. Despite the excitement of finding his own style and having his own record to plug, however, sales were marginal. A few more releases followed with some regional success, but still no breakthrough. Daily, sensing great promise in his new artist, then set up a recording date for Jones with Starday's biggest star, Sonny Burns. Burns was Jones's first duet partner and the two performed together quite often on the Houston Jamboree. But Burns ultimately burned himself when he missed one of those scheduled recording sessions.

Daily recalled the story in an interview with Martin Hawkins: "When we had them duet on a couple of discs it was done to help George's career, not Sonny's. These duets included 'Wrong About You' [which *Billboard* listed as a #5 territorial best seller in Houston] and 'Heartbroken Me.' And in fact, Sonny made his great mistake with drink. He was too drunk to turn up to a session in 1955, so George Jones cut 'Why Baby Why' (202) instead of him and it launched George to fame. He was nowhere before that session. Sonny just faded out and [many years later] he became a hair stylist in Nacogdoches. That was a great shame."[6]

Recording without his duet partner, Jones took a tip from Patti Page's recording success and dubbed his own vocal harmonies over his initial take. The trick worked and Jones singing career was officially launched. According to Jones, "I just did a lot of praying to the good Lord. I said, 'Get me one hit and let me just know the feeling of it to have my own hit.' And within just a few months we were very lucky with 'Why Baby Why.'"

Lucky? Perhaps, but it wasn't necessarily easy. If Burns was too drunk to even make it to the studio, Jones was not far behind. Houston fiddler Tony Sepolio, who claims to have put the "Why Baby Why" session together, remembered to researcher Andrew Brown: "I got the band for him. He called me. It took him all day to make it. I'm not used to that. I said, 'Yeah, I'll get you a steel guitar.' It was Herb Remington. The bass was Lew Frisby. And I got Doc Lewis on the piano. I got him a guitar player, I forget who [note: Glenn Barber remembers playing guitar on this session]. Man, it took him all day to make the darn thing. He'd get drunk . . . he went through a fifth of whiskey. He'd say, 'Wait a minute, I forgot the chords,' stop right in the middle of it. We'd start again, and then he'd say, 'Ah, that's not the words.' And I mean, I was up to here with him. 'Cause when I was with [Jerry] Irby, we'd make 'em boom-boom-boom. In one day, we made five 15-minute radio programs [transcriptions]. We might miss a note here or word there—we didn't care, we'd just keep going. And here's this idiot, man, toward the end he'd say, 'I forgot the words.' We took a break about lunch time. And he [Jones] was going through his fifth of whiskey. And I told Lew, 'Hey, if we can't whip him, let's join him.' So we went down to the corner and got us a six-pack of beer. I got frustrated with him. I swore that I'd never record with him again—and I never have. I told Jones, 'Man, don't ever call me again.' We got paid union wages, but it wasn't worth it."

Regardless of alienating several local musicians, Jones had just recorded his first hit session and Daily knew he was sitting on gold. Pierce recalls: "George had 'No Money in This Deal' that sold fairly well. We had two or three others that were getting airplay. The jockeys were saying good things about George. It wasn't long before Pappy called. 'I'm flying out to Los Angeles. We've just done a session. I'm coming out with material.' I met him at the airport, and we took

George Jones with his 1951 Packard, ca. 1956 (Courtesy of George Jones)

that tape over to Coast Records [to get pressed], and he played 'Why Baby Why' and 'Ragged But Right' and 'Seasons of My Heart' and one other which I think was 'Gonna Come Get You.' I said, 'This is just fantastic.' I just knew that we had hit material. I really worked hard on 'Why Baby Why,' and after we had gotten it up to #4, Webb Pierce covered it on Decca."

Jones's version stayed on the *Billboard* charts for more than four months (beginning in October 1955) and crawled all the way up to the #4 spot, though some thanks may be due to Webb Pierce who, along with Red Sovine, recorded the tune as an actual duet and scored a #1 hit. Don Pierce remembers: "Webb said, 'Now Pappy, I don't want to kill George Jones' record. You helped me get started in records.' There was enough loyalty there to say, 'Now, if we wait another couple of weeks, will that help [you] to get further established? After all, Red Sovine is doing most of the singing, but my name is gonna carry it to #1.' And so that's what he did, held it up for two or three weeks, and then [his] went to #1. I thought it was pretty nice that he called and cleared it with my associate Pappy Daily."

Despite Jones's current assessment that, "It was terrible! I don't know how that song ever clicked," according to Pierce "Why Baby Why" managed to sell 110–115,000 copies. Recognizing any sales over 50,000 to be a significant hit in the country and western market, Jones, Pierce, and Daily were ecstatic.

Jones's success continued with his next release, "What Am I Worth" (216), an upbeat number that splashed onto *Billboard*'s charts three months later and reached the #7 spot. Both songs were co-written by Darrell Edwards, a childhood friend of Jones and Coast Guard chief in Galveston. Jones tells, "I wrote a bunch of things by myself, like 'Just One More,' which was a big jukebox and disc jockey record, and most of my stuff was the drinking things back in those days, but I [also] did a lot of co-writing with Darrell Edwards, a friend of mine that was born in Saratoga, Texas, where I was a baby. He'd come up with these ideas and we'd sit down and we wrote 'em which is what we did with 'Why Baby Why' and 'Seasons Of My Heart' and 'What Am I Worth' and so on."

Jones's hot streak continued and several of his next records became Top Ten hits, including "You Gotta Be My Baby" (247), "Just One More" (264), and "Yearning" (279). In addition to his growing reputation as a talented young vocalist and performer, Jones was also establishing himself as an up-and-coming songwriter. Among his other popular self-penned Starday releases were "Hold Everything" (188), which became a #5 hit for Red Sovine, and "Seasons of My Heart" (202), a Top 10 hit for both Jimmy C. Newman and Johnny Cash. As Jones's stock continued to rise, however, the country and western market was reeling from the effects of the rock 'n' roll phenomenon. "Why Baby Why" may have sold 115,000 records, but it paled in comparison to recordings by Elvis Presley, which by 1956 were selling close to 20,000 a day. Indeed, a pivotal shift in American popular culture had taken place.

Presley began recording for Sam Phillips's Sun label in 1954 and Phillips strongly encouraged the blending of upbeat country material with the popular rhythm and blues sound of Memphis. Though not the first to record this upbeat hillbilly bop, Presley was most definitely among the first to cash in on it. With groundbreaking recordings such as "Baby, Let's Play House," "Blue Moon of Kentucky" and "That's All Right," Presley was on to something big and Phillips was quick to realize the new sound's potential. In short time, Phillips began recording artists such as Carl Perkins, Charlie Feathers, Warren Smith, Roy Orbison, Billy Lee Riley, Sonny Burgess, Jerry Lee Lewis, and others who had begun blending the genres. Thus, even without Presley's contract, which Phillips sold to RCA at the end of 1955, Sun Records quickly earned its reputation as *the* rockabilly label.

Pappy Daily also recognized the emerging trend and immediately encouraged his top act to take a turn at rockabilly (a term combining the words rock 'n' roll and hillbilly). In a 1971 interview with John Pugh, Daily explained, "I've always been a hillbilly and always wanted hillbilly music. But when you're making records for the public, you have to forget your own personal tastes, and stay on top of the market."[7]

Though Jones was reluctant to make the crossover, Daily was persistent. Initially, Daily asked Jones to sing soundalike, or copycat, recordings of the current Presley hits, which Daily and Pierce would then market with other soundalikes on their Dixie label. While recording these soundalikes Jones displayed a special knack with rock 'n' roll, and Daily further encouraged him to try recording his own original rock songs. As Jones explains: "Well, that stuff, that wasn't supposed to happen. But you know, as you get older, you do those things 'cause you need a couple three hundred dollars, you're hungry, and back in those days they was selling on the Del Rio Mexican station [XERF, though the Dixie soundalikes were primarily sold on DJ Randy Blake's program on WJJD in Chicago]. All night Paul Kellinger would sell eighteen top hits, whatever the top eighteen hits were going, well, he would sell them. But they fooled the people. They wasn't the real artists. It was people like me who was trying to get started. I could sing like Marty Robbins or whoever it was. I did 'Singing the Blues' and I even did 'One Woman Man' that Johnny Horton had out. But that's the way the Thumper Jones thing came about. I did record one rock 'n' roll thing because at the time I was hungry. I mean, I had no choice. Rhythm and blues and rock 'n' roll took over in the fifties and that's when I was getting started. So I tried one, 'Rock It' and 'Dad Gum It (How Come It), and I didn't want to use my name. That's how bad I hated it. Instead of using my name, they thought they'd just nickname me 'Thumper.'"

Released in mid-1956, the Thumper Jones single (240) failed to chart—or to sell. Though regarded by many record collectors as one of Starday's more significant recordings, Pierce did not know what to do with it. He had just spent the last three years building up a country music distributorship and establishing relationships with country music disc jockeys. All he knew was country music. Unfortunately for Starday, most country music jockeys showed little to no interest in promoting rock 'n' roll. Further, radio was undergoing a transformation to mostly Top 40 at this time. Singles like "Rock It" failed because it was considered "too rockabilly" for country programming and "too country" for the quickly growing Top 40 radio format. With little radio promotion and an artist unwilling to perform the songs live, the song quickly fell flat. Still, though the "Thumper" Jones record did not pan out as he had hoped, Daily recognized the power of the record-buying public and continued to produce rockabilly sessions for Starday. Another of the more unique rockabilly efforts came from Starday's most established songwriter, Leon Payne.

Regarded as one of the all-time great songwriters in the business, Payne found the majority of his successes in the late forties and early fifties, with hit songs recorded by Hank Williams ("Lost Highway," "They'll Never Take Her Love From Me"), Elvis Presley ("I Love You Because"), George Morgan, Hank Snow, and many others. His music career began as early as the late 1930s with an association with Bill Boyd's Cowboy Ramblers. His solo career began in 1939 on the Bluebird label and, after a stint with Nashville's Bullet Records, he began recording for Capitol Records in 1949. His first Capitol release, "I Love You Because," became a #1 hit record and stayed on the charts for thirty-two weeks despite simultaneous Top 10 cover versions by both Ernest Tubb and Clyde Moody. During the peak of this success Payne was living in Houston and befriended Pappy Daily, occasionally performing in Daily's Record Ranch. Though he eventually left Houston for San Antonio in 1952, Payne continued his association with Daily and signed with Starday Records in 1955.

Payne continued his success as a "hot" songwriter for Starday and among his first releases for the label were "You Are the One"/"Door Step to Heaven" (220), both of which became Top Ten hits for Carl Smith, as well as "All the Time" (250), which became a Top 20 hit for Kitty Wells in 1959. Despite the several successful cover versions of his songs, however, his own record sales were lacking and Daily eventually persuaded his blind friend to take a pass at rockabilly.

Much like Jones, Payne was unwilling to use his own name. Thus, Daily dubbed him as "Rock Rogers" for one release in May 1956; his frantic yelper, "Little Rock Rock" (245), was a mighty attempt at the new sound. Still, despite the strong backing vocals and hot guitar riffs of Hal Harris, there is a hint of uneasiness in Payne's vocals. Payne was yet another in the chain of many successful country acts to have the new teen sound forced upon them and, though he recorded within the genre admirably, he more than likely considered the rockabilly recordings an embarrassing departure from his own style. Ironically, it is for these, and several other recordings made during this era, that the Starday label remains so popular among rockabilly fans across the world.

Not every Starday artist was embarrassed to be associated with the new sound. Sometime in either late 1954 or early 1955, well before Jones's and Payne's efforts, Jack Starns and Pappy Daily put out the word that they were looking for a rock 'n' roll artist for Starday. Several leads followed, among them Sonny Fisher. Fisher later described to Ray Topping and Bill Millar his first encounter with the Starday label men. "We paid for our own sessions [at Gold Star Studios] and recorded 'Rockin' Daddy,' Hold Me Baby" (179), "Sneaky Pete,' and 'Hey Mama' (190) at the first one. There wasn't much there except a little turntable behind the glass [i.e., recording to disk], one or two microphones at the controls and I paid him [Bill Quinn] for the hiring [renting] of the studio. Quinn called Jack Starns and told him, 'There's a guy here doing stuff like Elvis,' and Starns came over to hear us. That's how we got on Starday. Jack Starns became my manager and I signed a bunch of papers, a one year contract with Pappy Daily."

Link Davis and his fiddle (Courtesy of Nathan Gibson)

By far the most progressive rockabilly recordings on Starday up to that point, Fisher's recordings were right on par with that of Sun Records in terms of both style and sound quality. Complete with slapping bass lines and Scotty Moore–esque riffs (though far bluesier) from guitarist Joey Long, Fisher and his group, the Rocking Boys, had the new sound figured out. Fisher explained his influences: "I grew up listening to Roy Acuff, Ernest Tubb, Jimmy Dickens, as well as the cowboy stuff by Gene Autry and Roy Rogers," but also added that, "[By 1954] everything we did came from R&B. We picked up the beat, the rhythm, everything from Joe Turner, Fats Domino, B. B. King, people like that. Then we heard Elvis and I recognized it as something a little different. . . ."[8]

Fisher was called back for a second session in the spring of 1955, this time with Starday's own Sonny Burns on rhythm guitar. Four more rockers were released, including "Pink and Black" (244) and "I Can't Lose" (207), and remain among the more popular rockabilly sides from Starday. Still, Fisher was not satisfied with the results. As Fisher noted: "Starns helped me by taking me 'round all the radio shows but I did get beat out of all my BMI rights. The records were played on radio but I never saw any money for that—just live performances. I had the impression they was doing good all over. My mother told me they were played out in California and I thought I was gonna get rich, but I didn't. Starday gave me one royalty check for $126 and offered me a two year contract. They told me I wasn't selling any records but other people told me they were selling fast. I thought they were giving me the runaround so I did not re-sign. That just might have been the worst decision of my career. I thought, I'll finish with little companies and wait for the big one to come along, of course it never did."[9]

Fisher was not alone in his skepticism. Countless artists from the early rockabilly era have been quoted saying similar things about how they were "ripped off" by their labels. Remarkably, at least one of the original Starrite royalty statements has survived to show another side to the story.

Link Davis eventually earned his place in rock 'n' roll history as the saxophone player on tunes such as the Big Bopper's "Chantilly Lace" and Johnny Preston's "Running Bear," but his interest in rock music began well before those recordings were made. Davis got his start playing music in the late 1920s, forming a trio with his siblings, and by the late thirties was playing fiddle in Cliff Bruner's Texas Wanderers. Davis soon became well versed in the western swing, Cajun, and blues genres and by the mid-forties had begun a career as a solo artist. As early as 1949 the Texas native recorded a swingin' western version of Roy Brown's jump blues classic "Good Rockin' Tonight," and the seeds of rock 'n' roll had been planted.

As the mid-fifties rolled around, Daily was eager to sign Davis to Starday where he could now record all-out rock 'n' roll. A session took place, four songs recorded, and in April 1956 Starday released "Sixteen Chicks" (235), a Bill Haley–inspired rocker complete with Davis's blaring saxophone solo and echo-drenched vocals. The tune, initially released with the country crooner "Deep in the Heart of a Fool," raised a few eyebrows and a short time later Starday re-released it with the more upbeat flipside "Grasshopper Rock" (242). Things seemed to be looking up for Davis and, according to the royalty statement, "Sixteen Chicks," sold roughly 1,600 copies. Though it did not break through nationally, sales were at least high enough to establish the record as a regional hit. Yet even after the success of "Sixteen Chicks" and three other releases, which include revered rockabilly tunes "Don't Big Shot Me" and "Trucker From Tennessee" (255), Davis was not paid a dime in royalties.

The standard royalty rate Starday paid to artists was one cent per record sold, as well as one cent per songwriter's credit. As of December 31, 1956, Davis earned a total of $166 dollars in royalties on his four records (including the Canadian release of "Sixteen Chicks"). But according to Davis's royalty

Link Davis's Starrite Publishing royalty statement dated 12-31-1956 (Courtesy of Link Davis Jr. and Andrew Brown)

statement, he was advanced $60 and the recording fees totaled nearly $200. After the pluses and minuses had all been tallied, Davis owed Starday $89, even with a moderately successful regional hit. Most likely Starday never collected the difference and instead took a loss on the session. All the artist usually remembers, however, is that they never got paid and were "ripped off." Because recording costs could run up to $200 per session (most Starday sessions probably fell in the $50–$100 range), it is safe to assume that Starday took a loss on most of its releases. With a royalty rate of just one cent, against $200 studio costs, an artist would have to sell at least 20,000 records (not counting airplay royalties) just to break even. Thus, it is easy to see where the "ripped off" theory originates.

The steep recording fees were largely unavoidable because Starday was no longer using Starns's living room as a studio. Instead, Daily began investing in Bill Quinn's Gold Star Studio in 1954, helping Quinn convert his recording business from a makeshift home studio into a professional recording center on Brock Street in southeast Houston. Sleepy LaBeef, who went on to record several rockabilly singles of his own for Starday, remembers: "Bill was recording in his living room and he got so busy cutting George Jones, Sonny Burns,

Sonny Fisher, Eddie Noack, and so many other artists that he made enough money so he could build a new studio—a Nashville-type studio. I think he was using Ampex [tape recorder]. He was getting a real good sound. I think what he was doing was comparable to what Sun was doing down in Memphis. [Quinn built an actual echo chamber for vocalists and he probably used the slapback tape echo effect that Phillips used.] He was certainly closer than anyone else to Sam [Phillips]'s sound."

As the rock era rolled on, independent labels were quick to develop their own rock rosters. Though none of their earlier rockabilly efforts caught on with the masses, Starday pressed on in its efforts to find a rival to Presley's rockabilly throne. Several more rockabilly records were released by Glenn Barber (including his 1954 stomper "Ice Water"), Rocky Bill Ford, Cliff Blakley, Rudy Gaddis, Bill Mack, Bob Doss, and others. There was even a Starday EP rumored to feature famed rockabilly Eddie Cochran alongside Joe Maphis, likely recorded in California and first released on Pierce's Hollywood label, credited as "Country Rockin' and Flyin'" by Buddy Dee (258). Still, despite the stellar sound production and performance, none of the releases sold well enough to make Elvis shake any more than he already did.

Perhaps the Starday rocker who came closest to the King was Presley's friend and touring buddy, Rudy "Tutti" Grayzell. Grayzell began playing music to impress a high school sweetheart but soon found that he impressed others along the way. He formed the Silver Buckles, a western-styled honky-tonk outfit, and began playing local clubs around San Antonio. In 1953 Charlie Walker, a local disc jockey and Imperial recording artist, arranged an audition with Fabor Robinson that resulted in a contract with Robinson's Abbott Records.

Despite superb backing accompaniment by country music legends Jim Reeves and Floyd Cramer, the sales of Grayzell's first releases were limited. The Abbott records did, however, allow Grayzell the opportunity to perform on the Grand Ole Opry and Louisiana Hayride. But instead of singing country music, Grayzell wanted to let loose and rock. Capitol Records gave him that chance in 1955 and changed his name to Rudy Gray. It was also around this time that Grayzell and Presley crossed paths. Presley was in San Antonio, looking for an opening act, when Walker urged him to stop by a club Grayzell was playing. Grayzell remembered, "This guy walks in wearing a pink jacket, white slacks, a black shirt and two-tone shoes. I was just a Texas boy and I'd never seen anything like it. He looked like something from outer space."[10]

Presley was also impressed. Grayzell elaborated: "I performed with Elvis for about a year and a half before he became famous. I knew he was great, but I didn't know how great. I had a lotta pictures of him and me together but gave most of 'em to chicks. You showed a picture of yourself with Elvis to these

Rudy "Mr. Personality" Grayzell's "Ducktail" publicity promo
(Courtesy of Rudy "Tutti" Grayzell)

dolls and baby, you were in! He was the one who really started callin' me "Rudy Tutti," so I billed myself that way for a few years."[11]

This experience surely affected Grayzell's recordings, for after his first release on Starday in 1956, his recordings took on a wild rock 'n' roll sound. "Duck Tail" (241), as slick as the pompadour he was touting, was later covered by Joe Clay, and Grayzell's "Let's Get Wild" (321) is just that. From the opening line about drinking, partying, girls, and "Lawdy Miss Clawdy," to the unintelligible mumblings about the Cuban cha-cha-cha and the Chinese mambo during the solo, Grayzell's record might have been *too* wild for radio. Whatever the reason, Grayzell's recordings were not reaching their target audience. Hoping for a better shot in the rockabilly market, Grayzell made the switch to Sun Records in 1958, but the fame and stardom his friend Presley had achieved still eluded him.

From 1954 to 1958 Starday released some of the earliest and best rock 'n' roll music ever recorded. It was raw, emotional, frenzied hillbilly bop at its finest, though Pierce and Daily never did figure out what to do with it. When initially asked about the early rockabilly records, Pierce matter-of-factly summed up the effort. "We tried it. It didn't work. We moved on." But when prodded,

Pierce elaborated, "I was not promoting the rockabilly stuff at all. I would say that whatever came in by way of rockabilly was sent in by Pappy Daily. We issued it but I didn't make any special effort in merchandising or promotions. We didn't have much success with it and I didn't even know which jocks would or wouldn't use it."

Though the Starday rockabilly 45s are highly regarded today, thanks in no small part to the European rockabilly revivalists, it is safe to say that Starday never made any money off their rockabilly waxings. Even the majority of country records they were pressing were selling less than a thousand copies. Thus, Pierce and Daily began looking for other ways to make money. One such development was the infamous Starday custom service.

Pierce had run a similar custom service for 4 Star in which anybody could send in a recording they had made, along with the nominal fee of $85, and 4 Star would press and ship 300 copies of that record to the artist on their own label. The deal proved to be quite profitable for both the artist, who could now sell their record at personal shows, and 4 Star, who not only made $85, but also retained the publishing rights to all the songs they pressed. It was through this custom service that 4 Star achieved one if its greatest successes. Slim Willet sent in a tape and ordered 300 copies of his new song, "Don't Let the Stars Get In Your Eyes." Not long after that run sold out, Willet ordered 5,000 more. Pierce took notice, and shortly thereafter 4 Star released the tune within their main series and it became a #1 country hit in 1952. Not only did it hit #1 in the country charts; far more profitable for 4 Star, Perry Como made it a #1 pop hit the same year.

Realizing the vast potential for new publishing material, new stars, royalties from airplay, and more income for the business, Pierce set up almost the identical service at Starday. He did, however, offer a few new features. Now, when an artist purchased 300 copies of a record, that artist would also receive 100 addressed record mailers. As Pierce boasted, "The envelopes were already addressed to the radio stations in a three state area. Put the record in there, tell the story, include a picture, and bang." The new service also touted a better quality vinyl and the opportunity to use the Starday logo on the record label, thus being able to bill yourself as a Starday recording artist without being signed to the label.

As he did with the 4 Star service, Pierce retained the option of signing an artist onto the main label if he was so inclined. According to the original promotional letter from 1954, Pierce wrote, "When we receive your material it will be carefully reviewed, and if it is suitable for making records, we will agree to make 300 flex records on your own label . . . provided, 1. You give us the option to use the recordings on STARDAY LABEL on a royalty basis. 2. You give STARDAY RECORDS AN OPTION for your services as

Arnold Parker, ca. 1956 (Courtesy of Arnold Parker)

a recording artist. 3. We be given publishing rights on the songs recorded."[12] Several songs appeared on both the custom and main label series, though only a handful of artists eventually made the crossover including Jerry Hopkins, Lucky Chapman, King Sterling, Hoyt Scoggins, Jimmy and Dorothy Blakley, Andy Doll, and Jimmy Simpson. Fees for the service were initially set at $115, but by the mid'-sixties had risen to $150 per 300 records.

The concept of vanity records—paid for and distributed by the singers or musicians themselves—was not groundbreaking. Both Columbia and Victor's Canadian division began pressing personal records as early as 1910. Still, Starday's service was easily the most successful custom service within country music and the records are highly sought-after today. Ranging from professionally recorded touring bands to amateurs singing in their kitchen, the custom series provided a refreshing alternative to major label production ideals and presented performers and bands recording their own music as they wanted it to be heard.

Though many of the artists using the service were little-known singers and groups, most were at least regional stars or held their own shows on radio or TV. The genres submitted encompassed all aspects of country music including bluegrass, sacred, hillbilly, rockabilly, western swing, and even a couple blues and southern gospel numbers as well. By the mid-1950s the custom series also afforded a lot of working country dance bands an opportunity to record with the new rock 'n' roll sound. Dozens of rockabilly sessions were sent in. Among the early highlights were Jimmy Johnson's "Woman Love" (Starday 561) (later covered by Gene Vincent as the flipside to "Be-Bop-A-Lula"), Lee Ogletree's "Crooked Dice" (Starday 536), Gene Terry and his Kool Kats' "The Woman I Love" (Rock-It 598), Luke Gordon's "Baby's Gone" (Starday 555), and Arnold Parker's "Find a New Woman" (Starday 570).

Arnold Parker's story is similar to many of the other artists who appeared in the custom series. As he recalls: "In the 1950s, we played country and western swing. Then, when rock and roll started getting so popular, to try to please a lot of the crowd, we had to start playing more and more rock and roll until it got to be about a 50/50 thing. In a Texas dancehall, with about 800 or 1,000 people, age ranging from teenagers to the sixties, most of the teenagers danced to country music, but they wanted to dance to rock and roll as well. It seems that it worked well because the older crowd enjoyed watching the younger ones dance and eventually some of them would try it too. When we recorded for Starday, we recorded at ACA Studios in Houston and it cost us about $360, which we paid. The songs were recorded and released in 1956. The song 'Find a New Woman' was written by Jack Hill, who played lead guitar in our band, the Southernaires. The country song on the other side, 'People Laugh At A Fool,' was written by me and was supposed to be the 'A' side of the record. Both sides played pretty well in this area, where we were known, for a few weeks and then actually the record was forgotten about."

And while several country artists took their turn at rock 'n' roll in the midfifties, one of the genre's greatest icons was still taking his turn at country. Today guitar enthusiasts remember Link Wray for his 1958 riot-inducing instrumental smash "Rumble," though his recording career actually began three years earlier and included three releases on the Starday custom label with his brothers Doug and Vernon.

Throughout the early to mid-1950s the group, which also included Shorty Horton and Dixie Neal, were billed as Lucky Wray and the Palomino Ranch Gang. After a move to the Washington, D.C., area in 1955 and a recording session at Ben Adelman's Empire Studio, six sides were released on the Starday vanity label as by Lucky Wray, with Link and Doug. Two other sides resulted from the session, including a rockabilly vocal take from Link, but were instead released on the Kay label later that year. At some time in 1955 it was discovered that Link had contracted tuberculosis and he subsequently lost a lung. From then on, "Lucky," an affectionate gambling moniker for Vernon, took on the role as lead singer and Link focused his energy fully on guitar. Link Wray recalled: "I first started playin' guitar when I was eight years old and there was this black man named Hambone who played bottleneck guitar and he taught me how to play the blues. I started from there. At first I wanted to play like Chet Atkins and the country pickers 'cause there was no rock and roll back then. And of course I loved Hank Williams. I also loved the jazz guys because I was just learning to play—Tal Farlow, Barney Kessel, Les Paul, Grady Martin, and all the early jazz guitar players. Because back then it was all just country, jazz, and pop. I guess that early stuff I was doin' with my brothers was mostly western swing, but real western swing had violins back then. I just did it with a guitar. . . ."

Though the Starday singles sold poorly, they were instrumental in helping Link and his brothers secure a spot with Milt Grant (a powerhouse teen TV and radio host similar to Dick Clark) as the house band on his show. It was there that history was made. Wray continued: "In Fredericksburg, Virginia, in 1957 there was a DJ who had a TV show where kids come and dance on his show and I'd play the record hops after the TV show. One night in 1957 this DJ brought the Diamonds on his show. They had the #1 song called 'The Stroll.' It was a slow dance and he said, 'Play me a stroll, Link,' and I said, 'I don't know a stroll.' My brother Doug, who was the drummer, said, 'I know the beat,' and he just started playin' the stroll beat and I just made 'Rumble.' I was just like, God . . . you know? I'm very spiritual and my God just zapped me with 'Rumble' and these kids all rushed to the stage and they were all screamin' over this instrumental right from the very first start. And then the DJ, he smelt money and they took me into the studio to try to record me but I couldn't get that same sound I had in Fredericksburg on stage, that rattly sound. So in the studio, I just took the speaker heads off and punched holes in it to get that sound."

Thus was Wray's guitar fuzz born. Wray is also credited with the invention of the "power chord," or simply 1-5 intervals, used to create the "Rumble" melody, which would forever transform rock and roll music. Wray adds, "It came out St. Patrick's Day 1958 [on Cadence Records] and four weeks later it was big in the charts. They banned it on a bunch of stations, 'cause there were gang fights and "Rumble" represented fighting, but it just got bigger. Dick Clark was playin' it all the time." Though Wray has yet to be admitted into the Rock and Roll Hall of Fame, artists such as Bob Dylan, Pete Townshend, Jeff Beck, Jimi Hendrix, Neil Young, Bruce Springsteen, and countless others have all gone on record citing Link Wray as a major influence, and *Rolling Stone* magazine included him in their list of the "Top 100 Greatest Guitarists of All Time."

Despite the excitement and steadily increasing rock 'n' roll sales, Pierce and Daily remained focused on the production and preservation of pure country and western music. Though Starday was technically a California-based label, it quickly became synonymous with East Texas honky-tonk. As Martin

Hal Harris at radio station KYOK, ca. 1955 (Courtesy of Andrew Brown)

Hawkins once described: "It would not be too far from the truth to say that the original Starday had its own style and its own sound—the 'classic' honky-tonk sound of the early '50s, employing the strutting rhythm, the prominent steel and the twin fiddle sounds heard otherwise only in Texas honky-tonks and bars and over the airwaves of the Louisiana Hayride show."[13]

Among the chief contributors to this unique Starday sound was studio session leader and guitarist Harold "Hal" Harris, brother of Clyde "Boots" Harris, Hank Williams's first steel guitar player. By the early 1950s Hal had his own radio show and band in Jackson, Texas. Harris made the move to Houston in 1953 and shortly thereafter had a radio job at KYOK as well as a weekly gig with the Houston Jamboree house band. The following year Harris purchased a brand new Fender Stratocaster. New to the market in 1954, the Stratocaster eventually became one of the most popular electric guitar models and reshaped the sound of music for generations to follow. Harris's Fender electric guitar became a familiar backdrop on both the Jamboree and the many Starday recordings. Starday artist James O'Gwynn recalled: "Hal was from Mississippi. He played a lot like Merle Travis, Travis-style, real good. He was a studio guy in Houston and most everybody [on Starday] used him."

O'Gwynn, whose real name was James Aucoin, also moved to Houston in 1953 and made his first recordings for Starday in 1956. As he tells, "I went down to Pappy Daily's myself in 1956. George [Jones] might have said something to him [O'Gwynn had been Jones's mechanic]. But I just went down to his [Daily's] office and talked to him. Had some cuts down, he listened to 'em, and he signed me. That's the way it was back then. You either got it or you didn't get it." O'Gwynn got the contract and his woeful lament "Losing Game" (266) quickly became a regional hit and helped earn him a four-year contract with the Louisiana Hayride. There he quickly became known as both "The Smilin' Irishman" and "The Pride of the Hayride."

Accompanying O'Gwynn on his recording session were the usual Starday sidemen: either Harris or Harold Sharp on electric guitar, Charles R. "Doc" Lewis on piano, Herbie Remington or Frank Juricek on steel guitar, Russell Vernon "Hezzie" Bryant or Tiny Smith on upright bass, as well as two or three fiddlers from the fiddle pool that included Ernie Hunter, Earl Caruthers, Joe "Red" Hayes, Kenneth "Little Red" Hayes, Link Davis, and others. The session, like most of the other early Starday sessions, took place at Bill Quinn's Gold Star Studios, now the oldest continuously operated recording studio in Texas (presently operating under the name Sugar Hill Studios).

Quinn began his company in 1941 as Quinn Recording, and started out recording radio commercials and birthday greetings. Soon, however, he realized there was a vast amount of unrecorded blues and country talent in East Texas and he began recording musicians such as Lightnin' Hopkins, Aubrey Gass, Wilson "Thunder" Smith, and Melvin "Lil' Son" Jackson. Quinn recorded his first hit in 1946 with Harry Choates's Cajun classic "Jole Blon," originally released on the Gold Star label. Quinn then leased it to the Modern label and the tune peaked at #4 spot on *Billboard*'s Most Played Juke Box Folk Records chart. Daily later purchased the Choates masters from Quinn and rereleased them on Starday.

Though Quinn engineered the Gold Star sessions, Daily remained in charge of producing the early Starday sides. In recalling his producing experiences, Daily once told John Pugh: "I've always looked for feeling in a song, because if country music doesn't have that true feeling, then it's no good. And if an artist is not sold on a song, he can't sell it. So I don't ever make an artist do a song or refuse to let him do one, because who am I to set myself up as a judge? . . . Producing is a lot more guess work than people realize. We can kick out the

Don Pierce and Pappy Daily at the Disc Jockey Convention, year unknown (Courtesy of Don Pierce)

dogs, but we can't really pick the hits. And I've missed a lot, really. But I used to think, 'How do I know this?' Well, my guiding thought has always been, 'Would I buy this as a customer?'"[14]

It was with that freedom that Daily's artists recorded, and the result was pure country music from the heart. From 1953 to 1957 over three hundred singles were released (in the main series and the custom press) and, aside from scattered rockabilly attempts, Starday produced one of the largest catalogs of honky-tonk and fifties country music ever assembled. Among the standout acts signed to Starday were Benny Barnes, Eddie Noack (a popular Houston artist who had previously been produced by Daily and signed to 4 Star), Fred Crawford (who also featured a young Buddy Holly as guitarist on at least one of his Starday sessions), Sid Ervin and his Western Melody Makers (who would later find success on Columbia as Sid King and the Five Strings), Smilin' Jerry Jericho, Les Chambers, Biff Collie, Chuck Mayfield, Bill Nettles, R. D. Hendon, Roy Drusky, Jack Newman, Smokey Stover, and many more.

By 1956 people had begun to hear of Starday. George Jones was considered among the fastest rising talents in all of country music. "Why Baby Why" was on the national charts, as were "What Am I Worth," "You Gotta Be My Baby," "Just One More," and "Yearning." Benny Barnes was riding high with the #2 hit "Poor Man's Riches"; James O'Gwynn was the hottest thing in Houston and on the Louisiana Hayride. Good things were happening for Pierce and Daily and people were beginning to take notice.

3

DON'T STOP THE MUSIC

Irving B. Green founded Mercury Records in Chicago in 1945. Among the first country acts to record for the new label were Wally Fowler, the Oklahoma Wranglers (later known as the Willis Brothers), Carl Story, Rex Allen, and others. By 1949 Mercury's country stable also boasted the likes of Dale Evans, the Masters Family, Eddie Dean, Bonnie Lou, Archie Campbell, and the legendary Flatt and Scruggs. Encouraged by Mercury's early successes in the more lucrative pop and rhythm and blues markets, Green advocated for an even stronger presence in the country music market. In 1951 Green hired Walter David "D." Kilpatrick [though often written in books and journals as "Dee" Kilpatrick, he has requested to be listed as "D."], formerly a Capitol Records salesman and producer, and appointed him the first full-time A&R man in the centralized recording center of Nashville, Tennessee, well before Nashville earned its reputation as "Music City USA." Kilpatrick brought to Mercury a passion for country music and he quickly assembled one of the most notable country stables of any label, adding artists such as the Carlisles, Jimmy Dean, Jerry Byrd, the Stanley Brothers, and Johnny Horton. Though Mercury was still largely considered a rhythm and blues label, thanks in part to the success of Dinah Washington and the Platters, both their extensive pop catalog (Tony Martin, Frankie Laine, Patti Page, and Lawrence Welk, among others) and their growing country catalog helped to establish Mercury as one of the five or six major record companies by the early 1950s.

Then 1956 happened. Elvis Presley was no longer just a hip-shaking, pelvis-gyrating country boy from Mississippi. Rock 'n' roll caught on and the entire country music industry was shaken to its core. According to Kilpatrick, "Country music saw some good times, and of course other times that were not so good, but that damn rock 'n' roll was just really tough on us." Kilpatrick himself was never fond of rock 'n' roll. In fact, he proudly boasts to have been the first person quoted as saying "Rock 'n' roll is the devil's music!" which he feverishly delivered in a speech, complete with pelvis gyrations, to a group of enraged and horrified onlookers during a League of Women Voters meeting in

Nashville organized by Jack Stapp. The exact date of that meeting is unknown; what is known is that fewer people longed for the harmony of the twin fiddles or the rhythm of a country boogie. Kilpatrick, like Daily, quickly realized that in order to stay competitive it was necessary to find rockabilly performers.

Green had been good friends with Sam Phillips and, when Phillips decided to sell Presley's contract to a bigger label, he offered it to Mercury for $50,000. Green, in one of the greatest missed opportunities of the century, declined the offer and instead opted to find his own version of Elvis. Roy Moss, Jimmie Skinner's protégé, was among the first to fill those shoes for Mercury in 1955, recording his first rockabilly singles shortly after Presley's historic Sun studio sessions that led to the nationwide frenzy. Not long after, many of Mercury's country artists were persuaded to record the new sound as well. Among them were Billy Wallace, author of the Webb Pierce classic "Back Street Affair," Don Johnston, Bing Day, George and Earl, Johnny "T" Talley, Royce Porter, Thomas Wayne, and others. Sadly, none of them showed nearly as much sales potential as the King. Success was limited, and Green was now ready to look elsewhere to boost his declining country sales.

Not only was Green ready to look elsewhere, he had to. By the end of 1956 Johnny Horton, who later attempted the rockabilly sound with much acclaim, had left for greener pastures with Columbia Records. Conway Twitty, who recorded for Mercury through 1957, released only teenybopper pop hits which occasionally rocked. It was not until after Mercury released Twitty that he waxed a string of rock 'n' roll recordings and later country recordings with colossal success. Desperation was even more apparent when D. Kilpatrick, the man who had developed the country division, announced that he too was leaving Mercury to replace Jim Denny as the manager of the Grand Ole Opry. Though unfortunate timing for Mercury, his move proved to be a saving grace for the Opry, which was slowly recovering from a scathing battle with its artists. Don Pierce recalls, "I could always work with Jim Denny, but I hated the guy when I first got here [Nashville] because I was well aware that he was using his position in the Grand Ole Opry to enrich himself in the publishing business. If the artist would do his songs [Cedarwood Publishing Company], they got the good bookings. They don't do his songs, they get the crap. And of course the artists were madder than hell about that. The Opry finally gave the job to D. Kilpatrick and all that stopped."

Mercury now had vacancies in both the A&R department and the country/rockabilly artist stable. Nashville's annual Disc Jockey Convention, held in November 1956, seemed like a logical place to find both. Cornbread, beer, and country music were the backdrop as various labels hosted parties to promote artists to disc jockeys, jukebox operators, and record distributors. It was a time of comradeship among industry leaders, performers, and friends, and

Don Pierce and Mercury president Irv Green during the 1956 Disc Jockey Convention in Nashville (Courtesy of Don Pierce)

also a time for wheeling and dealing. To combat the disastrous impact of rock 'n' roll on the country market, companies were looking for any way to make the bleeding stop, and Mercury was no exception.

Impressed by the continued chart success of Starday Records and its catalog, and perhaps even more intrigued by George Jones's ability to record both country and rockabilly (as Thumper Jones and later as Hank Smith on various EPs), Irv Green and Art Talmadge, then VP of Mercury, summoned a meeting with Daily and Pierce during the convention. As Pierce recalls, "Art said, 'We've given D. the job of getting a replacement for him, and we think the arrangement he's got would work pretty good. Pappy will be a Mercury distributor in Texas, and he will also book Grand Ole Opry talent for D. And Don, we'd like for you to replace D. as being in charge of our country music sales and headquarter out of Nashville, Tennessee.' So it was a deal with the Grand Ole Opry people and with Mercury Records and with me, so to speak."

Both Daily and Pierce were enthusiastic about the proposal. Daily was able to remain in Texas and continue doing what he had just recently started, distributing Mercury Records. He still searched for and recorded new talent, but now sent the masters to Nashville instead of Los Angeles. He could also further help his artists by booking them with the Grand Ole Opry talent throughout the Lone Star State. Pierce continued to schedule releases, compose notes, set up distribution and get the records into the hands of disc jockeys. He also produced many of the Nashville recording sessions. Hands were shaken, papers signed, and the two labels were merged.

The biggest adjustment to be made was moving Starday from Los Angeles to Nashville, something Mercury required and that Pierce was eager to do. Prior to signing the deal with Mercury, Pierce had cut back on the pressings done through Coast Record Company. Up until that point, Starday was still receiving rent-free office space at the Coast plant, with the understanding that they would press all of the Starday releases. Nevertheless, Daily and Pierce began looking for a more central pressing plant in an effort to cut back on shipping costs to distributors and to eliminate some of the breakage factor involved in shipping records. Pierce remembers, "That caused hard feelings with Coast, who felt like they helped us get started and now most of the pressing was going to Plastic Products in Memphis. There was some strain in our relationship, but we had to take our pressings back into the central part of the country."

Pierce, along with his assistant Murray "Jack" Frost, packed up the office and left the sunny beaches of California behind them. The completed move was first announced in *Billboard* on April 13, 1957. Once in Nashville, Pierce sought out a place to live. He remembers, "I bought a lot on the lake in Hendersonville for $5,000 and it happened to be right next door to Roy Acuff. The next lot over was owned by Governor Frank Clement and the lot behind me was owned by Silliman Evans Jr., who was the publisher of the *Nashville Tennessean*. I thought I'd died and gone to heaven." His other neighbors not far away would later include Johnny Cash, Kitty Wells and Johnny Wright, Roy Orbison, Bashful Brother Oswald, and a host of others within the industry with whom he would soon be barbecuing, boating, and fishing on a regular basis.

After securing a place to build a home, he and Daily bought a building to operate the Mercury-Starday business, as well as Pierce's rhythm and blues label Hollywood, which he continued to run separate from Starday. Rather than be a part of the newly forming Music Row downtown, Pierce and Daily opted to buy a building on Dickerson Pike (Highway 41), about six miles west of downtown Nashville. In doing so, Pierce could go about his daily business without fear of being closely supervised or having his marketing strategies

The Starday delivery van parked in front of the company office, studio, and warehouse on Dickerson Pike, Nashville, ca. 1962 (Courtesy of Don Pierce)

copied by neighboring competition. Pierce once explained to Colin Escott, "When I first came here, Murray Nash, who had worked for Acuff-Rose and Mercury and RCA, told me that the place to be was the old Cumberland Lodge Building on Seventh Avenue North, near WSM, but I said, 'Not for me. I want to be away from the business. These people are my competitors.' I didn't want to be seen as another outlet for these people to sell their songs. I told Murray, 'I'm your competitor. I'm interested in recording my songs, not your songs.'"[1]

Not only would the new location keep Pierce away from his competitors and music industry hawks, it also meant less of a commute to the golf course. For a total of $16,000, Starday now had an office to work from and a temporary residence for Pierce until his Hendersonville home was built. Pierce set up camp in the new office, and thus began a new phase of Starday Records.

The first release in the Mercury-Starday series was by the man who had first sparked the interest of Mercury, George Jones. The Mercury-Starday Country Series went into effect on January 1, 1957, and by January 2 they had released Jones's first major-label record: "Don't Stop the Music" (71029). The song picked up right where Jones had left off with his last Starday single "Just One More" (264). Tender, heart-wrenching ballads were quickly becoming Jones's favorite songs to sing. Though his upbeat country stompers and rockabilly sides more than likely played an important role in impressing Mercury, Jones himself never thought highly of them. As Jones once told journalist Pete Hunter, "I did some rock, had fun with it, but it didn't touch my heart. I was always looking forward to the next song so I could get back to a ballad."[2]

"Don't Stop" was the beginning of a completely unique singing style that would eventually help him to sell millions of records, but its initial sales clearly reflected the state of country music in the late 1950s. Pierce recalled that it was #1 on several top radio stations, and reached #10 on the *Billboard* country chart, but that it only sold about twenty-five to thirty thousand copies. The flip side, "Uh, Uh No" was an up-tempo Jones original. Undeniably country, it too reached *Billboard*'s charts, though it dropped off after just one week.

With a new label and a new record, Jones also found new management. Hal Smith, who also managed Carl Smith and Jimmy Newman, took over for Jones's first manager Bill Hall and Jones took to the open road to promote his new record. Just prior to the Mercury-Starday deal (August 1956), Jones joined the Grand Ole Opry cast and by the end of the year was also headlining on the Big "D" Jamboree. He began touring with Opry package shows in early 1957 and thus began the life on the road that Jones has battled publicly throughout his career. Though he had toured in support of his Starday records before, the demands of a major label and continuing chart success soon entrenched Jones in a career he was unprepared to manage. Depression set in often and alcohol was all that would ease the pain, much to the chagrin of Daily and Jones's wife. His alcoholism led to countless fights as well as financial difficulties throughout this time. All of this coupled with the fact that Jones still made his bed in Texas, despite the new position with the Opry and the deal with Mercury. This meant traveling back and forth, living out of the Clarkston Hotel when in Nashville, and splitting recording obligations between Bill Quinn's Gold Star Studio in Houston and Owen Bradley's Quonset Hut in Nashville.

Pierce and Daily preferred to record Jones in Texas. It was cheaper to record at Gold Star than it was in Nashville, which was quickly emerging as the recording center for country music. Further, Daily could attend and produce the Texas sessions and pitch new songs to his rising star. On March 31, 1957, Daily even sold his distribution companies to his sons, Bud and Don, so that he could spend more time on Mercury-Starday and with Jones. That meant even more opportunities to search for new talent and song material.

Jones was far more excited about the prospect of recording in Nashville, thinking that Nashville's top session men would be just the thing he needed to get a #1 hit. According to Jones, "Neither place in Texas [Starns's living room or Bill Quinn's Gold Star Studio] was worth a damn. When they talk about the Quonset Hut in Nashville competing with them, the Quonset Hut was the best damn studio in Nashville and still is the best to my knowledge, 'cause we put out some hits in that bugger!"

Don Pierce, who produced many of Jones's Nashville sessions, remembers, "George would come into town from the road and he'd call me and say, 'Don, I'm gonna be in for a couple days and I've got some stuff to record.' I'd say, 'Great.' Chet Atkins was a great help to me on those sessions. But in all honesty, George produced George. I didn't produce George. He'd picked all the

George Jones Mercury-Starday publicity photo, ca. 1957 (Courtesy of Nathan Gibson)

guys and said, 'Do it do-da this way' and 'Do-da that way' and that's how they did it."

It was during these quick stop-ins that Pierce got to know his young recording star personally. One of Pierce's favorite stories, as he told it to Escott, begins: "George was out in West Texas, got in trouble, and got thrown in the clink. Pappy Daily got him out and got him over to Houston for a gig that paid $2,500. George played the date, threw a party and got drunk. Pappy heard through another musician that George had thrown this party and flushed all of his money down the toilet. So when George came by later, Pappy said, 'Golly George, I get you out of jail, get you a date, I give you front money and buy you a new uniform and you go and flush $2,500 down the toilet.' George said, 'Pappy, that's a goddamn lie. It wasn't but $1,200.'"[3]

"Another time," Pierce remembers, "We took a trip to Cincinnati together and he played out at Verona Park and he'd been drinking some, so we got him onstage as early as possible and he just tore the crowd up. Then we took him to some downtown tavern, and he played a show there and did the same thing, and then he got his money and kept right on partying. The next day he was broke again. I remember we stayed at a hotel in Cincinnati and then he left, and he left the bill for me to pay, which was all right. He went down to Elizabethtown, Kentucky, to do another show and some women followed him and the party continued there." After the Elizabethtown show, Pierce headed back to Nashville by himself only to get a call the next day from Jones who was still broke and still in Kentucky. "I guess he ran out of money and I guess he was kinda mad at me because I wouldn't leave my office and drive back there to bring him back to Nashville." Pierce then suggested to Jones that he take the bus, which further outraged the singer. Pierce adds, "Ah well, I'm sure he was able to get transportation elsewhere."

The relationship between Pierce and Jones became, as Pierce describes, "rather strained during those years." Pierce attributes this to being the hatchet man. Daily was the "yes" man. If anyone ever had to say "no" to Jones, it would have to be Pierce. Pierce adds, "I was the one George would complain to if he wanted something. And from time to time when George would come in from the road to Nashville, and it would be late at night, he would call my home and if he had any gripes or things of that nature he generally unloaded them on my wife and she would relate them to me the next day."

That would be on a good day. On a bad day, George Jones might stop by the office and want to talk in person. According to Pierce, "One time George got to drinkin' some downtown and got to needing some money pretty bad and decided that if he went out to the Starday offices he could get some. And he came in there and he was pretty heavy under the influence and he started throwing things around and it was not a very nice scene. One of my employees called the police in Madison and they came over and told him to sleep it off."

That was Pierce's version of the story. Jones told the same story in his autobiography, though he remembered a few more details. Jones wrote: "I came in drunk one Saturday morning after driving all night from a show somewhere. I went directly to the office of one of Pappy Daily's assistants. I demanded that I be paid everything I was owed, but he couldn't say exactly how much that was. And the only number he seemed to know was eleven.

"'Well, just how many records have sold?' I demanded.

"'I'd say about eleven thousand,' the assistant said.

"'Well, how many advance orders do we have for our next release?' I asked.

"'Oh, I don't know,' he said. 'About eleven hundred.'

"I got sick of that real quickly. Someone said I was given nine hundred dollars, but I figured I had a lot more than that coming and I got rowdy. I wouldn't leave his side. If he moved behind his desk, so did I. If he went to the men's room, so did I. I threatened to whip him, and he took off out the back door. But not before calling the police."[4]

The police came and took Jones away and he slept the mood off. The very next day Jones went back to Pierce's office and apologized for acting up. "That's how it always was, because when he was sober and in his right mind, he was just the nicest and most humble fella you could hope to meet. Really, you couldn't help but love him," notes Pierce. Still, after Jones's book came out, Pierce wrote a letter to Jones explaining that he wasn't "Daily's assistant," but that in fact he was the president of Starday Records and that it was him who had driven across the country in his car promoting "Why Baby Why" and helping to make George Jones a star. Though he was not drunk when he wrote the book, Jones wrote back to Pierce the next day and apologized for that, too.

And so, Pierce put up with Jones's often brash behavior and remained cautious in his handling of the star singer. Jones was, after all, the backbone of the Mercury-Starday deal and recorded hit after hit. Strangely though, the Mercury-Starday years are often overlooked by Jones's many biographers and researchers. For most, his career began with "No Money in This Deal" and on to "Why, Baby, Why" and the rest of the Starday sides, and then skyrocketed upon the release of his first #1 hit, "White Lightning" on Mercury. In between the Starday and Mercury bookends, however, lies Jones' remarkable musical development of the Mercury-Starday period. The two dozen sides released by Jones under the Mercury-Starday banner highlight a youthful liveliness that was more mature than his Starday recordings, and yet he was still developing "The Voice" for which he eventually became known. The ease with which he drifted from his hardcore East Texas honky-tonk roots to the most heartwarming ballad to the most haunting gospel deliverance and then back to quasi-rockabilly novelty numbers, demonstrated his amazing versatility and flexibility. He was perfecting his craft of conveying raw human emotion in song and was, by this time, already one of the best.

Jones charted a total of four hit records for Mercury-Starday including "Uh, Uh No," "Too Much Water" (71096) (co-written by Capitol Records' budding star Sonny James, whose "Young Love" became a #1 hit in 1957), the heartfelt original "Color of the Blues" (71257), which peaked at #7 on the *Billboard* country chart, as well as the aforementioned "Don't Stop the Music." Irv Green and the Mercury brass were likely hoping for a rockabilly breakout within Jones, or at least some potential pop marketability, but Pierce and Daily were content allowing their country boy to write his own material, choose which songs to record, and create his own path toward success.

Their method paid off. Despite the extracurricular activities that have often overshadowed his professional career, George Jones went on to amass nearly every award that could be given to a country performer. Despite living out the

Roger Miller, ca. 1958 (Courtesy of Nathan Gibson)

ragged honky-tonk songs he wrote about, George Jones somehow managed to live through it all. In doing so, Jones sang his way to #2 on *Billboard*'s All-Time Country Music Recording Artist list. Jones truly earned his admission to the Country Music Hall of Fame and, according to Pierce, "With the passing of Johnny Cash, George is now acknowledged to be the #1 country music artist in the world. And he certainly should be."

But Jones's contribution to Mercury-Starday was not limited to his recordings. In fact, instead of having songwriters pitch their songs to him, more often Jones was pitching new songwriters to Pierce and Daily and helping to give his friends a shot in the business. One such friend was his then unknown pal Roger Miller, at the time a bellhop at the Andrew Jackson Hotel in Nashville. Miller was just getting acquainted with the Nashville music scene and had recently sung backing vocals on a Curtis Gordon Mercury-Starday session when Jones convinced Daily and Pierce to give Miller an audition. There, in an Andrew Jackson Hotel bedroom, Miller convinced the two men to record him singing his own songs, though they required the session take place in Houston. As Pierce recalls, "In Houston we could record Roger for $5 per song per man, whereas if we recorded Roger at that time, an absolute unknown newcomer, it would cost union scale in Nashville." According to Pierce, union scale at that time, as established by the American Federation of Musicians, was $41.25 per man per three hour session—a significant difference. Pierce suggested that Jones, who was going back to Houston to visit his wife anyway, and Miller drive to Texas together.

During this infamous road trip, Jones and Miller co-wrote several tunes, including Jones's classic recording of "Tall Tall Trees" (71176), which later became a #1 hit for Alan Jackson. Among the songs Miller saved for himself were "Poor Little John" and "My Pillow" (71212), which saw release in October 1957 as his first record. Pierce remembers that the disc "didn't sell well at all," but that Miller still played an important role in Mercury-Starday with his songwriting. Aside from his own release, Miller also wrote songs for several other Mercury-Starday artists, including Jimmy Dean, George Jones, Curtis Gordon, and Eddie Bond.

The Mercury-Starday years mark the beginning to one of the most illustrious songwriting careers ever launched in Nashville. After one more release on Starday in June 1958 (356), Miller left Nashville and returned to the Southwest. Later that year he was hired to front Ray Price's Cherokee Cowboys, an incarnation of Blackie Crawford's Western Cherokees band with a completely different lineup. After Price recorded Miller's "Invitation to the Blues," a honky-tonk shuffle that reached #3 on *Billboard*'s chart, Miller was signed as a writer for Tree Publishing Company and came back to Nashville. Shortly thereafter he was rewarded with a Decca Records recording contract. In addition to duets with Donny Young (better known as Johnny Paycheck) and Justin Tubb, Miller also recorded four more honky-tonk sides of his own. Again, sales were flat and Miller was dropped. An RCA contract and a year stint as Faron Young's drummer followed, though by 1963 Miller was again looking to leave Music City and give up on show business. To finance his move, Miller signed to Smash Records (a division of Mercury Records), where he was paid $100 per song he recorded. Among his first songs was "Dang Me," which became a #1 country hit and a Top 10 pop hit. He followed that with the #3 hit "Chug-A-Lug," the million-selling "King of the Road," "Engine Engine #9," "Kansas City Star," and "Husbands and Wives." Roger Miller was now a big-time star and in 1965 and 1966, Miller won eleven Grammys. His comedy and demeanor were infectious and his success was assured, eventually guiding Miller into the Country Music Hall of Fame in 1995.

Miller was not the only legendary recording artist Jones helped bring to Mercury-Starday. Another important newcomer was J. P. Richardson, later known as the Big Bopper. Richardson came to the attention of Pappy Daily while working as a disc jockey on KTRM in Beaumont (George Jones's former gig). He had initially taken a part-time job at the station to help finance a law degree, but soon was among the highest-rated jockeys in East Texas and thus gave up the legal aspirations. After a two-year stint in the army as a radar instructor, Richardson went back to work full-time at KTRM; in 1957 he set a record for the most consecutive hours of broadcasting—122 hours straight, with only ten-minute bathroom and shower breaks. This publicity stunt surely helped attract the notice of Daily. Presumably excited about the prospect of promoting his own discs on air, Richardson accepted Daily's offer to record for Mercury-Starday. His first recording session followed shortly thereafter, aside from an unreleased demo session he had made before going into the service.

Though Richardson is widely regarded today as a rock vocalist, his first record was pure honky-tonk, largely because Mercury-Starday was a country label. Because Richardson did not yet have a stage name, the record label credited him as Jape Richardson and the Japetts. The A-side was "Beggar to a King" (71219), a heartwarming, original ballad that failed to sell, though it later became a #5 hit for Hank Snow in 1961. The rookie effort was paired with another original, "Crazy Blues," which aggressively rollicked along while through his friendly Texas drawl he sang about killing either himself or his ex. The snappy drumbeat and voice echo bordered on rockabilly, but the swinging steel guitar and piano make it one of the best honky-tonk songs in the Starday catalogue. Unfortunately, it too fell on deaf ears. It would be Richardson's only release on Mercury-Starday.

With his very next release, recorded at Gold Star Studios and released on Pappy Daily's new D label, Richardson found his target audience. As Pappy Daily recalled to Martin Hawkins: "He was in Beaumont then, worked as a disc jockey at KRIC, and he'd been singing for a while. I'd been cutting him country, just country. Then one day in 1958 he called me and said he's coming in for a session on two pop songs, rock'n'roll stuff. He came in with Link Davis on saxophone, Eddie Noack on guitar, and I think Hal Harris and Doc Lewis. All country boys anyway. But they cut the rock tunes alright. The one J. P. liked was called 'Purple People Eater Meets the Witchdoctor,' so he took that song and gave me the publishing rights to the B-side, 'That's What I Like.' Well, I took the test disc home and played it a few times, and it seemed that not only was the B-side better but it had this recurring phrase, 'Chantilly Lace.' So I called J. P. and told him it was going to be the A-side. Well, he argued for a while. And he wanted the label to credit the artist as The Big Yazoo, because he'd been doing commercials under that name. But I named him the Big Bopper, thought that sounded better. The disc took off, selling 40,000 on D, so I licensed it to Mercury and it sold a million more. 'Chantilly Lace,' that was the real big one."[5]

Pappy Daily, Benny Barnes, and Don Pierce in 1956 (Courtesy of Nathan Gibson)

Less than eight months after waxing his first platter, Richardson had a coveted gold record and was headlining across the country. But tragedy struck the music industry on February 3, 1959, when his plane, also carrying Buddy Holly and Ritchie Valens, crashed into a snow-swept cornfield in Cerro Gordo County, Iowa. All three of the artists were at the peak of their career. Richardson was only twenty-four years old. Just one month after his death, Richardson's legacy was furthered when his original composition, "Running Bear" became a #1 hit for Johnny Preston and featured Richardson and George Jones doing the backing vocals. Simultaneously, Jones scored his first #1 hit with another Richardson tune. Jones recalls: "J. P. Richardson, the Big Bopper, was from my hometown of Beaumont, Texas and he wrote 'White Lightning' and another country thing called 'Treasure of Love, and I did those two on the session together and we came out with 'White Lightning' and I couldn't have been any more thrilled than anybody could be when it went to number one. But J. P. Richardson, he had just got killed in the plane crash before it came out and I really hated that and I would've liked for him to have seen and heard that record for himself."

But perhaps Jones's friend who caused the most excitement among the Mercury-Starday brass was Benny Barnes. Another in the hardcore East Texas honky-tonk tradition who came out of Beaumont, Barnes sang with a nasally, Hank Snow–influenced whine. Barnes came to the attention of Pappy Daily when Jones invited him to participate in one of Jones's Starday recording sessions sometime in 1956. There Daily overheard him singing a mid-tempo love song he had just co-written with Dee Marais entitled "Poor Man's Riches," and he was promptly rewarded with a Starday recording contract. Barnes was on the cusp of stardom after "Poor Man's Riches" (262) hit the *Billboard* charts in September 1956 and stayed there for over four months, crawling all the way to the #2 spot, Starday's biggest hit yet. Further of interest to Mercury, Barnes's single reached #1 in total country sales and sold more copies than any of George Jones's previous Starday hits. The success of "Poor Man's Riches" alone secured Barnes a spot on the Louisiana Hayride, regular appearances on the Big "D" Jamboree and, more importantly, brought him national recognition.

After promptly rereleasing "Poor Man's Riches" on the Mercury label and seeing the song covered by several hot artists, including George Jones, Red Sovine, and the Carlisles, the Mercury-Starday brass eagerly anticipated Barnes's next hit. But unlike Jones, even after the transition had been made from Starday to Mercury-Starday, Barnes continued to record at Bill Quinn's Gold Star Studio in Houston. Therefore, the Mercury-Starday sides still featured many of the celebrated Starday session sidemen including Hal and Charlie Harris on guitars, Joe "Red" Hayes, Ernie Hunter and Link Davis on fiddle, Herb Remington on steel guitar, Doc Lewis on piano, and "Hezzie" Bryant or Don Newton on bass. The result was Texas honky-tonk at its purest and finest, with a nasal resonance that made Barnes instantly recognizable. Unfortunately his voice, which became associated with the more traditional country sounds of Hank Williams and Lefty Frizzell, was of a kind not receiving massive amounts of airplay during the rockabilly spell cast over 1957. Not one of Barnes's subsequent releases on Mercury-Starday found the charts, and many began to write him off as a one-hit wonder. Pappy Daily remarked to Martin Hawkins, "I thought he [Barnes] was a fine singer. He was a great artist with a fine stage act. I never could understand why he didn't make it big."[6] Despite only moderate chart success, Daily continued to have faith in Barnes's talent and the two worked together for several years, making records for Mercury, D, and United Artists.

It was Barnes's non-musician friend, however, who came to play a much larger role in Mercury-Starday at this time. Dee Marais, an insurance agent in Shreveport who owned a recording studio and had made Barnes's first demo recordings, was instrumental in introducing Pappy Daily to Shelby Singleton, who was then managing his wife, Margie Singleton. Barnes and Margie Singleton began performing on the Louisiana Hayride around the same time in 1956, and shortly thereafter Shelby Singleton befriended Daily and convinced him to release Margie's first records on Starday. Though her first three records were all released in 1957, they were only released on the Starday label as opposed to Mercury-Starday. This was because Pierce had expressed an intense distaste for her voice, and he was the one who scheduled her releases. Pierce recalls: "I hated her records. Terrible! But my assistant Jack Frost cautioned me once to avoid any differences with Pappy when I complained about more stuff coming in on Margie and I'm sure glad he did." Her records were released on Starday, and a major confrontation with Daily was averted.

Not long after her first record came out, Mercury-Starday hired Shelby Singleton. Pierce had quickly realized there was no way he himself could possibly perform all the desired tasks that Mercury had in mind. According to a *Billboard* article detailing the Starday move to Nashville, Pierce was to spend "most of April, May and June visiting Midwestern, Eastern and Southern distributors and branches. He will concentrate on working with Mercury-Starday salesmen, one-stops and key country and western dealers on promotion of Mercury-Starday releases."[7] In addition to those duties, Pierce was to attend and report to the monthly meetings with Irv Green and Art Talmadge in Chicago. As Pierce remembers, "Once I got there [Chicago] they wanted me to do all the office work, produce several of the Nashville sessions, and do promotion across the country. But I didn't want to do all the promotion because it would mean their *entire* catalog, not just the country division. So Pappy recommended Shelby Singleton, and we hired him and he was great."

Singleton accepted his first full-time job in the music business as Mercury's Southern Promotions manager. Along with promoting the Mercury-Starday releases, he was also promoting, and later producing, artists such as Johnny Holiday, Sarah Vaughn, Dinah Washington, the Platters, Rusty Draper, and several other pop and R&B artists. Singleton tells the story: "I came to Nashville and met with the Mercury people and they hired me and the first person I ever went on the road with was Don Pierce. As I remember, I came to Nashville and we loaded up the trunk with records and got in the car, it was my car I think, and our first stop was in Richmond, Virginia. We had a distributorship there and from there we went to Washington, D.C. In Washington, Don borrowed my car to go someplace and he ran over somebody and knocked 'em down. Anyway, the police showed up and they were so nice that Don just gave 'em a bunch of the records as a gift. [The victim was OK.] It was on one of those trips that Don taught me, don't ever stop at a restaurant that advertises ice cream. Stop at one that advertises liquor instead 'cause it's a better

Willie Nelson's Starday custom single "No Place For Me" (Courtesy of Eric Jackson)

restaurant. The reason for that is, they don't have to make all their money on food, they can make it off the liquor, so the food would be better. . . . Don was full of advice like that."

Pierce continued to provide Singleton with good advice and, as Shelby Singleton's role in Mercury Records grew, so did his wife Margie's. Three of Margie's compositions, each co-authored with Shelby Singleton, were recorded by other Mercury-Starday artists: "Mine All Mine" (71119) by Benny Barnes, "Demon in My Heart" (71231) by Dorothy and Jimmy Blakley, and "Moonlight Magic" (71202) by "Country" Johnny Mathis. Although it would be several more years before she began her successful string of duets with both George Jones and Faron Young, she was one more in an impressive list of young artists to get their start from Daily and Pierce.

Another gifted songwriter's career was launched by Daily and Pierce on February 12, 1957, when Mercury-Starday released Leon Payne's recording of "Lumberjack" coupled with "A Million to One" (71063). The A-side became one of Payne's most popular songs, covered by Johnny Cash on his legendary 1961 album *Ride This Train*. But Cash was not the first to see potential in Payne's gem. When "Texas" Willie Nelson first heard "Lumberjack," he decided to record his own version, perhaps because it was among the few country songs to mention Oregon, where he was then living. Prior to living in Oregon, Nelson had jockeyed for various Texas radio stations and had befriended radio personality and recording star T. Texas Tyler. When Nelson informed Tyler of his recording ambitions, Tyler, who had been produced and befriended by Don Pierce while with 4 Star, phoned Pierce and asked if Starday could do anything to help the young jockey. Pierce, who was still operating the custom record service, in May 1957 offered to press up 300 copies of "Lumberjack" for Nelson (on the Willie Nelson Records vanity label) for a nominal fee, and those were then distributed throughout the Portland/Vancouver area.

The single, paired with Nelson's own "No Place For Me" (Willie Nelson 628), offered little indication of the aspiring songwriter's ability, and neither Pierce nor Daily saw fit to release it on the main series. Regardless, it was a foundation on which Nelson would quickly build. As Pierce remembers, "Shortly after that, Willie wrote that song 'Family Bible' and Claude Gray had a hit with it on D [1960]. It was then bumped up to Mercury. Willie sold it ... for $50. When Willie asked Faron to do 'Hello Walls,' he was willing to sell the song to Faron for $25 or $30 dollars [Young has said Nelson offered it to him for $500]. Faron said, 'No, you hang on to that.' And when Willie got his royalty for the sales of Faron's records on 'Hello Walls' he shipped an entire steer from Texas to Faron Young up here in Nashville."

Like Nelson, many artists recording for Pierce and Daily never made the transition to Mercury-Starday, although many saw releases on Starday. In 1957 alone, nearly eighty singles were issued under the Starday imprint. Why some singles were released on Starday and others on Mercury-Starday remains one of the great Starday mysteries. It is likely that the Starday imprint was being used as a local test run for releases, though Pierce could not recall any examples. Still, many highly touted artists did make the transition from Starday to Mercury-Starday including James O'Gwynn, Dorothy and Jimmy Blakley (though rockabilly releases by Jimmy's brother Cliff Blakley remained on Starday), Sleepy LaBeef, Jeanette Hicks, and "Country" Johnny Mathis. While recording for Starday, Mathis recorded duets with Les Chambers and was simply billed as Johnny Mathis. Confusion set in sometime around February 1957 when a pop vocalist with the same name emerged in *Billboard*'s pop charts and scored three Top Ten hits within the year. Eddie Noack later recalled, "I was listening to [The Louisiana] Hayride one night when this other Johnny Mathis came out and Johnny came on and said, 'People have asked me if I'm, y'know, if we're the same, the other Johnny Mathis and myself.' And he said, 'There's as much difference between us as there is between black and white,' and that's when he started calling himself 'Country' Johnny Mathis."[8]

Throughout 1957 Pierce kept busy scheduling releases for Mercury-Starday and running both the Starday custom service and his Hollywood R&B label. He also continued to operate the Dixie label, a label he and Daily created in either late 1955 or early 1956. Unlike the custom service, which increasingly began to use the Dixie label after 1958, this new Dixie label consisted primarily of soundalike recordings, or imitation records, made by the various Starday and Mercury-Starday artists and that were sold via radio only. Pierce explains: "I had a DJ friend named Randy Blake at WJJD in Chicago. While I was with 4 Star, we were furnishing him the *Hillbilly Hit Parade* that he sold by mail order. I talked to him on the phone and I asked, 'How you doing with Bill McCall?' 'Well, the breakage on Bill's records is just terrible.' I said, 'I can make a flex pressing, containing vinylite, and they are more flexible and will withstand a lot more handling and shipping.' He said, 'We'll give it a try. I want to have a set of Christmas songs, about 18 songs, and 12 of them to be just organ and chimes. That's what my people want, organ and chimes.' Well, I got a guy, C. Sharp Minor was his name [!], he played the organ for theaters in Los Angeles, and we made some tapes in his front room with organ and chimes. We furnished Randy the set and Randy sold probably 20-30,000 of them. . . . Randy said, 'Don, I'm ready for you to make me a *Hillbilly Hit Parade* set.'"

Pierce and Daily then began to furnish Blake with sets of either three 45s or 78s containing 18 songs total. Pierce further recalls, "We'd ship them out of Memphis and Randy would sell twenty to thirty thousand of a set. Then after those would die down, we'd get a new one made up. Randy became very important to us, and we made plenty of money with Randy Blake." The Dixie series began around 1956 and continued throughout the Mercury-Starday era and into the early 1960s.

Filling these *Hillbilly Hit Parade* sets were Starday and Mercury-Starday master recordings, often labeled incorrectly or with artists left entirely uncredited. Because most of the artists were merely copying the hit records of the day, few ever seemed bothered by the lack of recognition. George Jones sang a convincing Elvis Presley or Johnny Horton imitation. Leon Payne did Sonny James, Ernest Tubb, and Presley. James O'Gwynn could do a great Webb Pierce. Jimmy Blakley did a good Marvin Rainwater or Hank Williams impersonation. "Country" Johnny Mathis could sound similar to Hank Locklin and Porter Wagoner. Earl Aycock could be a convincing Johnny Horton. Benny Barnes did Johnny Cash and Hank Snow—and the list goes on. For many of the artists who went on to have successful careers, those recordings came back to haunt them.

George Jones, for example, admits to being embarrassed by his Elvis Presley soundalikes. Sleepy LaBeef, contrastingly, offers a different perspective. According to LaBeef: "Ten dollars a day. That's what we'd get paid. And it didn't matter if you did one [song] or five. Sometimes it was five and you still get ten dollars a day. And they put it out back then under a fictitious name. People like Wolfman Jack or Paul Kellinger at XERL [Del Rio, Texas], they would say, 'Friends, send in $3.98 and get these 18 big hits.' They were hit songs but they were not by the original artists. But they sounded like it. Johnny Cash. He came out a little later but he was easy to do. I did a couple of his. But the first part I was doing Hank Snow. Carl Smith. Earl Aycock would do the Everly Brothers and things like that. I've heard that George didn't want to do that early rockabilly stuff, but it was good. I thought it was good. I don't know why you'd be embarrassed by it. Maybe if you're the number one country singer you might be able to afford the embarrassment. To me, it's all just part of the ladder."

Many of those soundalike recordings were compiled, along with several Mercury-Starday sides, to complete a *Hillbilly Hit Parade* series of LPs, for which three volumes were released (one on Starday and two on Mercury-Starday). Pierce was fast becoming a believer in the market potential for the country LP and pushed hard for full-length country releases. Aside from the two *Hillbilly Hit Parade* LPs (MG20282 and MG20328), Mercury-Starday also released George Jones' second full-length album, *Grand Ole Opry's New Star* (MG20306); the first album by Jimmy Dean, *Jimmy Dean Sings His Television Favorites* (MG20319); and Carl Story's first album, *Gospel Quartet Favorites* (MG20323).

Dean, who grew up in Plainview, Texas, began entertaining while he was stationed at Bolling Air Force Base near Washington, D.C., in 1946, and formed his band, the Texas Wildcats, in 1949. Dean soon became associated with D.C. hillbilly impresario Connie B. Gay, who heavily promoted Dean and eventually directed him to a young Don Pierce. As Pierce remembers, "My association started with Jimmy Dean when I was still with 4 Star. I sent him a demo copy of 'Bummin' Around' and he made a record of it and it made the charts and that got him started. Later when we took over for Mercury-Starday, I recorded a session by Jimmy in the RCA studio and Chet Atkins was very helpful with the musicians and with the work."

Dean's initial recording of "Bumming Around" hit the charts on March 7, 1953, and peaked at #5. Two years later Dean signed a recording contract with Mercury and was produced by D. Kilpatrick. With the success of "Freight Train Blues" and other Mercury recordings, Dean secured a spot emceeing the regionally syndicated TV show *Town and Country Jamboree*, which featured regulars such as Patsy Cline, Billy Grammar, Roy Clark, and George Hamilton IV. Soon after Mercury and Starday merged, Dean was offered a job hosting his own CBS-TV show, *The Jimmy Dean Show*, which debuted in April 1957. His new show gained massive nationwide popularity and portrayed Dean as a smooth-talking, up-beat, happy-go-lucky Texas cornball.

His career was advancing rapidly when Dean and Pierce were reunited. In 1957 Dean recorded two sessions for the Mercury-Starday label. The new songs were well suited to his wit and charm and could easily fall into the good-time, toe-tapping, finger-snapping honky-tonk genre. His more promising Mercury-Starday recordings included "Happy Child" (71120), "Look On The Good Side," (71172) and "Nothing Can Stop My Love" (71240). As Dean wrote in his autobiography, "Among the young songwriters in Nashville whose songs I liked back then was Roger Miller. In fact, one distinction I'm proud to hold is that I cut the first song he ever had recorded, one called '[The Good Lord's] Happy Child.' I think it must have sold about two copies in North Dakota and then tapered off."[9]

Unfortunately for Mercury-Starday, a big new show also meant a big new label. As Kilpatrick recalled, "Jimmy was being managed by Connie B. Gay at the time I signed him and when I did, Connie came up with this line in the contract that said, 'If you leave, we leave.' I was about to sign it but I went to discuss it with Irv Green first and he said, 'Well, go ahead and sign it. You don't plan on going anywhere do you?'" Thus, when Kilpatrick left, so did Dean, who signed with CBS-affiliated Columbia Records.

The Jimmy Dean Show's initial run lasted only six months, but was revived again on network television from 1963 to 1966 on ABC and introduced, among others, Jim Henson's Rowlf the Dog to the masses. Throughout the sixties Dean found himself in both the country music and pop charts, often recording dramatic recitations such as "Big Bad John" (a #1 hit on both pop and country charts), "PT 109," "Little Black Book," and several others. But despite his reputation as a ham on television and live shows, it was sausage that captivated Dean's attention. Forming the Jimmy Dean Meat Company in 1968, Dean soon became known across America as the "Sausage King." Pierce adds, "I do feel that Jimmy is entitled to be in the Country Music Hall of Fame and it is a shame that he has not been so recognized. [Dean was admitted in 2010.] He was the first guy to take country music and put it on network TV. Then of course, he did very well in movies and other things. He's truly a very huge talent."

Dean was not the only country artist on the Mercury roster at the time of the merger. Also making the transition to the Mercury-Starday label were the Carlisles, Curtis Gordon, Eddie Bond, Tibby Edwards, Bill Wimberly, and Buck Ryan. Previously, under the production of D. Kilpatrick, many of the artists were advised to try rock 'n' roll, resulting in some great rockabilly records, notably by Gordon and Bond. Under the advice of Pierce and Daily, however, they all reverted back to pure country. In fact, Bond, who is often remembered for his Mercury rockabilly sides, including "Rockin' Daddy" and "Boppin' Bonnie" among others, dropped his band the Stompers and went back to recording country ballads. As Bond tells: "When I got involved with Starday, Pappy Daily and Don and all them, they would let me record country again, so I recorded several country songs for Mercury as well. I always liked country better. When

I was young, all I did was country and when we played night clubs and stuff, we were always playing country. 'They Say We're Too Young' (71067), now that's real country! That's got four fiddles on it. And another one called 'You're Part of Me' (71067). That's the country music I wanted to play."

Even though country music was far outsold by rock 'n' roll throughout 1957, Mercury-Starday did manage to find one major success in the country market. By the time Jimmie Skinner joined Mercury Records in early 1956, he had already recorded for Red Barn, Radio Artist Records, Capitol, and Decca. His quirky sense of rhythm and accented guitar playing endeared him to the masses (though likely not the session musicians) and his songwriting soon endeared him to the likes of Hank Williams Sr., Johnny Cash, Ernest Tubb, Jimmy Martin, and Fred Rose, among others. His first chart success came in 1949 when "Tennessee Border" made *Billboard*'s Top 20 charts for one week, though Skinner is most often remembered for his original song "Doin' My Time," later popularized by Flatt & Scruggs, Johnny Cash, and Don Gibson. Despite his gritty baritone voice and his often melancholy lyrics, there were no hits to speak of for the next eight years. During that time he continued to write and record his own brand of traditional country songs, a unique blend of blues, bluegrass, and honky-tonk influences, and his next chart hit, and the biggest in his career, would appear on Mercury-Starday.

The self-penned "I Found My Girl In the USA" (71192), released September 10, 1957, was written in answer to the August 1957 hit "Geisha Girl" by Hank Locklin; which was an answer to Bobby Helms's March 1957 hit "Fraulein"; which was basically an answer to Cowboy Copas's 1946 hit "Filipino Baby"; which was taken from Bill Cox's 1937 cover of the 1898 Charles K. Harris hit from the Spanish-American War. As sailors went from port to port, it seemed plausible that they might find a native darling. Skinner, though, hit a patriotic nerve with his country call about the difficulties of temptation overseas and the satisfaction of finding a lady friend back home.

The single entered the charts on November 4 and stayed there for over four months, peaking at the #5 spot. The flipside was a cover of Narmour and Smith's 1929 "Carroll County Blues," and featured Skinner's mandolin picker Ray Lunsford. Kilpatrick, who signed Skinner to Mercury, recalls: "Jimmie was a fantastic singer and he always brought with him this one musician, a mandolin player [Lunsford] who amplified the mandolin. His speaker was this damn cheap $15 radio that was old and tinny sounding, but it didn't matter. He [Skinner] could sell more records than anybody you ever see. There was just something about his voice that had a profound effect on middle-aged women. He had a noon-time show and those women would turn out in masses and beat down the place. That is one of the great mysteries in my life." Skinner followed up the success of his first major hit with another Top 10 Mercury-Starday

Carl Story with his Rambling Mountaineers, December 1956: (l-r) Bud Brewster, Carl Story, Willie Brewster and Claude Boone (Courtesy of Nathan Gibson)

charter, "What Makes A Man Wander" (71256), which spent two months on the *Billboard* chart.

Skinner was not the only artist on Mercury influenced by the bluegrass sound. In fact, Mercury's interest in mountain music began as early as 1947–48, when Carl Sauceman recorded two Bill Monroe–styled singles. Around the same time Mercury also signed Carl Story. Story was a fiddler who had joined Monroe's group on the Opry until Uncle Sam called upon his military services. After his tour of service ended in 1947, Story re-formed his original band, the Rambling Mountaineers, and began a long string of old-time stringband recordings. Ten years later when the Mercury-Starday deal went into effect, Story was still recording for Mercury Records and, with the exception of a brief period of secular country material (on Mercury and Columbia), was recording solely old-time gospel.

Over the years Story's Rambling Mountaineers included Red Rector, Claude Boone, and Tater Tate, but the addition of Willie and Bud Brewster, known as the Brewster Brothers, in the mid-1950s converted Story's stringband ensemble into a full-fledged bluegrass band. At Pierce's suggestion, the three Mercury-Starday singles, Story's first to feature the new bluegrass sound, each paired a gospel song with an instrumental flipside. Those instrumentals—"Mocking Banjo" (71088), "Banjo on the Mountain" (71143), and "Banjolina" (71218)—featured remarkable musicianship by the Brewsters, Lloyd Bell, Claude Boone, and Bobby Thompson on banjo. Don Pierce quickly became a fan of Story's, as he called it, "happy hand-clapping gospel revival-type" music. So much so that once Mercury and Starday were merged, Pierce strongly advocated for the release of a full-length album by Story and his band. *Gospel Quartet Favorites* (MG 20323), released in 1957, included the classic recordings of "Family Reunion" and "Light At the River." Though a handful of other bluegrass LPs were also released in 1957, researcher Jimmy Gutterman notes that Story's LP is, "One of the first-ever 12-inch bluegrass records."[10]

Aside from Story, A&R man Murray Nash also signed Lester Flatt and Earl Scruggs to Mercury Records in 1948. They too had been members of Bill Monroe's band, and went on to record some of their most famous recordings for Mercury such as "Foggy Mountain Breakdown," "Doin' My Time," and "Rollin' In My Sweet Baby's Arms." Three years later the duo took their music to Columbia Records and by 1952 Nash had also left Mercury. D. Kilpatrick, who had just joined the Mercury team and set up residence in Nashville, was then assigned the task of re-signing Flatt and Scruggs, at which he was unsuccessful. His next assignment was to find a suitable replacement and he did just that.

The Stanley Brothers were truly pioneers in the field. By the mid-1950s they had taken their old-time music and fused it together with a faster, more aggressive approach and were soon recognized as a full-fledged bluegrass band, though it was not yet called bluegrass. They had previously recorded for Rich-R-Tone and Columbia, but the Mercury recordings made by Ralph and Carter Stanley between 1953 and 1958 are largely considered to be the Stanley Brothers' finest. Ralph Stanley echoed that sentiment, simply stating, "Some of our best recordings were the Mercurys."[11]

Among those early bluegrass gems were eight sides released under the Mercury-Starday banner, including the 1957 Carter Stanley original "The Flood" (71064). The two brothers were stranded in Haysi, Virginia, as a massive flood tore through parts of Virginia, Kentucky, and Tennessee. Bearing witness to the immense tragedy, Carter immediately wrote the song and scheduled a quick recording session at radio station WCYB in Bristol, Tennessee. The brothers' record was released on February 14, 1957, just two weeks after the *New York Times* first reported the flood. Pierce later acknowledged that one of the advantages to merging Starday with Mercury was their ability to rush out "hot" record releases. With the advantage of two pressing plants (Chicago and St. Louis) at their disposal, "The Flood" was a perfect example of how quickly a song could go from just an idea to hitting the retail shelves.

The Stanley Brothers followed "The Flood" with several more classic recordings such as "Loving You Too Well" (71207), "I'd Rather Be Forgotten" (71258), and Ralph's instrumental banjo spectacular "Fling Ding" (71207). Yet, as great as the recordings were, they never scored the big hit. As Kilpatrick recalls, "The Stanley Brothers were not *really* hot then, but I could at least break even with them. I couldn't do too much with 'em 'cause it was so narrow with bluegrass then. Of course you had the tried and true bluegrass fans, but back then it just wasn't that damn popular." But he also adds, "Although the Stanley Brothers were not big sellers, sometimes I did pretty good with them. I could break even with costs for a bluegrass session if we sold around 25,000. It was a single monaural recording and if you had to, you could do it with just one mike. So I always broke even and maybe even made a little money too."

Though bluegrass "wasn't that damn popular," the Mercury-Starday country series was a significant introduction for Pierce, who was quickly becoming the genre's biggest fan. He began calling friends and distributors looking for any good bluegrass acts in search of a label, and several outstanding bluegrass records appeared on Starday by The Country Gentlemen, Hobo Jack Adkins and his Kentucky Pals, the Flat Mountain Boys, Harley Gabbard and Aubrey Holt, and others. Bill Clifton and Jim Eanes were fortunate enough to have releases under both the Mercury-Starday and the Starday banner in 1957.

Eanes had briefly been a charter member of Flatt and Scruggs's Foggy Mountain Boys, a member of Bill Monroe's early Blue Grass Boys, and also had solo recordings on National, Blue Ridge, Capitol, and Decca. As friend and fellow musician Matt Levine told historian Gary B. Reid, "Jim told me they [Decca] wanted to renew his contract, but he left because they did not promote him as they did other artists like Ernest Tubb, Webb Pierce, Kitty Wells, etc."[12]

Pierce signed Eanes to a recording contract in 1957, and his very first Starday release was "Your Old Standby" (297). The cut showed immense promise and was immediately covered by Benny Barnes and later by George Jones. The promise of "Standby" also helped Eanes make the transition to Mercury-Starday where he recorded a banjo-driven version of Jones's "Settle Down" (71229) in his casual, laid-back crooning style.

The other bluegrass artist Pierce brought to Mercury-Starday was Bill Clifton, whose recordings were actually given to Pierce by Kilpatrick because there was not enough flexibility in the Mercury release schedule. As Pierce remembers, "D. was leaving Mercury to take over operation of the Opry Artist Bureau. He said to me, 'Don, this is some good stuff. We just don't have any room for it right now. You can have it if you want it.'"

Pierce took the tapes, loved what he heard, and made room for it. Clifton, who had recorded for Blue Ridge in 1954, had already made a name for himself by 1955 when he published his *150 Old-Time Folk and Gospel Songs*, the first published songbook specifically for bluegrass musicians. He befriended old-time music legends such as A. P. Carter and Woody Guthrie and soon devoted his life to the music he loved. After an honorable discharge from the marines, Clifton began looking for a new label. As he explains, "D. [Kilpatrick] was

Bill Clifton's Mercury publicity photo, ca. 1957 (Courtesy of Bill Clifton)

really responsible for getting me on Mercury. We had done some shows and Carter [Stanley] told me that I should be on Mercury and he put me in touch with D. I went to Nashville and met him and played a demo of 'Little White Washed Chimney.' He really liked it but told me that he was going to the Opry and couldn't do it. He said, 'I won't have any connection in a month but Don [Pierce] is taking over and I'll advise Don that he should have you.'"

Pierce released Clifton's recordings—the first of which featured Ralph Stanley and the whole Clinch Mountain gang minus Carter—on Starday at the tail end of 1956. Once the merger was completed, Clifton's records were released on Mercury-Starday. Among those recordings are "Little White Washed Chimney" and "Pal of Yesterday" (71130), as well as "Lonely Heart Blues" and "Mary Dear" (71200). Bill C. Malone's 1980 *Collection of Classic Country Music*, compiled for the Smithsonian Institute, cites Clifton's heartfelt Mercury-Starday rendition of "Mary Dear"—a cover of Charlie Poole's 1929 recording of a 1902 pop song—as one of the 143 most significant songs in country music history.

Somehow, it too failed to sell. In fact, all labels were having a tough time selling bluegrass. As Clifton remembers, "They [Mercury and Mercury-Starday] were then virtually the only label for bluegrass and old-timey music. After all, the other labels had dropped just about everybody. The only exceptions, Decca still had Bill Monroe and Jimmy Martin and Columbia still had Flatt and Scruggs, while the Osborne Brothers had just signed with MGM."

But it was not only bluegrass artists with disappointing sales numbers. Even the occasional rockabilly efforts by Sleepy LaBeef and Curtis Gordon, though also highly regarded today, fell flat in sales. In fact, nearly the entire Mercury-Starday roster was struggling. By January 1958, almost exactly one year after the Mercury-Starday deal went into effect, many of the soon-to-be stars, such as Roger Miller and the Big Bopper, had yet to become stars. Even worse, some of those who had just become stars, such as Jimmy Dean and Charlie Walker, had just signed on with different labels. Walker, who had two releases on Mercury-Starday that went nowhere, jumped ship to Columbia Records where his first waxing, "Pick Me Up On Your Way Down," introduced a whole new shuffle beat to country music and became a #2 smash hit. With the exception of George Jones and Jimmie Skinner, Mercury became frustrated with the missed opportunities, disgruntled with the low sales figures and the lack of hit records, and disappointed with the quality of songs coming from the Texas talent pool. As Pierce told Escott, "There was some friction over publishing. Art Talmadge said that the publisher was always Starrite, our publishing company, and we weren't always using the strongest material from Nashville, and he was right about that."[13]

Pierce readily admits that he and Daily turned down many great songs to further their publishing interests. But he defends the position. According to Pierce, "George [Jones] got acquainted pretty quickly with Buddy Killen who was doing song work with Tree Publishing and of course Buddy wanted George to cut some of his songs. But I thought, 'Well gee, Pappy and I didn't bring him all the way into Nashville to start recording songs for our competitors when up to now, all the success that had been achieved had been with George's songs and our efforts on their behalf.'" He adds, "Why would we go to a publisher who 'lets' us be privileged enough to use their song and then put all of our money into promoting their stuff? Fuck that! We thought our copyrights were competitive, but they weren't selling."

At the same time, Mercury was finding grand success with Patti Page, the Del-Vikings, the Platters, the Diamonds, Jimmy Edwards, Sarah Vaughan, Dinah Washington, Louis Jordan, and much of their pop catalog. Further, while Pierce and Daily were busy running the Mercury-Starday country series, Mercury was dabbling with their own rock 'n' roll artists (including Conway Twitty, Narvel Felts, and Rusty Draper), who proved to be much more successful. It was decided by Irv Green that Mercury no longer needed the Mercury-Starday deal or even a country music division. Just like that, it was over. The decision was made and the country division of Mercury was terminated.

Green's decision effectively meant that Mercury, along with several other labels at the time, had completely given up on the country music market. What appeared to be the deal of a lifetime just a year and two weeks before, the merging of two great country music labels to promote honky-tonk, rockabilly, and bluegrass music to the fullest extent, instead came to a halt with very little warning. The last official release, a fittingly grim tale of a broken heart, was the Stanley Brothers' "A Life of Sorrow" (71258), released on January 15, 1958.

The breakup of Mercury-Starday was not all that painful for Mercury; they wanted to get rid of most of their country acts, and they did. Realizing his immense talent and sales potential, Mercury still held onto their contract with George Jones. In doing so, they also maintained a connection to Jones's manager and producer, Pappy Daily, who was also their Texas distributor. If ever Daily was to find another big hit song, Mercury would surely be the label to release it, regardless of the abortive Mercury-Starday deal. Green also held onto Jimmie Skinner and a couple of Daily's favorite acts, such as James O'Gwynn and Benny Barnes. As Pierce recalls, "Mercury took over George and I think four other artists and they cut everybody else they had out. Jimmy Dean is gone. Carl Story is gone. The Carlisles are gone. Stanley Brothers are gone. Chop chop chop chop chop. And they turned it all over to Pappy."

Because Pappy Daily still held onto his Mercury distributorship in Texas, continued to book Opry talent for D. Kilpatrick, and produced several Texas recording sessions for Mercury, not a whole lot changed for him. Shelby Singleton also remained on board with Mercury as the southern promotions manager. The other real change, besides dropping most of the country acts, was the axing of Don Pierce. Pierce received a phone call from Daily, who informed him that their deal was discontinued. During the same phone call, Daily also mentioned that George Jones would be staying with him. As Pierce remembers, "So there I was sitting in Nashville, and I'd lost the deal with Mercury, and I had lost George Jones, and I now had a severe problem with Pappy."

After weighing possible options, Pierce and Daily chose to divide the entire Starday catalog between them. In addition to the Starday releases up until that point, the catalog also included the Mercury-Starday series, the incredibly short-lived Square Dance Series (a blue label Starday series issued at Daily's request), the Dixie custom series, the Dixie *Hillbilly Hit Parade* series, and any other oddball master that was in their possession. In order to do so, Daily flew out to Nashville and sat in Pierce's office as the two men painstakingly sorted the files in the file cabinet. One by one, every song in the catalog was called out and placed into either the Daily pile or the Pierce pile. The master recordings as well as publishing rights to each song would be owned by the same person.

Pierce recalls: "We agreed that we would flip a coin for first choice, and then we would alternate, and whoever chose the song would automatically own the master that went with it. I drafted the papers, we didn't use any attorneys, and I thought everything was fine. We flipped a coin to see who would get first choice, and I won the flip, and I chose 'A' for 'A Satisfied Mind.' Pappy says, 'I thought that song started with "S,"' and I said, 'Well, in the song contract it says "A Satisfied Mind."'"

Clearly Pierce had the advantage going into the split. He knew the song's official titles. He knew what songs were played on the radio. He knew how many copies of each record had been sold. He had done all the promotion work on them and knew exactly which records could still get played on radio and those that had already run their course. Pierce chose specific songs, knowing that instrumental tracks were being used as background music on radio shows and that there was a recent spike in the airplay royalties from mountain and bluegrass music.

Daily, however, selected songs by the Texas musicians he liked the most, such as Benny Barnes, Sonny Burns, Eddie Noack, and James O'Gwynn. Though Daily left the meeting with several great songs, Pierce managed to walk with most of the important Starday hits including "A Satisfied Mind," "Ya'll Come," "Why, Baby, Why," and numerous other important copyrights. Aside from acquiring most of the hits and all of the bluegrass and mountain music, Pierce also got the Starday name. Pierce explains: "Here's my take on that. We just said, 'Well, we have the record name and the record publishing company,' and it was his turn to take a choice because we were alternating back and forth. And I think he was influenced by the fact that I had taught him how lucrative it was to be in the publishing business. So he took the name Starrite, which meant nothing, it was just the name of the company we used up to that time. And then when I acquired half of the Starrite catalog, I just put it all under the name of Starday Music. So it was something like, we were dividing up the company, he got to pick the name of the song company and I got to pick the name of the label. So I took the Starday label. Starday had acceptance then at that point, it had positive value."

When the last file had been pulled and sorted, the two men stood up. Hands were shook, papers were signed, and the two friends went their separate ways. The legendary tag-team duo of Pappy Daily and Don Pierce was effectively sawed in half. When the two men went to sleep that night, things seemed to be okay.

And they were, until the end of the next quarter when BMI released their royalty statements. When Daily realized that Pierce had made a whole lot more money, he was irate. Daily was under the impression that the split was going to be 50/50 and that each partner should be receiving the same amount of royalties. Papers were served after Daily hired an attorney to sue Pierce for his remaining share of the royalties.

In the meantime, Daily was able to make a dollar or two for himself with a new label he had started just before the Mercury-Starday split. Most likely founded in anticipation of the breakup, D Records featured most of the same acts as Starday in its early existence—Eddie Noack, Benny Barnes, Glenn Barber, Country Johnny Mathis, Margie Singleton, and several others. He also founded the Dart label. These labels served as talent scouts to find rock and country material that might interest Mercury.

Pierce continued to make a few dollars by focusing on his Hollywood rhythm and blues label, which by 1958 had released exciting records by King Perry, Johnny Fuller, Jesse Belvin, Johnny Taylor, Jimmy McCracklin, the Pyramids, the Feathers, Pee Wee Crayton, and others. In addition, Pierce still profited from the Christmas recordings he had purchased from Swingtime Records.

Daily and Pierce had been avoiding each other for months, running their own respective labels, when eventually their paths crossed in late 1958 at a music operators' convention in Chicago. Pierce and Daily met at the bar, had a few beers, and began arguing. When Herman Lubinsky, founder of Savoy Records, had finally heard enough, Pierce recalls: "He [Lubinsky] said, 'Look. You guys, you've been together all through these years. It's just no good for you to be on the outs. You all come with me up to my room and let's settle this thing.' And so we went up there, and I said, 'Pappy, now what's your problem?' And he said, 'Well, that building: we bought it for $16,000 and I just got credit for $8,000 for my share. But I had an appraisal on it, and it's worth $18,500.' 'Well, that's not a problem. I'll just pay you half the difference.' And he [Daily] said, 'With George, he's still under writer's contract for us—you'll have one-half of the songs that George writes for the duration of his contract, which has eighteen months to go, and then he will be totally with me.'"

In those eighteen months Jones began to find the success with rockabilly that had eluded him during the "Thumper" Jones stretch. On March 9, 1959, Jones scored his first #1 hit with the Big Bopper's up-tempo novelty number "White Lightning." Pierce, who was still producing many of Jones's Nashville sessions at Bradley's for the remaining months of the contract, produced the session and remembers, "We had several takes on the thing: we got up to #11, and each time it was taken off at the start by Buddy Killen playing string bass, who later sold his Tree Publishing Company for $38 million. Buddy said that the skin was coming off his fingers with all the runs that he had to make, and so we eventually decided to accept take number three, with a small flub in it where George says, 'One s-slug.' I didn't think it hurt the record any, and it certainly didn't, because it went to #1 right away."

Other artists also began having success with the now-free-from-Starday Mercury. Jimmie Skinner had a half dozen more hits in the next two years, including his popular rendition of "Dark Hollow." Benny Barnes had a hit with Eddie Edding's earlier Starday tune "Yearning." James O'Gwynn began a string of chart entries that would carry him through the next three years on Mercury, highlighted by the #7 hit "My Name Is Mud." When asked if Mercury suffered at all from the break with Starday, Singleton—who continued working for Mercury, eventually becoming the worldwide A&R head and rebuilding the entire country music catalog—thought not. "I think it probably helped Mercury if anything. All the A&R was not going through Starday anymore, it was going directly to Mercury. I was able to steal Faron Young from Capitol and I took Roy Drusky from Decca and a lot of the other acts. I could just wave some money in front of the acts and steal them away from other labels and I didn't have to check with anybody first."

With massive successes in pop, country, and rhythm and blues, Mercury was quick to recover, though it would take several years of hard work before Pierce could turn his blackbirds into bluebirds.

4

RANK STRANGER

For Pierce, the decision to stay in Nashville was obvious. He loved the city. He loved the people. He loved the food. He loved the business. He had built a new home. Despite the sour turn of events, there was at least a bright side: Pierce kept the office building he had bought with Daily. He still had half of a very active publishing catalog and was contracted with George Jones for another year and a half. According to Pierce, he was optimistic about his situation from the very outset and knew he could be successful on his own. "I had a lot goin' for me when I came to Nashville because I knew so much more about making records and distributing records," he explains. "The guys in town only knew one thing—the studio. But I knew everything. I did coast to coast. Start to finish. I could establish Starday here because I knew how to go from recording the artist to selling the product. These other guys would have to send stuff to New York to get it done but I could do it all right here."

It was with this confidence and swagger that Pierce began tying up loose ends and starting over in the spring of 1958. One loose end involved figuring out what to do with the Dixie 2000 rock 'n' roll series he and Daily had just recently constructed. The Dixie rock label was first announced in *Billboard* on January 27, 1958, as a way for Starday to release rockabilly and pop records on a regional scale and, if they were successful, make them available to Mercury Records. That plan never blossomed because the Mercury-Starday merger was terminated around the same time the new label debuted, and it was up to Pierce to follow through with the label's few scheduled releases. As he recalls, "Mercury never did any promotion for them. We issued those at our cost and expense in an effort to find material we could then send to Mercury. It was a regional scope, but it was a cut above the custom stuff, which is generally pretty crude. The Dixie stuff was pretty good stuff, but we only worked it in a limited area to see if it had any potential."

It did not take Pierce long to realize, however, that despite the quality of his material, he still had no knowledge of how to promote rock 'n' roll records—and that Mercury, who did, never showed any interest. The Dixie 2000 series came to an end after just twenty-six waxings. To Pierce, this was just another "something that we tried which didn't work out"; but to record collectors, these are among Starday's most popular and well-known rockabilly records. Among the more collectable platters released in the series were Eddie Skelton's fuzz-rocker "Gotta Keep Swingin'" (2011), Benny Joy's "Spin the Bottle" (2001), and Big "D" Jamboree star Groovey Joe Poovey's Jerry Lee Lewis–inspired rocker "10 Long Fingers" (2018).

The Dixie 2000 series should not be confused with the other Dixie records being released by Starday at the same time. Pierce continued to manufacture the *Hillbilly Hit Parade* sets as well as custom pressings, which later became known as the Dixie series. Perhaps inspired by the many artists who chose to use the Starday name on their private pressings, several artists later used the Dixie name on their custom records. The earliest artist known to do this was Tom Crooks and the Rock and Roll Four (Dixie 624) in April 1957, though many others followed shortly thereafter.

As the rock 'n' roll phenomenon continued throughout 1958 and 1959, hundreds of musicians contacted Pierce about pressing their Dixie custom rockers. Perhaps the most sought-after Dixie custom from this period came from a Louisville, Kentucky, man named "Orangie" Ray Hubbard. The record (Dixie 662), an original song entitled "Sweet Love," was his prize for winning a local talent competition, and has become one of the most infamous rockabilly records ever pressed. Hubbard shares his story: "Here's the way it goes: they were puttin' on this talent scout contest to promote this new radio station WBBL. So Clyde Brown calls in Zeke Clements. Zeke put on a talent scout contest and he copied it after *The Arthur Godfrey Show*. In other words, if you won, you won by applause meter like Arthur Godfrey did it. It was in a big theatre in Barberville, Kentucky, the Mitchell Theatre. And the way they did this, you couldn't just win once and be done with it. If you didn't get voted #1, you were allowed to come back the next week and perform. Well I went in and I won eight straight weeks. But the day they did the finals, they didn't do it by applause meter. They brought in judges. I find all this out after it was all over. Anyway, there was a tie that day with me and a guy named David Lundy. He's on the flip side of 'Sweet Love.' So we sent our tapes to Don Pierce. I did my tape in the radio studio in Louisville with Herman Criss on bass and Riley Tipton on lead guitar. I don't know where he did his. But we sent our tapes in and I thought we would each get a two-sided disc. But instead, they put Dave on one side and me on the other. They said, since we have a tie, we'll play the song on the radio every day. The man who gets the most requests is the winner. That was the end of it. I was promised a recording contract with Starday and Don Pierce. That was the prize, a promise of a record contract for giving up all your weekends. Well, at the time I think I may have gotten an oil change

Orangie Ray Hubbard and his group performing "Mean Woman Blues," backed by Barney Rapp's Orchestra at Cincinnati Gardens, ca. 1957 (l-r) Nelson Young, Bill Zekie Browning, Orangie Ray Hubbard, Clinton Doane, Herman Criss, Barney Rapp (Courtesy of Orangie Ray Hubbard)

for my car but it got a lot bigger than what they expected it to be. I've since heard it called the Holy Grail of rockabilly music."

Indeed it is collectable, valued in Jerry Osborne's *16th Edition 45 Price Guide* at $4,000 in excellent condition, though Hubbard notes he has been offered much more for his only remaining copy. As to why it might be worth $4,000, scarcity likely plays a large part. It is also one of the best rockabilly records released in the 1950s, featuring an Elvis-like swagger in the vocals, stellar finger-picked guitar solos, streaking steel guitar lines, accented drum fills and lyrics regarding "sweet love." Popular Cincinnati recording artist Rusty York even cut his own version of Hubbard's rocker, though York changed the words "sweet love" to "sweet talk." Still, the preceding description could be applied to numerous records worth a mere fraction of the stated value of Hubbard's "Sweet Love." Regarding the record's desirability, Hubbard offers his own explanation: "It's because of the sound that's on it. The cleanness of the sound. And I was offered a lot of money to show people how we could get that sound. But then nobody would pay me and I wasn't gonna show them how I did it. There was a cleanness, a separation from the music that none of the other rockabilly people ever got."

Other top-notch rockabilly records, by Art Buchanan, Hal Payne, Tony and Jackie Lamie, Groovey Joe Poovey, and others, poured in through the custom service, though they were never of much interest to Pierce. Despite the outstanding quality of the material or the "cleanness of the sound," Pierce knew country music, and only country music, and spent the rest of 1958 trying to figure out how to set up a successful all-country independent music label in Nashville. Of course, there would be challenges. Aside from the absolute beating given to the country music industry, courtesy of Chuck Berry, Buddy Holly, Bill Haley, Jerry Lee Lewis, Elvis, and the others, there was an even bigger challenge emerging from within the country music industry.

While some may argue that the downfall of "traditional" country music began when Elvis Presley shook his hips on television for the first time, an argument could be made that it instead began the day Chet Atkins suggested adding a full chorus to back up Jim Reeves's 1957 hit song, "Four Walls." Either way, the country music industry was changed forever and a new sound was born. It has since been dubbed the Nashville Sound.

In 1957 Steve Sholes, president of the country division for RCA and the man who helped bring Mr. Presley to national fame, moved to New York City to take over the then-thriving pop division of RCA. His replacement was a young guitar picker named Chester Burton Atkins. Atkins's vision for country music has been well documented. Put simply, he wanted to take raw, emotional hillbilly songs and smooth out their rough edges. This effect of sophistication could be achieved by adding choral backgrounds and string arrangements, and the outcome was a music made by country folk that was now marketable to the pop-loving city folk. Thus, the Nashville Sound was born. Full orchestras replaced the sound of twin fiddles and MGM found it to be in their interest to overdub and re-release Hank Williams Sr. recordings with orchestration. They were not making rock. They were not making pop. Rather, it was the beginning of an era that would find its heyday in the mid-sixties, much to the chagrin of Pierce and other traditional country enthusiasts.

The Nashville Sound was not limited to Atkins and RCA. Most major labels adopted the idea that, to compete in the ever-changing music market, they must adapt and therefore make the change from 1950s honky-tonk to the new sound. Owen Bradley of Decca was all for it. Taking over for Paul Cohen, who had been producing traditionalists such as Red Foley, Ernest Tubb, and Webb Pierce, Bradley became the country A&R man for Decca during the late fifties. His legacy includes creating a long line of pop-country hits for Patsy Cline, Brenda Lee, and Burl Ives. Even Don Law of Columbia Records, often associated with the hardcore honky-tonk sound of Carl Smith, Lefty Frizzell, and Ray Price, by the late fifties was launching the pop-country careers of Marty Robbins and Jimmy Dean. The unimaginable happened in the early 1960s, when Ken Nelson and his California-based Capitol Records—which had continually stood by traditional country music and represented the antithesis of the Nashville Sound, with artists including Hank Thompson, Tex Williams, and later Buck Owens—began releasing milder, smoother country music by Roy Clark, million-selling pop songs by Tommy Sands and Sonny James, and over-produced Ferlin Husky arrangements.

Thus, RCA did not want traditional country music anymore. Columbia could do without as well, Decca did not want it, and neither did Capitol. MGM was rereleasing orchestral Hank Sr. records and Mercury cut their entire country music catalog save four or five artists.

With the majors making the gradual shift to the smooth country crossover sound, at least one thing was clear to Pierce: it would be easy to sign the traditional artists who had been dropped and who did not want to adapt to the new style. In many cases, this meant that bluegrass acts were typically the first to go. No matter how hard they might have tried, the major labels could not find a way to add a full string orchestra to a Bill Monroe record and make it sound good. Presumably, the Anita Kerr Singers would have had a terrible time trying to blend in with the mountain sound of the Stanley Brothers' high and lonesome wails. Because he had always been fond of bluegrass and no longer had to contend with Daily's distaste for the sound, those were the first acts signed to Pierce's reinvented Starday label.

By the late 1950s, bluegrass music, named after its founder Bill Monroe's Blue Grass Boys, had a rather small, though loyal, fan base. Pierce felt drawn to the music. He knew it was a niche market, but that meant there *was* a market, and that somebody should supply it. In just a few short months Pierce had acquired the services of nearly every major bluegrass act on the circuit. By 1959 Starday had earned its reputation as *the* bluegrass label; by 1960, Pierce had amassed the largest active bluegrass catalog in the world. Among the acts signed were the Stanley Brothers, Bill Clifton, Jim Eanes, Carl Story (all from the defunct Mercury-Starday series), the Country Gentlemen, the Lewis Family, Buzz Busby, Jim and Jesse, Bill Harrell, Charlie Moore, and several other popular acts. Because Pierce was the only entrepreneur actively seeking out bluegrass (with the exception of Syd Nathan of King Records), he was also able to sign or lease recordings from a slew of new and less well-known bluegrass acts such as Bill and Mary Reid, the Wright Brothers, Connie and Joe, John Reedy, Hoyt (who had first appeared on Starday in 1954) and Tyrone Scoggins, the Flat Mountain Boys, Vern and Ray and the Carroll County Boys, Ken Clark and his Merry Mountain Boys, and many others.

Pierce did not have to lure the bluegrass musicians to Starday with pockets full of cash, because most of the acts had either been dropped by majors or were just looking to get their records out on any label. Instead, they came to

Carter and Ralph Stanley, the Stanley Brothers, ca. 1962 (Courtesy of Don Pierce)

him and he quickly snatched them up. Pierce remarked on signing the early acts: "It was easy. I had a one-page agreement. Other labels had lots of pages and legal jargon. My contract was simple to understand. My lease agreement was a royalty agreement with each artist for the recordings that they made, and as part of that agreement, they gave me the option for twelve more sides. And that's all, one page. It's better than tying a guy up for three years and he wants to get loose and then you have hearings and all that sort of thing. If the guy's got a better chance to go, let him go. As long as he takes care of what he owes me."

Pierce recalls that many of the artists were impressed with the agreement and, without the worry of being tied to a long-term contract, signed it without hesitation. It was with such ease that Pierce finagled a contract with Ralph and Carter Stanley. According to Pierce, the Stanley Brothers stand today among the "big three" of first-generation bluegrass bands with Bill Monroe, the father of bluegrass music, and Flatt and Scruggs with their Foggy Mountain Boys. Arguably the first to take Monroe's sound and find independent success with it, the Stanley Brothers were seasoned professionals by the time they joined Starday, having recorded for over twelve years on Rich-R-Tone, Columbia, Blue Ridge, and Mercury Records.

Pierce recalls: "I was first aware of them from their first recording of "Little Maggie" on the Rich-R-Tone label of East Tennessee. I was still in L.A. at the time. There's no question, they were among the absolute foremost in the bluegrass field. When the Mercury-Starday series got under way, I got to know them, and we recorded the Stanley Brothers in Nashville. Later, when Mercury decided to concentrate mostly on George Jones, fortunately the Stanley Brothers became available to me."

Shortly after the Stanley Brothers signed their recording contract with Pierce in mid-1958, they were lured to the larger King Records label by Pierce's friendly Cincinnati competitor Syd Nathan. Pierce made sure to exercise his option for twelve more sides after the initial contracted twelve, but due to his friendly relationship with the Stanley Brothers and Nathan, there was no deadline pressure for the remaining recordings. Therefore, throughout the late fifties and early sixties the Stanley Brothers alternated recording between Starday and King, and their releases appeared on those labels simultaneously.

The Stanley Brothers recorded twenty-eight songs for Starday, and Pierce was able to lease more recorded material from both Jimmie Skinner and King Records. The material was then stretched to fill ten singles, four LPs, several extended-play 45s, and over twenty bluegrass compilation albums. Among the standout tracks was their upbeat version of Charlie Poole's "If I Lose" (546), a remake of Ralph Stanley's solo effort "Little Maggie" (522), "Riding That Midnight Train" (494) with Bill Napier on mandolin and Chubby Anthony on fiddle, and their legendary recording of "Rank Stranger" (506), which became their biggest seller on Starday and is considered one of the Stanley Brothers' all-time greatest recordings.

"Rank Stranger" was also among the first of many Starday recordings to bear the name York as songwriter. The classic tune was actually penned by famed gospel songwriter Albert E. Brumley, though the copyright had not yet been claimed. Therefore, the label credits were given to William York, a BMI pseudonym for Pierce. This, of course, upset a fair share of artists who thought Pierce to be "stealing" the arrangement credit. According to banjoist Roni Stoneman, "We [Ernest V. Stoneman and the Stoneman Family] were invited to come to Nashville and record for Starday Records and I was very young [twenty-two years old]. This was a very exciting time for us. They took us to the Starday Studio and we did a couple albums, two or three. It was a long day. They took us out, took a picture, then took us back in and started working again. We featured Scotty on some fiddle tunes, did 'Orange Blossom Special,' and Scott played his heart and soul on it. Well, when it was released it came out as 'Orange Blossom Breakdown,' arranged by York. We said, 'Who's York?' They said, 'That's Don Pierce's surname.' I said, 'He didn't play no fiddle. How can he put soul into a fiddle tune?' So here we were . . . Scott never read music, none of the Stonemans ever read music, but we played our music with our every bit of soul and inner beings because that's all we ever knew to do. We just loved what we did. And then York claimed it. Why would he want to steal our stuff? How dare him? I've never received one red cent from Starday and I don't believe any of the Stonemans have. We should have taken some lawyers with us to Nashville!"

Jim and Jesse with their Starday-era backing band ca. 1958: (back row, l-r) Vassar Clements, Jesse McReynolds, Don McHan, Jim McReynolds, Bobby Thompson, and (seated) Chick Stripling (Stripling did not play on the Starday recordings) (Courtesy of Jesse McReynolds)

Although Pierce certainly had his fair share of critics, most artists accepted his arrangement credit deal. "If a song was in the public domain and it was an arrangement that I controlled, or that I put out, I would submit it to BMI and they would send me credit or credit to William York," Pierce defends. "And some of that stuff, anything that wasn't nailed down by another publisher, I figured was in the public domain. If I'm spending my money to manufacture the product and send it out to all the radio stations and that sort of thing and do the artwork and nobody else controls the copyright, I'll claim it. That's all. If it wasn't nailed down, I'd grab it."

Pierce then signed Jim and Jesse McReynolds who, like the Stanley Brothers, were a brother duo from Southwest Virginia. Jim and Jesse and their Virginia Boys began their career in the late 1940s; by 1952 they were signed to Capitol Records, where they quickly established a reputation for tight harmonies and intricate cross-picking mandolin work. After being dropped by Capitol in 1955, they continued performing and touring but made no commercial recordings until their association with Starday in 1958. By that time they were doing radio and television work, touring and appearing on the Suwannee River Jamboree in Live Oak, Florida. Jesse McReynolds recalls: "We recorded a few songs

The Country Gentlemen: (l-r) Eddie Adcock, John Duffey, Charlie Waller, and Jim Cox (Courtesy of Nathan Gibson)

down in Jacksonville and then brought them to Nashville to shop around. But no one was taking any interest as rock 'n' roll was taking over at that time. We shopped it to a few different people and somehow ended up at Starday's front door. Don Pierce was a great help to us and all of bluegrass music when no one else wanted it, and I appreciate everything he did for us." That sentiment would be repeated by countless others over the next few years.

The tracks Pierce picked up included "Pardon Me" (412), "Hard Hearted" (412), and "Border Ride" (433), all recorded in October 1958. Backing Jim and Jesse on their three Starday sessions were Bobby Thompson on banjo, who had accompanied Carl Story on his "Family Reunion" Mercury session, Don McHan on bass and vocals, and Vassar Clements, formerly with Bill Monroe, on fiddle. Their association with Starday lasted for nearly two years and a total of fourteen sides. By 1960 Jim and Jesse had secured a sponsorship by Martha White Flour, who also sponsored Flatt and Scruggs at the time. The sponsorship led the duo to a recording contract with Columbia Records (from 1960 to 1969) and a long-lasting membership with the Grand Ole Opry.

Ben Adelman, a Washington, D.C., music promoter, also played a large role in creating the Starday bluegrass catalogue. According to Pierce, Adelman was the Pappy Daily of the bluegrass-dominated D.C. area. Pierce explains, "If you're in Texas and you want to make a record, you go see Pappy Daily or someone like that. Conversely, if you're in the D.C. area and you want to make a record, you go see Ben Adelman." Adelman and Pierce became friends during Pierce's California days when Adelman sent country material to 4 Star. Because Pierce was among the few label owners showing an interest in bluegrass music, Adelman now sent material directly to Starday for release. During this time, Pierce kept publishing rights to all of the music he was releasing as singles. Adelman received his monetary thanks for helping establish acts in the form of partial songwriting credit. Adelman set up a pseudonym, Cindy Davis, who is credited as co-author on many early Starday bluegrass releases.

Among the first acts Adelman directed to Pierce was the newly formed Country Gentlemen. In July 1957, tenor John Duffey filled a concert vacancy left by an injured Buzz Busby. Duffey and Busby's band jelled quickly and, after six months, signed a recording contract with Pierce. Throughout their early Starday years, the Country Gentlemen had a revolving cast of players, but the core of the group consisted of Duffey on mandolin or dobro and Charlie Waller, the guitar-picking lead vocalist. Duffey was born and raised in Bethesda, Maryland, the son of an opera singer. Waller was born in Texas and grew up picking cotton and guitars in Louisiana. Despite the difference in upbringing, the men bonded and found their bluegrass niche performing with a high lonesome trio sound. The earliest recordings for Starday, recorded in December 1957 in Ben Adelman's basement, featured banjoist Bill Emerson singing baritone along with Waller and Duffey.

Eventually, more than forty sides were recorded for Starday, with several more songs leased from Folkways albums as singles. With the release of "Hey, Little Girl" (367), "High Lonesome" (367), "New Freedom Bell" (455), and several other revered early recordings, the Country Gentlemen were established as one of the premier progressive bluegrass acts in the country.

Buzz Busby, the mandolinist whose absence created the opportunity for the Country Gentlemen, was another major bluegrass contributor to Starday. Busby, born Bernarr Graham Busbice, was an established bluegrass star in the D.C. area. After a childhood farming in Louisiana, he moved to Washington to begin a career with the F.B.I. In either late 1951 or early 1952, he formed a trio with fiddler Scotty Stoneman and guitarist Jack Clement. Clement was later replaced by Pete Pike, and the group secured a radio show, won a National Country Music Championship Competition in Virginia and, as a result, Busby

Buzz Busby publicity photo (Courtesy of Nathan Gibson)

hosted a television show called the WRC-TV *Hayloft Hoedown*. Though relatively short-lived, the show helped the popularity of bluegrass in the D.C. area and gave Busby instant star status, which led to better bookings. After a short stint on Boston's Hayloft Jamboree and recordings on the Sheraton label, Busby secured a spot on the highly influential Louisiana Hayride. He made one recording for the obscure Jiffy label, but by 1956 had returned to the D.C. area to team up with local scenesters such as Stoneman, Waller, Emerson, and Eddie Adcock. Busby was involved in a serious car accident on July 4, 1957. Miraculously, after being pronounced dead at the scene, Busby was revived by medics, and shortly thereafter signed a Starday recording contract arranged by Adelman.

Although only twelve sides were released on Starday with Busby's name, he played on several other Starday sessions. Those twelve sides have become legendary among bluegrass fans because they capture raw emotion unlike any other bluegrass act of the 1950s. Like George Jones, Busby often wrote about personal conflict and the drama in his life, and those struggles are clearly reflected in his voice. His recordings were strongly influenced by Bill Monroe and in a 1980 interview with Eddie Stubbs, Busby referred to "Lonesome Wind" (409) by saying that he even "out-Monroed Monroe" on that one.[1]

The man who did the most to preserve and promote bluegrass music in the late 1950s, aside from Pierce himself, was Bill Clifton. Another

Mercury-Starday act to make the transition to Starday, he went on to make not only a significant contribution to Starday, but to all of early bluegrass music. Clifton, whose birth name was William August Marburg, did not grow up with the hardships often associated with early country musicians. Instead, he grew up in a very wealthy family in Baltimore County, Maryland; received a masters degree in business administration from the University of Virginia; became a Marine Corps officer; and later spent two years as a registered stockbroker.

While attending the University of Virginia he founded his Dixie Mountain Boys and changed his performing name to Bill Clifton. Clifton explains: "Well, I come from a family in Baltimore where my grandfather served as ambassador to Belgium under Taft or Wilson. His brothers were rather distinguished and I was gonna work on WBAL and my father said I couldn't use the family name. 'In your hometown, you're not gonna play hillbilly music and use the family name.' So I picked out ten names out of thin air. Some were two syllables, some one. Scott was my favorite initially, but I ended up with Bill Clifton. It was all just random."

The success of Clifton's earliest Starday recordings—including "When You Kneel at Mother's Grave" (417), "You Go To Your Church (I'll Go To Mine)" (417), and "Gathering Flowers From the Hillside" (447)—earned him a devoted legion of fans, who voted him into the 1959 *Cash Box* magazine poll's "Most Promising Newer Country Recording Artists." Pierce soon found it profitable to release Clifton's music on full-length albums as well as singles, and found that the LPs outsold singles both in the United States and overseas. Pierce gathered enough material (with the help of a few leased tracks) to fill seven full-length Clifton albums on Starday and its subsidiary, Nashville. Among his most popular albums are *Mountain Folk Songs* (SLP 111) and the tribute to his friend A. P. Carter and the group that first inspired him, *The Carter Family Memorial Album* (SLP 146). The latter album, recorded in 1961, was among the first memorials dedicated to the Carter Family and helped bring their importance in country music to the forefront.

Later that year Clifton made another significant contribution to the bluegrass cause: he organized an all-day bluegrass show, on July 4, 1961, at Oak Leaf Park in Luray, Virginia, featuring himself and several Starday bluegrass acts (including Jim and Jesse, the Stanley Brothers, and the Country Gentlemen) as well as Mac Wiseman and the legendary Bill Monroe. The show was successful, attracting a large crowd and helping to unify the various bluegrass acts on the circuit. Clifton recalls: "Monroe had been adamant about not being on stage with any former Blue Grass Boy. He felt that anyone who left his band was not welcome to share the stage with him. I told him that I invited Mac Wiseman and the Stanleys. I said, 'These people have been your lead singers at times and you have to recognize that we're all in the same boat. We can't be enemies. We're playing similar music and we can all help each other and perform with each other," and Bill agreed." The concert also gave Clifton valuable festival experience, which helped him two years later when he became one of the organizing directors of the 1963 Newport Folk Festival.

Shortly after the Newport festival, Clifton moved to England, where his popularity was on the rise. Clifton explains: "Don went around the world and made a trip to London and wowed the Decca people, who decided to license everything I had out, and they put it all out over there. He [Pierce] did that with a lot of people. They weren't in the market to buy that stuff, but he sold it to 'em. He said, 'It's gonna be a good thing.' Britain didn't outsell the U.S. market but it certainly was a nice addition and it allowed me to work over there. *Country Music Magazine* and several others, actually it was called *Country Western Express* originally, was doing annual polls on who is the best at this and that, and I kept coming out at the top of the polls in best bluegrass and I never understood that. After several years I wrote to the editors and said, 'I'd like to come over,' and I asked if there was any work over there and they didn't know. But I kept getting favorite of the year and they said it had to do with my enunciation and that they could understand my way of speaking. Bill Monroe had a way of clipping his words and some of the others were hard to understand. Lester Flatt did the same thing at times. Carter had his own way of singing altogether, probably the finest voice in bluegrass, very emotional. But enunciation was always very important in school. It was just something you had to do in school. Not swallow words. And that was probably the reason my recordings were more popular at times."

After the move to England, Clifton continued touring and tirelessly promoting bluegrass and his own Starday Records. Clifton adds: "I wouldn't have been able to move if Don hadn't gotten there first. They [Clifton's records] were also released in France, Belgium, Holland, and others. I'm sure he had things in South Africa also. And then of course he did the same thing in Tokyo that he did in London and knocked 'em off their seats and created such an excitement around bluegrass. He was just a natural salesman and he certainly brought the Japanese into the picture."

Indeed, the network of distributors was growing. In 1959 Pierce changed his motto from "Starday—Country and Gospel" to "Starday—Country and Gospel International." But even as the international network grew, Pierce continued to build his bluegrass empire within the United States. He credits his initial success to several key distributors who kept ordering and selling the bluegrass material. Among the most notable were the Schwartz Brothers of Washington, the first distributors to achieve large success with Starday's bluegrass and gospel albums, and Lou Epstein of the Jimmie Skinner Music Center in Cincinnati, who always featured the Starday catalog and encouraged Pierce to stay with it.

But Pierce was not interested in building a purely bluegrass label. Instead, he made his one-page contract available to any artist who did not want to mold to the new sound of Nashville; this included a fair amount of traditional old-timers and newer country acts who wanted to uphold their "country" identity. Anything and everything was fair game, from gospel to bluegrass, honky-tonk to cornball comedy, Hammond organ versions of "The Battle of New Orleans," even countrified sermons from the pulpit. Just as they had been in 1957, several Starday singles were released regionally in early 1958, though similar to most of the 1957 releases, without any network distribution or advertising, they simply drifted off into obscurity.

October 1958 marked a turning point for Pierce. Instead of continuing with the same release numbers on singles, he skipped from release number 376 by the Southlan Trio (consisting of Vernon Smith, Lewis Shumate, and Barney Smith and sometimes referred to as the Southland Trio) to 401 by Benny Barnes. The numerical skip marked a concerted effort to put the past behind him and begin anew. He then set out to develop a talented roster, build a national and international distributorship, and reconnect with country music disc jockeys. Unfortunately for Pierce, when he finally set out on his own, he was literally on his own. Jack Frost, Pierce's long-time assistant and friend, had grown unhappy in Nashville, perhaps discouraged with the prospect of starting a music business all over again, and moved back to California.

As Pierce became inundated with bills, papers, contracts, royalty statements, release notes, recording session schedules, and errands, he began looking for help to run his company. On one of his routine trips to the First American Bank in Nashville, it was recommended that Pierce hire a friend of his bankers, Dorothy Cole. Pierce met with and hired Cole that week and the two of them worked together tirelessly to establish the new Starday. "Dot" Cole continued to work for Starday until Pierce retired from the business, becoming the longest active employee for the label.

By 1959 Pierce had leased recordings from a handful of honky-tonk musicians including Bill Browning (author of "Dark Hollow," a national hit for both Luke Gordon and Jimmie Skinner), Lattie Moore, Denver Duke and Jeffrey Null (who previously had recorded one bluegrass session for Mercury-Starday), Darnell Miller, Jack Kingston, and a young Dave Dudley. Despite the fading popularity of the honky-tonk sound, Pierce worked to prolong the trend. After all, as the 45 record sleeves boasted, Starday was "Preserving the Heritage of American Country Music." Though he never defined what that heritage was, Pierce was clearly more interested in promoting the older country music sounds than the modern ones. Once word spread that Pierce was revamping Starday, country music traditionalists now had a new door to knock on. Among the first at Starday's doorstep was Billie Morgan, a raspy-voiced thirty-six-year-old mother of four.

Morgan grew up and lived in Nashville, though her singing style is more commonly associated with the Texas honky-tonk sound. Nashville session fiddler Dale Potter recognized her talent and brought her to the Starday offices. Potter knew that Pierce was looking for the more traditional country artists and was impressed with her songwriting credits, which by 1959 included over 150 songs. Pierce was also impressed and signed her on the spot. Her first recording session was three days later and within ten days her first record, "Life to Live" (420), co-credited with Potter, was released in January 1959. The song, a stirring answer to Stonewall Jackson's "Life to Go," hit the *Billboard* charts on March 23, 1959, peaking at #22. Though only a modest hit, it significantly gave the new Nashville-based Starday its first taste of national radio exposure.

Margie Singleton was another up-and-coming star on Pierce's revamped Starday. Singleton had been a major source of conflict between Pappy Daily and Pierce at Mercury-Starday. Daily loved her music; Pierce couldn't stand it. Daily wanted more releases by Singleton. Pierce wanted them to stop. Yet, after Daily and Pierce had split, Pierce continued releasing records by Singleton on Starday. She was given a boost in Louisiana Hayride appearances, where she was now plugging her own Starday hits, and her popularity was on the rise. Her first release of 1959 (her fourth on Starday) was the tender balled "Nothin' But True Love" (443), which hit the *Billboard* chart on August 3, 1959, and peaked at #25. Her follow-up, the soft-spoken, vibrato-laden "The Eyes of Love" (472), was released six months later and stayed on the charts for over three months, climbing to #12.

Phil Sullivan was another exciting young star with a couple of upbeat Texas-style honky-tonk releases in Starday's early Nashville incarnation. Sullivan was the brother of John and Rollin Sullivan, the comedy duo dubbed Lonzo and Oscar (Lloyd George played the role of Lonzo from 1945 to 1950), and was among the earliest acts signed to Pierce's one-page contract. Pierce recalls: Jim Denny wanted us to do Lonzo and Oscar. You know, they had that 'I'm My Own Grandpa' [originally released on Victor in 1947 but rerecorded and issued as Starday 463], which by the way we weren't selling anything at all. They were a comedy act and nobody was interested in their records. But they had this thing 'Country Music Time' [543]. I wasn't real anxious to do anything with Lonzo and Oscar because I didn't think they had any sales potential for singles, but they'd been on the Opry for twenty years or so and I thought that they had enough stature that they would sell something in album form."

Though Pierce was hesitant to release singles by Lonzo and Oscar (although they had eight on Starday), he enthusiastically released three singles by their third brother using their band, the Peapickers. Phil Sullivan recorded up-tempo piano-driven honky-tonkers, and his second release, "Hearts Are Lonely" (437), hit the *Billboard* charts in June 1959 and peaked at #26, another early hit for Pierce's born-again label. A third record was released and Pierce considered Sullivan to be one of his "rising stars," but his life was tragically ended in an automobile accident later that year, in which Oscar's wife also died. The tragedy was only the first of several that would haunt Starday in the following few years.

By the end of 1959, Pierce was still looking for his first *big* Nashville record. Without the advantage of a Top Ten record to depend on, and facing a year and half worth of operation expenses, Pierce began searching for ways to cut corners financially. To get his product from the studio to the record racks, Pierce had to front money for studio time at Bradley's, or wherever else he could secure studio time, and pay the session men. He then paid to print and press up the records. He paid for packing materials and office supplies, as well as Cole's salary, and he paid the postage to mail singles to each and every radio station he could imagine. By 1959 Starday was servicing more than a thousand big and small stations across the country.

To the rescue came Tommy Hill. Toward the end of 1958, Pierce was introduced to the young fiddler backstage at the Grand Ole Opry. Hill had grown up just outside San Antonio and spent his early days picking guitar and singing with Big Bill Lister on San Antonio's KTSA. His first musical break came at age nineteen when Smiley Burnette heard him singing with his brother and brought them both to California to appear as extras in several of his movies. Unsatisfied with riding horses in circles and pretending to be a bad guy in Hollywood, Hill returned to San Antonio—only to find Webb Pierce passing through town without a fiddle player. Hill offered his musical services and was invited to travel to Shreveport and play with Pierce for a few months. During that time, Webb Pierce took a liking to Hill's original composition "Slowly" and recorded it a number of times for Decca, eventually reaching *Billboard*'s top position and earning country music's prestigious Song of the Year award in 1954. This song and several others established Tommy Hill as a well-known songwriter rather than a performer.

For his role in helping Webb Pierce, Webb's manager Tillman Franks (later a Starday recording artist himself) helped Hill secure a recording contract with Decca Records. During one of his 1953 recording sessions Tommy brought his sister with him to demo a tune he had just written for Kitty Wells entitled, "Let the Stars Get in My Eyes," an answer to Slim Willet's "Don't Let the Stars Get In Your Eyes." Decca took a stronger interest in his sister Goldie than they did Tommy. Hill had written a #1 hit, but it was his own sister who would be heard over the airwaves.

Don Pierce and Tommy Hill in the Starday Studio (Courtesy of Howard Vokes)

Hill moved to Nashville in 1954 and was still hoping to make it as a country music solo artist when Fred Rose signed him to his new label, Hickory Records. After stints backing Hank Williams Sr. and fronting Ray Price's Western Cherokees and later Jim Reeves's Blue Boys, Hill was excited to be stepping out of the background and into the limelight. After several solid but non-charting releases on Hickory, Hill was again backing other performers on the Grand Ole Opry stage. It was there, backstage at the Opry, where Don Pierce and Hill developed their friendship. Pierce recalls one day mentioning to Hill that he was looking for some help cutting corners at Starday. Hill told Pierce that he was looking for a job and a new label. "He asked me if he could work at Starday and I said, 'Sure,'" remembers Pierce. "He started out just packing the records in the shipping department part-time."

Pierce also agreed to release some of his solo sides, and Hill's first Starday release, "Oil on My Land" (429), was released in April 1959. He followed that with several scattered album tracks and even two albums of country fiddle instrumentals. It was a simple suggestion from Hill to Pierce, however, not his recordings, that would forever change Starday Records: If you're looking to cut back on your recording costs, why not build your own studio?

Soon Pierce and Hill were meeting several times a week, discussing studio possibilities, and before long Hill became a full-time Starday employee. Though Hill had no previous studio engineering or design experience, he advised Pierce on what to build and what equipment he would need; when all was said and done in May 1960, Starday had built a giant concrete square recording studio onto the back half of the office building. Not only was Hill responsible for operating the new studio, Pierce also credits him with bringing Starday its first Nashville hit.

Frankie Miller explains: "I recorded 'Black Land Farmer' [the spelling on the original single listed Black Land as two words, though later reissues often used Blackland] in Houston. I had the master kicked around [in] my car about two years before we ever got it on Starday. Tommy Hill was up in Nashville. I went to Nashville with a guy named Howard Crockett [real name Howard Hausey, co-author of Johnny Horton's 1956 hit "Honky Tonk Man"]. I had this song out in the car. Tommy was working with Don on some stuff. He wasn't working with him exclusively at that time, but he was working for Atco Publishing and a guy named Ray Scribner up there in Nashville. And ol' Howard said, 'Tommy, you wanna hear a good country song?' Tommy said, 'Yeah.' He said, 'Frank, go down and get that copy of 'Black Land Farmer' and bring it up here and play it for Tommy.' I said, 'Oh man. Hell, rock and roll is so strong. They don't wanna hear no country record.' But Tommy said, 'Yeah, go get it.' And I went down and got it and played it and Tommy's eyes lit up. He took it out to Starday and Don Pierce and the next day they offered me a recording contract."

At a time when Pierce was trying to re-establish Starday as the only purely country label in Nashville, Miller's "Black Land Farmer" (424) was an ideal song to promote to radio stations. The laid-back tune embodied Pierce's perception of country music values, with Miller's nasal voice humming and crooning about farming, the Good Lord's blessings, and a hard-working man making an honest living. Miller remembers recording it at Bill Quinn's Gold Star Studios with "a local musician in Houston named [1950s and 1960s Starday artist] Glenn Barber, he played guitar on my session. My brother Norman played the coconut shells to sound like a horse walking. I bought the shells on the way to the studio and we hollowed 'em out to make the horse's hooves [and] we put a mic down there by the coconuts." Other musicians present included Jimmy Robinson on steel guitar, "Hezzie" Bryant on bass, Henry Bennett on fiddle, and Jack Kennedy at the piano.

The single was released on March 9, 1959, and marked a joyful reunion between Pierce and Miller. Pierce remembers: "I first became acquainted with Frankie Miller's recordings when I was working at 4 Star in Los Angeles. He made some good sounding records for us but we never had much luck. Later when we got Starday going in Nashville I was offered some sides that he had cut and one of them was 'Black Land Farmer.' I liked the song right away and always thought that Frankie had a real good country voice and he was a very good artist to work with in every way."

Tommy Hill and Frankie Miller recording "Family Man," August 1959 (Courtesy of Frankie Miller)

Miller's music career began in 1950 after filling in for Hank Locklin on Houston's KLEE. After a few superb recordings on the Gilt-Edge label, Miller recorded for Pierce at 4 Star and later signed with Columbia Records. By the time he signed with Starday Records, Miller had already guested on the Grand Ole Opry, the Louisiana Hayride, and was a regular on Fort Worth's Cowtown Hoedown. But it was "Black Land Farmer" that truly established Miller and put him on the country music map. Despite the "throwback" sound and comparisons to Hank Williams Sr., Miller's style and lyric resonated with country music fans across the nation: "When the Lord made me he made a simple man, / not much money, not much land. / He didn't make me no banker or legal charmer, / when the Lord made me he made a black land farmer." The record was an immediate hit.

The tune, complete with humming intro and chorus, hit the charts in April and stayed there for almost five months, eventually peaking at #5. Shortly after its release, Miller began recording new material for Starday. Like most Nashville Starday sessions that took place prior to May 1960, when the Starday Studios first opened, Miller recorded at Owen Bradley's Quonset Hut located at 804 16th Avenue South near downtown Nashville. Miller remembers: "It was an old Army Quonset hut, one of those tin buildings that's round-shaped that they used during World War II. And what a sound they got! The engineer's name was Selby Coffeen. He did all my sessions at Bradley's. Tommy Hill was there and he would always play on all the sessions. He would lead them too. Lightnin' Chance played bass on some of 'em and Junior Husky played on the others. And Grady Martin played guitar on all of 'em at Bradley's. I used him some at Starday and I used Hank Garland also. Steel guitar I used mostly Jimmy Day if he was in town 'cause I knew Jimmy from back in Texas. Jimmy was a friend of mine, but sometimes he was out so we used [Buddy] Emmons and on several sessions at Starday we used Pete Drake. On piano I used Pig [Robbins] on most of 'em. Also Dean Manuel on a couple sessions. He was a friend of mine and a good piano player. I used him on two or three sessions for Starday."

Miller's followup tune was another home-spun story about a man who could not go out and party with the boys, but instead had to make money and raise his family. "Family Man" (457) was released the following September and entered the charts on October 5. "Family Man" became his second Top 10 hit, climbing to #7 on the *Billboard* charts and staying for another five months. Miller recalls: Bobe West wrote that one. He had some conflict with Don Pierce later on. I did an album and did about four or five of his songs. He [West] said Don could have the publishing so when I got back to Fort Worth after I recorded, well, he'd given the publishing to a company down here in Fort Worth. They [the publishing company] called Don. Don called me. He said, 'Get to Fort Worth and find out what's happening with those songs.' So, I got back to Fort Worth and they wanted part of the publishing on it. Bobe did and he was in with Howard Crockett. And I said, 'You guys promised me that Don Pierce could have the publishing on 'em. That's the only reason I cut the songs.' And I had some witnesses with me at the time they said we had the publishing. So Don said, 'Well hell, we'll get 'em up here in Davidson County in Nashville and we'll rip 'em!' But they come across and said 'OK.' We got it all squared away and then they released all the songs."

"Family Man" landed on both the *Billboard* and *Cash Box* charts and confirmed Miller as one of the hottest country acts in the nation. Miller won the *Cash Box* award for Most Promising New Country Artist in 1960 and, according to Miller's sources, fell just two votes behind Buck Owens in the *Billboard* voting for the same category (paradoxically, neither artist was really "new").

Pierce and Miller had found success with a clean, wholesome image, and Miller continued to record down-home, earthy songs. With his second release after "Family Man," Miller again found himself in the national charts, this time with "Baby Rocked Her Dolly" (496) reaching *Billboard*'s #15 spot. According to Miller, "We definitely tried to keep a family image. 'Black Land Farmer.'

'Family Man.' The next one we had was 'Reunion.' And then 'Baby Rocked Her Dolly' which was a good chart song for me, one that Merle Kilgore wrote. He originally wrote it for Johnny Horton. Well, I was gonna record next week and we was doing the Louisiana Hayride one Saturday. Johnny was in the restroom and I went in and asked him, 'Johnny, you got any songs boy? I need some material. I'm fixin' to record next week.' He said, 'I got a good song here for you. Merle Kilgore wrote it for me but I'm not going to be able to cut it anytime soon.' So he taught it to me backstage at the Louisiana Hayride and I recorded it the next week. That was another Bradley's [Owen Bradley's Quonset hut] cut."

Miller continued to record for Starday into the mid-sixties, though he never reached the level of stardom attained by his *Billboard* rival, Buck Owens. In fact, only two more hits followed "Dolly"—and one of them was "Black Land Farmer" a second time. Apparently a television station started playing the original version in Houston and teens began dancing the "Black Land Farmer." During its second life in 1961, "Black Land Farmer," the most country song Don Pierce could find and promote, even crossed over to *Billboard*'s pop charts and peaked at #82. As befuddling as that may be, it is even harder to imagine what the dance might have looked like. Pierce adds, "I still have no idea how in the hell anybody could dance to that song."

Of course, Frankie Miller was not the only Starday artist with a pure and wholesome image. After all, Pierce's motto was "Starday—Country and Gospel International," and he actively sought new gospel and sacred acts. According to Pierce, "Country and gospel music go hand in hand. Most often they use the same instrumentation and nearly all country artists include some gospel numbers in their repertoire." Pierce also knew that the genres could be equally lucrative. He further explains: "The removal of Starday from L.A. to Nashville was a whole different ballgame. I was soon well aware of the huge market for sacred. I got really started with Randy Blake of Chicago, WJJD—50,000 watts. [Radio stations with 50,000 watts of broadcast power were known as "clear channel" stations, no relation to the later Clear Channel radio conglomerate.] *Suppertime Frolics* was the show. Man, he had a powerhouse show! Well, he used to use the Chuck Wagon Gang and he wanted me to put together a package for radio mail order. Eighteen songs, three songs on each side of a 45 rpm record. So you had three of 'em. He wanted a country set, a Christmas set and a gospel set [Pierce had already been supplying the *Hillbilly Hit Parade* and Christmas sets]. I had material from Story and the Stanley Brothers and things like that from Mercury but I went out and I got the Blackwood Brothers, the Lefevres, the Sunshine Boys, the Statesmen, and others. I told them, 'Look, whatever Randy does up there, it's completely in addition to what you're already doing. It doesn't take anything away from your market because it's all

WLW–Cincinnati disc jockey Randy Blake (Courtesy of Nathan Gibson)

mail-order, it doesn't get in the stores.' And they were willing to lease their material to me, which in turn, I used for Randy. That's really how I got started in the sacred stuff and man, it sold like crazy."

Pierce credits various country music radio shows, such as the Grand Ole Opry, for emphasizing the role of gospel music within American country music and increasing its popularity. Pierce also points out that there are, in his opinion, several different styles of gospel music. In an interview with the *Music Reporter* in 1962, Pierce explained his three different categories for sacred material: a traditional country artist who records sacred material, mountain sacred music (or bluegrass sacred), and gospel quartets. For the sake of brevity on records and album covers, Pierce simply lumped it all under the umbrella title of gospel.

Among the first true gospel quartets to be released on Starday were the Jubilaires Quartet, the Melody Quartet, Anna Lee and the King's Messengers, Kirby Buchanan (accompanied by the Jordanaires), the Sunshine Boys, and the Oak Ridge Quartet. The Oak Ridge Boys, as the quartet later became known, actually began their career playing shows around Knoxville, Tennessee, in the early 1940s as the Country Cutups. For a brief period of time, members of the Cutups recorded for Capitol as part of Wally Fowler and the Georgia

The Sunshine Boys publicity photo, April 1965 (Courtesy of Don Pierce)

Clodhoppers, though Fowler decided to re-form the group around 1945 and stick solely to gospel music. After regular weekend gigs at the atomic energy plant in Oak Ridge, the group became known as the Oak Ridge Quartet and began appearing on the Grand Ole Opry and recording as early as 1947.

The Oak Ridge Boys have always had a revolving cast of members and, by the time they arrived on Pierce's doorstep, Wally Fowler, the leader, was no longer in the group. Instead, Fowler was recording live transcriptions of his Gospel and Spiritual All Night Singing Concert at the Ryman Auditorium (SLP 112 and SLP 301) for Starday. Fowler had left the quartet in 1956 and sold the Oak Ridge name to Smitty Gatlin, then the group's lead singer. Gatlin reorganized the group a year later and became labelmates with Fowler in 1959. Other members of the Starday-era group included Herman Harper, Ronnie Page, and "Little" Willie Wynn. Backing them on their Starday recordings was their regular piano player, Tommy Fairchild, and Hank "Sugarfoot" Garland on lead guitar.

The Oak Ridge Quartet recordings were also among the first to be made at the new Starday Sound Studios in May 1960. By 1961, Pierce had gathered enough recordings to piece together their first full-length album, *Master*

Showmen of Song (SLP 130). Shortly after its release the group renamed themselves the Oak Ridge Boys, and in 1965 Starday released another full-length album *The Sensational Oak Ridge Boys From Nashville, Tennessee* (SLP 356), featuring their new sound, complete with a full country backing band and smoother singing styles. The shaggy, bearded boys from Oak Ridge eventually found their way into the hearts of America in the late 1970s, peaking in 1978 when they won the Country Music Association's Vocal Group of the Year award as well as Instrumental Group of the Year, *Billboard*'s Number One Country Music Group of the Year, *Record World*'s Number One Vocal Group of the Year, *Cash Box*'s Country Vocal Group of the Year, four Grammy Awards, and fifteen Dove Awards.

The first gospel quartet signed to Starday was the Sunshine Boys, touted as "America's Number One Spiritual Quartet." Despite having a rather boastful title, they were the first gospel quartet to sell a million records, backing Red Foley on his immortal classic "Peace in the Valley." By the time Pierce inked them to Starday in 1958, they had recorded records under their own name for Decca and had appeared in nearly twenty Hollywood films. The Sunshine Boys membership was also ever-changing; the 1958 group consisted of Ace Richmond, Fred Daniels, Ed Wallace, and Burl Strevel. The guitar work on their first Starday recordings was by Sid "Hardrock" Gunter, among the earliest rockabilly pioneers (his 1950 recording of "Birmingham Bounce" on the Bama label is often recognized as one of the earliest rock 'n' roll records), and distinguishes the Sunshine Boys from the other quartets as a more aggressive, rocking gospel group. Gunter was later replaced by featured guitarist Gerald Wallace. The Sunshine Boys' first LP, *The Word* (SLP 113), was released in 1959 and was followed by five more full-length albums.

While he was signing new acts and restructuring the label, Pierce also decided to restructure the way he released material. Preferring to release various gospel groups on EPs (multiple songs per side of a 7" 45 rpm single), as opposed to the traditional two-song singles, Pierce set up a new EP series starting in the 100s. Secular material was later released within the EP series, though the early EPs were comprised of four to six gospel and sacred songs and often were packaged with multicolor sleeves. Among these early gospel and sacred EPs were releases by Bill Clifton, Jim Eanes, George Jones, Carl Story, and the Stanley Brothers. There was also a plethora of gospel bluegrass EPs by Hoyt Scoggins, Jimmie Williams and Red Ellis, the Acorn Sisters, Bill and Mary Reid, John Reedy and the Stone Mountain Trio, Roy Shepard and the Tri-State Singers, Don and Earl, the Southlan Trio, the Upchurch Family, and many more, as well as several by more well-known gospel and sacred bluegrass acts such as Wayne Raney, Charlie Moore and his Dixie Partners, and the Lewis Family.

The first EP (SEP 101) consisted of four tunes by Carl Story and his Rambling Mountaineers, another Mercury turned Mercury-Starday turned Starday act. Shortly after Mercury dropped their country acts, Pierce, who had befriended the high tenor Story, snagged him and began a long relationship between Story and Starday. Based on the popularity of his first Mercury LP, Pierce immediately compiled enough songs for Story's second LP, *America's Favorite Country Gospel Artist* (SLP 107). Many of those songs were bluegrass versions of his popular Mercury offerings. The album became quite popular with bluegrass fans and, over the next ten years, Starday released twelve full-length albums by Story and his band. Among his most successful recordings for Starday were bluegrass remakes of his previous Mercury hits such as "Why Don't You Haul Off and Get Religion" (SLP 152), "You Don't Love God (If You Don't Love Your Neighbor)" (SLP 219), "Mighty Close To Heaven" (SLP 219), and "Everybody Will Be Happy" (SLP 137). As to why Story and his band were so successful, Pierce notes: "They sang with the spirit and that beat. They had a sincerity to their sound that got people in that old-time religion feeling."

Another man of great importance to Starday's gospel outpouring was Wayne Raney. Pierce reminisces: "Wayne Raney . . . now there was a hoss! WCKY— 50,000 watts! And he sold so goddamn many of our gospel sets and *Hillbilly Hit Parade* sets and stuff like that. I first met Wayne when I was in Cincinnati and I called on him. He was a disc jockey on WCKY and I needed airplay. Wayne was familiar with the work I was doing with Randy Blake in Chicago on the gospel sets for mail order and he told me that he wanted to do some work with me being as Randy Blake had passed away. Wayne Raney knew radio and Raney knew the country gospel business and so we started to make gospel sets for radio mail-order sales. Wayne would listen to the various gospel recordings on Starday and largely select what he thought would be the best for sales and he was uncanny. He knew how to pick those songs. I'd have all that stuff stacked up and he'd throw this one out and that one out. He'd find one and he'd know it was something he could use. As you know, he had long been active with Lonnie Glosson and the sale of harmonicas on Mexican radio stations so he certainly knew how to sell country gospel music. He was a great disc jockey and he had all those chickens he raised out there [Concord, Arkansas] and in the meantime he was doin' that mail-order business. I mean, Wayne was a real good businessman. Sharp as a tack."

Aside from Raney's business ventures, he was also an established singer and extraordinary harmonica player. By the time Raney joined the Starday ranks, he was already established as a top-rated disc jockey, a well-respected salesman, and a great songwriter and performer, having scored three Top 15 hits before 1950: "Lost John Boogie," "Jack and Jill Boogie," and the #1 classic "Why Don't You Haul Off and Love Me."

Don Pierce and Wayne Raney listening to Mother Maybelle Carter while choosing songs for the *Hillbilly Hit Parade* sets (Courtesy of Don Pierce)

After several years of boogie and secular country material for King (and a brief stint with Decca), Raney joined Starday and recorded some of the gospel music he had been selling on his shows. Eighteen gospel songs were recorded by Raney with his wife, Loys, and their three children. Those tracks were compiled for their first album, oddly mistitled *16 Radio Gospel Favorites* (SLP 124), highlighted by the comical-but-serious declaration "We Need a Lot More of Jesus (And a Lot Less Rock and Roll)." The tune, covered by numerous artists including Pat Boone, the Greenbriar Boys, Cowboy Copas, the Sunshine Boys, and Linda Ronstadt, has become a gospel classic and even became a minor country hit for Skeeter Davis several years later.

Charlie Moore was another well-known picker who recorded bluegrass gospel for Starday. Moore's professional career began in 1956 as part of Cousin Wilbur Wesbrook's popular band in Asheville, North Carolina. Moore organized the Dixie Partners in 1957, which consisted of Moore on guitar and lead vocals, Ansel Gutherie on mandolin and vocals, Duck Sisk on fiddle, Bob Ellis on bass, and Curly Ellis on the five-string banjo. By the time they recorded their first records in 1958, Moore was a disc jockey at WHBB in Belton, South Carolina, host of the Saturday night television show, *Carolina Promenade Party*, and host of his own bluegrass gospel show on WSPA in Spartanburg.

Two four-song gospel EPs were released (SEP 103 and 116), mostly original songs from their television appearances, with individual tracks appearing on several other EPs. In 1960, when Moore teamed up with the former Stanley Brothers mandolinist Bill Napier, he finally found commercial success. After signing to King Records in 1962, Moore and Napier became widely popular capitalizing on the truck-driving song phenomenon with "Truck Driving Queen," "Long White Line," and the poignant, yet politically not-even-close-to-correct, "Hot Rod Kids and Women Drivers," all of which were later leased and rereleased by Starday.

By the end of 1959 Starday had reestablished itself as a powerful Nashville-based independent label, and Pierce was recognized for his extensive efforts on behalf of both Starday and the future of country music. Citing Pierce as "One of the dominant and most effective forces in helping country music maintain a traditional identity," *Billboard* dubbed Pierce the 1959 Country and Western Man of the Year, an award voted on by country music disc jockeys nationwide. Pierce was presented with the award in November at the 12th annual Country Music Festival and Disc Jockey Convention in Nashville.

Specific reasons for the award included his signing many traditional country acts dropped by the major labels and his promotion of country music overseas. Not only did Pierce sign older acts, he began recording and releasing full-length albums, which at the time was considered an enormous financial risk. Pierce contends: "When I saw that my buyer was an adult, and we were getting away from 45s and going to LPs, I went heavily into LPs. And at a time when the major companies felt that, 'Well, if we're not selling our 45s much, why spend any more money on album art?' In the meantime, I'm filling this void. And I'm also doing a big job with the Armed Forces overseas through the army. Those guys come home and they still want the product. The guys from the Grand Ole Opry, they go to Germany, they see those racks over there loaded with Starday and can't find anything by the other labels. . . . It cost us a lot of money for the artwork and it cost a lot of money for the printing, but there was a market for it and so we supplied that market."

The Armed Forces Network proved to be a strong supporter of Starday Records, largely because Starday was among the very few labels supplying them with free records of all their releases. Surprisingly, Pierce was the only entrepreneur in country music actively going overseas and creating new markets, despite stressing the importance of pushing country music overseas in several pamphlets he made available to the Country Music Association. In fact, Pierce had been a founding member of the CMA, organized in November 1958 by industry executives, their goal to unite and promote country music. He even served as the organization's secretary for four of its first five years. In 1961 the group established and operated the Country Music Hall of Fame. All the while Pierce openly shared his ideas on how to promote country music with other board members.

Bringing American country music to the world, however, was not without difficulties. On behalf of both the CMA and Starday, Pierce took several trips around the globe enthusiastically promoting his beloved music, though occasionally it was less enthusiastically received. Pierce recalls: "The first time I went to England [1959] we bought Starday of London Publishing Co. and leased my material over there and I took a film of the Grand Ole Opry over there with me to London. We had this big reception and we brought in all the disc jockeys from the BBC and had some whiskey and then played 'em that Opry tape and they just started laughing and laughing. They said it was the worst crap they'd ever heard in their life and that it would never sell in England." He quickly adds with a chuckle, "They were wrong."

His determination paid off. By November 1959 Pierce not only had established his U.S. distribution network from coast to coast but had also reached agreements with distribution companies in Japan, Germany, Britain, and South Africa. In the next five years over one hundred Starday albums were released in England, Holland, Germany, Italy, South Africa, Australia, and Japan, and nearly every album in the catalog was released and manufactured in Canada by Sparton Records. By 1965 Starday material was also released (often on other labels such as London, Ember, Quality, Oriole, Top Rank, White & Gillespie, and many others) in New Zealand, France, Spain, Scandinavia, and Yugoslavia. In addition to his growing international interests, Pierce also stressed to the CMA the importance and profitability behind making Nashville the publishing headquarters for country music throughout the world. He argued that, "By making Nashville the headquarters which would handle all overseas representation for all the copyrights originating in Nashville and the South, Nashville would also become one of the biggest music centers in the world." People were quicker to catch on to this idea, and before long WSM disc jockey David Cobb's Nashville nickname stuck: "Music City, USA," first used during a 1950 radio broadcast.

Billboard's Country and Western Man of the Year award was a great honor for Pierce. It was a sincere thank-you from country music jockeys and fans, both for preserving bluegrass and traditional country music and for making it readily available to small rural stations as well as 50,000 watters. Pierce adds: "That meant a lot to me because that's when country music was struggling with rock 'n' roll. The major companies had greatly reduced their rosters and they weren't spending any money on the airplay unless the station subscribed to their services and all that. And here I am, a little guy, servicing 1,200 to 1,400 stations and keeping country music going. So that's why the country disc jockeys voted for me ahead of RCA, CBS, Decca, and everybody else. Nobody else was doin' much of anything."

5

SUNNY TENNESSEE

By 1960 Pierce had earned the esteem and admiration of music executives on Nashville's downtown Music Row as well as fans and disc jockeys. Respect for Starday was further cemented with the grand opening of the Starday Sound Studios in May 1960. Prior to its opening, Nashville studio time was hard to come by. Pierce's studio was soon booked solid as well. The studio quickly became one of the top four recording outlets in Nashville, alongside Owen Bradley's Quonset Hut (which was sold to Columbia Records in 1962), RCA Victor, and Fred Foster studios. Though the Starday studio had initially been Tommy Hill's idea, it was Pierce's friend and golfing buddy, John Story, who made the idea a reality. Pierce remembers that Story, a stockbroker, approached Pierce about helping with studio costs. "I said, 'What did you have in mind?' He said, 'Well, I have an investor and we will put up the money and I will have 25 percent and my customer will have 25 percent and Starday will have 50 percent.' I got Glenn Snoddy, and for $25,000 he built a complete recording studio. I put up the building to house the studio, and the money went for the equipment in the studio." Still in operation today by Gusto Records, it is now the oldest continuously operating recording studio in Nashville, Tennessee.

Though Story's contribution to the studio was significant, it was also brief. Just a short while after the studio opened, Story passed away. Pierce explains:, "It was a little later on when John Story and myself and Silliman Evans, the publisher of the *Tennessean*, used to barbeque and party together. One day we were at my cottage up on the lake, and we were having a party and John was there, and wanted to ride the horses. I wasn't able to break away from the party, but John took Morning Glory, my horse, and he got out on Shute Lane, and apparently was racing the horse. There's a curve at the end of the Southern Shores place on Shute Lane that turns sharply to the right, and apparently he lost control and fell off, and one foot was caught in the saddle. He was dragged on the road and was killed. It was a tragic, tragic accident and much regretted."

Tommy Hill at the recording controls and Junior Husky playing bass (Courtesy of Don Pierce)

When Story's estate was settled, Pierce purchased Story's share in the studio, as well as his investor's share, and took on full ownership. Shortly thereafter Hill and other Starday employees began experiencing strange goings-on in the studio. According to multiple employees, faucets would turn on and turn off when no one was in the lavatory, the sound of footsteps would be heard where no one had walked, and occasionally Story's voice would call out for a friend during late-night recording sessions. Adding to the lore of the oldest operating studio in Nashville were the many ghost stories of friendly John Story who is said to have moved into the studio to become the resident spirit.

Tommy Hill had only limited experience with home recording machines prior to taking the helm at Starday Sound Studios, but proved to be a quick learner. After helping Pierce acquire the necessary components, Hill's involvement with the studio became a full-time obligation. Pierce placed his full trust in Hill and gave him sole control of all studio production. Although he tried to stay out of the studio as much as possible, Pierce still expressed to Hill exactly what he was looking for in the finished product. Pierce recalls: The recordings I would leave entirely up to Tommy. We'd agree on what we'd record and he was in charge. Rarely did I have much criticism for him. All he knew was this: I want to hear the melody. I don't want no hot licks in there. I want to hear the melody. And another thing I said to him, 'Get that singer separated in the booth where the music does not override being able to understand everything that the singer sings.' And that's one thing about Starday's stuff: you could hear that singer and you could understand the goddamn lyrics! Musicians did not play hot licks unless they were playing an instrumental. If they were accompanying the singer, they would just accompany the singer and I don't want to put jazzy stuff in there. That's my rule. I said, keep it simple. Because these guys are excellent musicians and they like to take off and go, but with me, I said that's not what we're all about. We're selling that song and that artist, we're not selling hot licks. That was my code and Tommy followed it and we were successful."

Hill himself recorded only sparingly throughout his tenure at Starday, but quickly garnered a reputation as one of Nashville's top producers. He was also instrumental in setting up the Starday studio house band, composed mainly of Hill's closest friends living in Nashville. Though it would change somewhat throughout the years, the earliest session men regularly scheduled were Roy "Junior" Huskey on bass, Harold Weakley or Willie Ackerman on drums, Jerry Shook or Hank "Sugarfoot" Garland on electric guitar, Jerry Smith or Dean Manuel on piano, and almost always Pete Drake on steel guitar.

After two years of running the studio alone, Hill hired Jack "Hoss" Linneman as his engineering assistant. Linneman had previously recorded in his home studio in Sacramento, California, but moved to Nashville in 1951 as a musician looking for electric guitar, steel guitar, and dobro work. After being called upon as a session man at Starday on multiple occasions, Hill and Linneman became good friends. With Linneman's hiring, there were two new members in the house band: "Hoss" Linneman and his son, Billy. The elder Linneman, who often sat in on sessions with his dobro, remembers: "When I started working over there, Junior Huskey was playin' all the bass and my son would go over there during the sessions and watch. He finally bought a bass from Junior for $100 and he just picked that thing up and started playing it. First thing you know, Billy could get a better tone than Junior. So as it turned out, we had two separate bands we would use. My son would play on about half the stuff and Junior on the rest. Well, Junior would often get drunk and do all kinds of bad things. Well, he got drunk one time, took my son's bass, and knocked the soundpost out of it. I just threw a big temper tantrum on that and that was the end of Junior playing bass at Starday."

Despite having two talented house bands and a growing roster of top talent, there were still many challenges to be met in the Starday studios. Linneman explains: "Tommy wasn't really an electronics or acoustics man, but he had a great ear, and with the equipment they had when I came there, he did a really fantastic job. Originally all they had in there were a couple of Altec mixers, which was really just PA equipment. But I built a real board in there with higher-class equipment and we slowly started getting equipment and reorganizing the studio itself. It was actually a very bad studio. The main thing wrong with the studio is that it was basically square. Every which way. And it had a lot of deadening stuff in it. And of course a studio with a lot of dead stuff in it is a dead studio because only the high frequencies would get absorbed easily."

Aside from having a "dead studio," Hill and Linneman also had to contend with trucks driving by, slowing to a halt at the stoplight out front and popping their airbrakes. In addition to the occasional air-brake outtake, they also had to contend with radio feedback bleeding through the amplifiers from WLAC, a 50,000-watt rhythm and blues station just up the road from the studio. When Linneman (who later founded Hilltop Records) arrived at Starday in 1962, his recording expertise greatly enhanced the studio. He built a separate sound booth, added reflective walls throughout the studio, and rewired the electronics to help minimize the radio feedback. Prior to Linneman's arrival, Hill had to get creative with how he recorded the various artists. Frankie Miller remembers: "I cut the very first session there. Tommy Hill engineered it and he didn't have any echo set up or anything. So we went up in the attic and put a speaker at one end and a microphone at the other and that's how we got our echo."

Shortly thereafter, Hill and Linneman built their infamous echo unit to enhance recordings. As David McKinley, who became Hill's assistant engineer at the studio in 1971, remembers, "They built an echo unit. You listen to some of the early Red Sovine and Cowboy Copas stuff. They used it on Red's vocals a lot and it was a box. It was like an acoustical delay with a lot of coils inside this thing that delayed the signals and made this echo sound and it was wonderful. It's really something. RCA was calling. Columbia was calling. All the majors were calling out here, 'What have you guys done to get this vocal sound on Red Sovine?' It's unbelievable! So Tommy and Jack thought, 'We've got a fortune here. We'll start building these boxes and making these echo units.' So Jack Linneman took the box apart to see what he'd done. You have to know the guy to understand this. He built it and now he takes it apart to see what he'd done to make a whole bunch of 'em and sell 'em. Linneman could never get the thing back together again. So, it was gone. Couldn't build any more. Couldn't put the original back again. And that's a true story."

Fortunately, before that minor tragedy struck, hundreds of recordings were made with the echo unit. Among the first to benefit from the special echo was Lloyd Estel Copas, better known as Cowboy Copas. Copas grew up on a corn and tobacco farm near Blue Creek, Ohio. While in his teens he adopted the "Cowboy" moniker and, for the remainder of his life told friends and audiences that he grew up on a ranch near Muskogee, Oklahoma, as his Starday album

Cowboy Copas posing for the cover of a collection of sacred songs (Courtesy of Don Pierce)

liner notes affirm. Copas's music career began in 1927 when, at age fourteen, he joined a local group, the Hen Cacklers String Band, as vocalist and guitar picker. Seeking more exposure, Copas teamed up with a champion fiddler named Lester Vernon Storer, who developed a stage act as Natchee the Indian, and the two began playing together and entering talent contests. After a move to Cincinnati, a regular gig performing on WLW's Boone County Jamboree, and a radio job at WNOX in Knoxville, he eventually replaced Eddy Arnold as featured vocalist in Pee Wee King's Golden West Cowboys. King, who was already an established Grand Ole Opry act by 1943, then brought Copas to Nashville and the Opry stage.

Copas's recording career began in Cincinnati with Syd Nathan's brand new King label. His first release, King's sixth, was "Filipino Baby." Released in 1944, the record suffered from poor pressing quality and inspired Nathan to build his own manufacturing plant. The tune was rerecorded, released again in the summer of 1946, and became a #4 hit. Over the following years came several more Top 10 hits, including "Signed Sealed and Delivered," the first ever recording of "Tennessee Waltz," "Tennessee Moon," "Candy Kisses," "The

Strange Little Girl," and "'Tis Sweet To Be Remembered." A strong tenor and unique timbre made his voice instantly recognizable to radio listeners and his prowess with the waltz numbers soon earned him the nickname "The Waltz King of the Grand Ole Opry."

For some inexplicable reason, the hits suddenly stopped in 1952. While Copas continued to record for King, perform on the Opry, and travel the country, his songs were not charting. By the mid-fifties his touring schedule was cut back; and in 1957 he signed to Dot Records to try his hand at rock 'n' roll as Lloyd Copas. After the Dot recordings proved conclusively that Copas was not cut out to be a teeny-bopper, most people considered his career to be over. Copas still desired a career in the industry but found it near impossible to do so and support his wife and three children. About that time Jim Denny approached Pierce about signing Copas to Starday. Pierce recalls: "Jim asked me if I was interested in recording Cowboy Copas. I said I sure was. 'I'd record him in a New York minute!' And he said, 'Well, Copas needs a label.' I said, 'I have always admired his voice. When I first heard it as a record salesmen in California it really knocked me out.'" A deal was then arranged in which "We would make sessions and do two Cedarwood songs and two Starday songs and we would get $500 from Cedarwood to help us with the promotion."

The idea for Copas's first LP, *All Time Country Music Great* (SLP 118), was to rerecord some of Copas's early hits and show off his versatility. The album included duets with his daughter Cathy, a couple of waltzes, an instrumental flat-top guitar blues, uptempo mountain songs, a couple of sacred numbers, and a few more originals. The result was a resounding success. Pierce continues: "So we had a session, and I wanted to do an album. In those days, if you said you were going to do an album, the union would let you do six songs in a three-hour session. If it was for singles, you were limited to four songs in a three-hour session. We had six songs lined up, and we put four of them down. But the fifth song that we got ready to do was a song called 'Alabam.' Well, it sounded real good, and we had Grady Martin playing guitar on the session, one of the greatest session musicians who ever lived as far as I'm concerned, and he said, 'Don, forget about trying to do six songs. This song—something can be done with this. Let me go out to the car and get my tambourines.' Tambourines? I think he went out there and took a snort, came back with his tambourines which Cathy Copas beat against her legs forming a very unique sound, and letting Copas play his open-string guitar on the runs. It was great!"

As soon as the album had been pressed, Copas brought an advance copy over to WSM disc jockey Ralph Emery. Pierce recalls: "I got a call from Cowboy Copas. He said, 'Don, I was on Ralph Emery's show last night and he put the needle on "Alabam," and the lights went up and he got calls from all over the country. We have to do something.' I said, 'I'll have pressings in seven days.'"

At the time, Pierce was hesitant to release "Alabam" as a single because it was recorded during an album session and he did not want to pay the union overtime wages. After much deliberation, Pierce went ahead with the single release (501) and was rewarded immediately. "Alabam" hit the *Billboard* charts on America's birthday, 1960, and stayed there for the next thirty-four weeks. At a time when Copas was struggling to stay afloat financially, he was overjoyed when he received his first BMI royalty check on "Alabam" for over $1,800. It also came at a very opportune time for Pierce, as the song's success helped re-establish his strong distributorship. Pierce adds, "I have to thank Ralph Emery. When I mentioned it to Ralph much later, he told me, 'Don, I had been hearing that songs that I played on WSM on the all-night show were getting recognition even when they weren't out on records. I wanted to test it. The record was not on the market or being played anyplace else, so it couldn't be heard anyplace but here.'"

The song became Copas's first #1 hit, the biggest hit of his career, and held the #1 *Billboard* spot for three months. *Country Song Roundup* and other trade publications proclaimed Copas "The Greatest Comeback of the Year," and Pierce estimates that "Alabam" sold between 125,000 and 130,000 copies. Copas was again on his way—and it makes sense that "Alabam" would be the song to make it happen. The origin of the tune, a tale of people having a whale of a time at a turkey roast in Alabama (among other things), is just as perplexing as the origin of Copas himself. The lyrics at times seem nonsensical, and many suggest that he just made them up as he went. Others say he took each verse from a different folk song and added "I'm goin' back to Alabam" at the end of each one. Copas had told Pierce that he learned the song from his father. According to Copas's son Mike, "The origin of 'Alabam' will forever remain a secret. Cope is the only one that knows for sure." He then adds, "Personally, I like the story that he wrote it one very cold New York morning on his way to work the 5:00 morning show at a local radio station. Although he was born and raised in Ohio, he thought about a warmer climate and penciled the words of 'Alabam.'"

To be fair, Copas owed much of the "Alabam" success to Frank Hutchinson, a West Virginian country blues singer and slide guitarist. Though the lyrics were slightly altered by Copas, the song's melody and structure were lifted directly from Hutchinson's 1927 Okeh recording of "Coney Isle." Regardless of how the resulting song developed, what is certain is that it reestablished Cowboy Copas as a country music star. The affable Ohioan was now recognized as a top guitar picker in Nashville and began to back several other musicians on their Starday sessions. Pierce remembers that Copas went from making $100 a night to over $400 per gig and that he also became one of the first Opry acts to bring a chair with him on stage. Pierce adds, "He would sit and play his

George Jones backstage with Cowboy Copas (Courtesy of Don Pierce)

acoustic guitar, which became wildly popular with the [Opry] crowds. People just couldn't get enough of his Martin flat-top, thumb-pickin' style."

"Alabam" was followed by several similar tunes and a number of them charted. "Flat Top" (542), a rollicking number in which Copas describes a trip of his to Nashville on a Saturday night, was a cross between "Alabam" and Chuck Berry's "Johnny B. Goode." In the song, Copas met a boy who played the flat-top guitar and so he requested the song "Alabam" or another called, "Sunny Tennessee." The tune hit the charts in April 1961 and reached *Billboard*'s #9 spot. It was followed by "Sunny Tennessee" (552), surely the same tune Copas had requested of the boy in "Flat Top," and it too charted in 1961, peaking at #12. His very next release was a remake of his 1948 classic "Signed, Sealed and Delivered" (559), and that too topped *Billboard*'s Top 10. Copas was again among county music's hottest acts and was Starday's biggest seller.

But Copas was not the only artist to make a career comeback on Starday. In 1960 Pierce signed another former King Records artist, Moon Mullican, also known as the "King of the Hillbilly Piano Players." Mullican soon was back in the *Billboard* charts for the first time in nearly a decade with his own version of the blue-collar standard "Ragged But Right" (545). The tune entered the charts in May 1961 and peaked at #15. Though the comeback was not as dramatic as that of Copas, it was another well-deserved break for an established veteran.

Copas and Mullican also shared an interest in helping to get Don Pierce's neighbor, Tennessee Governor Frank Clement, re-elected. Each cut a side promoting the popular governor and the two sides were released together on the Dixie label (594) in 1962. Pierce recalls: "It was our good fortune when we moved to Nashville to have as our next-door neighbor Roy Acuff and the next neighbor over was Governor Frank Clement. I became acquainted with him and his family and we certainly enjoyed their friendship. When he got ready to run for governor a second time, I stopped by his house and we visited and I asked him if it would be helpful if I made a recording that he could use on his campaign stops. He was enthusiastic about that and he wondered what I had in mind. 'Well, I'll work up something and get back to you.' It was strictly something that I wanted to do for him. I got some help from Marijohn Wilkin, who was writing for Cedarwood Publishing Company. She came in with a good song idea, and Moon made a recording called 'Good Times Are Gonna Roll Again (In Sunny Tennessee).' They used that at campaign stops and Frank Clement was re-elected."

Though it was a fun project to help a neighbor, releasing singles was becoming more and more infrequent. In 1960 Starday released a total of fifteen albums and sixty-three singles; by 1962 those numbers had changed dramatically, with Starday issuing fifty-five long-play albums and fewer than forty singles. Despite the sharp decline, Starday still released great 45s throughout the early sixties. Among them were truck driving classics by Tom O'Neal and Jimmy Simpson; honky-tonkers from Little Jimmy Dempsey, Bob Steele, and Lonnie Mullins; and bluegrass releases from Connie and Joe, Buzz Busby, Jim Eanes, and the Country Gentlemen to name a few. There were even some country-rockers from Bill Browning, Dave Dudley, Bill Parsons, and Hardrock Gunter (leased from Emperor). But the real rockers were still originating from Starday's custom service.

The Dixie custom series was still going strong in 1960, and released over eighty singles that year. Among them are some of the best, and today's most highly sought-after, rockabilly records from the 1960s: Tommy Nelson's "Hobo Bop" (Dixie 814), The Hi-Tombs' "Sweet Rockin' Mama" (Cannon 832), Red Moore's "Crawdad Song" (Red 840), and many more. A few releases showed enough promise to cross over onto the Starday label. Among them was another political campaign song. In October 1959, Kilgore utilized Starday's custom service to release his recording of "Jimmie Bring Sunshine" (J-I-M 808), a Johnny Horton–esque ode to Louisiana's "Hard-working Governor," Jimmie

Davis. According to Kilgore, that record proved to be instrumental in securing a victory in the gubernatorial candidate's bid for a second term. When Pierce first heard the song, which had been produced by his good friend Shelby Singleton, he immediately liked it and rereleased it on the Starday main label (469). Kilgore remembers, "Don really worked on it and the flip side, 'Dear Mama,' flipped over and I started getting airplay. It went up to #12 on *Billboard* and I think it made #12 on *Cash Box* too. That was my first chart record ever."

It is remarkable that that statement is true considering Kilgore's reputation for writing big hits. Among his most well-known songs are "More and More," a #1 hit for Webb Pierce in 1953; Johnny Horton's #1 hit "Johnny Reb"; Claude King's #1 hit "Wolverton Mountain"; as well as co-authoring Johnny Cash's immortal "Ring of Fire" with June Carter. Yet, throughout his own recording career with Imperial, Mercury, Columbia, Starday, Starday-King, Warner, Elektra, and others, Kilgore's only singles to break the Top 50 in the *Billboard* charts were on Starday. Kilgore recalls: "I was on Mercury for a couple years and then Shelby let me off Mercury and I got on Columbia Records. And Don Pierce said, 'Listen, why don't you come in and do an album for us since you're between labels?' I said, 'That's a great idea,' so I went in and cut an album on Starday, '*There's Gold In Them Thar Hills*'" [SLP 251].

The first single after "Dear Mama" paired "Love Has Made You Beautiful" with "Getting Old Before My Time" (497). Both sides charted and the "Love" side peaked at #10. Though they did not chart, Kilgore points to his covers of "The Death of Abraham Lincoln" (SLP 251) and "Pinball Machine" (644) among his personal favorite recordings. Unfortunately for Kilgore, the switch to Columbia Records proved to be unsuccessful. He returned to Starday in the late 1960s as Merle Kilgore, "The Boogie King," and also worked part-time for the label. He tells the story: "I went to work for Starday years later [late 60s] for Hal Neely [President of the Starday-King merger]. I was workin' the Hank [Williams] Jr. roadshow and I was open all week 'cause we worked Fridays and Saturdays and Sundays. So I went out and just kind of interned, you know. Producing the records and running the country division for Starday-King. I was out there for almost two years. Then they moved me up to where I was director of the country market there. It was like learning a whole new part of the business that I really hadn't had the chance to experience."

Kilgore was not the only artist to find success through the Starday custom service. In 1959 a North Carolina truck driver sent in a recording about another truck driver whose pinball addiction caused him to lose his wife and family. That record, Lonnie Irving's first, was initially released in January 1960 on the custom Lonnie Irving label (Lonnie Irving 827) with 300 copies pressed. The song caught on in Cincinnati and Irving submitted an order for 10,000 more copies. Pierce quickly took notice.

Lonnie Irving holding a pinball and wearing his "Pinball Machine" custom hat (Courtesy of Eddy Arnold Irving)

Lonnie Leon Irving was born on June 11, 1932, and grew up in Leaksville, North Carolina. He learned firsthand about the hardships of the truck driver while driving for Hennis Truck Lines and penned several songs about his experiences. When he returned home from the road he began looking for a way to record his creations. To the rescue came Jim Eanes, Starday recording artist and disc jockey in Martinsville, Virginia. How Eanes and Irving met is unknown, but Eanes quickly scheduled and produced Irving's recording session. Eanes's band, featuring Roy Russell on fiddle and Allen Shelton on banjo, provided the backing and were joined by Frank Burroughs (misspelled as Frank Burris on the record label) on electric guitar. "Pinball Machine," first released on Starday as "Pinball" (486), grabbed the attention of the record-buying public and Irving found immediate success with his heartfelt tale. The tune charted in March 1960 and stayed on the charts for more than four months, reaching *Billboard*'s #13 spot.

Two more truck-driving singles were released before Irving passed away. He had been diagnosed with leukemia on October 2, 1959, and told he had less than six months to live. Irving passed away in December 1960, but lived

Loyd Howell and the Blue Stars performing at Budrow's Lounge, ca. 1965 (Courtesy of Loyd Howell's family)

long enough to travel to Nashville and accept his 1960 BMI songwriter's award for "Pinball Machine." As Pierce remembers, "That was the big one, 'Pinball Machine.' I remember he came in to the BMI banquet and got his award and he was so happy and he let me know that it was hard for him to make the trip because he was in later stages of leukemia."

Realizing that a lot of the custom material sent in to Starday had strong commercial potential, Pierce decided to set up a label that would serve as a cross between the custom series and the Starday main series. Shortly after the success of "Pinball" in the summer of 1961, Pierce founded a subsidiary label, Nashville Records. Just as they had for the custom service, artists would generally pay for their own studio sessions. But as was the norm for his Starday productions, Pierce would usually pay for the pressing, shipping, and promotion. The goal was to establish another successful line of singles that, similar to the rock label Dixie, could be shopped around on a local level.

The label proved successful, and soon Pierce was releasing fifty to seventy-five Nashville singles annually. Almost entirely recorded at the Starday Sound Studios, the music ranged from rockabilly to gospel to bluegrass to honky-tonk and even countrypolitan, but it all fell into the cornucopia of country music; and in Pierce's eyes, these were a cut above the custom recordings. Because most of the sessions were recorded at Starday, a large majority of the

Nashville releases through 1968 were produced by Tommy Hill. Hill scheduled sessions, hired musicians if needed, and, if he felt the singer had talent, would convince Pierce to release the record on Nashville. Consequently, most of the releases had either one or both sides published by Tronic Publishing, the publishing company jointly owned by Pierce and Hill.

Several outstanding records emerged from the series. Among the standout artists were Bobby Hodge, Johnny Nace, Marvin Jackson, The GT's, the Casuals, Lyle Collins, the Kenetics, and several others. Perhaps the brightest glimmer in the series was the rockabilly-charged stomper by Loyd Howell titled "Little Froggy Went A-Courtin" (NV 5028). Howell's drummer had sent several demos to Starday. Pierce promptly responded in a personal letter to Howell dated June 2, 1961: "Mr. Howell . . . We just can't offer anything on Starday at present as we are overloaded with material . . . [but] if you wanted to come out to Nashville and record at our studios, we could consider the use of completed masters that would be available to us on a lease basis for use on our new Nashville label."[2]

Howell and his band, the Blue Stars, drove to Nashville and recorded "Froggy" live to four-track. The traditional folk song had been recorded previously with a rockabilly beat, by Bob Gallion in 1959, and both Danny Dell and Jimmy Dawson in 1960, but Howell's version is arguably the best. The growling guitars and heavy drum backbeat proved that rock 'n' roll was very much alive in Michigan in 1960, though Howell recalls that it was the country flipside, "They Don't Know," that became a regional hit for them around Detroit. Despite the regional success, the record was never released on Starday. Howell remembers: "I remember that initially [after the Nashville session was made] Tommy gave us the option of being on Starday or Nashville. I liked the Nashville label, the red label, better and so we went with Nashville."

Other musicians did make the jump from the Nashville series onto the Starday main series, where they could receive wider exposure. Some of those artists even went on to record full-length albums, such as Tennessee's Hammond organ stylist Jimmy Richardson (*Sweet with a Beat* [SLP 126] and *Jimmy Richardson and His Swinging Hammond Organ* [SLP 145]), Schenectady, New York, guitar-pickin' yodeler Pete Williams (*Sings All Time Country Hits* [SLP 359]), South Dakota's "Maestro of Music" Buddy Meredith (*Sing Me A Heart Song* [SLP 225]), and legendary country musicians Buddy Starcher (*Buddy Starcher and His Mountain Guitar* [SLP 211] and *History Repeats Itself* [SLP 382]) and Smokey Rogers (*Gone* [SLP 332]). Artists who recorded singles for both the Nashville and Starday labels include Hawaii's Polly Hutt and the Crackers, Howdy Kempf (often billed on Starday as Howdy Kemp), Ken Clark and his Merry Mountain Boys, Paul Wayne, Jimmy Simpson, Hobo Jack Adkins (who also recorded for Starday prior to the Mercury-Starday deal), Mike Miller and

Jack Casey with the Stone Mountain Boys, Big Bill Johnson, and Luke Gordon (Johnson and Gordon recorded custom records under the Starday banner).

Not only did the Nashville label provide a testing ground for newer artists, many of the songs were used as demos for the Starday main label artists or filler tracks for some of Starday's later concept albums. The label also was used as another way to reach the bluegrass market. In addition to the aforementioned bluegrass artists, numerous outstanding bluegrass records were released on the Nashville label by Jimmy Gately and Harold Morrison, Lowell Varney, Bill Luttrell and the Ozark Playboys, Jay Johnson and Earl Taylor and the Stoney Mountain Boys, Jim Greer and the Mac-O-Chee Valley Boys, the Justice Brothers, Robert White and the Candy Mountain Boys, Delmer Sexton, George Winn and the Bluegrass Partners, and others.

In many cases these releases coincided with a massive boom experienced within the bluegrass market. As Pierce kept busy stockpiling bluegrass masters throughout the late fifties and early sixties, America was falling in love with the five-string banjo, and a folk explosion resulted. The resurgence could be attributed to several factors, including a rise in pop music featuring the tenor banjo (e.g., Johnny Horton's "Battle of New Orleans'"), though its proponents viewed the current folk music as a more mature and sophisticated alternative to rock 'n' roll. The phenomenon originated on college campuses where popular folk groups such as the Kingston Trio, the Chad Mitchell Trio, the Limelighters, the Brothers Four, the Clancy Brothers, the Weavers, and the New Christy Minstrels—all of whom utilized the five-string banjo—organized picking and singing hootenannies. The "roots craze," as it was later called, caught on, and campus hootenannies were soon booked solid with folk singing groups, folk jazz, jug bands, and bluegrass bands. The common denominator between the differing styles was the banjo.

The trend persisted throughout the early sixties; bluegrass bands were booked at New York's prestigious Carnegie Hall (resulting in the Starday album *The Country Gentlemen, Live at Carnegie Hall*, [SLP 174]), and nearly every major news source had a feature on bluegrass music. In 1960 it was reported in *Time* that banjo sales had increased by over 300 percent from previous years and that the five-string banjo had become the most popular instrument in the country. Pierce credits the banjo's increasing popularity and the entire "bluegrass boom" to one man: Earl Scruggs. In a story in *Billboard*, Don Pierce quipped: "Earl Scruggs developed a specific style of [three-finger] five-string banjo pickin' that constitutes the basic sound for true Bluegrass music. . . . As the folk music craze hit America, the banjo got an additional shot in the arm." Folk songs recorded with a banjo began to appear on the American pop hit parade and, Pierce noted, "This in turn put the spotlight on America's folk music, or the roots, so to speak. Their music became accepted outside of country music circles, and the boom for bluegrass was under way."³

More and more people discovered bluegrass music throughout the early sixties. Fortunately for Pierce, by the time the scene had exploded, Starday was known as *the* bluegrass label. By 1962, over forty bluegrass and banjo albums represented nearly one third of Starday's album catalog. But rather than simply reissue the older recordings again and again, Pierce continued to sign new talent and release bluegrass music in both single and album form. Aside from steady album releases by bluegrass favorites the Stanley Brothers, Bill Clifton, Carl Story and the Lewis Family (as well as one by Story with the Lewis Family), Pierce also released newly recorded LPs by the Lonesome Pine Fiddlers, Hylo Brown (including one by Brown with the Lonesome Pine Fiddlers), the Kentucky Travelers, Ernest V. Stoneman and the legendary Stoneman Family, the Southlan Trio, Red Ellis and his Huron Valley Boys, as well as another LP by Red Ellis with Jimmie Williams.

Pierce also began to issue the rural comedy, or cornball humor, records that would come to be associated with Starday. Once again ahead of his time, Pierce began releasing country comedy material well before the televised days of *Hee Haw*, when the style became both nationally accepted and campy. He knew that comedy had been a part of country music shows since country music shows had been a part of the entertainment world. He knew millions of Americans grew up listening to the down-home humor of Will Rogers, Andy Griffith, Bob Burns, and countless others. Most importantly, the albums were cheap to produce and very few other labels were doing them. With Pierce specializing in country music, it seemed only fitting that he should specialize in country comedy as well.

Pierce did not see much of a market for comedy singles, but he knew he could sell it in album form. The key was to issue albums with bright and hokey album art and market them to Grand Ole Opry audiences, where cornball humor was heard on a regular basis. Pierce also wanted to further Starday's image as a wholesome, good-for-the-whole-family label, and found country humor to be clean, family-friendly comedy. As Pierce justified in the liner notes of his first comedy LP: "Many people are tired of the sick humor of several present day comedians. We think a return to a more countrified type of humor is preferred by many people who remember the 'old days on the farm,' or who like to revel in the difficulties of the 'country boy who goes to town.'" That first album, *Button Shoes, Belly Laughs and Monkey Business* (SLP 148), was by Benjamin Francis "Whitey" Ford, one of the masters of country comedy and better known to his fans as the Duke of Paducah. Pierce's liner notes go on to say, "Ford first saw the light of day in Desoto, Missouri, on May 12,

1901. For a teething ring, they gave him a corn cob. The cob wore out, but the corn lingers on."[4]

Ford's first Starday album effectively captured the quick-witted one-liners he had perfected in vaudeville shows, medicine shows, and country music tent shows since the 1930s. Like the majority of the Starday comedy albums, *Button Shoes* was recorded at the Starday Sound Studios in front of a live audience. Anybody from off the street was welcome to attend the "Starday Night Club," as Ford called it, though space was presumably limited and the crowd was usually dominated by Starday employees and their friends. By the time Ford retired, he had a library of over half a million jokes, which he categorized under 450 subjects and sold to the producers of *Hee Haw*. The Duke's legacy was furthered in 1986 with his induction into the coveted Country Music Hall of Fame.

Archie Campbell, also known as the "Mayor of Bull's Gap, Tennessee," was another successful country comic signed to Starday and who later enjoyed success on *Hee Haw*. *Country Song Roundup* hailed Campbell's *Bedtime Stories For Adults* (SLP 167) as the #1 country comedy album in sales in 1965. Pierce recalls: "Archie came by and said, 'I made these things for Chet and them and Decca turned it down and do you want it?' 'Well, yes, I want it.' And we did good business with it. So then we began to take a few others. We didn't get any huge sales [from country comedy] but we did a decent business with it. There was a market for it, that sort of thing, and nobody else was doing it."

Lester Alvin "Smiley" Burnette was another legendary comedian brought to fill the Starday comedy roster. Unlike the other Starday comedians, Burnette gained his reputation through a rather lengthy film career, spanning over 170 western movies. Burnette's Hollywood career began when Gene Autry hired Burnette to be his first sidekick, Frog Millhouse, in December 1933. By the late thirties and early forties Burnette's popularity was nearly equal to Autry's, and he was recognized as a true American icon. He later went on to appear alongside Roy Rogers in seven more films and made numerous solo efforts on film.

Burnette's Starday album, *Ole Frog* (SLP 191), one side of which was music and the other side live standup material, gave Burnette the opportunity to rerecord several of his classic ARA and Bullet 78s on modern equipment and also to showcase his knack for storytelling. After the success of Burnette's LP, Pierce released a cavalcade of country comedy albums by Lonnie "Pap" Wilson, Minnie Pearl, Gene Martin, Johnny Bond, Lonzo and Oscar, and several others.

About the same time the comedy albums were getting hot, Pierce was also heavily invested in the recording of instrumental albums. There were country guitar albums, numerous banjo albums, steel guitar albums, fiddle albums, dobro albums, piano albums, and even country organ with saxophone albums. Because Pierce liked his vocal recordings kept simple, this was the musicians' opportunity to turn loose in the studio, and the results were often astonishing. The first instrumentalists Pierce went after were the bandmates of his dear friend and next door neighbor, Roy Acuff. Pierce remembers: "We recorded all the Smokey Mountain Boys. Roy would never let anybody else do that but me. He'd rather have them on Starday than have them on Hickory [the recording branch of Acuff-Rose music publishing]. 'If they're on Hickory,' he says, 'They're lost. You'll never find one. If they're on Starday, they're in your face all the time. Don knows how to put out an album that will sell and Wesley [Rose] don't know how to do crap.'"

Among the Smokey Mountain Boys who recorded their own Starday albums were Benny Martin (*Country Music's Sensational Entertainer* [SLP 131], though he left Acuff's band in 1951), Gene Martin (*Country and Western Confidential—A Backstage Expose* [SLP 226]), Bashful Brother Oswald (*Bashful Brother Oswald with his Banjo and Dobro* [SLP 179]), Jackie Phelps (*Golden Guitar Classics* [SLP 265]), Shot Jackson (an instrumental LP with Buddy Emmons titled *The Singing Strings of Steel Guitar and Dobro* [SLP 230]), as well as an entire album dedicated to the Smokey Mountain gang dubbed *Country Music Cannonball* (SLP 276). That particular album included numbers by Cousin Jody, Howdy Forrester, Jimmie Riddle, June Stearns, and the rest of Acuff's gang. Pierce elaborates: "Last week on WSM [in 2004], they played some of the duets between Shot Jackson and Buddy Emmons with Shot playing the dobro and Buddy playing the steel. They did this medley of waltzes and this guy on WSM said, 'Boy there's just nothing like Starday.' And when you get a whole album of Buddy and Shot together . . . Oh my God, it's fantastic! We were out at my home when I lived next door to Roy and they were both out there and we talked about it then. I said, 'Go on in the studio. I'll tell Tommy and we'll do that.' And I agreed to do a Kirby Oswald [Beecher Ray Kirby, otherwise known as Bashful Brother Oswald] thing on him as well. We did everything with Roy and his band. Roy let us do anything. It always made Wesley Rose mad but Roy just said 'Fuck you, Wesley!'"

Starday also began recording the bands of several other major label stars around this time: Jim Reeves's Blue Boys and featuring his pianist Dean Manuel (*Town and Country Piano* [SLP 196]), as well as Hank Snow's Rainbow Ranch Boys featuring Fiddlin' Chubby Wise (*Tennessee Fiddler* [SLP 154]). Other instrumental albums followed by Leon McAuliffe (often spelled McAuliff, who first made his name with Bob Wills's Texas Playboys), Jerry Rivers (of Hank Williams's Drifting Cowboys), Pete Drake, Little Roy Wiggins (a former member of Eddy Arnold's band, the Tennessee Plowboys), Cecil Campbell, Buddy Starcher, and several others.

Among the more established musicians to join Starday was Arthur "Guitar Boogie" Smith [not to be confused with Grand Ole Opry star Fiddlin'

Arthur Smith, who also recorded for Starday]. Smith had three Top 10 boogie instrumentals on the MGM label prior to 1950 and Pierce was excited to add him to the Starday roster. Though he mostly recorded instrumental LPs for Pierce, rerecording many of his previous hits, Smith also made two gospel albums and another consisting of novelty numbers. Included in the latter was a parody of Rolf Harris's hit "Tie Me Kangaroo Down, Sport" titled "Tie My Hunting Dog Down, Jed" (642), which brushed *Billboard*'s Top 30 spot for three weeks. He also wrote and recorded a song specifically for Pierce. Pierce recalls: "One time I asked him for a song about golf and he made one called 'The Master of the Game (Duffer's Dream)' (634). It's funny. I couldn't sell it to anybody, but . . . Arthur was a tremendous musician, remarkable personality, and a very smart businessman. He could play that fiddle and he could play that guitar and write songs."

Not only was it financially beneficial to have instrumentals available to disc jockeys for voiceovers between songs, Pierce also felt that it was important to release the material in album format. In a letter to *Billboard* in 1964 Pierce wrote: "I think the phrase 'Superiority by Specializing' might describe Starday's approach to the country music album market. We strive for superiority and the only way we can successfully compete against the larger and better established labels is by specialization. Country music has been a growing trend for several decades and Starday recognized this. The country music buyer was slower to change from the 78 rpm speed to 45 rpm speed. Likewise, being largely rural, he was a little late in accepting the long play album. The reluctance to accept the long play album when it first became popular in the early 1950s, when coupled with the advent of rock and roll and the subsequent decline of country music single sales (as many teenagers switched to the rock and roll sound) made most of the major firms feel that issuing country music albums was like 'throwing good money after bad.' The feeling in some quarters seemed to be that if country single sales were down, then why fool around with albums."

Pierce goes on: "Starday took a different viewpoint. We felt the reason that the dollar volume in country singles was down in the early 1950s was because part of the country music teenage market had been lost to the rock sound, part had been lost in the transition from 78 to 45 to 33 1/3 speed, and a great deal more had been lost because no one was endeavoring to supply the natural preference of the country music fan to buy long play albums for home use. The basic error derived from not having a real 'profile' of the average country music buyer as he existed. The average country music buyer is an adult with a home, with a family; he's probably a so-called 'blue collar' worker rather than a farmer, though farmers will always be a strong backbone for the country music field."[5]

Pierce later adds, "[Once] we found that the country music buyer was an adult and preferred the long play records more than they did the single

Martin Haerle holding Starday's *Country and Western Golden Hit Parade* and explaining the benefits of double pocket albums (Courtesy of David Haerle)

records, we found that we had a very strong market for that. I think we pioneered that. We were very active in the album business and it was very good for us." But Pierce doesn't take all the credit for Starday's success with long-play albums. Instead, he credits a twenty-year-old disc jockey from Germany who pushed him in that direction. "Martin Haerle came to me after I had been in Nashville for just a couple years. He had tried to catch on with Acuff-Rose and they didn't have a spot for him. He had a thick accent. He says, 'I come to work for you, Don. I know your catalog. I know your music. I know the G.I.s over in Germany. They's crazy about it. I'm from Stuttgart and we had those [Armed Forces Radio] shows down there and all that.' He was wild about bluegrass. I said, 'Martin, I don't know how much money I can pay you.' He says, 'Well, pay me for half time and I'll work for full time.' He says, 'My mother has some money and she sends me money from time to time.' So we got started that way for about 6o sixty days and pretty soon I knew I had to have the guy. He was brilliant . . . he really got me charged up about LPs and great jackets. He encouraged me to spend the extra money to do the four-color jackets. Most people were doing two or three color covers and they weren't

The Starday brass reviewing their Country Music Hall of Fame series: (l-r) Tommy Hill, Don Pierce, Martin Haerle, and Herb Schucher (Courtesy of David Haerle)

imaginative at all. But Martin and I, we saw the value of a good-looking jacket and we scored big when we came into the double pockets." Haerle became Pierce's right-hand-man for several years before briefly serving the company as vice president. Pierce continues, "The guy was really, totally dedicated. He came up with a lot of the ideas for album art. He made a great contribution. Later on he formed his label out on the West coast and made me the godfather of [Haerle's] CMH label."

Once Haerle had convinced Pierce to invest in full-length country music albums, as opposed to singles, they searched for a way to make their albums stand out from the competition. For starters, Pierce believed in "A scholarship and a bargain." He believed that descriptive liner notes should accompany every album and he often provided studio and session information on the back cover. He was also a fan of including extra photos of the artists making the record in the studio. He proclaimed Nashville "The Musical Heart of America," which he proudly emblazoned on the back of every album, and included full-color record sleeves offering Starday catalogs on the inside. He even added "Since 1952" to the Starday logo, though this was a bit of a fib since Starday was technically founded in 1953. According to Pierce, "Johnny Sipple, who wrote for *Billboard* and worked for Mercury, is the guy who told me to put on the label: Founded 1952. He says, 'Let 'em know that you're not in and out of business like 99 percent of the other labels, that there is some longevity and substance to the operation.' It started to mean something come along 1965. There was very few labels sustaining. Labels come and go all the time."

The only thing left to do was design a flashy front cover to catch the viewer's eye. The first few Starday album covers were designed in Cincinnati at the Royal Plastics plant, a subsidiary of King Record Company, where Starday LPs were mastered, plated, and pressed. The earliest Starday LP artwork was done by Nikki Ames, though she considered herself to be more of a producer than an artist. She eventually hired her brother-in-law, Dan Quest, to design the album covers. Quest was a graduate of Carnegie Mellon Art Institute and had served as a photographer while enlisted in the military. After a few years of design work at King, also designing covers for other independent labels including Starday, Pierce persuaded the young artist to move to Nashville and take on the Starday line full-time. Once in Nashville, Quest set up the Dan Quest Art Studio near Music Row and began creating bold and innovative album covers. While other country labels were busy gearing their artists toward the larger and more sophisticated pop audience, Starday was doing the exact opposite. Working with Pierce, Haerle, and *Tennessean* photographer Terry Tomlin, Quest's album covers never misguided their audience as to what they might hear. Whether posing the artist holding a pig, sitting in front of a barn, rocking in a chair with a rooster on his lap, riding a horse, or just going fishing, Starday albums screamed "Hillbilly!"

Pierce felt that the hillbilly approach would also help sell and promote the Grand Ole Opry legends and old-timers. Although it was unlikely he would score any #1 hits with the Opry old-timers, Pierce knew that, as long as the LPs were packaged with flashy four-color covers, the albums could sell. According to Pierce, "We felt that [Opry old-timers] needed some expression for their many years of work on the Grand Ole Opry. We didn't sell a whole lot of it [Opry-artist LPs], but I felt that their music should be recognized." Not only recognized, but also preserved. Among the long-time Opry legends to make new albums for Starday were Stringbean [David Akeman], the Old Hickory Singers, Sam and Kirk McGee, the Crook Brothers, Fiddlin' Arthur Smith and the Dixieliners, Robert Lunn with his Jug and Washboard Band, Lew Childre, Curly Fox, and Texas Ruby, as well as several live Grand Ole Opry tribute albums.

Sadly though, 1963 began with immense tragedy for both Starday and the Grand Ole Opry. On March 5, a plane crashed carrying Patsy Cline, her manager Randy Hughes, Hawkshaw Hawkins, and Cowboy Copas. Ironically, the four were returning from Kansas City, where they had played a benefit performance for the family of a country musician who had just lost his life. As the entire country music industry grieved, Starday fans were left listening to Copas's final recording session, which produced "Goodbye Kisses" (621). Much like Hank Williams, whose last single before he passed on was "I'll Never Get Out of This World Alive," Copas's final "Goodbye" to all of his dreams had a similar prophetic tone and became a posthumous hit.

Unfortunately, tragedy continued. Just a short while later another Starday recording artist, Texas Ruby, was killed in an explosion in her home. Eerily, Texas Ruby's last Starday recording, "Love Me Now (While I'm Still Here)'" on *Fantastic Fiddlin' Fun and Songs* (SLP 235), also cast a foretelling shadow. Shortly after the explosion, country music lost another beloved musician when Starday artist Dean Manuel's plane, also carrying Jim Reeves, crashed in 1964.

A seemingly endless chain of bad luck and sorrow carried over to 1964. Country music had lost several of its biggest stars and Pierce had lost one of his closest friends. He adds, "Cowboy Copas was my buddy and I still miss that fellow. Whatever we would ask Copas to do, he would try to do it. And he helped us in the studio on recording sessions. He was just beloved by everybody at Starday and we were just totally devastated when he lost his life on that ill-fated airplane trip. We went ahead and issued a memorial album on Copas and he will always be in our thoughts. A wonderful, wonderful person."

6

GIDDY-UP GO

Despite the recent tragedies, by 1964 country music was enjoying a massive surge in popularity, both within the United States and overseas. Once viewed as a small independent label on the outskirts of town, Starday was now considered to be one of the hot trendsetters during the resurgence. Yet even with the industry recognition and the growing success of their longplay albums, major labels still dominated the singles market. In the first eight months of 1964, 190 songs hit *Billboard*'s charts. Among those, 139 were released by major labels (Columbia, RCA Victor, Decca, Capitol, and Mercury), compared to only six on Starday. Because most radio stations were still operating on a singles format, Pierce was still lacking, with the exception of "Alabam," the big chart hits. There were, however, several notable minor hits.

Benny Martin, a veteran fiddler and inventor of the 8-string fiddle, was another of the many Opry members to join the Starday ranks and brought with him an impressive music résumé. After joining the Opry and accompanying Robert Lunn, Curly Fox, and others, Martin joined Bill Monroe's Blue Grass Boys in 1948, a year later joined Roy Acuff's Smoky Mountain Boys, and was then persuaded to join Lester Flatt and Earl Scruggs on the WNOX Midday Merry-Go-Round in Knoxville. Before signing with Starday, the thirty-two-year old Martin had also played in Johnnie and Jack's Tennessee Mountain Boys and spent six years as a solo artist for Mercury, Decca, and MGM. The revered fiddler finally experienced his first and only chart success as a solo artist with his Starday recording of "Rosebuds and You" (632), which skimmed *Billboard*'s Top 30 for one week only in May 1963.

Tillman Franks was another beloved country performer who found solo success on Starday, though he is more often remembered as a legendary producer, manager, bass player, and songwriter. Before he joined Starday as a recording artist, Franks had previously managed Webb Pierce, Bill Carlisle, Johnny Horton, and several others, ran the Louisiana Hayride Artists Service Bureau for three years, had co-written Johnny Horton's "Honky-Tonk Man" and "One Woman Man" among other hits, and had played bass on the

Louisiana Hayride with countless other bands. But like Benny Martin, he had never scored a hit record of his own. At the time of his Starday releases, Franks was busy managing and promoting Claude King, whose recording of "Wolverton Mountain" eventually became a #1 hit. In the meantime, two of Franks's four Starday sides also made the charts. The first, "Tadpole" (651), credited to Tillman Franks and the Cedar Grove Three, hit the charts in December 1963, and five months later his recording of "When the World's on Fire" (670, with the Tillman Franks Singers) also reached the Top 30. They were his only two releases on the label and the only two chart records under his own name.

The minor hits kept rolling through 1964. Frankie Miller reached the charts again with another homespun humming lament about American life entitled "A Little South of Memphis" (655). Glenn Barber, who had previously recorded rockabilly favorites "Shadow My Baby" (249) and "Feeling No Pain" (249) for Starday in the mid-fifties, was back on Starday and in the charts with his two-sided platter "Stronger Than Dirt" b/w "If Anyone Can Show Cause" (676).

Though Starday had a few more hits, they were modest at best. Fortunately, Pierce's investment in the LP proved to be financially successful, based on his claim that Starday's total gross from the sale of country and sacred records increased by at least 30 percent each year from 1958 to 1964. Still, the emphasis on LP releases severely hindered the release of singles. Pierce realized that, in order for his business to be lucrative without that big, special hit single, he would have to seek alternate forms of revenue.

Among the most important alternatives was the formation of the Country Music Record Club of America in 1963. The CMRCA, as it was often referred to, certainly was not the first record club to capitalize on country music mail-order sales. Goddard Lieberson, President of Columbia Records, had started his record club in August 1955, and RCA Victor and Capitol followed suit with their own clubs in 1957. The CMRCA was, however, the first country-music-only record club.

The idea was not new to Pierce. In 1959 *Billboard* published a letter from Pierce suggesting that "Someone should form a country and gospel record club, and a country and gospel one-stop that is centrally located and stocked so that dealers and operators can purchase those 'hard-to-get' records."[1] Surprisingly, nobody took the bait, and four years later Pierce wound up doing it himself. He explains: "It was Martin Haerle who really made me go into the Country Music Record Club of America. He says, 'Don, it's like this. These people, they live in the country, and they don't come to record stores. They're used to buying everything by mail order.' He says, 'The way to get to them is to form the Country Music Record Club of America,' which I did, and Minnie Pearl became the Honorary President and the initial forward boosting it was from my neighbor Roy Acuff himself. Roy says, 'Friends, you think a needle in haystack is hard to find? Have you ever tried to locate a store that carries your favorite country music record albums? Now, *real* American music shouldn't be hard to find and some of my friends here in Nashville are doing something about that." We put an ad in the *Billboard* and we just got flooded. We got mailing lists from people like Randy Blake and others that did mail order and then we'd mail that catalog to them and tell 'em they could join and be members of the CMRCA and we'd give 'em a card that says they were supporting American country music and then we'd give 'em a little lapel pin put in there with a guitar on it so they could identify with country music. Boy we just killed 'em!"

Other benefits included window decals, country music playing cards, the occasional free Starday record, exclusive Golden Classics records, and the club's own *RFD* newsletter featuring photos of "Cindy Lou." Cindy Lou was actually Starday employee Lucille Paradise, who posed for the photos which appeared above Pierce's overhyped text explaining the benefits of the club and the goings-on in the Nashville scene. The club actually was run not by Paradise but by Elizabeth Casey, and it proved quite popular. The first enrollment in the club was received from Diane Mimms of Raleigh, North Carolina, in November 1963; by the end of the year the club boasted over 20,000 members. Two years later that number had doubled and included members from every state as well as nine foreign countries.

The same year Pierce started the CMRCA, he also set up a new line of economy albums in which he could rehash and recycle songs that had stopped selling for Starday. Using the label name he had created two years earlier for singles, Pierce set up a line of albums on the Nashville label. Starday was not the first label to tap the budget market, but it was the first to establish a budget label within the country music industry. Pierce recalls: "We saw that we could recycle stuff and sell it for $1.98, as opposed to $3.98 [the going rate for Starday LPs]. That's when we got started with the rack jobbers and Handleman [a music distribution business based in Michigan that stocked the shelves of retail chains]. They [Handleman] wanted the top-of-the-line stuff, but they also did a big job with the budget stuff. So we started the Nashville line and did well with it. Wherever we could put racks, we'd do it. My first order from the Handleman Company was $38,000 worth of albums and I used that money to put the additions on the building and studio and I paid for it with cash from just one order from Handleman."

The new building additions became the Starday warehouse, and soon every available market was flooded with their albums. Pierce still counted on the retail stores and his distributors. He still had the radio-only mail-order business. He now had his own record club and even had Starday records sold through the Columbia and Capitol record clubs. Pierce also pioneered the use of rack jobbers—all-metal racks displaying Starday and Nashville records. Pierce says:

"We took the records to the people and got fantastic results in big cities as well as the rural areas. We put them in supermarkets, department stores, hardware stores. Anywhere you can imagine a record being sold, we sold it." And the spur-of-the-moment country music album purchase was born.

Noting the success of the Nashville budget LPs, Pierce then formed a budget label for singles. Pierce wrote, in a promotional pamphlet for the new label, "Starday has always been a pacemaker in creating new and unique methods of merchandising country music. Creation of Starday's 'Country Juke Box Oldies Series' fills the need for great country favorites of yesteryear and is now available to juke box operators featuring classic country." Using both Starday material and songs leased from other labels—including hits by Patsy Cline, Buck Owens, Johnny Cash, Hank Locklin, and others—the singles soon found their way into stores and jukeboxes, and offered fans the opportunity to buy new copies of out-of-print country records, some of which originally had been released only as 78s.

Pierce kept busy creating new products but also recognized that his distributors were the most important component in selling his country music merchandise. Thus, Pierce called for a meeting with all thirty-six of his nationwide distributors in July 1966 so that he could personally show them around Nashville and detail the recent changes within Starday. The invitation read: "Down through the years, artists, song writers, publishers, disc jockeys and others in the music field have been feted by the Nashville music trade—and rightly so. However, we here at Starday feel strongly that the record distributors have been overlooked."[2]

"That was the first National Record Distributor Sales Meeting to be held in Music City, USA," Pierce remembers. "These are distributors that we brought in from all over the United States to attend a seminar and we showed them Nashville, brought them out to the guest cottage, let them go out fishing, fed them, swimming, boating. My distributors were my customers so we wanted to acquaint them with the Starday saga and Nashville and the Grand Ole Opry and get them excited about this country music stuff and get them enthusiastic for selling this Starday product. It cost us a lot of money but it was well worth it."

These innovations in merchandising were followed by others. Starday also became the first to package country music albums in box sets, the first to use gatefold album covers [LPs that open like a book cover] for country albums, the first country label to record in front of live audiences, and on and on. Pierce soon earned a reputation as a carnival huckster, willing and able to sell anybody on country music, and never accepting "No" for an answer. In fact, Pierce recalls hearing that his good friend Tex Ritter was even warning others to be careful what they said around Madison, Tennessee, "Because Don Pierce might try to record it, put it out on an album and sell it." Indeed the reputation was warranted. By the end of 1963, sales had grown to the point that Pierce estimated he would sell around 2.5 million records in the following year and that in 1965 he would gross more than $1.5 million.

Pierce knew that he would not attain such lofty goals by merely promoting his own records. Instead, he would have to become Nashville's most fervent cheerleader for Music City, the Grand Ole Opry, and anything having to do with country music. As much as the country music industry could grow, thought Pierce, so too could Starday Records. With this in mind, he began searching for other ways to promote country music, outside of running his record label. Among the first, and most promising, investments he made was in the booming industry of country music exploitation films.

The first bona fide film of the genre was Paramount's *Country Music Holiday*, released in black and white in 1958, which featured Ferlin Husky, Lonzo and Oscar, Faron Young, June Carter, and several others. MGM responded with their 1963 *Hootenanny Hoot* starring Johnny Cash, George Hamilton IV, and Sheb Wooley, to name a few. Others followed, including *Country Music on Broadway, Country Music Caravan, Tennessee Jamboree, Second Fiddle to a Gold Guitar*, and more. A genre was born and, by 1964, with country musicians hungry for the exposure, several independent filmmakers were jumping at the opportunity to pack the drive-ins with their low-budget country music masterpieces.

One such man was Ron Ormond, an independent filmmaker and producer who—along with his wife and son, June and Tim—moved from Hollywood to Nashville in 1965. Ormond's film career, which began in the 1940s with an extensive list of western films starring the "King of the Bullwhip" Lash Larue, had, by the time he arrived in Nashville, already earned him a distinction as one of the kings of "B" movies. The Ormonds immediately began searching Nashville for investors for country music films. Tim Ormond, also a supporting cast member, explains: "When they moved, Mom talked to her banker at the time and he told her that Don Pierce had money and perhaps she should talk to him. Turns out my parents knew Don from before [in what capacity is unknown], so they approached him as an investor and he was happy to be involved."

Excited to support this new trend in country music, Pierce invested in Ormond's Atlanta Productions and even offered his own land, Five Coves Farm, as a shooting location. Pierce details: "Ron located in Nashville and was interested in making some pictures that would use country music stars. We got together and we made a couple of movies out on my farm on Cages Bend where we had the parties after the golf tournament. The first movie we made was called *The Girl From Tobacco Row* and it starred Tex Ritter and Minnie

Pearl and a few other people from the Grand Ole Opry." That star-studded cast also included Martha Carson, Earl "Snake" Richards, Gordon Terry, Rita Faye, Ralph Emery, Jimmy and Mildred Mulcay, Smiley and Kitty Wilson, Fiddlin' Arthur Smith and the Dixieliners, the Haywood Mountaineers, the Skylarks, and several other traditional country acts. The film also included a background score by Tommy Hill and Moon Mullican's Starday recording of "Ragged But Right" with overdubbed vocals by Richards.

The film was successful at drive-ins across the South and was quickly followed up by *Forty Acre Feud*, a Calhouns vs. the Culpeppers political showdown featuring Ferlin Husky, Minnie Pearl, Ray Price, George Jones, Loretta Lynn, Roy Drusky, Skeeter Davis, Bill Anderson, Hugh X. Lewis, Del Reeves, and Starday's own Willis Brothers, among others. Ron Ormond told *Billboard:* "We don't put them in movies simply because they're country singers. They have so much untapped talent it's amazing.... Most musicians make good gun toters. Instead of toting guitars, I put guns in their hands."[3]

Several other movies were shot at or around Pierce's home, though his involvement in the Ormonds' movies ended after *Feud*. By 1966 the Hillbilly Hollywood fad had become oversaturated; the Ormonds went on to produce several successful non–country music "B" movies during the sixties including *Please Don't Touch Me, White Lightnin' Road*, and the cult classic *The Monster and the Stripper*, also known as *The Exotic Ones*, featuring a shirtless Sleepy LaBeef as the dreaded swamp monster.

Because Pierce was known to invest in multiple country music–related ventures, he was also approached with an opportunity in stock car racing. Pierce explains: "Webb Pierce and Faron Young came to me one day at Starday and said, 'Stock car racing is getting so popular, and people like to see the crashes and all. Down in Georgia they've started a very popular thing called the Figure Eight Demolition Derby.' We went to the old Sulphur Dell ballpark that was no longer used by the Nashville baseball team, we bought it and started the Figure Eight races where they would take old jalopies and crash into one another. We had a lot of fun with it." Tuesday and Saturday nights were for racing and there was even one particular race which pitted numerous country music personalities against each other including Faron Young, George Jones, Hubert Long, and Bobby Lord, among others. Even Tommy Hill, a hot rod enthusiast since his youth in San Antonio, kept busy preparing for the derbies by customizing his own Starday jalopy, which he dubbed the "Country Music Cannonball."

Unfortunately, the novelty of the Figure Eight quickly wore off with fans; after just six weeks, the track began to run short of money. Initially, Pierce fed more money into the kitty, but after just a couple months Pierce withdrew as an investor and the races stopped altogether. Despite the short life of Sulphur Dell Speedways, the races caused a buzz around Nashville, and Pierce strongly

Starday employees Chuck Chellman and Tommy Hill showing off the "Country Music Cannonball," Starday's entry in the Figure Eight races at Sulphur Dell (Courtesy of Don Pierce)

encouraged his friend Johnny Bond to cash in on the trend by recording a concept album for Starday all about racing. Capitalizing on his previous success with "Hot Rod Lincoln," Bond agreed and recorded an album entitled *Famous Hot Rodders I Have Known* (SLP 354), which featured two songs ("Around and Around the Figure Eight" and "The Great Figure Eight Race") specifically about the Figure Eight races at Sulphur Dell.

Pierce continued to search for new ways to promote country music and Nashville. One of his more profitable ventures was the formation of Nashville's first jingle company. With easy access to both musicians and studio space, and a firm belief that country music could help sell any product, Pierce co-founded Custom Jingles of Nashville along with his friends and fellow vice presidents, Eddy Arnold and Little Roy Wiggins. Vic Willis of the Willis Brothers trio was made president and Charles Mosley became the secretary and treasurer.

The company was instantly in demand and within a short time had produced jingles for Fender, Krispy Kreme, Kellogg's, Pillsbury, Luzianne Coffee, Ford, Gunther Beer, Bubble Up, Lava Soap, Red Fox Chewing Tobacco, Wiedemann Beer, and many more. Every available recording time slot in the Starday studio was quickly filled with jingle sessions and clients were ecstatic to hear Dolly Parton, George Morgan, Marion Worth, the Jordanaires, Barbara

Dottie West Starday publicity photo, ca. 1960 (Courtesy of Nathan Gibson)

Mandrell, Hank Snow, Faron Young, or Jan Howard sing their own company's jingle. Other artists included on the Custom Jingles payroll included the Light Brothers, Red Sovine, the Willis Brothers, Bobbie Staff, Rex Allen, Jimmie Riddle, D. J. Fontana, Curtis McPeake, Jerry Rivers, Floyd Cramer, Danny Davis, Dottie West, and a laundry list of Nashville's A-Team session men.

Aside from the occasional jingle sessions, Dottie West also made her earliest commercial recordings for Starday. West had studied music at Tennessee Tech and moved to Cleveland, Ohio, upon graduation. Alongside her steel guitar–slidin' husband Bill, West appeared on the Landmark Jamboree and made several trips to Nashville in hopes of landing a record deal. Starday employee David McKinley recalls: "Dottie was driving by here [the Starday studio] on a Saturday. She passed the place and she stopped her car and she walked in the front door and Tommy just happened to be in his office and she said, all decked out in her curly red hair, and she walks in and says, 'I wanna be a country singing star.' And Tommy, in his old-fashioned style says, 'Oh, you think you can sing?' She goes, 'Yeah, I can sing.' He took her right back into the studio and put on a tape and had her sing and that's how it began."

Pierce heard the results and signed the young singer to Starday in 1960. In addition to her own recordings, West also sang several duets with Cowboy Copas, backing vocals for Leon Payne and others, as well as jingle sessions. Pierce recalls: "Dottie came to Nashville out of Ohio with her husband, and they stopped by the studios. They wanted to know about getting on records. She made some sides for us and later on we did an album [*The Country Girl Singing Sensation* (SLP 302)]. She was a very friendly person and it was nice to have her around the studio. I recall when John Story, who was a co-owner of the studio, would dance with her in the studio. We were delighted when she went on and had great success later on."

Though her Starday records failed to bring her much attention, West paired up with Chet Atkins as producer in 1964 and became the first female country artist to win a Grammy Award with "Here Comes My Baby." She joined the Grand Ole Opry that same year, and her career was well under way. By the end of the 1970s the cute country farm-girl look was replaced with spandex pants, hoop earrings, and high heels. The image makeover resulted in multiple CMA awards and several #1 hit duets with Kenny Rogers including "Every Time Two Fools Collide," "What Are We Doin' In Love?," and "All I Ever Need Is You."

As the Starday side projects continued to reap rewards, Pierce continued to pursue more and more country-related business opportunities. In the mid-1960s Pierce placed an ad in *Billboard*'s annual issue *The World of Country Music*, describing Starday as a "Country music one-stop service,"[4] and advertised everything from phonograph records, premiums, jingles, music publishing, recording studios, and custom pressing to waterfront real estate, registered quarter horses, radio-TV mail order, tobacco farming, and even Angus cattle.

Sensing the growth of the country music industry in and around Nashville, Pierce in 1965 purchased and operated 1,700 acres of waterfront land for subdivision purposes on Old Hickory Lake, fourteen acres of tobacco farms, over 120 head of prime beef cattle, and a herd of registered quarter horses. He even became vice president of Citizen's Bank in Hendersonville. Yet his proudest contribution to Nashville, outside of Starday Records, was his golf tournament. Pierce explains: "In 1964, the Country Music Association, where I was a Director, asked me for about the third time if I would start a golf tournament that would help create desirable publicity for country music and the Association. I thought it over, and I had by this time acquired Hal Neely's services to assist me in the operation of Starday, and I felt that I could do this job."

The first task was tracking down the golf pros to see if they would be interested. Pierce continues: "I went with Peck Leslie, who is the professional at my home club of Bluegrass Yacht and Country Club, to a club in North Palm Beach [Florida] where Cary Middlecoff had a house. Peck introduced me to Cary, who had twice won the National Open. We talked for awhile and played some golf. I asked Cary if I could successfully get some of the tour professionals to play in a golf tournament in Nashville during the month of October and associate with some of the stars of country music. Cary, being a Tennessean, was enthusiastic . . . and he proceeded to give me the names and numbers of people like Sam Snead, Tommy Bolt, Byron Nelson, and many others that were very prominent on the PGA Tour."

With a few stars on board for the tournament, it was then up to Pierce to secure a course, which Bluegrass donated, create the rules, accommodate everyone's schedules, round up the remaining celebrities, hunt for publicity, and raise a $10,000 purse. Among the stars Pierce convinced to compete in the first couple of tournaments were baseball greats Jim Bunning and Dizzy Dean, as well as non-country musical artists Perry Como, Pat Boone, and Lawrence Welk. Golf pros included Nelson, Bolt, Mason Rudolph, Johnny Pott, Lou Graham, and several other top draws. Pierce also secured the participation of as many country music stars as possible, which over the years included Roy Acuff, Minnie Pearl, Ray Price, Buck Owens, Eddy Arnold, Chet Atkins, Porter Wagoner, Ernest Tubb, Charlie Walker, Teddy Wilburn, Jimmy C. Newman, Grady Martin, the Glaser Brothers, Bob Luman, Pee Wee King, Glen Campbell, Wilma Burgess, Charlie Pride, and many more.

Pierce recalls that preparing the tournament took three long months, but that it proved to be a huge success in promoting country music and the CMA. Don reflects, "I did a lot for Nashville with golf and a lot for golf in Nashville. The Music City Pro-Celebrity helped pave the way for professional golf to come to Nashville, both the Seniors and the LPGA. When those pros came in and got to socialize with Minnie Pearl and Ernest Tubb and Dizzy Dean, they just loved it! They came down to the Opry and we had parties for 'em out at my lake. People would play all night long. Glen Campbell, Perry Como. That was a great thing for Nashville. A great thing for golf. A great thing for country music."

The tournament also turned out to be a great thing for Don Pierce. Each team was to include one golf pro, one country music star, and one country gentleman. Because Pierce was responsible for creating each team, he matched himself up with an old golfing buddy. "The tournament was a lot of fun. I was paired with Dutch Harrison and with Bobby Lord, who was then doing a daily show for WSM and was a Grand Ole Opry star. It was particularly gratifying to me because way back in 1936 I had caddied for Dutch Harrision," Pierce continues. "Then 30 years later, I invited him to play in the tournament in Nashville for the CMA and we won the tournament together."

Although the tournament was costly to his business and extremely time consuming, Pierce loved combining his two favorite passions: golf and country music. He continued to run the tournament through 1967, drawing over 20,000 fans to the course in the final year and raising a purse of $25,000.

Don Pierce, E. J. "Dutch" Harrison, and Bobby Lord, winners of the 1965 Music City Pro Celebrity golf tournament (Courtesy of Don Pierce)

Despite the growing popularity, Pierce says the CMA greeted him with only "Very faint fucking praise."

To say the least, Pierce was upset. Pierce elaborates: "I operated it for three years, and then for some reasons not known to me, it was decided by my co-sponsors, the *Nashville Tennessean* and the Country Music Association, to take the event into Nashville and play it at Harpeth Hills course and do the entertaining downtown." Aside from taking the tournament and parties away from Pierce, he was further upset when he was not even invited to sit on the board of directors the following year. His baby had been taken away from him and he had no say in the matter. Consequently, relations between Pierce and the CMA were tense for many years to follow.

Although extremely disappointed by these events, Pierce could go back to working full-time on Starday. Refocusing his attention from his other country-related interests, Pierce decided it was time to protect the most lucrative aspect of his label, the publishing division. In a 1964 article published in *The Country Music Who's Who,* Pierce explained, "Starday's publishing operations are separated from its record activities so that a greater effort can be made to develop a staff of strong country music songwriters and to better exploit the Starday music catalog. Vic Willis and Lee Emerson have joined with Eddie Wilson to head up Starday's song department. This insures better material for Starday artists to select from and a lot of material that Starday is now able to offer to other labels."[5]

Starday continued to gain steam, and by 1965 more and more songwriters pitched their songs to the label. Pierce finally broke down and opened a Starday office on Music Row. Realizing the advantages of a central location for music publishing, Pierce bought a new building at 813 18th Avenue in downtown Nashville. As he explained in the following year's *Country Music Who's Who*, "Starday's new location will be called the Starday Townhouse and it will be a workshop headed by famed country music composer, Joe "Red" Hayes. Hayes, composer of 'A Satisfied Mind' and many other country song hits, left the Hank Thompson band to join the Starday organization as professional manager for Starday Music, Bayou State, Tronic, Kamar, Golden State, and other affiliated music publishing catalogs."[6]

The grand opening of the Townhouse took place during the 1965 Country Music Disc Jockey Convention and was met with great enthusiasm. Hayes's responsibilities included searching for new song material as well as managing the current domestic and foreign catalogs. Perhaps the most successful body of work within Pierce's publishing interests was that of Buck Owens. Pierce relates: "It was a time when I was just getting started with my publishing overseas and Buck wasn't active in that direction at all. I was offered an opportunity to control the foreign rights to his catalog but I wasn't sure if it was a good idea. The Aberbachs [Julian and Jean Aberbach, founders of Hill and Range Publishing Company] convinced me that I should go ahead and do it and with an advance of $500 we were able to pick up 'Act Naturally' and 'Together Again' and some other very successful songs and we split the international publishing royalties 50/50. The first check I got off that material was for $13,000."

Shortly after this transaction, the Beatles covered "Act Naturally," released in 1965 and reaching #47 in the pop charts, on the flip side of their giant smash success "Yesterday." Ray Charles then had a hit with Owens's tender ballad "Together Again." Indeed, Pierce's investment was solid. The foreign rights to Owens's catalog proved to be an enormous moneymaker and before long Owens wanted them back. Pierce remembers: "We were out at a convention and he had hired a lawyer to contact me and see if he could get out of that contract because he wanted to start his own publishing company for overseas. His lawyer says, 'I'll put it to you straight: Buck wants out of his contract. What will it take?' I said, 'Nothing.' I said, 'Buck was good enough to give me those six big songs for a $500 advance and "Act Naturally" was on the back side of "Yesterday" by the Beatles. I'd done pretty well. I will give him the release' and

I just turned it over because I think in the business we should try to get along with one another in every way possible."

Owens was quick to thank Pierce. Pierce continues: "One day he had stopped by the Starday offices and we visited in the warehouse and he bought some of the albums that we had issued on him using a bad picture of Buck on the front [*The Fabulous Country Music Sound of Buck Owens* (SLP 172)]. We had six tunes that were done by Buck that we had leased from Pep Records and we did six other Buck Owens songs by various Starday artists. You know, we wanted to put together an album on Buck but we only had six songs. But he never got mad at us. He just wanted to sell the damn albums at his shows and Capitol wouldn't sell him his records. We sold records to our artists for one dollar a piece. It was a very pleasant meeting and then Buck furnished us with a better picture [for later reissues] and we were criticized by Capitol Records for using it. Capitol was irate. But when they realized that it had been furnished to us by Buck's mother, why everything ended up smoothly."

Other albums by artists who had started out on Starday but who had achieved greater success with another label were quick to follow. In addition to the Dottie West album were several George Jones albums and even a Roger Miller album [*The Madcap Sensation of Country Music* (SLP 318)]. These albums were comprised of early Starday recordings, or other leased material from the artists' early careers, repackaged with flashy artwork to look as though it was a newly recorded album. As one might guess, most artists did not take to the concept as well as Owens.

Roger Miller was among those who took exception to Pierce's practice. As Miller's successes continued to stack on top of one another, Pierce was quick to rummage through his files to see what he might find. In doing so, he uncovered Miller's early Starday and Mercury-Starday sides, as well as several soundalike recordings he had made. Because Miller was paid a flat rate for his soundalike sessions, Pierce did not even have to pay royalties for their use. Pierce then devised a plan. He wrote a letter to Miller offering to pay him the royalties anyway, provided Miller re-record some of the songs he had written that were now in the Starday publishing catalog. Knowing that nearly everything Miller recorded in the mid-sixties became a huge hit, Pierce eagerly awaited a reply. Miller, however, did not respond. Pierce waited a few weeks and then sent Miller a letter explaining that his royalties would be forthcoming. As Pierce later told the *Nashville Tennessean*, "My sentimentality got the best of my saltiness. We're using the guy's name to sell records, so we ought to pay him."[7]

Much like Owens, Miller was quick to give thanks. Pierce recalls that, "One time Roger left the road that he was doing a bunch of appearances with Andy Williams and he came to Starday and reacquainted with all the staff and we spent an entire afternoon together. Then he went on to greater and greater fame and we were always delighted with his successes."

Though unlikely to release any other Roger Miller albums, Pierce did find another way to reuse that material time and time again. In the early 1960s, Starday pioneered the use of the concept album in country music. Pierce explains: "We found that when we issued album number 117 [*Country Music Spectacular*], a double pocket country album with 20 different artists, it just took off. From then on we said, 'Well, we'll do sacred albums. We'll do bluegrass albums. Then we'll do our concept albums. We found that we could find a place in the market for records with several artists all based on one concept. When we were at our peak, the majors just weren't that interested in the same stuff. We did sort of pioneer the multi-artist albums. I think we were about the only ones who did. I was able to pick up masters everywhere and I used 'em. I got Gene Autry. I got Flatt and Scruggs. I got Patsy Cline. I got Johnny Cash. I didn't record them, I just leased them. Many of the record companies that recorded those artists had had their sale on those records. They were not very much interested in issuing country music LPs and the records were no longer selling for them so they were willing to lease that material out in exchange for a royalty payment to labels that would put them back out in the market place and that's what I did."

Those leased songs, many of which came from the Pickwick label, were then released on albums centering around topics such as death and sorrow, railroad culture, prison life, boozing, cheating, truck driving, and more. The Starday shish-kebabs consisted mainly of "Tex Nobody" [a term used by Pierce, Linneman, and several other Starday employees to describe an unknown recording artist] recordings from the Nashville and Dixie custom labels, previously recorded Starday material that was no longer selling, and the leased tracks. By far, the most successful concept albums were those centered around truck driving.

After Lonnie Irving's trucking hit "Pinball Machine," Pierce began suggesting to other artists that they record truck-related material. By 1963 Pierce had amassed enough material to fill an entire album based on the topic. *Diesel Smoke, Dangerous Curves* (SLP 250), a compilation of fourteen trucking songs, was released and became Starday's best-selling album yet. As of June 1967 the album had sold over 51,000 copies and was still one of Starday's hottest sellers. Realizing the emergence of a new market, Pierce quickly compiled more albums and by 1970 the truck-driving concept album market was flooded with fourteen different compilations from Starday.

The genre was hot, but definitely not new. Truck driving had been a prominent theme in country music beginning with Cliff Bruner's 1939 classic "Truck Driver's Blues." Several more trucker-themed records followed in the forties and fifties, including Link Davis's early Starday number "Trucker From Tennessee" (255). Prior to these, railroad-themed songs were central to country music. America's fascination with travel songs has been around as long as country music. Yet, for some reason, by the mid 1960s, the nation was smitten with trucks and the glory of the open road. Dave Dudley, Red Simpson, Dick Curless, Del Reeves, C. W. McCall, and a handful of others soon became synonymous with gearjammers and freight haulers. As to why Starday was the label to find the most success with it, A&R man (and Patsy Cline's husband) Charlie Dick has his own theory. According to Dick, "Don just had the best album covers in country music. 'Cause we had all the good looking women. The best lookin' women all worked at Starday. We did a bunch of shots down the road at Truck City and those truck drivin' covers are great! My second wife, Jamie Ryan, was on the cover of a bunch of 'em."

Those truck-driving album covers have since become legendary, often portraying Starday employees (and sometimes models) in skimpy spandex outfits hanging on to trucks or getting picked up in a truckstop. They were bold and they were sexy. They were kitschy, funny, and tacky at the same time. These Picassos of the country music album art world were largely thanks to Suzanne Mathis. Mathis teamed up with Dan Quest in 1963 and brought with her a keen sense of design that at a glance made Starday records instantly recognizable as Starday Records. Her use of bright colors, artist names at the very top of every album (so that the records could be easily identified in record racks) and tightly-clad sexy women in spandex all contributed to the total Starday package. Mathis adds, "I just loved, loved working at Starday. I loved Don. He was a great boss. My sister worked there too (Joan Proctor, who also modeled on several album covers) and we loved him. We had so much fun taking those pictures and making those album covers. Don and Martin would get these ideas and then we'd just go do it."

Mathis, like many others, got her job at Starday through her neighbor and accordionist, Vic Willis. The youngest of the Grand Ole Opry's Willis Brothers trio, John "Vic" Willis was both a recording artist and a song scout for Starday throughout the mid-sixties. He was also a career counselor on the side. He convinced Pierce to employ several of his friends and at one point he even had Shot Jackson's daughter, Alene, and all three of the Willis Brothers' wives working at Starday.

The Willis Brothers—Charles "Skeeter," James "Guy" and John "Vic"—began playing professionally in 1932 and already had an impressive résumé before joining Starday in 1960. Aside from making their own recordings for Mercury, Coral, Sterling, and RCA Victor (as the Oklahoma Wranglers), they also backed the immortal Hank Williams on his first recordings for the Sterling label (as the Original Drifting Cowboys), as well as Eddy Arnold for eight

"Skeeter" (fiddle), "Guy" (guitar), and "Vic" Willis (accordion), the Willis Brothers (Courtesy of Don Pierce)

years at the peak of his career (1948–57). By the time they joined the Opry in 1960, they were again known as the Willis Brothers and that same year began a relationship with Starday.

Their first two albums were purely western trios, spliced with historical anecdotes for added effect, and are among their most popular albums. But it was their third album *Give Me Forty Acres* (SLP 323), highlighted by the title track "Give Me 40 Acres (To Turn This Rig Around)," that popularized them in the truck-driving genre. The tune, a catchy ditty about an Alabama truck driver dealing with the perils of Boston city traffic, became the group's first and only Top 10 hit of their career. The tune stayed on the charts for five months and the Willis Brothers were even featured in the Ormond film *Forty Acre Feud* singing their hit song. They followed this success with several other Starday albums dedicated to truck driving and life on the road. Pierce remembers: "The Willis Brothers were almost a Starday institution since their wives

Red Sovine recording in the Starday Sound Studio (Courtesy of Don Pierce)

all worked over there and we made a lot of albums with them and we had some success with 'Give Me 40 Acres.' These people were the first to back up Hank Williams on his first recordings and they did a series of television shows, electrical transcription shows with Eddy Arnold. Vic produced that Jean Shepard number that did so well for her, 'Second Fiddle (To An Old Guitar)' [on Capitol Records], and we were the publisher for that song. And Vic did a lot of producing for a lot of the Starday people."

The truck driving phenomenon continued to sell, and "Give Me 40 Acres" was soon eclipsed by an even bigger Starday trucking hit. Woodrow Wilson "Red" Sovine's musical career began in the late 1930s, though by the early forties he had given up on music and taken a job at a local hosiery mill. After eight years of managing hosiery, Sovine was again ready to try his hand at music, and took on his first full-time gig with the Echo Valley Boys in 1947. After replacing Hank Williams on the Louisiana Hayride and establishing a contract with MGM, his records began to chart and get noticed. He joined the Grand

Ole Opry in 1954 and made his first recordings for Decca that same year. The following year his version of George Jones's "Why Baby Why," a duet with Webb Pierce, became Starday's first song to reach the pole position. Shortly thereafter Sovine covered another of Jones's Starday tunes, "Hold Everything," and carried it to #5 in 1956. Unfortunately for Sovine, the well went dry shortly thereafter. By 1959 he was looking for a new label.

Pierce remembers, "Again we had acquired an artist through the kindness of Jim Denny. It was Jim Denny, who had managed the Opry Artists Bureau, that asked me if I would like to have Cowboy Copas and I said I certainly would and we got lucky with Copas on 'Alabam.' Then he brought me Red Sovine, who was looking for a label. My deal with Jim was to do a Cedarwood song on one side of the records; Jim would send $500 to help promote. I told Jim I sure would like to have Red. We recorded a lot of material and we considered him, along with Cowboy Copas, to be the biggest stars on Starday. It was a pleasure doing business with him in every way. We got lucky with a hit and Red stayed with us from then on and we had a wonderful relationship."

The aforementioned hit was none other than "Giddy-up Go" (spelled "Giddyup Go" on the single [737], but hyphenated on the LP release [SLP 363]), the 1965 #1 hit recitation about a truck driver meeting up with his long-lost son at a truckstop. Tommy Hill wrote the heartbreaking story specifically for Sovine, who was looking to do more recitations. Sovine's heartfelt renditions on Decca, including the Top Five hit "Little Rosa," had already established him as one of the great spoken-word artists of the day, alongside T. Texas Tyler and Red Foley. It was his Starday tearjerkers, however, that earned him the well-deserved nickname, the "Ol' Syrup Sopper."

Several versions of the "Giddy-up Go" story have been told, with varying degrees of accuracy, but few are as engaging as that of Jack "Hoss" Linneman who engineered the session. According to Linneman: "It's really a fascinating story. Of course, Tommy had written the thing. I didn't know anything about it and in one of the sessions we was doing, we had about fifteen minutes left and we had fellows that we'd normally used. So Tommy said, 'Hey, I've written this thing for Red Sovine and I don't know if we should do it or not.' And we told the band, if they did something they'd get paid and all this other crap. What he wanted was 'Home Sweet Home.' He didn't know if we should do it or not and I said to him, 'Well, we got everything set up and there's plenty of time, let's go ahead and do it.' He said, 'OK.' So that could've been a critical point where it never would have happened. But everything about it is so accidental. So the band starts playing 'Home Sweet Home' and it had a terrific feel to it. They would all nod to each other and take turns with fills and such. And Tommy said to me, 'Fade it.' I didn't fade it. 'Course then I was thinking it's OK if it's too long, we can just fade it down. Tommy said again, 'Fade it.' I still didn't fade it. By this time it had gone on for a long time so finally the band just looked at each other and they just came up with a nice beautiful ending.

"So, it was about a week later that Red did the lyrics. Tommy gave the words to Red and he came out to do the thing and he and Tommy were there so I put the track on and began making adjustments here and there to get going so we could go through it one time for practice. We started through it and then Tommy gets a phone call. He goes back out in the hallway and I'm still up there making final adjustments and Red is out there reciting the thing and he finishes it and here comes this nice beautiful ending right on cue. See if I would have faded it, we would've had big problems. So all that was just one great big accident there. So Tommy came back just as it was finishin' up and he says, 'Well, let's listen to it.' So we listened to it and nobody could find a darn thing wrong with it. So that was it. It wasn't even presumably a master take. I hadn't even finished all the adjustments. The producer wasn't even there. And the track being the exact length. Red had never even read through it!

"But now the accidents are going to keep happening. See, I would take the master tapes uptown where they cut the master acetate. You know, we sent it away for plating. Of course, normal procedure, when we mastered and got it all right, we cut the two master acetates. One for plating and the second one which we would bring back to the office, basically so Don and Tommy could listen to it and be sure that's what they wanted. Well that thing was sittin' up on Don's desk and Tommy came in and he picked up a whole stack of records. He was lookin' for something else. See, he wasn't supposed to pick up Red Sovine. And at that time, WENO was a big station and so he takes 'em over to WENO and they play this 'Giddyup Go' and here come the phone calls. They finally had to tell the people, 'OK, we're going to play it every hour on the hour so we don't need you to call in anymore.' And they also called back to Tommy or Don and said 'Hey, you got the biggest monster hit there ever was,' so from there on the records hadn't even been pressed up cause I had just pressed the master a few hours ago.

"So they were sent off, pressed someplace down in Mississippi at that time. So anyhow, they rushed the whole thing through. They got fifty records up there fast. According to Tommy's story [in the Nashville Musician's Union newsletter], we cut fifty acetates. That would not only take you several days but the cost would be astronomical. But they pressed up fifty real quick and so they were sent out to the major stations and then Red was someplace in Minnesota at the time and he don't know any of this. Tex Ritter went up there to do a show with him and Tex says, 'Wow! You got a monster hit record.' Red said, 'I had a cold,' and Tex told him to have colds more often!"

Several minor hit songs followed, as well as several albums of classic honky-tonk country, but it was the spoken word recitations that proved most popular.

Minnie Pearl posing with her miniature poodle and Red Sovine on the wings of her and husband Henry Cannon's plane (Courtesy of Don Pierce)

In July 1967 Starday released "Phantom 309" (811), another eerie tale penned by Hill about a hitchhiker being picked up by an all-around good guy/ghost trucker who drove his truck over a cliff to save a school bus full of children blocking the road ahead. Once again Sovine was in *Billboard*'s coveted Top 10. A few other chart-scrapers followed, mostly tear-inducing truck driver recitations, yet "Giddy-up Go" remained his most popular.

So popular in fact, that a followup to "Giddy-up Go" was quickly written and rushed out. Again Hill penned the words, but this time he wrote it from the mother's point of view and asked comedienne extraordinaire Minnie Pearl to record it. Though not even remotely funny, "Giddyup Go—Answer" (754) was the first and only chart record in Pearl's illustrious Hall of Fame career, which had already included twenty-five years on the Grand Ole Opry. "Answer" entered the charts in March 1966 and reached *Billboard*'s Top 10, a well-deserved hit indeed. Pierce recalls: "There is none finer than Minnie Pearl. We made her the honorary president of our record club and she made two or three albums for us at our place with a live audience [four albums in total: *Howdee* (SLP 224), *Lookin' Fer A Feller* (NLP 2043*)*, *America's Beloved* (SLP 380), and *The Country Music Story* (SLP 397)]. We'd bring down a bunch of BBQ and a keg of beer and put all these people in the studio, usually Starday employees—their friends and like that, for the sound effects. She'd go in there and do her comedy thing and we made an album out of it. Then of course she did those recitations with great success. Wonderful person."

In addition to the "Giddy-Up Go" songs, Starday had an even bigger recitation record in 1965. In fact, the only record Pierce ever released that eclipsed "Giddy-Up Go" in sales was Johnny Bond's 1965 remake of his 1951 spoken-word classic, "10 Little Bottles" (704).

When Bond signed with Starday he was fifty years old and already a country music legend. His 1938 composition "Cimarron" became a western swing standard, and his association with Gene Autry brought him to Hollywood. After a twenty-year relationship with Columbia Records came to an end, Bond was ready to find a new home. Pierce retells the story: "I had met Johnny when I was still in L.A., and later in Nashville he came to me and he wanted to record. Columbia had apparently dropped him and he was available and he was of course associated with Tex Ritter in many ways and Johnny Bond was also very friendly with Jimmy Wakely. Johnny always had good ideas and good songs and so we generally arranged it so that Starday could publish half of the material that he did. He was a very good connection for me then because he knew almost everybody in the business, and if Johnny Bond was doing business with you, you certainly took on a position or a stature that you wouldn't have otherwise."

Bond signed with Starday in 1961 and the original plan involved Bond re-recording his Columbia western classics. Sales were limited, though Pierce remembers getting a visit from a wildly enthusiastic Tommy Hill in 1964. "We was at the Disc Jockey Convention and I went back to Belle Meade Country Club to accept several song awards from the previous year from BMI. I got back to our hospitality suite that we always had at the Hermitage Hotel—we would serve beer and cornbread and it was quite a popular thing with the disc jockeys from all over the country who came to Nashville for the convention—and Tommy Hill said, 'Something crazy happened. We had this show at Studio B. Johnny Bond did a recitation on '10 Little Bottles' with the audience laughing at him. Don, the way it sounded, we should issue it.' We did, and it went to #1 [#2 in *Billboard*] and although Johnny Bond had had it years before on Columbia, this version on Starday was the first time he had ever had a #1 record."

Johnny Bond reading over a recitation with Tex Ritter in the background, ca. 1964 (Courtesy of Don Pierce)

The live recitation featured many disc jockeys laughing at the woes of a "drunken" Johnny Bond and, presumably excited about hearing themselves on the airwaves in the background, they gave it enough plays to keep it in the charts for over five months. Pierce remained puzzled at the whole phenomenon. "I thought that record was terrible. Horrible! But we decided that we would issue it and it sold nearly a million copies for us. The biggest record seller we had on Starday was '10 Little Bottles' by Johnny Bond. I really hate the song, but it took off big time and I remember the first royalty check that I sent to Johnny Bond was just around $20,000. He told me that was the biggest royalty check that he had ever had in thirty years of recording. I am quite proud of that. Johnny is now in the Hall of Fame and he certainly deserves it."

To complement the newfound success Starday had accomplished with singles, Pierce quickly issued concept albums based on those hit songs. Starday's best-selling album became Bond's drinking recitation LP, *10 Little Bottles* (SLP 333), which sold over 100,000 copies in the first two years. The album investment continued to pay off, and Pierce signed more and more traditional country acts with the intent of releasing them on full-length albums. Among the new crop of country music legends to appear on Starday LPs in the mid-sixties were Jimmie Skinner, Joe and Rose Lee Maphis, Justin Tubb (son of country music icon Ernest Tubb), Alex Campbell and Ola Belle, Wilf Carter (also known as Montana Slim), Patsy Montana, Floyd Tillman, Pee Wee King and Redd Stewart, Howard Vokes, T. Texas Tyler, and Clyde Moody. Pierce was also able to lure several old-timers out of retirement and back into the studio, including Leon Payne, Lulu Belle and Scotty, Smokey Rogers, Charlie Monroe, and even the Blue Sky Boys. Though the LP sales were not as good as the previously mentioned hit singles, Pierce not only made a small profit, he also made a significant contribution to what he considered the preservation of the older, more authentic country music.

His efforts were loudly applauded in trade journals throughout the industry. In 1965 *Country Song Roundup* proudly proclaimed, "We of CSR sincerely feel that Don Pierce and Starday Records are rendering a great service to the country music fan. . . . Since 1958, Pierce has pioneered in the production, packaging and sales of country music, believing that the material is basically adult in its appeal. All through the rock and roll era, Starday never deviated from a strict country policy, and its point of view that LPs were the best way of merchandising country music."[8]

Pierce was grateful for the acknowledgment, and in 1965 pledged a continued effort "To produce and sell more country and sacred music than any other label with the largest and most diversified album catalog of country and sacred music ever assembled and to promote and sell Nashville, Tennessee, 'Music City U.S.A.'"[9]

7

A SATISFIED MIND

Nineteen sixty-six was a good year for country music. Several of the trade publications declared it so and Pierce could certainly agree. With the successes of "Giddy-Up Go," "Ten Little Bottles," the various truck driving albums, Pierce's side-project golf tournament and various business adventures, Starday experienced its most successful year. Yet, buried deep within the pages of the trade publications were several smaller, less noticeable articles about the decline of bluegrass music's popularity. Though Pierce had played a significant role in promoting bluegrass music throughout the late 1950s, in addition to capitalizing on his stockpile of bluegrass recordings during the folk boom, he found that by 1966 the bluegrass fad had passed. Despite his best efforts to repackage previous hits and older Starday material with new and exciting cover art, its day had come and gone.

"The bluegrass got caught up in the protests for the Vietnam War," says Pierce. "They all started using the 5-string banjo in all these protest things in the colleges and they would bring in bluegrass bands. At that point I saw my sales going down and I didn't do as much bluegrass after that. It was great for a while, but I always associated the downturn for me, of losing bluegrass, with the protests."

Pierce made his interpretation even clearer in a 1967 letter to *Bluegrass Unlimited*. "For a while I felt that the college trade and the more sophisticated city trade would create a boom for bluegrass music sales. It sure didn't happen that way for us. The people that bought bluegrass by mail order from Jimmie Skinner, Wayne Raney, Starday and other sources, seemed to identify bluegrass with so called 'beatniks,' 'draft dodgers,' 'civil rights demonstrators' and the like, including subversives, homosexuals, pill and dope takers and, as a result, bluegrass sales to the country music market took one hell of a beating."[1] Pierce went on to explain that his letter did not necessarily reflect his own views, but instead was a cross-section of comments he had heard.

Regardless, his remarks created heated debate in the issues that followed. Noted historian Neil Rosenberg was the first to strike back. "I think Mr. Pierce has misinterpreted the reasons for the drop in sales in bluegrass in the past two or three years.... I stopped buying Starday Records because I got tired of getting repackaged recordings I already had.... Starday's catalog is out of date. One of the attractions of Starday in the early sixties was that some exciting groups were recording for them. Starday built up a big backlog of recordings by these groups, but the vast majority have been released, over and over—on Starday and Nashville and on numerous drugstore pirate/pseudonym labels. They are at the end of the repackaging line, and virtually no one records fresh exciting material on Starday anymore."[2]

Pierce took exception to Rosenberg's accusations and responded in the following issue. "I think it is important to bear in mind that we cannot produce music purely for the sake of art or as a hobby. I have 22 people on my payroll and I must sell to distributors who are handling thirty or forty competing labels," wrote Pierce. "I simply cannot get independent record distributors and rack jobbers to make an effort on bluegrass. This precludes me from making further investments. I would like to change the situation but I don't know how I can wave a wand and change the law of supply and demand in the competitive market place."[3] The debate raged on for several issues, but one thing was clear: Bluegrass wasn't selling. In fact, according to a summer of 1967 *Billboard* article, bluegrass was no longer being programmed in the bluegrass regions of Kentucky.

Even more unfortunate for Pierce, by 1967 his country music albums were not selling as well either. Though Starday released several new high-quality, high-fidelity (and stereo) recordings—by Frankie Miller, Arthur "Guitar Boogie" Smith, Joe Maphis, Johnny Bond, T. Texas Tyler, the Willis Brothers, and more—the novelty of the country music album had worn off. Even with the added distribution of Bud and Don Daily, who in 1966 began Starday distribution in Texas for the first time since the rift with Pappy, sales continued to drop. According to Pierce, "The market just got too damn flooded."

Other labels were quick to observe Pierce's album success, including that of concept and budget albums, and his marketing efforts that were previously considered risky and innovative by 1967 were considered industry norms. Other record clubs had popped up and nearly every label was offering their country music to rural communities via mail-order. In the two years that followed "Giddy-Up Go," Pierce watched his album sales and airplay royalties shrink drastically. Though Starday had pledged to remain true to authentic roots music, the rest of Nashville gravitated to the more successful pop country sound and were reaping big benefits from country music's boom years.

Adjusting to the steady decline of sales, Pierce developed a new plan and cut back heavily on album production. He was in search of another hit record and, after signing several new and promising country artists, he released a barrage

Betty Amos Starday publicity photo, ca. 1967 (Courtesy of Nathan Gibson)

of promising singles and freely distributed them to over 2,000 radio stations. Emerging from Pierce's new cast of all-star hopefuls were Orval Prophet, Adrian Roland, Onie Wheeler, George Riddle, Eddie McDuff, Kenny Roberts, and Howdy Kempf, to name a few. Sadly, nothing stuck with the public.

Roland, who Pierce considered to be one of the great up-and-coming country music talents, tragically perished in a Texas plane crash shortly after signing with Starday. McDuff was another promising star who passed away after just three releases on the label. The recordings of Riddle, known mostly through his association as bandleader for George Jones, and Wheeler, remembered mostly as a Sun rockabilly artist and the man who passed away while singing on the Grand Ole Opry stage, are highly regarded today, but at the time of their release they too passed unnoticed.

Betty Amos was perhaps the most successful songwriter among the new additions brought to Starday. Formerly a member of the Carlisles, she had sung on several hit records including "Is Zat You, Myrtle" and had written songs recorded by Jean Shepard ("Second Fiddle (To An Old Guitar)"), Ernest

Tubb, Loretta Lynn, and Goldie Hill. Amos recalls: "Goldie Hill and I were good friends and Tommy, her brother, was at the Hayride [in the early 1950s] and so later he wanted me to come out there to Starday to record. Bill [Carlisle] always was very nice to me. You know, I was just a kid when I went with him so he was like a second daddy to me and he guarded me with his life. But I wanted to go out on my own with my own group. The humorous things were good for their time but I wanted to do some different things and stretch my vocal chords."

Amos then formed a trio with her best friend Judy Lee and her sister Jean and did just that. Dubbed as Betty Amos with Judy and Jean, the trio released a series of rocking bluegrass and upbeat country ditties for Starday. Among their more popular recordings was their playful rendition of "The Cat and the Rat" (756) and their bluegrass truck driving anthem, "Eighteen Wheels A Rollin'" (692). According to Amos, "Actually, my dad was a trucker. He drove an eighteen-wheeler. I didn't even know how many wheels were on them things until I called my dad to ask him 'cause I wanted to write a truck driver song. I also wrote 'Blazing Smoke Stack' with my father, Ronnie Amos, which was recorded by the Willis Brothers. He knew all those trucker phrases and things. Anyway, we were starting to do a little more uptown then but Tommy Hill would always say, 'Ladies, keep it country!'" Though "Keeping it country" is noble in the mind of the traditional country music purist, it was also likely the reason Starday was not making the charts. Regardless, Hill and Pierce pressed on, determined to keep Americana roots music in the limelight.

Another of Pierce's brighter hopes was Kenny Roberts, the "King of the Yodelers," who in 1966 reinvented one of the Starday catalog's best songs. In 1950 Roberts had been a household name in country music; according to Roberts, his 1949 recording of "I'll Never See Maggie Alone" had sold over one million copies. He continued recording throughout the 1950s for Coral and Decca, and came to Starday in 1965. Pierce recalls, "Coral had pretty well stopped releasing country stuff and he was needing a label and he came down to Nashville and we made an album by him and I liked that song 'Tying the Leaves' [769] and some of those other things that he could do and I gave him this song that Bill Mack had wrote called 'Blue.' We had done a record by Bill Mack on 'Blue' [360] and I liked the song very much but we didn't have much success with it and we gave it to Kenny and Kenny made a real good record on it [788]."

Roberts remembers: "I was doing a show out in Michigan and the Willis Brothers saw me and they talked Don into signing me to Starday and even backed me up on my first records. Then Don gave me that song 'Blue' and I

Kenny Roberts singing and playing his 12-string guitar for Tommy Hill in the Starday Sound Studio, ca. 1965 (Courtesy of Don Pierce)

made a record on it and I was the one who added the yodel to it. Later on, LeAnn Rimes covered my version with the yodel in it and it became a huge hit."

Pierce knew the song had hit potential and pushed Roberts's record as best he could. Alas, the airplay did not come and it was soon retired. Thirty years later, LeAnn Rimes broke onto the country scene when her rendition of "Blue" became a Top 10 *Billboard* hit and won her a Grammy Award for Best New Artist of 1996. At the time, rumors swirled that the tune originally had been written for Patsy Cline and that she was killed in the plane crash just before she was to record it. In actuality, the tune was both written and recorded by Starday rockabilly and legendary disc jockey Bill Mack in either late 1957 or early 1958. Alas, even the hits were not becoming hits for Starday.

Things were looking bleak when George Morgan arrived at the Starday Studio door. Morgan, a Grand Ole Opry member since his 1948 #1 hit "Candy Kisses" took the nation by storm, had just been dropped by his longtime label Columbia Records. "The Candy Kid" was an Opry favorite and had amassed over a dozen Top 20 hits, but by 1967 he had not had one in a long time. Pierce remembers: "He became available to us after Columbia had quit recording him and George I think wanted to get maybe the same kind of luck that we had with Copas and Red Sovine."

George Morgan and Hal Neely reviewing lyrics during a recording session (Courtesy of Don Pierce)

Indeed their stories were similar, except that Morgan never scored the big #1 hit record for Starday. Times had simply changed too much. Over the next two years Morgan charted five hits in the Top 60, highlighted by his #31 rerecording of "Sounds of Goodbye" (850) and the truck-driving anthem "Shiny Red Automobile" (814). Regardless of his Starday shortcomings, his place in country music history was furthered in 1959 with the birth of his daughter, country music star Lorrie Morgan, and again in 1998 with his election to the Country Music Hall of Fame. Pierce adds: "He [Morgan] made some very good records for us and it was always fun for him to come around. He was a practical joker and always poked fun, and although we didn't have any big sales with him, I sure was delighted when he was elected into the Country Music Hall of Fame."

Pierce may have been delighted years later, but at the time the hits still eluded Starday, and he was losing money. As he keenly observed, the country labels finding the most commercial success were those willing to cater to the pop market. There was no way around it. The gap between old and new country was clearly divided, and artists such as Sonny James, Bill Anderson, Jeannie Sealy, and even Dottie West were succeeding with the new sound. Pierce, finally willing to concede this fact and take his chances with the new sound, signed a handful of pop stars to Starday in 1968. Pierce recalls: "Snooky Lanson had been a big pop star on the Hit Parade from New York and he was a native of Nashville. After he'd retired back to Nashville we made an album on him [*Nashville Now* (SLP 426)] and he was a pretty nice guy. At one time he was certainly one of America's biggest pop stars. And of course, Guy Mitchell was a big pop star, made a lot of records for Columbia. And he came into Nashville with several handlers when he was looking to our label and trying to revive his career. After a lot of negotiating around we finally made some albums with Guy [*Traveling Shoes* (SLP 412) and *Singin' Up A Storm* (SLP 432)]."

Other acts followed, including Billy Golden, Bobby Harden, J. David Sloan, and Rudy Lyle. Pierce was sure that at least one of these artists would break open for him and that it would likely be Mitchell. After all, Mitchell had charted over twenty-five pop hits from 1950 to 1960 and was a movie and TV star. In fact, Mitchell did chart three records for Starday, but none cracked *Billboard*'s Top 50. Pierce's frustrations were mounting when he received a phone call that sounded too good to be true. "We were approached by some people from Los Angeles who said they had some unreleased smashers on Glen Campbell. And without even seeing them first, we were well aware of their value and we payed $10,000 dollars," according to Pierce. The only catch? Nobody could listen to the "smashers" until they were paid for in full. It was a risk, but Pierce was keenly aware of Campbell's sales potential.

Campbell was a reputable studio musician, having played on records by Elvis Presley, Frank Sinatra, Ricky Nelson, Bobby Darin, and the Monkees, and also spent a brief time in the Beach Boys as Brian Wilson's onstage replacement. His solo career began in 1961 and by 1967 he had become the hottest act in country music. His rendition of "Gentle on My Mind" won him a 1967 Grammy for Best Country and Western Recording and his followup, "By the Time I Get to Phoenix" helped him win two more Grammy Awards in 1968. "Glen had become a huge star and we knew that everything he was doing was selling like hotcakes. So we picked up some tracks that we recognized as being demonstration recordings of songs," notes Pierce. "They were terrible! But we released them anyway and when the album came out, of course Glen complained and I heard Capitol complained too. He sued us and Glen's lawyer, who was a Nashville lawyer that I knew, asked me to explain to him what constituted a demonstration record. I told him as far as I was concerned, anytime an artist sang in front of a microphone, knowing that the music was going to be recorded and available for reproduction, that he had just made a phonograph record. And I didn't see any distinction between a commercial record and a demonstration record. In both cases, the artist sang into a microphone material to be recorded and replayed at another time. And I felt that a recording was a recording. And we proceeded on that basis and we eventually settled

Glen Campbell's *Gentle On My Mind* publicity photo for Capitol Records, ca. 1967 (Courtesy of Nathan Gibson)

the case for about 10, or 12,000 dollars. Glen played in the golf tournament that I created and it ended up on a friendly basis."

When all was said and done, two full-length albums, *Country Soul* (SLP 424) and *Country Music Star #1* (SLP 437), were released and made to look like new recordings by Glen Campbell. Despite the drab, Glen-less (Pierce didn't dare ask Campbell for a proper photograph) album covers and subpar recordings, they actually sold quite well. According to Pierce's sales reports, over 27,000 copies were sold within the first three months. The experiment was apparently quite lucrative. In 1971 Hal Neely, then Starday president, wrote the following in an office memo to Pierce: "Please note that we have settled this claim on the basis of $12,000 plus royalties. A total amount of $21,012.61. Needless to say, this is a *very good* settlement. It is exactly what we agreed to do back before the action started."[4]

Though the action proved beneficial, it was also not likely to be duplicated. Things continued to unravel at Starday. Fewer hits were denting the charts; in 1967 through 1969, fewer than twenty albums were released each year. Tommy Hill, sensing a change, left his role as Starday's A&R man in 1968 and joined MGM. Shortly thereafter he founded Stop Records with his friend Pete Drake. Starday engineer "Hoss" Linneman also left to start his own record label, Hilltop Records. A plethora of engineers and producers filled out the remaining recording sessions. Life at Starday had taken a significant turn for the worse.

Try as he might, Pierce could see no way out. His independent empire of traditional country music was breaking apart at the seams. Pierce retells: "When we were mailing 2,200 radio stations all of our singles and I saw my performance royalties from BMI going down instead of up, I knew something was happening. One, the majors were again in full swing and releasing a whole lot of product and releasing it to all the small stations as well as the large stations without requiring them to pay a subscription fee. So I could see that airplay was changing and that I didn't have access to the airplay that I did before. . . . And I saw my album sales going down and I could see what was happening and I agreed to sell out."

Several other factors contributed to Starday's decrease in BMI performance royalties. Country music radio legend and Disc Jockey Hall of Famer Tom Perryman suggests that "The downfall of independent labels, in my opinion, was when *Billboard* magazine started the quote, 'Reporting Stations.' So, in other words, unless you had records in the charts of these so-called reporting stations, you never got into the national charts of *Billboard*. You could be #1 on every small station or every station in the country, but unless you were one of the so-called reporting stations, you never got into the charts. To me, that was the beginning of the control of the charts by the major record companies."

Former Starday vice president Chuck Chellman agrees with Perryman. "A weird thing about the music business, there really was a period where everything in the world revolved around *Billboard* magazine. And country radio had followed Top 40 radio in playing 40 records. But to all these reporting stations that reported to *Billboard*, they all had sixty slots. So we were always fighting for those extra twenty, which meant, they weren't playing the records on the air, they were just reported to *Billboard*. So we would get a lot of records into *Billboard*s Top 100 country records, and we could get 'em up to the 38's or 39's without the record ever being played on the radio. Just gather enough reports, and I didn't like that. So then a client would call me from L.A. or New York and they'd say, 'I need twelve reports out of your area,' and I'd say, 'OK.' I'd go to twelve radio guys and they'd say, 'Oh yeah buddy, you got it. I'll report it.' Then the accountant would call me up and say, 'What the hell is going on? You only got three reports.'

"Well, number one, the record is never getting on the radio. But it would get into the charts and the artist would think he was doing great. The publisher would think he was doing great. But the record was not even on the air. I was the old-fashioned guy. I just couldn't see gettin' all these reports and not even getting the record played. Artists would call me up and say, 'How's my record doing?' I could say, 'Great! I got it on WSM A-rotation.' 'Oh, but they're not a reporter. Well I got WHAS in Louisville, that's another 50,000 watter. We're doing great.' 'But they're not reporting.' I'd say, 'The record is on the radio.' They'd say, 'I don't care about that. I want reports.' So this reporting thing got to be more important than the music."

It became clear to Pierce that the independents could no longer compete with the mighty major labels. The time had come to try and sell Starday. Pierce had sensed this trend as early as 1967 when he casually mentioned to a few friends that he would be willing to sell his label. Offers immediately poured in. Randy Wood of Dot Records, then connected with Paramount, made the first offer, though Pierce would not let go of his publishing rights at that time and the deal fell through. Roulette then entered a bid of two million dollars, but Pierce was not fond of the company. Pierce remembers: "They were just high flyers and I didn't like it. I went up to New York and saw their operation and I didn't like it. Their deal was $500,000 down and $1.5 million in Roulette stock. But I didn't think much of the Roulette stock." As it turned out, "They went broke not long later and it would've been a disaster if I'd have gone down with it."

Offers continued through March 1968, when Pierce received word that his close friend, mentor and competitor Syd Nathan had passed away in Miami. Pierce remembers: "Syd had heart trouble. His eyesight was very poor. He was gradually slowing down and then he passed away. That left King Records being owned by his widow and she needed to sell the company. So, after the NARM convention in Miami that year, the people that were operating the King plant, Johnny Anderson and others, came down. We went down to Marathon in the Florida Keys and had a meeting down there. We discussed whether it would be feasible for Starday to acquire King Records." Pierce had originally considered buying the King label and running it himself, but quickly changed his mind. "I wasn't so sure I would get along with Mr. [James] Brown and I realized that I knew very little about pressing plants, plating plants, label printing, or taking care of thirty branch offices. So, I decided I did not want to own King Records."

With the idea of purchasing King Records abandoned, Pierce refocused his energy on making Starday more competitive in the shifting market. One option was to get public underwriting for Starday and make it a public company through JC Bradford and Company. Pierce says: "I was well-acquainted with them, as I had bought a lot of securities from them. Starday, I should point out, consisted of six corporations: Starday Records, Starday International Sales, Starday Sound Studio, Madison Music Publishing, Nashville Music Agency, and the Country Music Record Club of America. I used several corporations to achieve lower tax rates. JC Bradford said they could take me public. It would cost about $50,000, but it would be quite lucrative to me. We were going to go ahead with it until one day Mr. Luke Simon of JC Bradford, who was one of the top two or three executives there, suggested to me that I might want to give consideration to selling Starday to Lin Broadcasting Company."

Simon then introduced Pierce to Fred Gregg, owner of Lin Broadcasting, and a match was made. Pierce explains: "Lin Broadcasting owned several broadcasting stations, very successful ones, and were a very strong company with headquarters in downtown Nashville. Fred was acquiring companies, and we had a nice talk. He said he was very much interested in acquiring Starday Records and that he knew that it was a very successful operation. I mentioned to him that he could also acquire the King Records Company. We told him of the importance of King and, because Hal Neely [who was then vice president of Starday] had formerly been one of the chief operators at King Records, he could operate both Starday and King on behalf of Lin Broadcasting Company."

King Records had started out primarily as a hillbilly label in the fall of 1943, with artists such as Cowboy Copas, Moon Mullican, the Delmore Brothers, Hank Penny, Grandpa Jones, Homer and Jethro, Wayne Raney, the Carlisle Brothers, and many more. The Cincinnati label grew rapidly and Syd Nathan began signing rhythm and blues acts. Among the roster of R&B giants at King were Wynonnie Harris, "Bullmoose" Jackson, Ivory Joe Hunter, Hank Ballard, and of course, "The Godfather of Soul" himself, James Brown. Others followed such as Little Willie John, Bill Doggett, Freddie King, and Earl Bostic, and by the early 1960s King was one of the most important independent record labels in the United States. In addition to their thirty branch offices and pressing and plating plants, King also owned and utilized two recording studios in Cincinnati and Macon, Georgia.

Gregg liked the idea of buying the "package deal" and agreed to purchase Starday for two million dollars. This time around Pierce agreed, rather reluctantly, to include all of his publishing rights (including more than fifteen thousand songs) in the final selling price, but managed to keep all of the land holdings he had acquired through the company as well as over $250,000 in retirement trust funds that he had established for his employees. Because Gregg had agreed to purchase King Records as well, Pierce went to setting the deal in action. Pierce explains: "So it was decided that we would make an attempt to buy King Records and I sent Hal Neely up to Cincinnati with a cashier's check for $100,000 of Starday money as earnest money to acquire King for two and a half million dollars."

Before the deal was completed, Pierce remembers that "In order to close out the deal with King, I had to collect for all of the receivables that were due to Starday up to the date of the sale. And a lot of those receivables took many months to come in, especially from overseas. There were also the unpaid accounts from distributors." Once everything had been accounted for, the final purchase price of Starday was $2,700,000. Harlan Dodson, Pierce's attorney and Nashville's Chamber of Commerce president, drew up the purchase agreement, and Pierce and Gregg signed it while having lunch at Shoneys.

The sale was consummated in 1970 and Pierce received a check for one million dollars cash and notes for the remainder plus interest. Pierce remembers how everything got wrapped up: "I must say, Lin performed 100 percent and I put most of the cash into municipal bonds. I realized later that I had overlooked putting in the contract that I was to retain all the land, and I had overlooked that a part of my music holdings was my overseas publishing. So I went back to Fred and said, 'You recall that I said I'd sell you only my music business.' 'That's right.' 'Well, then we have to change the papers to where I retain all the land,' and he agreed to that. 'And I agreed to sell you my music business, and I neglected to put in my overseas publishing interests, and so I will deed them over to you.'" Although that meant giving up the worldwide publishing rights to songs such as "A Satisfied Mind," "Tall Tall Trees," "Blue," and several other top sellers in his catalog, Pierce held on to the land holdings, which provided a foundation for his future business plans.

By late 1968 Hal Neely was operating both labels as Starday-King, which also controlled and distributed King and Starday subsidiary labels including Federal, Bethlehem, Nashville, Look, Hollywood, and Deluxe. Despite the vacancies left by the departure of Starday engineers Hill and Linneman, many Starday artists continued to record for the newly merged Starday-King, such as the Willis Brothers, Red Sovine, Johnny Bond, Kenny Roberts, Merle Kilgore, and more. Several other prominent country music recording artists were also signed to the merger including Rose Maddox, Tommy Collins, New Grass Revival, Larry Sparks, and J. D. Crowe, to name a few. The label's strongest and best-selling asset, however, was not country.

James Brown, the "Hardest Working Man in Show Business," both recorded and produced numerous hit singles for the merged labels including "Get Up (I Feel Like Being A) Sex Machine" (Starday-King 6318), "Super Bad" (Starday-King 6329), "Mother Popcorn (You Got To Have A Mother For Me)" (Starday-King 6245), and "Brother Rapp" (Starday-King 6310), among many others. Both "Sex Machine" and "Super Bad" were recorded in 1970 at the Starday Sound Studios, and Brown continued to record there even after his association

James Brown performing his Starday-King recording "World" on the ABC-TV show *The Music Scene*, September 1969 (Courtesy of Nathan Gibson)

with Starday-King ended. Rumor even has it that Brown demanded the outer facade of the Starday Studio be painted from its original white color, when Pierce sold the label, to its current shade of brown.

Non-country artists on the Starday-King roster included many of Brown's protégés: Marva Whitney, Vicki Anderson, and Lyn Collins, as well as longtime associates Bobby Byrd and Leon Austin. Other standout artists appearing on Starday-King and its affiliates were Hank Ballard (now produced by Brown), Hal Singer, Marie "Queenie" Lyons, the Manhattans, Arthur Prysock, Charles Spurling (whose band included brothers "Bootsy" and "Catfish" Collins), and many more. Pierce's Hollywood label, which had become dormant by the early sixties, was also revived in either 1966 or 1967 and released approximately three dozen highly collected soul and funk classics from the Presidents, Sam Baker, Earl Gaines, Freddie Williams, Eugene Evans, L. H. and the Memphis Sounds, Dan Brantley, and others. Several of the deep soul and blues tracks appearing on the Hollywood label at that time were penned by (and in some cases accompanied by) country musicians including Jerry Reed, Merle Kilgore, Pete Drake, and Scotty Moore (Elvis Presley's first guitarist). Bobby Smith produced the majority of the Starday-King Macon sessions, Henry Glover and Buddy Scott produced most the Cincinnati sessions and the Nashville producing duties were split between Hal Neely, James Brown and William Hoss Allen.

The Starday-King venture was short-lived. The R&B, soul, and funk material from King was selling, but the country market was still grinding to a halt. Sovine hit the charts in 1970 with a few minor truck-driving hits, including "Freightliner Fever," though nothing reached *Billboard*'s Top 40. In an effort to stay afloat, several of the country artists began recording more commercial country pop and rock material, such as Kenny Roberts's yodeling rendition of Creedence Clearwater Revival's "Green River" (908) or Jack Kane's countrified take on George Harrison's "Something" (919), but with no chart success. Album sales were down. Single sales were down. And with over 125 employees working for Starday-King, Lin had a massive hole in the bucket. The future outlook was grim, and before long Lin Broadcasting wanted out of the recording industry altogether.

The label's most valuable commodity, James Brown, was the first to go. His contract and catalog were sold to Polydor in July 1971. A few months later, Lin found a buyer for the rest of Starday-King: Tennessee Recording and Publishing, a New York–based triumvirate consisting of Lieber and Stoller, Freddy Bienstock, and Starday-King president Hal Neely, who together purchased the label for a reported $1.4 million (with Lin taking a loss of several million). Jerry Lieber and Mike Stoller were well established in music circles, having together written "Hound Dog," "Stand By Me," "Yakety-Yak," and many other classic rock 'n' roll hits, in addition to their production work with the Drifters, the Coasters, and others for Atlantic Records. Freddy Bienstock, along with his brother Johnny, was a very successful New York song publisher who had formerly been associated with the Aberbachs at Hill and Range. Neely, who orchestrated the triumvirate and eventual sale, held onto his position at the helm of Starday-King. Pierce says, "Arrangements were made for the Bienstock brothers to handle the music publishing interests from New York, and Neely would handle the Starday-King recording interests in Nashville." Unfortunately, the industry's downward trend continued. Neely, desperate to turn things around, began recording larger bands with fuller arrangements, though Starday-King only spiraled further into debt. Pierce adds, "After about a year and a half, the operation in Nashville was deeply in debt and the Bienstock brothers came down and discontinued Hal Neely."

Tennessee Recording and Publishing now wanted out of the Starday deal, but only partially. The publishing rights they would keep, but the music could go. Pierce says: "Those guys [the Bienstocks] are only interested in the music publishing. That they won't give up. Imagine what they made off 'Blue' and 'Tall, Tall Trees' last year. They hold those copyrights and they know that those copyrights don't argue. They just grow money. But they're not in the record business. Take the records and get as much of it in the market place as possible. But we'll do the publishing."

Without the ability to press and distribute records, the Bienstocks began their search for someone interested in purchasing and reissuing the master recordings. Gayron "Moe" Lytle found himself in the right place at the right time. When Tommy Hill's Stop record label stopped, Hill took his assets and created Gusto Records in 1972. Aside from reissuing prior Starday material, Gusto continued to record Starday artists such as Sovine, Jimmie Skinner, Carl Story, as well as Jimmy Martin, Mel Tillis, and Mike Lunsford. After two years Hill partnered with Lytle, and they jointly operated Gusto Records. A year later Lytle, who also ran GML, Inc., began looking to expand his music collection.

Pierce recalls: "Tommy told me that Moe Lytle went to New York and the Bienstocks wanted $500,000 for the Starday and King masters and that they would not sell the publishing rights under any circumstances. It's just a cash cow. Plus the overseas, oh yeah. Moe went up there and laid down a check, according to Tommy Hill, for $375,000. They said, 'You're out of your mind.' He picked up the check and said, 'I'll be at my hotel room.' They got to talking about it, realized the Neely thing didn't work out right and they didn't have anywhere else to go. They didn't know what to do with the masters. They don't know a goddamn thing about records. They got all these songs but they needed somebody to use those masters. So they took the $375,000. Imagine that! The whole King and Starday catalogs. Of course things were low ebb then. They weren't like they are now. It was just a different ballgame then."

As owner of the Starday and King catalogs, Lytle continued reissuing material on Gusto throughout the mid- to late 1970s, and Tommy Hill continued to produce and engineer new recording sessions. It was, in fact, in this incarnation that Starday had its first-ever million-selling record. In 1976 Gusto released another tender, heartwarming recitation by Red Sovine about a truck driver who, this time, took a few hours out of his busy day to fulfill a crippled boy's dream of one day riding in a big rig. As he had done with "Giddy-Up Go," Hill penned "Teddy Bear" (Starday-Gusto 142) just for Sovine and the song instantly shot up to *Billboard*'s pole position. Hill and Sovine teamed up again for a much brighter follow-up recitation, in which the crippled boy could suddenly walk and the driver was later saved from a burning wreck by his newly adopted dog, "Little Joe" (Starday Gusto 144). Another hit. These were followed up with recitations about a homeless child who died on Santa's lap at a shopping mall and another about a seven-year-old paperboy who has to work to feed his mother and his abusive, alcoholic father. With such tearjerkers pouring over the airwaves, it's hard to imagine truck drivers able to see through their tears long enough to stay on the road.

Toward the end of the 1970s Sovine's success began to dwindle. In 1979 Hill sold his share of Gusto Records to Lytle, who continues to reissue the Starday material. Lytle later acquired the Scepter/Wand and Musicor catalogs and continues adding to what is believed to be the largest independently owned vault of master recordings anywhere in the world. Now under the name of King Records, Lytle's International Marketing Group (IMG, Inc.) is also believed to be the largest grouping of independent record labels. Recent years have seen well-researched liner notes accompanying bluegrass and old-time reissues of Buzz Busby, Jim Eanes, the Country Gentlemen, the Lewis Family, Jim and Jesse, Hylo Brown, Stringbean, and the Blue Sky Boys, as well as box sets on the Stanley Brothers and a Best of Bluegrass compilation covering both Starday and King material. In the United Kingdom, Ace Records has released CDs covering the early Starday and Dixie rockabilly era, and the UK-based Jasmine label has issued CDs of the early Texas honky-tonk period. Germany's Bear Family label continues to release beautifully documented boxed collections featuring Starday recordings from Roger Miller, Frankie Miller, Cowboy Copas, Bill Clifton, and others.

As for Pierce, his interests became quite diverse. Shortly after the Starday sale was completed, Pierce invested in a beautiful new home on Old Hickory Lake. Shawnee Waters, as Pierce and his wife Lari dubbed it, was designed by both Lari Pierce and Braxton Dixon—who had built Johnny Cash's home just a few houses away—and later served as the set of Sonny Bono's 1979 film, *Murder in Music City*. Pierce was kept on the Starday-King payroll for two years after the sale as an advisor, but played virtually no role in the decision-making process. Initially, he went into land development, but was hit hard by the 1976–80 real estate recession. Pierce branched out into a number of varied financial endeavors including the continuation of his tobacco farms, operating several manufacturing plants for automobile parts, opening a Shoney's Restaurant and a Captain D's Restaurant, as well as several other business ventures. In the early 1980s, Pierce partnered with his close friend Ernie Fitzgerald, a builder who had built Twitty City for Conway Twitty, and the two developed the land that Pierce had acquired during his Starday tenure.

Pierce and Fitzgerald's working relationship continued through the next twenty years, though Pierce could not stay out of the country music industry forever. He relates: "It occurred to me that maybe I could contribute something to the industry that had been so good to me, and further aid and abet the continuing relationship that I wanted to have with the people in the business that I had come to know and admire. So, I created the Golden Eagle Master Achievement Awards. We started it in 1989 and at the annual R.O.P.E. [Reunion of Professional Entertainers] banquet I tried to select people that I felt had been so great for the country music industry that they deserved to be in the Country Music Hall of Fame, but had not yet been voted in. I felt that maybe this award, given as much publicity as I could get for it, might help those people get the honors that were properly due them."

Don Pierce presents Porter Wagoner with the Golden Eagle Master Achievement Award in 1993. Also pictured are comedian Speck Rhodes (far left) and music manager Don Warden (far right). Photo by Gordy Collins (Courtesy of Gordy Collins)

The first Don Pierce Golden Eagle Awards were given to Webb Pierce and Carl Smith in 1989. Though it may have taken the Country Music Hall of Fame voters a few years to take notice, each artist was eventually honored with the prestigious recognition (eleven years later for Webb Pierce, thirteen for Smith). The following year the Golden Eagle, essentially a Lifetime Achievement Award, was given to Ray Price and Faron Young. They too joined the Hall of Fame years later. Other Golden Eagle recipients who later went on to be inducted into the County Music Hall of Fame include Porter Wagoner, Johnny Bond, Conway Twitty, Bill Anderson, Ferlin Husky, Jimmy Dean, and Roy Clark. Other Golden Eagle recipients still awaiting induction into the Hall include Red Sovine, Merle Kilgore, and Pierce's Starday partners Pappy Daily and Tommy Hill, among others. Perhaps one day even Don Pierce will himself be inducted into the Country Music Hall of Fame. He was nominated in 1988, though not elected, and there are many who are still trying to make that happen. Only time will tell.

Through R.O.P.E., Pierce continued his ties to country music; he also made a sizeable donation to the new Country Music Hall of Fame building which opened in downtown Nashville in May 2001. Still, Pierce was happy to be retired from the music industry. He became more interested in real estate and land development, perfecting his golf swing, and spending time with his family.

According to Pierce, "It [the music industry] was just changing and that's why I cashed in my chips, so to speak. I could see what was happening. My performance money from BMI was going down and down and down, all the while we were servicing 2,200 radio stations. The market was getting cluttered and there was less and less airplay for the more traditional type music I made."

And so, Pierce retired. His $333 investment had been turned into a $2.7 million dollar country music enterprise in less than twenty years. On April 3, 2005, Don Pierce passed away at the age of 89, leaving behind a wife, daughter, granddaughter, and a legacy in the country music business that shall not be forgotten.

Don Pierce was not only a country music maverick: founding member of the Country Music Association; founder of the Golden Eagle Master Achievement Award; founding member and president of the Starday Recording Company; a barking businessman who could usually be found with both feet propped up on his desk, a cigar in his hand, and a piece of good advice on the way. He opened up country music's acceptance overseas. He initiated the country music concept album. He pioneered budget labels, rack-jobber placement, country music record clubs, custom service recordings, and countless other trends in music marketing. He will be remembered as a man who tirelessly promoted country music through its darkest hours and who preserved traditional American music for future generations. He was a constant supporter and lover of bluegrass and mountain music; a proud cheerleader for the city of Nashville, Tennessee and all of traditional country music; a man who midwifed the careers of George Jones, Willie Nelson, Roger Miller, the Big Bopper, Jimmy Dean, Dottie West, and many others; and who strongly promoted veterans in the field and gave new life to the careers of Johnny Bond, Cowboy Copas, Red Sovine, the Stanley Brothers, the Blue Sky Boys, Moon Mullican, the Willis Brothers, Minnie Pearl, and so many more.

When Don Pierce left the music business, he left behind the largest country music album catalog in the world. When he left the world, Pierce left us with the legacy of a country music pioneer. In recounting his life experiences for this book, even he was surprised by everything that he had done. One particular morning as we sped along the shoreline of Old Hickory Lake in his boat, he pointed out all the mansions now sitting on property he once developed. The lake was remarkably quiet; I was struck by the surreal imagery. As I enjoyed our morning trip around the lake, a trip he had surely taken thousands of times before, he leaned over to me and asked, "Can you believe all of this came from the simple twang of a guitar string?" Indeed, it was impressive.

Later that day, back at his office, we got to listening to some Starday recordings I had brought with me to Nashville. I told him that my favorite Starday LP was Kenny Roberts's *Indian Love Call* (SLP 336), because it had led to my

Don Pierce, ca. 1957 (Courtesy of Don Pierce)

friendship with Kenny and my further exploration of the label. Pierce told me that his favorite album was *Opry Time in Tennessee* (SLP 177) because, according to Pierce, it told the story of country music in Nashville. The LP was released at a time when Pierce was still reinventing Starday in Nashville and establishing a strong relationship with the Grand Ole Opry and other Nashville operations. After hearing his explanation, it made perfect sense. Pierce was Nashville's proudest resident and country music's loudest cheerleader. Thus, when I asked him what his favorite single was, I was a bit surprised when he did not name a song from the same Nashville era. Without hesitating, Pierce told me that there was one particular Starday song he felt summed up his life and experiences in the country music business. After listening to it, I could only agree. Don Pierce was truly a man with "A Satisfied Mind."

NOTES

CHAPTER 1
1. Cooper, 130.
2. *Ibid.*, 140.
3. *Ibid.*, page unknown.
4. Hawkins, "Martin Hawkins on the Starday Label," 13.
5. Daily, 44.
6. Escott, "The D Singles," page unknown.
7. Starns, 15.
8. Duff, ix.
9. *Ibid.*, x.
10. Escott, *Tattooed on Their Tongues*, 69
11. Brown, "On the Road with Blackie Crawford and the Western Cherokees: The Bobby Black Interview," 3.
12. Jones, Carter, 45.
13. Millar, "Talk Back with Noack Pt. 1," 18.
14. Hawkins, "Martin Hawkins on the Starday Label," 12.

CHAPTER 2
1. Gillett, 28.
2. Horstman, 224.
3. Escott, *Tattooed on Their Tongues*, 70.
4. Daily, 46.
5. Jones, Carter, 46.
6. Hawkins, "Martin Hawkins on the Starday Label," 12.
7. Pugh, 3.
8. Millar, Topping, page unknown
9. *Ibid.*
10. Tottenham, unknown.
11. Davidson.
12. Pierce, "Letter to Professional Vocalists and Bandleaders."
13. Hawkins, "Martin Hawkins on the Starday Label," 11.
14. Pugh, 1–2.

CHAPTER 3
1. Escott, *Tattooed on Their Tongues*, 72.
2. Escott, Cup of Loneliness, 10.
3. *Ibid.*, 12.

4. Jones, Carter, 61–62.
5. Hawkins, "Martin Hawkins on the Starday Label," 13.
6. *Ibid.*
7. *Billboard*, "Starday Moves to Nashville," page unknown.
8. Millar, "Talk Back with Noack Pt. 1," 6
9. Dean, 67.
10. Gutterman, 15.
11. Reid, "Stanley Brothers and the Clinch Mountain Gang 1953–1958, 1959," 1
12. Reid, "Jim Eanes and the Shenandoah Valley Boys," 5
13. Escott, *Tattooed on Their Tongues*, 72.

CHAPTER 4
1. Reid, liner notes to Buzz Busby CD *Goin' Home*, 6.

CHAPTER 5
1. Pierce, personal letter to Loyd Howell, 1.
2. "Bluegrass—The Brightest, Freshest Sound," 84.
3. Pierce, Duke of Paducah LP liner notes, 1.
4. Pierce, "Superiority Via Specialization," 97.

CHAPTER 6
1. Pierce, "Let's Stick Together," 161.
2. Pierce, "Letter to Distributors."
3. "Hollywood calls . . . Nashville Answers," 70.
4. Advertisement, 1967 *Billboard The World of Country Music*, 129.
5. "Starday's Country Music Record Club Spearheads Another Year," 12.
6. "More Country Music Success at Starday in 1965," 8.
7. Daughtrey, 7.
8. "Don Pierce and Starday Records," 24.
9. "More Country Music Success at Starday in 1965," 8.

CHAPTER 7
1. Pierce, letter to March *Bluegrass Unlimited*, 8–9.
2. Rosenberg, *Don Pierce: The Rise and Fall of Starday*, 4–5.
3. Pierce, letter to June *Bluegrass Unlimited*, 7–8.
4. Neely, private memo.

RECOMMENDED LISTENING

After completing this book, I realized that it might be useful for me to point readers to where they might hear some of the records about which they have just read. Sadly, much of the Starday catalog remains out of print. Additionally, I recognize that many music listeners have long since abandoned their record players and have no interest scouring eBay for records every day. With that in mind, I have attempted to compile a list of some of the more notable CD reissues that are readily available in stores or online. This list is in no way meant to be comprehensive, but should provide the reader with a good place to start tracking down these precious recordings. The numbers in parenthesis correspond to the label's CD release number.

As mentioned in the final chapter, reissues continue to be made available from International Marketing Group Inc. (gustorecords.com). Over the years these reissues have appeared on the Starday, Gusto, King, and Hollywood labels. In the past twelve years, Lytle and company have paid considerable attention to their massive bluegrass holdings. The following bluegrass CDs and box sets are enhanced with high quality remastering as well as detailed liner notes. The *Best of King and Starday Bluegrass* box set includes two CDs dedicated to each label, 100 songs in total, and provides a nice sampling of the bluegrass talent on Starday.

Smilin' Jim Eanes – *Your Old Standby: Complete Starday Recordings* (2-CD set) (Starday 3507)
Jim and Jesse – *Dixie Hoedown: Their Complete Starday Recordings* (KSCD 0210)
Blue Sky Boys – *Are You From Dixie: Complete Starday Recordings* (Gusto 0549)
Carl Story – *Angel Band: Early Starday Recordings* – (Gusto 0548)
Hylo Brown – *Lovesick and Sorrow: 16 Greatest Starday Recordings* (Gusto 0124)
Stringbean – *Barn Yard Banjo Pickin'* (2-CD set) (Gusto 0956-2)
The Lewis Family – *Born of the Spirit* (2-CD set) (Gusto 0953)
Buzz Busby – *Going Home: Greatest Starday Recordings* (Gusto 0123)
Various Artists – *The Best of King and Starday Bluegrass* (4-CD set) (KG 0952-4)
The Stanley Brothers – *The Early Starday and King Years 1958–1961* (4-CD set) (KBSCD 7000)
The Stanley Brothers – *The Complete Starday and King Instrumentals* (2-CD set) (King 5121)

Additionally, numerous budget reissues (liner notes are minimal if at all existent) have been produced. The following are just a few of these affordable CDs worth tracking down for the music alone.

Benny Martin – *22 Favorites* (Gusto 2119)
Pete Drake and his Talking Steel Guitar – *For Pete's Sake, 18 Songs* (Gusto 0685)

The Stoneman Family – *28 Classics* (Gusto 0697)
The Willis Brothers – *20 Great Truck Driving Songs* (Gusto 0841)
Johnny Bond – *Ten Little Bottles* (Gusto 2128)
Minnie Pearl – *The Starday Years* (3-CD set) (Gusto 3509)
The Lonesome Pine Fiddlers – *Starday Collection* (Gusto 2130)
The Lonesome Pine Fiddlers – *Bluegrass Collection* (Gusto 2131)
Howard Vokes – *Songs of Tragedy and Disaster* (Gusto 5122)

Finally, various Starday LPs have been reissued as budget CDs and often include reproductions of the original artwork, though not in every case. Almost all of them include the same songs in the same order as the original LP. The following is a numerical list of Starday LPs that have been reissued on CD from Gusto. Artist names and album titles can be accessed in the record listing portion of this text.

105, 122, 132, 142, 147, 150, 157, 159, 160, 170, 173, 174, 175, 179, 181, 191, 192, 195, 205, 206, 209, 215, 219, 246, 260, 285, 302, 312, 316, 336, 340, 350, 351, 356, 367, 389, 432, 450, 463, 480, 489

Bear Family (bear-family.de), based in Germany, sets the gold standard for country music reissues. Their CDs most often feature stellar sound quality, plentiful tracks, beautiful artwork, insightful and extensive liner notes, and detailed discographies. Only recently have Starday recordings been made available to Bear Family, and my hope is that this trend continues. The Frankie Miller 3-CD set includes a 98-page booklet, many unreleased Starday recordings and demos, and is well worth tracking down.

Frankie Miller – *Blackland Farmer: The Complete Starday Recordings, and More* (3-CD set) (BCD 16566)
Cowboy Copas – *Settin' Flat on Ready* (BCD 16990)
Rudy Grayzell – *Let's Get Wild* (BCD 16837)
Sleepy LaBeef – *Sleepy Rocks* (BCD 15981)
Roger Miller – *A Man Like Me* (BCD 16760)
Benny Barnes – *Poor Man's Riches* (BCD 16517)

Ace Records (acerecords.co.uk) is another label known for high-quality reissues. Their interest in Starday has primarily been centered on rockabilly and their two volumes of Starday Dixie Rockabilly are must-haves for any fans of the genre. All but two of the twenty-eight tracks on *Rarest Rockabilly & Hillbilly Boogie* stem from the Starday catalog, and *Rockabilly Shakeout* includes more of the best of Starday rockabilly. In 2005 Ace abandoned their rockabilly-centric exploration of Starday and issued an excellent compilation of Red Sovine's country and honky-tonk material.

Various Artists – *Starday Dixie Rockabillies, Vol. 1* (CDCHD 704)
Various Artists – *Starday Dixie Rockabillies, Vol. 2* (CDCHD 708)
Various Artists – *Rarest Rockabilly & Hillbilly Boogie/Best of Ace Rockabilly* (CDCHD 311)
Various Artists – *Rockabilly Shakeout* (CDCHD 191)
Red Sovine – *Honky Tonks, Truckers and Tears: 1964–1980* (CDCHD 1052)

RECOMMENDED LISTENING

In recent years the Jasmine label (jasmine-records.co.uk) has issued several outstanding Starday compilations. The affordably-priced 2-CD set, *Hillbilly Bop, Boogie and the Honky Tonk Blues Vol. 3*, covers nearly fifty honky-tonk standards from Starday's early era. *You All Come* is comprised of selections from the first twenty Starday releases in 1953. *Hixville* takes a look at the country releases in the custom series. All highly recommended.

Various Artists – *Hillbilly Bop, Boogie and the Honky Tonk Blues Vol. 3: 1954–1955* (2-CD set) (JASCD 3583-4)
Various Artists – *Hixville: We'll Have A Time Yes-Siree! (Custom Pressings Vol. 1)* (JASCD 452)
Various Artists – *You All Come! East Texas Honky Tonk* (JASCD 3555)

I also recommend Time Life's (timelife.com) compilation on George Jones, primarily because it includes a previously unissued track from Jones's first ever recording session. Included are fifteen tracks of vintage George Jones.

George Jones – *Early Hits: The Starday Recordings* (M19487)

Bear Family issued a wonderful 8-CD box set on Bill Clifton in 2001 entitled *Around the World to Poor Valley*. This collection included virtually all of Clifton's Starday recordings. If price is a concern, I recommend Rounder Records' (rounder.com) fifteen-song reissue of Clifton's early Mercury-Starday and Starday efforts.

Bill Clifton – *The Early Years 1957–58* (Rounder 1021)

The Cactus label has issued three CDS of early Starday honky-tonk and hillbilly material as well as releases by Sonny Burns and Eddie Noack. These may be tougher to find, but all are worth looking for.

Various Artists – *Starday Hillbilly, Vol. 1* – Cactus STACD1
Various Artists – *Starday Hillbilly, Vol. 2* – Cactus STACD2
Various Artists – *Starday Hillbilly, Vol. 3* – Cactus STACD3
Sonny Burns – *The Starday Recordings* – Cactus SB 1
Eddie Noack – *The Starday and D Sessions* – Cactus EDCD 1

Many years ago Collector Records, based in Holland, released the most extensive interrogation of the Starday custom series to date. Six CDs, thirty songs each, were filled with obscure rockabilly and honky-tonk private pressings. Like the Cactus CDs, these may take more effort to find but are well worth the hunt.

Various Artists – *Dixie Rock and Roll* (CLCD 4410)
Various Artists – *Great Dixie Rock and Roll* (CLCD 2222)
Various Artists – *Dixie Boppin' Country Billies* (CLCD 3333)
Various Artists – *Dixie Boppin' Country Billies* (CLCD 4444)
Various Artists – *Great Dixie Boppin' Country Billies* (CLCD 5555)
Various Artists – *Great Dixie Boppin' Country Billies* (CLCD 6666)

My final recommendations are the first three rockabilly CDs I ever owned. In 1993, the Texas Gold label issued three CDs, thirty songs each, covering Starday's main and custom series rockabilly outpouring. I would recommend seeking out the Ace rockabilly reissues first, but if the price is right, these are welcome additions.

Various Artists – *The Starday Story Volume 1* (TG 931)
Various Artists – *The Starday Story Volume 2* (TG 932)
Various Artists – *The Starday Story Volume 3* (TG 933)

RECORD LISTING

While writing the history of Starday Records, I became very interested—obsessed, actually—in hearing the music I was to be writing about. Unfortunately, much of this great label's output remains locked away in a vault. Thus, the only way to hear many of these tunes is to seek out the records themselves. In attempting to do so, there were many highs and lows. For example, I can think of very few things as exciting as discovering a record that I previously did not know existed. However, tracking down these rare records can be exceedingly difficult. When I began this project, there was not any reliable discography or record listing published for the records I was trying to collect [though several inaccurate listings were readily available online]. I spent countless hours scouring the Internet, searching for keywords such as label names Starday, Hollywood, Nashville, Dixie, and King, in addition to Starday-affiliated publishing companies such as Starrite, Starday Music, Tronic, Golden State, Kamar, Bayou State, etc. From many years of record research, I was fortunate enough to discover many Starday recordings and I have been able to compile a substantial listing of the Starday catalog.

Some parameters had to be set. It would be nearly impossible to compile a complete listing of every single record that Starday issued or had a partial role in creating/distributing/promoting. For the purposes of this book, I have only tried to complete a listing of Starday records from 1953 to 1970, the era in which my collaborator Don Pierce was associated with the label. I did not attempt to complete listings for the Starday-King singles and albums or the Starday-Gusto incarnation that followed. In addition, I left out many Starday-King affiliated labels including Federal, Deluxe, Look, Volunteer, and others; there simply was not enough time to research them all. Also, many singles released within the above stated time frame were also left out of this listing. These include short-lived ventures such as the Starday Square Dance 1000 series, the Dixie Hit Parade 300 series, and the instrumental disc jockey EPs. Early on in my research I spent considerable time piecing together a listing of Pierce's Hollywood rhythm and blues label, but because Pierce ran it separately from Starday I opted against its inclusion (despite the last twenty-four Hollywood releases stating "A Product of Starday Records" at the bottom of the label). Most regrettably, I was unable to finish a listing for the Starday EP series. This is an important part of the Starday story. I did make an attempt, but my listing is too sparse for publication. I simply couldn't do it all.

Instead, I have tried to provide an accurate listing of *most* of the Starday and Starday-related records issued from 1953–70. Included are listings for Starday singles, Starday albums, Nashville singles, Nashville albums, Mercury-Starday singles, Mercury-Starday albums, the Starday Juke Box Oldies Series, the Dixie Rock series, and the infamous Dixie custom releases. In total, more than 2,600 records are listed. I am forever grateful to several contributors for their efforts in making this listing possible. Following are a few notes regarding each listing.

Various Starday single label shots (Courtesy of Nathan Gibson)

Starday Singles – compiled by Nathan Gibson, with thanks to Allan Turner and the *Hillbilly Researcher*

As I mentioned in the introduction, Allan Turner of the *Hillbilly Researcher* deserves special recognition. Many years ago the good folks at the *Hillbilly Researcher* published a booklet entitled *Starday: The Texas Years*, which provided a nearly complete discography for Starday singles #101–376. According to page 31, "Listing compiled by Big Al Turner from information supplied by Alan Bennett, Yvan Biamon, John Burton, Don Dawn, Dick Grant, Dave Howe, Jan Jerrod, Cees Clop, Bob Jones, Henri Laffont, Lars Lundgren, Dennis Morraine, Ian Saddler, Tom Sims, Menno Smith, Roger Smith, Mike Smythe, Brian Taylor, Phillip J Tricker, Russell Turner, Richard Weize."

During my Starday scavenger hunts I found several records not listed in that booklet, and have added them accordingly. I then went about compiling my own list of records

#401–984, creating a complete list of Starday singles (including those released on the Starday label during the Starday-King era). Realizing that a full discography (with master numbers, songwriter's information, studio dates, release information, etc.) would be beyond the scope of this book, I set out with the "simple" task of creating an accurate listing of the Starday catalog and personally verifying the accuracy of each and every listing. I did this by searching through the archives at the Country Music Hall of Fame with the generous assistance of Senior Historian John Rumble; purchasing every Starday record I could find; and combing through record store bins and searching eBay. I attempted to misspell every word that appeared misspelled on the original label (for example, Howdy Kempf's name appears on various labels as either Howdy Kemp or Howdy Kempf) and present each listing as it originally appeared. Though multiple spellings may exist on different pressings of the same release, I provide the spelling from the label that I could visually verify. Unfortunately, I was not able to track down a copy of every 45, though I came close. The following is a list of records that I have seen listed for sale online without photos or that have appeared in other Starday single listings but have not been verified by myself: #417, 430, 971, 972, 973, 976, 978, and 980.

101 – Mary Jo Chelette – Cat Fishing / Gee, It's Tough to be Thirteen
102 – Blackie Crawford – Mariuch (Mottie-Ooch) / The Western Cherokees – Cherokee Steel Guitar
103 – Bob Heppler – If You Don't Mind / I Don't Like It
104 – Arlie Duff – You All Come / Poor Ole Teacher
105 – Blackie Crawford with the Western Cherokees – Huckleberry Pie / The Western Cherokees – Hot Check Baby
106 – Arlie and Lois Duff – A Million Tears / Stuck-In-A-Mud Hole
107 – Bob Heppler – Handle With Care / One Step Ahead
108 –
109 – Patsy Elshire – Someday I Know He Will / Two Can Play the Game
110 – Bill Potter – I Lost My Gal / Nobody Knows
111 – Bill Potter – Honk Your Horn / Cry Not For Me
112 – Mary Jo Chelette and the Western Cherokees – You Can Be the One / Son of Mexican Joe
113 –
114 – Sonny Burns – Blue, Blue, Rain / Tho' You're In My Arms
115 – Patsy Elshire – You Can't Play In My Play House / Pieces of A Heart
116 – Blackie Crawford – Stop Boogie Woogie / The Western Cherokees – Left Over Love
117 – Jack Rhodes with Al Petty – Al's Steel Guitar Wobble / Jack Rhodes and Freddie Franks – Gipsy Heart
118 – Sonny Burns – Too Hot To Handle / Powder And Paint
119 – Billie Harbert – Ain't That Whiskey Hot / Mortgage on Your Heart
120 – "Smilin'" Jerry Jericho – Let's Call It Off / Moanin' In the Morning
121 – Mary Jo Chelette – He Likes Me / Where Are You Darling
122 – Patsy Elshire – Girl With a Past / You Sent Her An Orchid
123 – Patsy Elshire – Throw Away the Glass (Answer to There Stands the Glass) / Mary Jo Chelette – You Can Be the One (Answer to Let Me Be the One)
124 – Fred Crawford – Time Will Take You Off My Mind / Empty Feeling In My Heart
125 – Jimmie Walton "The Tennessee Country Boy" – High As a Georgia Pine / Baby You're the One

126 – Blackie Crawford and the Western Cherokees – If They Tell You / The Western Cherokees – Popcorn
127 – The Duff Trio – When the Saints Go Marching In / Country Singing (Alongside the Road)
128 – Earney Vandagriff – Where You Been / Alabama Blues
129 – Cotton Henry and the Oklahoma Hillbillies – Alibying Sweetie / Eskimo Nell
130 – George Jones – No Money In This Deal / You're In My Heart
131 – Sonny Burns and the Western Cherokees – A Place For Girls Like You / Heart Like a Dollar Sign
132 – Arlie Duff with the Western Cherokees – Let Me Be Your Salty Dog / Back to the Country
133 – "Smilin'" Jerry Jericho – Lovin' Up A Storm / I Can't Give You Anything But Me
134 – Corky Carpenter – My Heart Would Like To Know / Chapel of Memories
135 – Ann Raye – Brazen Ringless Hand / You Can't Go Riding (In My Wagon Anymore)
136 – Jack Tucker and his Oklahoma Playboys – Itchin' For a Hitchin' / I Was Only Fooling Me
137 – Les Chambers and his Mountaineers – Too Much Pride / Lonely Heart Waltz
138 – Hoyt Scoggins and the Dixie Cowboys – Born of the Spirit / My Mother Was Good and Faithful
139 – Marvin Lacy "The Tune Twister" – I Want To Know More About You / Lost Chicken
140 – Chuck Mayfield – Washing On the Line / Face in the Clouds
140 – Chuck Mayfield – Washing On the Line / Lucky Me [issued twice with alt. flip sides]
141 – Al Petty with the Rainbow Riders – Steel Guitar Special / Al Petty with Gene Tabor – Country Saturday Night
142 – Pat Patterson and his Missouri Hillbillies – Mister Hillbilly / First You Buy the Beer
143 – Dick Stubbs – Wired For Sound / Hillbilly Swing
144 – Jimmie Walton "The Tennessee Country Boy" – I'll Live That Name / What Will the Future Bring
145 – Fred Crawford – First On Your List / Love With Such a Past
146 – George Jones and Sonny Burns – Wrong About You / George Jones – Play It Cool Man—Play It Cool
147 – Sid Ervin with the Western Melody Makers – If Tears Could Cry / Western Melody Makers – Who Put the Turtle In Myrtle's Girdle
148 – Bob Jones – I Got By / You'd Better Behave Baby
149 – De Wayne Higdon and the Drifters – Take Your Time (Cause Every Minute Counts) / Does Anybody Know
150 – Don Payne – Pogo the Hobo / Forever
151 – Anne Ray – I Think Of You / One Year Has Passed
152 – Sonny Burns – Another Woman Looking For a Man / Waltzing With Sin
153 – Hoot and Curley with the Western Cherokees – Hurry, Hurry / Another Man's Wife (My Mother)
154 –
155 – Joe Price – Pay Attention Please / Keep the Wolves Away
156 – Fred Crawford – Never Gonna Get Married Again / Each Passing Day
157 – Al Petty with the Rainbow Riders – Steel Mill / Cecil Ray with Al Petty on Steel Guitar – I May Not Be Much of a Fellow
158 – Les Chambers and his Mountaineers – Kiss Like That / Lonesome
159 – Eddie Noack – Don't Trade / Take It Away Lucky

160 – George Jones – Let Him Know / Let Me Catch My Breath
161 – Chuck Mayfield – Lucky Me / Helpless Hands
162 – George Jones – You All Goodnight / Let Him Know
163 – Eddie Eddings and the Country Gentlemen – Smoochin' / Yearning (To Kiss You)
164 – Red Hays – A Satisfied Mind / Doggone Woman
165 – Sonny Burns and George Jones – Heartbroken Me / Sonny Burns – Tell Her
166 – Glen Barber – Ice Water / Ring Around the Moon
167 – R. D. Hendon and his Western Jamboree Cowboys – You Traveled Too Far / Return My Broken Heart
168 – Hoot and Curley – Country Lovin' / Part of Your Heart
169 – Eddie Noack – Left Over Lovin' / I'll Be So Good To You
170 – Fred Crawford – You Gotta Wait / I Just Need Some Lovin'
171 – Cotton Henry – Two Times Two / Let's Be Sweethearts Tonite
172 – Pat Patterson and his Missouri Hillbillies – Here Comes All My Love For You / Racetrack of Love
173 – Hoyt Scoggins and the Georgia Ramblers – Trudy / Muddy Old River
174 – Bill Nettles – Wine-O Boogie / Gumbo-Mumbo (Papa Had To Go)
175 – Sonny Burns – Invitations / Let's Change Sweethearts
176 – Arlie Duff – Fifteen Cents A Sop / Courtin's Here To Stay
177 – Joe Price – Typhoon / It Makes Me Happy
178 – Biff Collie – What This Old World Needs / Lonely
179 – Sonny Fisher – Rockin' Daddy / Hold Me Baby
180 – Les Chambers with Dick Stubbs and his Mountaineers – Sneakin Out (In the Middle of the Night) / Bald Headed Daddy (Here Today—Gone Tomorrow)
181 – Les Chambers and Johnny Mathis – Will It Always Be / Everybody Else Does (Why Can't I)
182 – Jerry Hopkins – My Everlasting Love / Mamma Baby
183 – Jess Thomas – Weekly Rasslin' Match / Take Two Aspirins
184 – Chuck Mayfield – Trinidaddy / Tell Me Sweet
185 – Roy Drusky – Mumbling To Myself / Such A Fool
186 – Melvin Price and his Santa Fe Rangers – The Pace That Kills / Maybe It's Because I Love You
187 – Harry Choates – The Original New Jole Blon (English) / The Original Jole Blon (French)
188 – George Jones – Hold Everything / What's Wrong With You
189 – Sonny Burns – Six Feet of Earth / You'll Look A Long Time
190 – Sonny Fisher – Sneaky Pete / Hey Mama
191 – Earney Vandagriff and the Big "D" Boys – Guest Star In Heaven – A Tribute to Hank Williams / I Know I'm Falling In Love
192 – Smokey Stover – You Wouldn't Kid Me, Would You / It's Easier Said Than Done
193 – Hoot and Curley – That's My Style / Hillbilly Heart
194 – R. D. Hendon and his Western Jamboree Cowboys – Big Black Cat / Four Walls (Around My Heart)
195 – Hoot and Curley – Battered Old Raincoat / You Get What You Pay For
196 – Glenn Barber – Poor Man's Baby (And A Rich Man's Dream) / Married Man
197 – Jack Hammons – Mr. Cupid / That's the Way To Fall In Love
198 – Gene Tabor – A Real Gone Jesse (I'm Hot To Trot) / I'm Not the Marryin' Kind
199 – Fred Crawford – Can't Live With E'm (Can't Live Without E'm) / What's On Your Mind

200 – Jimmie Blakley and Dorothy Blakley – You Left Me With the Blues / Take My Heart
201 – Eddie Noack – Wind Me Up / If It Ain't On the Menu
202 – George Jones – Why Baby Why / Seasons of My Heart
203 – Biff Collie "The Bellerin' Bowlegged Boy" – Goodbye, Farewell, So Long / Look on the Good Side
204 – Jimmy Lee Durden and the Drifters – What Can I Say / Reconsider
205 – Jack Derrick – Rainbow of Love / Waitin' and Watchin'
206 – Les Chambers and Johnny Mathis – Give Me a Little More / Les Chambers – Real Sincerely
207 – Sonny Fisher – Rockin' and a Rollin' / I Can't Lose
208 – Leon Payne – I Die Ten Thousand Times a Day / We're on the Main Line
209 – Sonny Burns – A Real Cool Cat / Frown on the Moon
210 – Bob Jones – I Can't Bear To See You Go / It Died In Your Heart
211 – Chuck Mayfield – Are You Trying To Tell Me Goodbye / Hog Sloppin' Time
212 – Harry Choates – Poor Hobo / Opelousas Waltz
213 – Eddie Noack – Fair Today, Cold Tomorrow / Don't Worry Bout Me, Baby
214 – Glenn Barber – Ain't It Funny / Livin' High and Wide
215 – Leon Payne – Christmas Everyday / Christmas Love Song
216 – George Jones – What Am I Worth / Still Hurtin'
217 – Rudy Gaddis – Uranium Fever / My Tears Are A Measure
218 – Fred Crawford – Just Another Broken Heart / Me And My New Baby
219 – Buddy Dee and his String Band – Swamp Water Drag / Cherokee Rag / String Band Rag / Shuffle the Blues
220 – Leon Payne – You Are the One / Doorstep To Heaven
221 – Jimmy Blakley and Dorothy Blakley – Sorry For You / Ping Pong
222 – Jack Newman – Full of Love / Afraid To Call
223 – Sonny Burns – Satan's A-Waitin / Girl of the Streets
224 – Harry Choates – Port Arthur Waltz / Honky Tonky Boogie
225 – Eddie Noack – When the Bright Lights Grow Dim / It Ain't Much But It's Home
226 – Melvin Price and his Santa Fe Rangers – One Man's Love / Gonna See My Baby
227 – Carl Stuart – Let 'Em Talk / I Did Care, I Do Care
228 – R. D. Hendon and his Western Jamboree Cowboys – Don't Push Me (Let Me Fall) / We Smiled
229 – Rudy Grayzell – The Moon Is Up (The Stars Are Out) / Day By Day
230 – Biff Collie "Bellerin' Bowlegged Boy" – Doodle Doo / Empty Kisses
231 – Bill Mack – Fat Woman / Kitty Kat
232 – Leon Payne – Two By Four – Impersonation of "You Know Who" / You Can't Lean On Me
233 – Larry Nolen and his Bandits – Ship Ahoy / Lady Luck
234 – George Jones – I'm Ragged But I'm Right / Your Heart
235 – Link Davis – Sixteen Chicks / Deep In the Heart of a Fool
236 – Benny Barnes – No Fault of Mine / Once Again
237 – Neal Merritt – What's the Difference / You Had To Do Me Wrong
238 – Johnny Nelms – A Tribute To Andy Anderson / Everything Will Be All Right
239 – Jimmie Lee Durden and the Drifters – I Miss Her So / Since Yesterday
240 – Thumper Jones – How Come It / Rock It
241 – Rudy "Tutti" Grayzell – Duck Tail / You're Gone
242 - Link Davis – Sixteen Chicks / Grasshopper Rock

243 – Fred Crawford – Rock Candy Rock / Secret Of My Heart
244 – Sonny Fisher – Pink and Black / Little Red Wagon
245 – Rock Rogers – That Ain't It / Little Rock Rock
246 – Eddie Noack – For You I Weep / You Done Got Me
247 – George Jones – You Gotta Be My Baby / It's OK
248 – R. D. Hendon and his Western Jamboree Cowboys – The Waltz of Texas / Lonely Nights
249 – Glenn Barber – Shadow My Baby / Feeling No Pain
250 – Leon Payne – All the Time / One More Chance
251 – Biff Collie "Bellerin' Bowlegged Boy" – Joy Joy Joy / All of a Sudden
252 – Bill Mack – Cat Just Got In Town / Sweet Dreams Baby
253 – Rocky Bill Ford – Have You Seen Mabel / Mad Dog In Town
254 – Sonny Burns – If You See My Baby / Think Again
255 – Link Davis – Don't Big Shot Me / Trucker From Tennessee
256 – George Jones – Taggin' Along / Boat of Life
257 – Amos Como and his Tune Toppers – Hole in the Wall / Heartbroken Lips
258 – Buddy Dee – Country Rockin' and Flyin' / Harry Choates – Drag That Fiddle / Musical-Aires – Skip Along Guitar / Lucky Chapman – Blue Grass
259 – Larry Nolen and his Bandits – Golden Tomorrow / I Wonder
260 – Neal Merritt – No One But You / Someday You'll Pay
261 – Jack Newman – At Last / Let It Happen
262 – Benny Barnes – Poor Man's Riches / Those Who Know
263 – Johnny Tyler – Lie To Me, Baby / County Fair
264 – George Jones – Gonna Come Get You / Just One More
265 – Bob Doss – Don't Be Gone Long / Somebody's Knocking
266 – James O'Gwynn – Losing Game / If I Never Get To Heaven
267 – Leon Payne – Sweet Sweet Love / A Prisoner's Diary
268 – Louisiana Lannis – Much Too Much / Muscadine Eyes
269 – King Sterling & His Blue Grass Melody Boys – Too Many Taverns / Don't Hang Around
270 – Rudy "Tutti" Grayzell – Jig-Ga-Lee-Ga / You Hurt Me So
271 – Jeanette Hicks – Extra-Extra / Cry Cry (It's Good For You)
272 – Fred Crawford – Lucky In Cards / I Learned Something From You
273 – Harry Choates – Allons A Lafayette / Draggin' That Fiddle
274 – Smokey Stover – Now / My Building of Dreams
275 – Link Davis – Bayou Buffalo / Would You Be Waiting
276 – Eddie Noack – The Worm Has Turned / She Can't Stand the Light of Day
277 – Harry Carroll – Two-Timin' / Checkerboard Lover
278 – Tibby Edwards – I Don't Want To Say I Love You / Fool That I Was
279 – George Jones and Jeanette Hicks – Yearning / Jeanette Hicks – So Near (Yet So Far Away)
280 – Bill Mack – It's Saturday Night / That's Why I Cry
281 – Neal Merritt – I've Got To Cry / The Funniest Feeling
282 – Slim Watts – Tu-La-Lou / Painted Lady
283 – Larry Fox – Guilty Heart / Don't Hold Me Close
284 – Harry Choates – Tondelay / Basile Waltz
285 – Jimmy Lee Durden – Time Heals Everything / No Mistake
286 – Jimmie Logsdon – No Longer / Can't Make Up My Mind
287 – Margie Singleton – One Step (Nearer To You) / Not What He's Got

288 – Peggy Upton and Danny Buck – What'cha Gonna Do Tonight / Our Love Is Not the Same
289 – Bill Boyd and his Cowboy Ramblers – Big D / Texas Star
290 – Bill Clifton, Dixie Mountain Boys – Flowers from the Hillside / Take Back the Heart
291 – Hoot and Curley – You Little Devil / Lonesome and Lovesick
292 – Sleepy La Beff – I'm Through / All Alone
293 – Link Davis – Slippin' and Slidin' Sometimes / Allons A Lafayette
294 – Eddie Skelton – Let Me Be With You Forever / My Heart Gets Lonely
295 – Special Disc Jockey Release – George Jones and the Jones Boys – No Money In This Deal / Slim Coxx – Mocking Bird Special / Dorothy Blakley – Tickle the Ivories / Herbie Remington – Remington Swing / Dorothy Blakley – Raggin' the Piano / Herbie Remington – Ragged But Right
296 – Ray Lunsford – Carroll County Blues / Mt. Vernon Rag
297 – Jim Eanes and the Shenandoah Valley Boys – Your Old Standby / Don't Stop Now
298 – King Sterling – Not Much / What Will Your Answer Be
299 – Jimmy Blakley – Crazy Blues / Jimmy and Dorothy Blakley – Runaway Heart
300 – Hobo Jack and his Kentucky Pals – Four Little Words / Mountain Music
301 – Utah Carl – Sometime / Lovin' You
302 – Arlie Duff and the Duff Family – What A Way To Die / You've Done It Again
303 – Bill Boyd and his Cowboy Ramblers – Lone Star Rag / Rambler's March
304 –
305 – Orville Couch – You're Dreamin' / King For A Day
306 – Peggy Upton and Danny Buck – Alone, Sorry and Blue / Knocking
307 – The Flat Mountain Boys – Choo Choo Coming / I Could Love You (All the Time)
308 – Harlin and Stanley and the Wright Brothers – Carolina Mountain Home / What Can I Do
309 – Margie Singleton – My Picture of You / Love Is A Treasure
310 – Jack Cardwell – Hey Hey Baby / Once Every Day
311 – Dave Woolum – It's So Nice / Done Gone and Done It
312 – Jim Eanes and the Shenandoah Valley Boys – No Need To Be Lonely / Walk Slowly
313 – Bill Mack – Cheatin' On Your Mind / Million Miles Away
314 – Fred Crawford – By the Mission Wall / You're Not the Same Sweet Girl
315 – Eddie Skelton – That's Love / No Sweetheart Tonight
316 – Eddie Noack – Think Of Her Now / Scarecrow
317 – Fiddlin' Rufus Thibodeaux – Cameron Memorial Waltz / Mean Audrey
318 – Jimmy and Dorothy Blakley – Pair of Crazy Hearts / Making Believe You're Mine
319 – Sleepy Jeffers and the Davis Twins – My Blackbirds Are Bluebirds Now / The Davis Twins and Sleepy Jeffers – Pretending Is a Game
320 – The Marksmen – Don't Gamble With My Heart / You Hurt Me So
321 – Rudy "Tutti" Grayzell – Let's Get Wild / I Love You So
322 – Utah Carl – Stormy Skies / Don't Go Wrong
323 – Margie Singleton – Take Time Out For Love / Beautiful Dawn
324 – King Sterling with the Scott York Singers – Raindrops / Crying For You
325 – Bill and Mary Reid and the Melody Mountaineers – In the Valley / She Can't Stand the Light of Day
326 – Orville Couch – I Will If You Will / Five Cent Candy
327 – Hobo Jack – Lonesome Old Road / Just Wishing

328 – Harley Gabbard and Aubrey Holt, the Logan Valley Boys – You'll Never Find Another / Burning the Strings
329 – Lucky Hill – I'm Missing You / Wait For Me
330 – Lonnie Smithson – Me and the Blues / It Takes Time
331 – Link Davis – Big Coonie (Two Step) / Waltz of the Jambalaya
332 – Herby Remington – Slush Pump / Station Break
333 – Ray and Lindy – Hey Doll Baby / Love Must Be In the Air
334 – Eddie Noack – Dust on the River / What's the Matter, Joe?
335 – Gary Bryant – My Kind of Girl / Since You're Gone
336 – Cecil Bowman and the Arrows – Blues Around My Door / Too Late
337 – Tommy Riddle – Starlight Starbright / Stolen Love
338 –
339 – Sunshine Boys – Lead Me (To That Rock) / Peace In the Valley / (My Soul's Been) Satisfied / Then I Met the Master
340 – Cactus Pryor – Sputnik (part one) / Sputnik (part two)
341 – Nelson Young and Trio – So Easy To Fall In Love / Sunrise
342 – Ray Anderson and the Home Folks – Dreaming / Sputniks and Mutniks
343 – Bill and Mary Reid and the Melody Mountaineers – I Want To Be Wanted / Beautie Cutie
344 – The Country Gentlemen – Dixie / Backwoods Blues
345 – Andy Doll, 7 Men and 17 Instruments – You Can't Stop Me From Dreaming / That's Life (Ho Ho)
346 – Short C&W Instrumentals – Tommy Jackson – Fiddlin' Joe / The Country Gentlemen – Banjo in the Backwoods / Roy Russell – Fiddle on the Hill / Herbie Remington – Station Break / Dobber Johnson and the Louisiana Bluegrass Boys – Pickin' Cotton / Dorothy Blakley – Ragtime Piano Polka
347 – The Country Gentlemen – Charlie Waller, Bill Emerson, John Duffey – Backwoods Blues / It's the Blues
348 – Ray and Lindy – Little Miss Love / I Give Up
349 – Darnell Miller – Cardboard Sweetheart / She's Gone
350 – Hobo Jack Adkins – Now That You're Gone / Baby Tell Me Why
351 – Jubilaires Quartet – What A Friend . . . / Oh Come Unto Me
352 – Cliff Blakley – Want To Be With You / High Steppin'
353 – The Sunshine Boys with guitar acc. by Sid (Hardrock) Gunter – Jubilee's A-Comin' / When I Looked Up (And He Looked Down) / I Believe In the Man In the Sky / This Heart of Mine
354 – Ray Anderson – Give Me the Flowers Now / My Old Clay Home / The City of Shut Ins / Old Time Church
355 – Buzz Busby and the Bayou Boys – Talking Banjo / Lonesome Road
356 – Roger Miller – Can't Stop Lovin' You / You're Forgetting Me
357 – Dorothy Blakley – Piano Polka / Dorothy and Jimmy Blakley – Slowpoke Rag
358 – The Lewis Family – You Can't Do Wrong (And Get By) / Where There's a Will / A Voice from Heaven / The Old Gospel Ship
359 – Lonnie Smithson – Quarter In the Jukebox / Will You
360 – Bill Mack – Blue / Faded Rose
361 – Carl Trantham with the Rhythm All Stars – Deedle Deedle Dum / Our True Love
362 – Ballard Brothers – Craving Your Loving / Nobody But You
363 – Hobo Jack Adkins – Will They Have A Resting Place / Kentucky School Bus
364 – Dave Dudley – Careless Fool / Cry Baby

365 – Cousin Jody and his Country Cousins – Beyond the Next Hilltop / Lady Cop / Jody's Chimes / Blues In Reserve
366 – Short C&W Instrumentals – Bill Wimberly's Country Rhythm Boys – Swing Fiddle Rag / Bill Clifton and his Dixie Mountain Boys – Cedar Grove / Al Petty – Steel Guitar Twist / George Jones' String Band – Opry Rag / Bill Wimberly and Thumbs Carlisle – Springfield Guitar Social / Allen Shelton – Bending the Strings
367 – The Country Gentlemen – High Lonesome / Hey, Little Girl
368 – The Raindrops – I Don't Want A Sweetheart / The Raindrops, featuring Johnny Harrison – The Golden Stairway
369 – Cliff Blakley – Get Off My Toe / I'm Not Going Steady Anymore
370 – Ken Hammock and his Tennessee Valley Gang – Now or Never / Gotta Find Some Way
371 – Brewster Bros. and Four Bros. Quartet – Cross Over Jordan / Brewster Bros. – Dixie Rag
372 – Lenze and Oscar – Deep Thinking / Lonzo and Oscar – Have A Little Faith In Me / Peapickers Quartet – Talk With Jesus / Lonzo and Oscar – Things Look Silly
373 – The Raindrops featuring Johnny Harrison – I Don't Want a Sweetheart / Blue
374 – The Raindrops featuring Johnny Harrison – But I Love You / Raindrops
375 – Dale Johnson and the Rhythm Kings – Can't Do Nothin' At All / Want You, Need You
376 – The Southland Trio – Angel Band / Gone Home / Insurance (Beyond the Grave) / Shout and Shine
377–400 –
401 – Benny Barnes with the Echoes – You Gotta Pay / Heads You Win (Tails I Lose)
402 – Jack Kingston – Go Away (And Leave Me) / When the Bright Lights Grow Dim
403 – Lattie Moore – Why Did You Lie To Me / You Never Looked Sweeter
404 – Opry Star Lonzo and Oscar – Deep Thinking / Have A Little Faith In Me
405 – Cousin Jody – Beyond the Next Hilltop / Blues In Reserve
406 – Stanley Brothers – Gonna Paint the Town / That Happy Night
407 – Jim Eanes with the Shenandoah Valley Boys – Don't Make Me Ashamed / Blue Sunday
408 – Country Gentlemen – Dixie Look Away / Buzz Busby – Mandolin Tango / Bill Emerson and John Hall – Deep South / Bill Wimberly Band – Thumbs Guitar Boogie / Dobber Johnson – Swamp Fever / Bill Emerson and John Hall – Banjo Whiz
409 – Buzz Busby – Lost / Lonesome Wind
410 – Phil Sullivan with Lonzo and Oscar's Peapickers – Luckiest Man In Town / Love Never Dies
411 – Carl Story and his Rambling Mountaineers – Angel Band / Old Country Baptizing
412 – Jim and Jesse and the Virginia Boys – Pardon Me / Hard Hearted
413 – Stanley Brothers and the Clinch Mountain Boys – Holiday Pickin' / Christmas Is Near
414 – Jim Eanes with the Shenandoah Valley Boys – It Won't Seem Like Christmas / Christmas Doll
415 – Charlie Waller and John Duffey with the Country Gentlemen – The Devil's Own / Rollin' Stone
416 – Jack Kingston – Don't Trade / You
417 – Bill Clifton – When You Kneel (At Mother's Grave) / You Go To Your Church (I'll Go To Mine)

418 – Bill Mack – Long, Long Train / I'll Still Be Here Tomorrow
419 – The Kentucky Travelers – Living My Life In Vain / Old Kentucky Hills
420 – Billie Morgan – Life To Live / Thinking All Night
421 – Red Kirk – Dark Streets / I Wonder
422 – Darnell Miller with the Swing Kings – Royal Flush / Mommy, Will My Doggie Understand?
423 – Rusty York with Willard Hale – Don't Do It / The Lock On Your Heart
424 – Frankie Miller – Black Land Farmer / True Blue
425 – Buzz Busby – Going Home / Me and the Juke Box
426 – Jim Eanes and the Shenandoah Valley Boys – Orchids of Love / Road Walked By Fools
427 – Carl Story with the Rambling Mountaineers – Shout and Shine / A Beautiful City
428 – Anna Lee and the King's Messengers – Never Walk Alone / A Thousand Times No
429 – Tommy Hill – Oil On My Land / Walls Of Stone
430 – The Southlan Trio – Have They Forgotten Jesus? / I'm Going Home
431 – Bill Clifton and the Dixie Mountain Boys – Corey / I'll Wander Back Someday
432 – Bill Browning and his Echo Valley Boys – Don't Push—Don't Shove / Dark Valley Walls
433 – Jim & Jesse and the Virginia Boys – Let Me Whisper / Border Ride
434 – Charlie Waller and John Duffey with the Country Gentlemen – I'll Never Marry / Travelin' Dobro Blues
435 – Billie Morgan – Too Weak (To Go Home) / Billie Morgan and Eddie Hill – Move Over
436 – Lonzo & Oscar – Gotta Find Julie / Hills of East Tennessee
437 – Phil Sullivan – Hearts Are Lonely / Rich Man—Po Boy
438 – Stanley Brothers and the Clinch Mountain Boys – Trust Each Other / Beneath the Maple (On the Hill)
439 – Buddy Starcher – The Battle of New Orleans / Pale Wildwood Flower
440 – Wayne Raney with his Talking Harmonica – Country Express / The Stanley Brothers – Banjo In the Hills / The Country Gentlemen – Mountaineers Fling / The Country Gentlemen – Orange Blossom Fiddle / Bill Clifton – Dixie Ramble / Rusty York and Willard Hale – Banjo Breakdown
441 – Lattie Moore – Too Hot To Handle / Just A Waitin'
442 – Ken Clark and the Merry Mountain Boys – Pretty Love / Buckskin Coat
443 – Margie Singleton – It's Better To Know / Nothin' But True Love
444 – Bill Clifton and the Dixie Mountain Boys – You Go To Your Church (I'll Go To Mine) / When You Kneel (At Mother's Grave)
445 – Bill Harrell and his Virginia Mountaineers – Tragic Highway / Love Is A Stranger
446 – Denver Duke and Jeffrey Null – Trouble Number Two / I'll Say I Do
447 – Bill Clifton and the Dixie Mountain Boys – Take Back the Heart / Gathering Flowers (From the Hillside)
448 – Hobo Jack Adkins – Union Man / Country Boy Went To Town
449 – Carl Story and his Rambling Mountaineers – Old Gospel Ship / Set Your House In Order
450 – The Kentucky Travelers – Dreaming / That Old Moon
451 – Little Jimmy Dempsey with his Cherokee Country Boys – Honky Tonk World / Answer From Your Heart
452 – Buzz Busby – Reno Bound / Where Will This End

453 – Bill Mack – Johnny's Gal Frankie / Loneliest Fool In Town
454 – A Sermon by Rev. Barney Pierce – Gossip / Hell Bound Train
455 – Charlie Waller and John Duffey with the Country Gentlemen – New Freedom Bell / The Hills and Home
456 – Jim Eanes and the Shenandoah Valley Boys – Budded Roses / Log Cabin In the Lane
457 – Frankie Miller – Family Man / Poppin' Johnny
458 – Jim and Jesse and the Virginia Boys – Nobody But You / Have You Lost Your Love For Me
459 – Darnell Miller – Back To You / Mark of Cain
460 – Starcher Buddy – Running Away (From the Blues) / Buddy Starcher – Billy the Kid
461 – Lex Thomas – Man Alone / Dixie Line
462 – Phil Sullivan – You Get A Thrill / I Could Never Be Alone
463 – Lonzo and Oscar – I'm My Own Grandpa / Bare Face - Bird Brain
464 – Billie Morgan – Country Girl At Heart / Treatin' Me (The Way You Do)
465 – Carl Story and his Rambling Mountaineers – I'll Be a Friend / I Heard My Mother Weeping
466 – Stanley Brothers with the Clinch Mountain Boys – Another Night / Highway of Regret
467 – Williams Brothers – Old Birmingham Jail / So Remember Me (also released as by The Edwards Brothers)
468 – Ken Clark & his Merry Mountain Boys – South Pacific Shore / Candy Man
469 – Merle Kilgore – Dear Mama / Jimmie Bring Sunshine
470 – Jimmy Jay – Run Wild (While You're Young) / You're Cheap As You Can Be (But You're Everything To Me)
471 – Buddy Starcher – Cryin' / Ace of Hearts
472 – Margie Singleton – The Eyes of Love / Angel Hands
473 – Lex Thomas – Call Me / St. Louie On the River
474 – Bill Clifton and the Dixie Mountain Boys – When Autumn Leaves Begin To Fall / Walking In My Sleep
475 – Cal and Ivan – Lazy (Part 1) / Lazy (Part 2)
476 – Cowboy Copas – Black Cloud Risin' / Mom and Dad's Affair
477 – Bill Clifton – Dixie Mountain Express / Country Gentlemen – Travelin' Dobro / Ken Clark – Merry Mountain Hoedown / Earl Mitton – Snowflake Breakdown / Jim and Jesse –Dixie Hoedown / Cal and Ivan – Lazy
478 – The Barnette Brothers – Gonna Lean On the Lord / Say No To Sin
479 – Denver Duke and Jeffrey Null – Dear Lord, Let Me Die / I'm Gonna Get You
480 – Bill Harrell – Eatin' Out of Your Hand / A Heart Never Knows
481 – Frankie Miller – The Money Side of Life / Reunion (With Dinner on the Ground)
482 – Jim Eanes – Celebration / Road of No Return
483 – Buzz Busby – Cold and Windy Night / Don't Come Runnin' Back To Me
484 – Kirby Buchanan – Timbrook / His Hand On My Shoulder
485 – Kirby Buchanan – Timbrook / A Satisfied Mind
486 – Lonnie Irving – Pinball Machine / I Got Blues On My Mind
487 – Charlie Waller and John Duffey with the Country Gentlemen – A Letter To Tom / Darling Alalee
488 – Bill Browning – Down In the Hollow / Country Strings
489 – Billie Morgan – I Had To Talk To Someone / I'll Accept What I Can't Change

RECORD LISTING

490 – Connie and Joe, the Backwoods Boys – My Dollie Would Cry / Toil, Tears and Trouble
491 – Lonzo & Oscar – I Lost An Angel / Blue Love
492 – Carl Story and his Rambling Mountaineers – (I Heard My Name) On the Radio / Sweeter Than the Flowers
493 – Cowboy Copas – That's All I Can Remember / South Pacific Shore
494 – Stanley Brothers and the Clinch Mountain Boys – A Little at a Time / Ridin' That Midnite Train
495 – Ken Clark – Big Man / Days That Once Have Been
496 – Frankie Miller – Rain Rain / Baby Rocked Her Dolly
497 – Merle Kilgore with recitation by Jimmy Jay – Getting Old Before My Time / Merle Kilgore – Love Has Made You Beautiful
498 – Bill Clifton and the Dixie Mountain Boys – You Don't Think About Me (When I'm Gone) / Mail Carrier's Warning
499 – Dave Dudley – It's Gotta Be That Way / Where Do I Go From Here
500 – Bill Harrell – One Track Mind / I'll Never See You Anymore
501 – Cowboy Copas – Alabam / I Can
502 – Margie Singleton – My Special Dream / For the Love of Jim
503 – Jimmie King – Over My Shoulder / That Old Girl of Mine
504 – Jim Eanes and the Shenandoah Valley Boys – I Gotta Know / There'll Come A Time
505 – Lonnie Irving featuring Frank Burris, Guitarist – Gooseball Brown / An Old Fashioned Love
506 – The Stanley Brothers – Rank Stranger / Gathering Flowers For the Master's Bouquet
507 – Benny Martin – Hobo / Her Baby Girl
508 – Lonnie Mullins – Thirteen Miles (From the Tennessee Line) / I'll Be Your Fool Again
509 – Paul Wayne – Angel on Paper / Stolen Love
510 – Red Sovine – One Is A Lonely Number / Burna the School
511 – Ray Hendrix – My Last Memory / Last Night
512 – Connie and Joe, The Backwoods Boys – Home Is Where the Heart Is / Lonely Years
513 – Frankie Miller – Young Widow Brown / Strictly Nuthin'
514 – Carl Story and his Rambling Mountaineers – Someone's Last Day / Ship That's Sailing Down
515 – Charlie Waller and John Duffey and the Country Gentlemen – Helen / Poor Ellen Smith
516 – The Kentucky Travelers – Will There Be A Rainbow / When You're Out of My Arms
517 – Dottie West – Angel On Paper / No Time Will I Ever
518 – The Willis Brothers, Oklahoma Wranglers – Pretty Diamonds / Billy the Kid
519 – Benny Martin – Dime's Worth of Dreams / Pretty Girl
520 – Lonnie Irving – Trucker's Vitus / I Wish I Had My Heart Back
521 – Red Sovine – If I Could Come Back / No Money In This Deal
522 – The Stanley Brothers and the Clinch Mountain Boys – Little Maggie / God Gave You To Me
523 – Lonzo and Oscar – Takin' A Chance With You / Punkin Raiser
524 – Cowboy Copas – I Have A Friend / The Hem of His Garment
525 – Frankie Miller and Dottie Sills – Two Lips Away / Out of Bounds
526 – Bill Parsons – Hot Rod Volkswagen / Guitar Blues
527 – Moon Mullican – New Jole Blon / Farewell

528 – Cowboy Copas with his guitar and string band – Settin' Flat on Ready / Cowboy Copas with the Cathey Copas Trio – Midnight In Heaven
529 – Bill Clifton and the Dixie Mountain Boys – Bed On the Floor / Railroading On the Great Divide
530 – Justin Tubb – One Eyed Red / I'd Know You Anywhere
531 – Carl Story and his Rambling Mountaineers – Get Religion / Jerusalem Moan
532 – The Willis Brothers, Oklahoma Wranglers – Little Footprints In the Snow / Y'all Come
533 – Merle Kilgore – Just Another Song Now / Daddy's Place
534 – Billy Todd – Lonely Hearts / Drop Me Gently
535 – Jim Eanes and the Shenandoah Valley Boys – Mark of Cain / Borderline
536 – Benny Martin and Joanne Martin – No One But You / Benny Martin – You Are the One
537 – Frankie Miller – Richest Poor Boy / I'll Write To You
538 – Jimmy Simpson – Old Timer / The Alcan Run
539 – Bob Steele – Let Me Talk To You / Nothin' To Lose
540 – Red Sovine – Why Baby Why / Little Rosa
541 – Paul Wayne – Dreams / Troubles (On My Mind)
542 – Cowboy Copas – Flat Top / Cowboy Copas with the Cathey Copas Trio – True Love (Is the Greatest Thing)
543 – Lonzo and Oscar – Country Music Time / Can't Pitch Woo (In An Igloo)
544 – Bill Parsons – A-Waitin' / The Price We Pay For Livin'
545 – Moon Mullican – Ragged But Right / Bottom of the Glass
546 – The Stanley Brothers and the Clinch Mountain Boys – If I Lose / Don't Go Out Tonight
547 – Dottie West – I Should Start Running / I Lost, You Win, I'm Leaving
548 – Bill Clifton and the Dixie Mountain Boys – I'm Rollin' On / I'll Be All Smile Tonight
549 – Justin Tubb – My Heart Keeps Getting In the Way / One For You—One For Me
550 – Frankie Miller – A Little Bit's Better (Than Nothing At All) / Lookin' Around Downtown
551 – Cousin Ezra and the Lonesome Pine Fiddlers – Why Do You Treat Me the Way You Do / Two Kinds Of Blues
552 – Cowboy Copas – Sunny Tennessee / Cowboy Copas and Cathey Copas – Dreaming
553 – Red Sovine – Brand New Low / Heart of A Man
554 – Jim Eanes and the Shenandoah Valley Boys – Mary Was A Little Lamb / You Made Me What I Am
555 – The Willis Brothers – Tattooed Lady / The Willis Brothers with T. Tommy "The Big Daddy" – Everlovin' Dixieland
556 – Moon Mullican – Just Plain Lonesome / The Way You're Treatin' Me
557 – Archie Campbell – Grab A Little Sunshine / Sergeant York
558 – Charlie Waller and John Duffey with the Country Gentlemen – Red Rockin' Chair / I Know I've Lost You
559 – Cowboy Copas – Signed Sealed and Delivered / New Filipino Baby
560 – Justin Tubb – How's It Feel / Your Side of the Story
561 – Bill Clifton and the Dixie Mountain Boys – Bring Back My Blue Eyed Boy To Me / Cannonball Blues
562 – Moon Mullican – I'll Sail My Ship Alone / Mona Lisa
563 – Lonzo and Oscar – Honey Babe / The Touch of You
564 – The Lonesome Pine Fiddlers – Eatin' Out Of Your Hand / Lonesome Pine

565 – The Stanley Brothers and the Clinch Mountain Boys – Carolina Mountain Home / A Few More Seasons
566 – Frankie Miller – The Cat and the Mouse / It's Not Easy
567 – Red Sovine – Color of the Blues / Hold Everything
568 – Archie Campbell – A Womans Work Is Never Done / Settin' My Tears To Music
569 – The Kentucky Travelers – Beyond A Doubt / Wishing
570 – The Willis Brothers with T. Tommy "The Big Daddy" – Big Daddy / The Willis Brothers – It's the Miles
571 – Buck Owens – There Goes My Love / It Don't Show On Me
572 – Red Allen and the Kentuckians, Frank Wakefield on mandolin – Trouble Round My Door / Beautiful Blue Eyes
573 – Cowboy Copas – A Thousand Miles of Ocean / Sal
574 – Dottie West – My Big John / Men With Evil Hearts
575 – Pete Drake – Pleading / The Spook
576 – Arthur "Guitar Boogie" Smith – Guitar Boogie Twist / Napoleon's Retreat
577 – Frankie Miller – The Picture at St. Helene / Gotta Win My Baby Back Again
578 – Hylo Brown – Hills of Georgia / Picture in the Wallet
579 – Red Sovine – East of West Berlin / Thanks For Nothing
580 – Bill Clifton and his Dixie Mountain Boys – March Winds / Give Me Your Love
581 – Hardrock Gunter and Buddy Durham – Hillbilly Twist / As Long As You're Happy
582 – Justin Tubb – They Painted A Picture For Me / Walking the Floor Over You
583 – Stringbean – Down At the Opry / Chewin' Chewing Gum
584 – "Little" Roy Wiggins – Love Theme / Thru the Night
585 – Cowboy Copas – Seven Seas From You / Cowboy Copas and Cathy Copas –There'll Come A Time Someday
586 – Smiley Burnette – Old Fishin' Pole / It's My Lazy Day
587 – The Stanley Brothers and the Clinch Mountain Boys – Come All Ye Tenderhearted / Choo Choo Comin'
588 – Buck Owens – Down on the Corner of Love / Right After the Dance
589 – Ramona Jones – Don't Sell Daddy Anymore Whiskey / Fiddler Joe
590 – Arthur "Guitar Boogie" Smith – Heartaches / Foolish Questions—Silly Answers
591 – George Jones – Boat of Life / The Acorn Sisters – Where Will I Shelter My Sheep
592 – The Willis Brothers – Sally's Bangs / Honey, Do You Love Your Man
593 – Hylo Brown – Rose of Love / Take A Look
594 – Moon Mullican – Good Times Gonna Roll Again (In Sunny Tennessee) / Cowboy Copas – The Ballad of Frank Clement (The Living Legend of Tennessee) [released on blue Dixie label]
595 – Cowboy Copas – Sold the Farm / Table In the Corner
596 – Moon Mullican – Ain't Nothin' Like Lovin' / Good Times Gonna Roll Again (In Sunny Tennessee)
597 – The Lonesome Pine Fiddlers featuring the Goins Brothers – Mountain Flower / Little Glass of Wine
598 – Red Sovine – She Can't Read My Writing / Rose of Love
599 – The Stoneman Family, fiddle by Scotty Stoneman – That Pal of Mine / The Stoneman Family, vocal by Scotty Stoneman – Talking Fiddle Blues
600 – Archie Campbell – Fools Side of Town / Root Beer
601 – Hylo Brown – Time / The Girl in the Blue Velvet Band
602 – Bashful Brother Oswald – Beneath the Willow / Black Smoke

603 – Buddy Meredith – Secret Sin / I Miss You All Over (More Than Anywhere)
604 – The Willis Brothers – Morning Glory / Yankee Dollar
605 – Melvin Morris – Spending Nights in Nashville / Still
606 – Cowboy Copas – Bury Me Face Down / Heart On the Run
607 – Tom O'Neal – Too Many Tickets / Sleeper Cab Blues
608 – Bill Clifton and the Dixie Mountain Boys – There's a Star Spangled Banner Waving Somewhere / Sinking of the Maine
609 – Archie Campbell – Don't You Ever Fret / The Master's Hand
610 – Paul Wayne – Turned Her Back / You're Just Filling In
611 – Tommy Hill's Nashville String Band, Shorty Lavender and Buddy Spiker on fiddles – Twin Fiddle Polka / K. C. Train Whistle Blues
612 – Cowboy Copas – Family Reunion / Smoke On the Water
613 – Hylo Brown – The Prisoner's Song / Treasures From the Past
614 – The Lonesome Pine Fiddlers – Hello Mr. Banjo / Coal Dust Blues
615 – Arthur "Guitar Boogie" Smith – Hospitality Blues / Philadelphia Guitar
616 – Red Sovine – Sittin' and Thinkin' / A Million To One
617 – Buddy Meredith – A Heart Is No Plaything / Here I Am Again
618 – Johnny Bond – How To Succeed With Girls (Without Half-Way Trying) / Don't Mention Her Name
619 – Carl Story and his Rambling Mountaineers – Rank Stranger / A Picture From Life's Other Side
620 – Leon Payne – Joe Lopez / You Stood Me Up This Morning ('Cause I Let You Down Last Night)
621 – Cowboy Copas – Goodbye Kisses / The Gypsy Girl
622 – Hylo Brown – Daddy's Place / Seasons Of My Heart
623 – Benny Martin – Rosebuds and You / Sinful Cinderella
624 – Archie Campbell – My Baby's Home / A World Full Of Women
625 – The Willis Brothers – Ax Cabin / Pvt. Lee
626 – Curly Fox – The Old Grey Mule / Texas Ruby – Shanty Street
627 – Jimmie Skinner – Trouble Walked In / Old Bill Dollar
628 – The Country Gentlemen – Copper Kettle / Sunrise
629 – Tom O'Neal – I Stumble, I Fumble, I Fall / Blue Endless Highway
630 – Bobby Sykes – Run, Johnny, Run / A Place For Girls Like You
631 – The Lonesome Pine Fiddlers – Too Hot To Handle / I Walked To the River
632 – Red Sovine – I Forgot To Keep Her With Me / Waltzing With Sin
633 – Paul Wayne – I've Lost My Biggest Race / Whole Lot of Blues
634 – Arthur "Guitar Boogie" Smith – Master of the Game (Duffer's Dream) / Travelin' Blues
635 – Howdy Kempf – One Last Time / Take My Hand Take My Heart
636 – Johnny Bond – True Love (Is So Hard To Find) / Cimarron
637 – Leon Payne – Close To You / Log Train
638 – Hylo Brown – Take A Look At That Rain / Tiny Doll
639 – Gene Martin and June Stearns – Three Sides to the Story / June Stearns – Just Another Song
640 – Glenda Raye – Don't Be Surprised / You Sent Her An Orchid (And You Sent Me A Rose)
641 – Cowboy Copas – Break Away, Break Away / Louisian
642 – Arthur "Guitar Boogie" Smith – Guitar Hop / Tie My Hunting Dog Down, Jed
643 – Archie Campbell – Don't Let Love Die / Crying In My Pillow
644 – Merle Kilgore – Pinball Machine / Old Smokey

645 – The Willis Brothers – Truck Driver's Queen / Who's Next On Your List
646 – Benny Martin – 2 – 1: Lonesome (Two Take Away One Equals Lonesome) / Down In the Shinerry
647 – Jimmie Skinner – Yesterday's Wrongs / Try To Be Good
648 – Howard Vokes – The Miner / Death On the Highway
649 – Johnny Bond – Let the Tears Begin / Three Sheets In the Wind
650 – Red Sovine – Dream House For Sale / King of the Open Road
651 – Tillman Franks and the Cedar Grove Three – Tadpole / Pretty Little Girls
652 – The Blue Sky Boys, Bill & Earl Bolick – Don't Trade / Kentucky
653 – Clyde Moody – Nobody's Business / Waltzing In the Arms of A Friend
654 – Bobby Sykes – Good Girl Bad / I Should Start Running
655 – Frankie Miller – A Little South of Memphis / Too Hot To Handle
656 – Arthur "Guitar Boogie" Smith – The Stuttering Song / Back To His Hole He Went
657 – Howdy Kempf – I Can't Tell My Heart To Let You Go / Only For You
658 – Cowboy Copas – Autobiography / The Rainbow and the Rose
659 – Hylo Brown – The Hole In the Wall / The Room Over Mine
660 – Gene Martin & June Stearns – Family Man / We've Got Things In Common
661 –
662 –
663 – Wayne Raney – Mail Order Heart / Don't Try To Be What You Ain't
664 – Stringbean – Big Ball In Nashville / Little Pink
665 – Johnny Bond – Have You Seen My Baby / What Have You Done For Me Lately
666 – Leon Payne – September Memory / Six Foot Six
667 – The Blue Sky Boys – A Satisfied Mind / Why Not Confess
668 – Pee Wee King and Redd Stewart – Goodbye New Orleans / Waitin'
669 – Jimmie Skinner – The Cork and the Bottle / Let's Say Goodbye Like We Said Hello
670 – Tillman Franks Singers – Uncle Eph / When the World's On Fire
671 – Clyde Moody – Where There's Smoke (There's Bound To Be Fire) / Whispering Pines
672 – Red Sovine – Old Pipeliner / Peace of Mind
673 – Frankie Miller – Out of This World / 15 Acres of Peanut Land
674 – Cecil L. Boykin – She Walked Away / Gonna Get On the Riverboat
675 – Rose Lee Maphis – Remember (I'm Just As Close As the Phone) / Joe and Rose Lee Maphis – Hoot 'N Annie
676 – Glenn Barber – Stronger Than Dirt / If Anyone Can Show Cause
677 – Wayne Raney – Strictly Nothing / Love Thief
678 – Johnny Bond – Hot Rod Surfin' Hootlebeatnanny / Don't Mamma Count Anymore
679 – The Homesteaders – Leaving But I Won't Be Long / Sing Me a Sad Song
680 – Hylo Brown – Silent Partner / Sad Prison Song
681 – The Willis Brothers – Give Me 40 Acres (To Turn This Rig Around) / Gonna Buy Me A Juke Box
682 – Pee Wee King and Redd Stewart – When the Lights Go Dim Downtown / Stay Away From Me
683 – Joe Maphis "The King of the Strings" – Hot Rod Guitar / Lonesome Jailhouse Blues
684 – Adrian Roland – Toc Tic / Exactly Like Him
685 – Cowboy Copas – Pretty Diamonds / An Old Man's Story
686 – Wilf Carter (Montana Slim) – Grandad's Yodelling Song / The Little Shirt My Mother Made For Me
687 – Jimmie Skinner – This Old Road / Things That Might Have Been

688 – Carl Story – The Old Country Preacher / Listen To Your Radio
689 – Wayne Raney – Young Widow Brown / I Stumble, I Fumble, I Fall
690 – Johnny Bond – Bachelor Bill / My Wicked, Wicked Ways
691 – Frankie Miller – It Took A Lot of Love / Mean Old Greyhound Bus
692 – Betty Amos with Judy & Jean – More Than Your Money / Eighteen Wheels A Rolling
693 – Howdy Kempf – Baby Take Me / I Don't Believe
694 – Ken Cameron – Just One More Time / Say You Will
695 – The Homesteaders – Carry Me Down This River / Comin Back For More
696 – Dean Manuel with the Blueboys and Pete Drake's steel guitar – Maggie / Ida
697 – Hylo Brown – Walk Slowly Darling / When the Bright Lights Grow Dim
698 – Pee Wee King & Redd Stewart – Ten Thousand Crying Towels / The Urge
699 – Glenn Barber – Dancing Shoes / Knock Knock
700 – Adrian Roland – Better Judgment / Until My Ink Runs Out
701 – Arthur "Guitar Boogie" Smith – I Like 'Lasses / Flat Top Hari Kari
702 – Clyde Moody – Dark Midnight /What It Means To Be Lonesome
703 – Willis Brothers – Too Early To Get Up / Blazing Smokestack
704 – Johnny Bond – 10 Little Bottles / Let It Be Me
705 – Benny "Big Tige" Martin – Stick Your Finger In A Glass Of Water / The Other Me
706 – Pete Drake and his Talking Steel Guitar – Invitation to the Blues / Rick-A-Shay
707 – Cecil Boykin – Cabin In the Pines / Billy Blue Jeans
708 – Cowboy Copas – Black Eyed Suzie / Won't You Ride In My Little Red Wagon
709 – Frankie Miller – Big Talk of the Town / I Can Almost Forget
710 – Joe & Rose Lee Maphis – Hot Time In Nashville / Rose Lee Maphis – I've Come To Take You Home
711 – Jimmie Skinner – Hard Working Man / How's It Been (Since Last Heartbreak)
712 – The Homesteaders – White Rain / Diamonds For Ruby (Rubies For Pearl)
713 – The Willis Brothers – A Six Foot Two By Four / Strange Old Town
714 – Betty Amos with Judy and Jean – Steeplejack / Suzie-Suzie
715 – Hylo Brown – Outlaw Girl / I Wonder What You'll Find
716 – Kenny Roberts – Guitar Ringing / Tavern Town
717 – Joe "Red" Hayes – I Grew Up Loving You / Sunset Years
718 – Roger Miller – Playboy / Poor Little John
719 – Howdy Kemp – Heart Keep Your Big Mouth Shut / Angels Don't Love Like You Do
720 – Ken Clark – We're Too Far Apart / Standing On the Outside
721 – Johnny Bond – Sick Sober and Sorry / The Man Who Comes Around
722 – Glenn Barber – Loneliest Man In Town / She's Out of Our World
723 – Slim Jacobs – That's Truck Drivin' / Tommy Hill's String Band – Cajun Call
724 – Dottie West – Walking In the Dark / I'd Be Lying
725 – Benny Martin – Weekend Willie / One Way Or the Other
726 – Larry Kingston – Women Do Funny Things / Losers Shoes
727 – Archie Campbell – Green Stamps / The Three Little Pigs
728 – Joe and Rose Lee Maphis – Your Little Black Book / Don't Pass Me By
729 – Cowboy Copas – Waltzing With Sin / Blue Kimona
730 – The Willis Brothers – Pinball Anonymous / When I Come Driving Thru
731 – Johnny Bond – The Great Figure 8 Race / Sadie Was A Lady
732 – Adrian Roland – Weasel In the Henhouse / Two of Us Sorry
733 – The Homesteaders – Calico Bay / One Man's Sugar (Is Another Man's Salt)
734 – Coy Jackson – The Birds and Bees / What It Takes (To Make A Grown Man Cry)

RECORD LISTING

735 – Betty Amos with Judy and Jean – Franklin County Moonshine / I Can Almost Forget
736 – Kenny Roberts – If I'm Blue / Fly Away Mockingbird
737 – Red Sovine – Giddyup Go / Kiss and the Keys
738 – Jimmie Skinner – Twenty Beers / To Tell the World
739 – Frankie Miller – Bringing Mary Home / The Country Music Who's Who
740 – George Riddle – When "It" Hits the Fan / Sad Tale of Woe
741 – Glenn Barber – Let's Take the Fear (Out of Being Close) / Happy Birthday Broken Heart
742 – Hylo Brown – Trickle Down Teardrops / Someone To Care
743 – Benny Martin – I'll Never Get Over Loving You / Hello City Limits
744 – Larry Kingston – Foot In My Mouth / I'm a Flop
745 – Joe & Rose Lee Maphis – Ridin' Down Ole 99 / Turn On the Bright Lights
746 – Lule Belle and Scotty – I'll Be All Smiles Tonight / Try To Live Some (While You're Here)
747 – Rusty Diamond – I Guess I'd Better Get Up and Go Home / Rusty Diamond with Maryanne Mail – The Lonely Sentry
748 – The Willis Brothers – Love Thy Neighbor / Swing Til My Rope Breaks
749 – Johnny Bond – They Got Me / Silent Walls
750 – Cowboy Copas – Cowboy's Deck of Cards / Beyond the Sunset
751 – Pete Drake with his Talking Steel Guitar – Y'all Come / My Abilene
752 – Stringbean and his 5 String Banjo – Crazy Viet Nam War / Hey Old Man (Can You Play A Banjo)
753 – Howdy Kempf – Go Find Another Fool / Doc Doc Can You Tell
754 – Minnie Pearl – Giddyup Go—Answer / Minnie Pearl's Giddyup Go Boys – Road Runner
755 – George Riddle – What Have I Gotta Do / Set Up Another
756 – Betty Amos with Judy and Jean – The Cat and the Rat / If Mommy Didn't Sing
757 – Red Sovine – Long Night / Too Much
758 – Johnny Bond – Fireball / Over the Hill
759 – T. Texas Tyler "The Man with a Million Friends" – Texas Boogie Woogie / Just Like Dad
760 – The Willis Brothers – Three Sheets In the Wind / Waltzing With Sin
761 – Gene Brown – One For All—All For One / That's How Sure I Am
762 – Larry Kingston – Down the Drain / If Your Lips Move
763 – Buddy Starcher – Little Red Riding Hood / Ace of Hearts
764 – Minnie Pearl – Live Some While You're Here / What Is An American
765 – George Kent – Water — Whiskey and Gas / The More I See
766 – Red Sovine – I'm the Man / I Think I Can Sleep Tonight
767 – Onie Wheeler – Dancing / Mr. Free
768 – Polly Hutt and her Crackers – Why Buy the Cow / You'll Never Love Him (Like I Do)
769 – Kenny Roberts – Anytime / Trying the Leaves
770 – Hank Malcolm – Mary Turn Around / Yellow Bellied Sap Sucker
771 – Orval Prophet – The Traveling Snowman / Big River Joe
772 – Larry Edwards – Over the Wall / The Thirteenth Month of the Year
773 – Harold Lowry – Leatherneck / One Step More
774 – Red Sovine & Minnie Pearl – Alabam / Minnie Pearl & Red Sovine – Nobody's Business
775 – Howdy Kemp – Bundle of Love / It's Over Now
776 – Johnny Bond – Hell's Angels / A Way of Life
777 – Frankie Miller – Charlie's Got A Good Thing Going / A Tough Row To Hoe

778 – Betty Amos with Judy and Jean – Almost Persuaded / Why Don't You Be My Baby
779 – Red Sovine – Class of 49 / I Hope My Wife Don't Find Out
780 – Jack Lionell – She Wasn't You / Don't Let It Keep You From My Door
781 – Paul Wayne – Everything But Love / Keep the Fool You Made Me
782 – The Willis Brothers – Goin' To Town / Ain't It Funny (What A Little Drink Can Do)
783 – T. Texas Tyler – By the Way (I Still Love You) / It's A Long Road Back Home
784 – Bobby Wooten – Goin' Deer Huntin' / Deer Huntin' Widow
785 – Onie Wheeler – I Closed My Book Last Night / Playing Tricks
786 – George Riddle – This Town's Poorest Fool / Your Sweet Love Came Along (Just In Time)
787 – Roy Wiggins – Annette / You Are the One
788 – Kenny Roberts – Sioux City Sue / Blue
789 – Wade Jackson – Sippin' On A Sud / A Poor Boys Dream
790 – Johnny Bond and Red Sovine with the Giddyup Go Boys – The Gear Jammer and the Hobo / The Giddyup Go Boys featuring Joe "Red" Hayes and Little Hank Singer – Sweet Nellie
791 – Dottie Moore – The Hand That Rocks the Cradle / Losing Him by Loving You
792 – Betty Amos with Judy and Jean – Have You Ever / Raven Black
793 – Frankie Miller – Fickle Hand Of Fate / She's My Antibiotic (In White)
794 – Red Sovine – I Didn't Jump the Fence / Don't Let My Glass Run Dry
795 – Eddie McDuff – Country Comes To Town / Colored Glass
796 – The Willis Brothers – Bob / Show Her Lots of Gold
797 – Gene Brown – When Our Front Door Is Shut / Skeleton In Everybody's Closet
798 – Shirley Wood – This One Belongs To Me / When It Happens
799 – Mike Lane – Letter To a D.J. / I'm Not Allowed To Talk To Strangers
800 – George Kent – 100% Pure Lonesome / Nice Guy
801 – The Lewis Family – His Blood Now Covers My Sin / When I Reach That City (On the Hill)
802 – Tommy Dee – Roger, Ed and Gus (America's Astronaut Heroes) / School For Fools
803 – Johnny Bond – Your Old Love Letters / Si Si
804 – George Morgan – I Couldn't See / Look At the Lonely
805 – Kenny Roberts – Just Look Don't Touch / Singing River
806 – T. Texas Tyler – Crawdad Town / Injun Joe
807 – Betty Amos with Judy and Jean – He's Gone and Left Us / One More Step
808 – George Riddle – I Can Love You More / The Lovin' Land
809 – Wade Jackson – I'll Take You Back / A Big Wing Ding
810 – Larry Kingston – Moving Hand of Fate / Scratch Your Dog
811 – Red Sovine – Phantom 309 / In Your Heart
812 – The Willis Brothers – The End of the Road / Somebody Knows My Dog
813 – Johnny Bond – Don't Bite the Hand That's Feeding You / I Ain't Gonna Go
814 – George Morgan – Shiny Red Automobile / Have Some of Mine
815 – Warren Robb – I Can't Stand the Light / Before the Past Destroys Me
816 – Ray King – Big Wheel / You're Gone
817 – Betty Amos with Judy and Jean – Gotta Be Careful / An Ordinary Girl
818 – Eddie McDuff – You're A Cheater / Give A Little
819 – Guy Mitchell – Every Night Is a Lifetime / Traveling Shoes
820 – George Riddle – Some Real Good Reasons / Hanky Panky In Our Sugar Shack
821 – Jimmie Skinner – The Kind of Love She Gave To Me / I'd Rather Take the Blame

822 – Gene Brown – China Girl / If You Want Her You Can Have Her
823 – Red Sovine – Tell Maude I Slipped / Not Like It Was With You
824 – Arthur Smith – British Back Beat / Lynn's Gone
825 – George Morgan – Barbara / Sad Bird
826 – Johnny Bond – Bottom of the Bottle / I'm Gonna Raise Cain (While I'm Able)
827 – Billy Golden – Life's Little Pleasures / A Loser Makin' Good
828 – Guy Mitchell – Irene Good-by / Alabam
829 – Snooky Lanson – Take Your Time / Woman Gone Bad
830 – Willis Brothers – Ode to Big Joe / Drivin's In My Blood
831 – Red Sovine – Twenty-One / Sparkling Wine
832 – Warren Robb – Temporarily Mine / Push-Ups From the Ceiling
833 – Ray King – Where He Lives / Curves and In Betweens
834 – George Morgan – Living / Rosebuds and You
835 – Charlie Hamilton – I'll Never Leave San Antonio / Bad Dreams
836 – Jimmie Skinner – The Story of Bonnie and Clyde / The Stanley Brothers – Bonnie and Clyde's Getaway
837 – Pat & Darrell – Our Sleeper Cab Home / Hippie Dippy Dan
838 – Carol Lee – I Don't Believe / I'm Surprised At Me
839 – Bobby Stephenson – You're the One / I Know You're Going Away
840 – Billy Golden – Wild Wild Thing / Born Loser
841 – Tommy Faile – A Certain Little Girl / I Don't Have To—But I Do
842 – Red Sovine – Good Enough For Nothing / Loser Making Good
843 – Eddie McDuff – Part Time / Day After Never
844 – Gene Brown – Get It Over / God Made A Woman
845 – Snooky Lanson – It Ain't Easy / World of Memories
846 – Guy Mitchell – It's A New World Every Day / Frisco Line
847 – Johnny Bond – Invitation to the Blues / Down To Your Last Fool
848 – Willis Brothers – Moonlight Ride In A Diesel / Diesel Drivin' Donut Dunkin' Dan
849 – Billy Golden – Good Enough For You / I Was Born To Be In Love With You
850 – George Morgan – Sounds of Goodbye / The Ballad of the Grand Ole Opry
851 – Kenny Roberts – Country Music Singing Sensation / Fugitive of Love
852 – Red Sovine – Normally, Norma Loves Me / Live and Let Live and Be Happy
853 – Glen Campbell – For the Love of a Woman / Smokey Blue Eyes
854 – Rudy Lyle – Can I Come Back Again / Brown Eyes Crying Over Blue
855 – Snooky Lanson – Every Night Is A Lifetime / The Ever Present Past
856 – Warren Robb – Pretty Pictures In Your Mind / More Woman Than You
857 – Red Sovine – Between Closing Time and Dawn / The Father of Judy Ann
858 – Carol Lee – With Each Thought Of You / Number Eighty Two
859 – Billy Golden – I Don't Know A Lot of Things / Me and Mine
860 – George Morgan – I'll Sail My Ship Alone / Live and Let Live and Be Happy
861 – Arthur "Guitar Boogie" Smith – What Is An American? / Psychoanalsis
862 – Snooky Lanson – Anytime / What Could I Do With Your Memory
863 – Willis Brothers – Alcohol and # 2 Diesel / My Ramblin' Boy
864 – Red Sovine – Whiskey Flavored Kisses / Blues Stay Away From Me
865 – Warren Robb – Magical Light Of Love / (How Long Does It Take) A Memory To Die
866 – Guy Mitchell – Get It Over / Just Wish You'd Maybe Change Your Mind
867 – Red Sovine – The Pledge of Allegiance / I Know You're Not An Angel
868 – Arthur "Guitar Boogie" Smith – Guitar Unlimited / Summer Theme

869 – Kenny Roberts – Artificial Flowers / Gonna Whistle Me A Tune
870 – Gene Dunlap – Six Steel Bars / One Brick At A Time
871 – Ralph Loveday and the Kinfolks – I'm Not Two Faced / You Should See Me Tomorrow
872 – Red Sovine – Who Am I / Three Hearts In A Tangle
873 – Lois Williams – He's the Man / A Corner Of Your World
874 – Willis Brothers – Buyin' Popcorn / One Thousand Acres
875 – Bobby Harden – Except For One / The Wild Ones
876 – Sylvia Mobley – Treating You Cool / Swapped For the Bottle
877 – Lois Williams – A Girl Named Sam / We've Got Another Chance
878 – Guy Mitchell – Smokey Blue Eyes / Heartaches By the Number
879 – Karen Wheeler and Bobby Harden – We Got Each Other / The Love For A Child
880 – Warren Robb – Wild Seed In the Wind / The Face of Love
881 – J. David Sloan – Something Ain't Right / Angeline
882 – Red Sovine – Chairman of the Board / Truck Driver's Prayer
883 – Judy West – Just A Bend of the Road / Tomorrow (I'm Going To Have A Talk With My Heart)
884 – Willis Brothers – Gypsy Rose and Me / Cold North Wind
885 – Red Sovine and Lois Williams – Castle of Shame / Why Don't You Haul Off and Love Me
886 – Lois Williams – From Miss to Mistake / You Low-Down Son of a Gun
887 – Tiny Harris – Blackland Farmer / Georgia Manhunt
888 – Lewie Wickham – Little Bit Late / Hank and Lewie Wickham – Endless Love Affair
889 – Red Sovine – Money, Marbles and Chalk / I Know You're Married But I Love You Still
890 – Kenny Roberts – You Left Too Much / The Bottle Holds The Man
891 – J. David Sloan – Love Can't Always Be the Way You Want It / Heaven Help My Soul
892 – Mayor Ronnie Thompson – Sittin' On the Dock of the Bay / It Couldn't Happen Again
893 – Johnny Bond – It Only Hurts When I Cry / The Girl Who Carries the Torch For Me
894 – Carl Tipton – High Heels With No Soul / Sophie Tipton – Tiger Let Me Hear Your Roar
895 – Rose Maddox – The Bigger the Pride / Faded Love
896 – Red Sovine – Mr. Sunday Sun / Freightliner Fever
897 – J. David Sloan – Young Widow Brown / Sleep Woman Sleep
898 – Charlie Collins – I've Been on the Road Too Much / Monkeys Out of Men
899 – Lois Williams – I Fell In Love With A Feller (On the Hee Haw Show) / What It Takes (To Make A Big Girl Cry)
900 – Warren Robb – Everybody's Got A Little Evil On Their Mind / A Better Way To Die
901 – Larry Downey – It's Never Too Late / Deep In the Heart of My Woman
902 – Lewie Wickham – Hippy Love Song / How Come My Dog Don't Bark (When You Come Round)
903 – The Willis Brothers – There Goes My Farm / Nashville's Ace In the Hole
904 – Gene Henslee – Life To Legend (A Tribute to Bob Wills) / Things I Want To Be
905 – Peter Breck – She's A Woman / Mornin' Road
906 – Judy West – Nashville Wives / Yes, I Know That I'm Alive
907 – Tommy Collins – The Roots of My Raising / Cigarette Milner
908 – Kenny Roberts – Green River / The Best Part of My Years

909 – Tiny Harris – King of the Highway / If I Hear It From You
910 – Mayf Nutter – Simpson Creek (Won't Never Run Clean Again) / Public Service Programming Aid, Subject: Pollution
911 – Jimmy Wolford – I Woke Up In A Tree (stereo) / I Woke Up In A Tree (mono)
912 – Beverly Wilkes – One Man Woman / Lonely Room
913 – Lois Williams – Don't Take My Child Away / I'm Looking For A Man, Boy
914 – Mayor Ronnie Thompson – Help Keep Our City Clean / Downtown Country Girl
915 – Red Sovine – Enough To Take the Me Out of Men / I'm Waiting Just For You
916 – Johnny Bond – Take Me Back to Tulsa / Here Come the Elephants
917 – Jim Single – Bobby Joe (mono) / Bobby Joe (stereo)
918 – Red Sovine – The Thought Of Losing You / The Unfinished Letter
919 – Jack Kane – Satisfied Mind / Something
920 – Wayne Walker – When Passion Calls / Nobody Knows But Me
921 – Rose Maddox – The Two of Us / Get It Over
922 – Mayf Nutter – Country's Gone / Nashville Wives
923 – The Willis Brothers – For the Good Times / Women's Liberation
924 – Kenny Roberts – Pretty Flowers / Pistol Packin' Mama
925 – Jack Kane – Pray Together, Stay Together / Bottle of Wine
926 – Red Sovine – Violets Blue / Get In Touch
927 – Texas Bill Strength – Nervous As A Cat / Hillbilly Hades
928 – Jim Single – What's Been Wrong For Me (Now Seems So Right For You) / A Rollin' Heart Gathers No Hurt
929 – J. David Sloan – Songbird / One Toke Over the Line
930 –
931 – Johnny Bond – The Late and Great Myself / The Bottle's Empty (& Other Sad, Sad, Stories)
932 – J. David Sloan – Country Boy / Everything
933 – Red Sovine – I'll Sail My Ship Alone / Happy Birthday, My Darlin'
934 – Red Sovine – Beautiful Life / I Am A Pilgrim
935 – Jack Ward – Treat Her Right / A Very Hurt Man
936 – Bobby Stephenson – Let It Rain / Jerry Lee You Told On Me
937 – Max Powell – It's Time To Say Goodbye Again / What's This World Coming To
938 – The Willis Brothers – She's Living In Sin (On the Back Side of Town) / You Make My Heart Want A Dip of Snuff
939 – J. David Sloan – Everything / I'll Have To Be With You Again
940 – Jack Ward – Baby You Got It / Lonely Minutes
941 – Bobby Spicher – The Last Sad Song / Stormy Monday
942 – The Tadpole Creek Opinion – The Bussing Song / Reach Up and Take Hold (Of the Saviour's Hand)
943 – Jack Ward – Shop Around / Morning Noon & Night
944 – Max Powell – I'm Not Alone / It's Time To Say Goodbye Again
945 – Pete Street – Drinkin' Man / Say There Blue Bird
946 – Polly Ann – You'll Come Back To Me / Living For You But Dying For Him
947 – Kenny Roberts (King of the Yoddlers) – Mule Skinner Blues / Ding Dong Bell
948 – Jim Stocks – Sugar Cane Sandy / A Loser Coming Home
949 – Jim Single – Help / Walking Uninvited (Through My Mind)
950 – Big Merle Kilgore (The Boogie King) – The Great Drinkin' Bout / Good Rockin' Tonight

200   RECORD LISTING

951 – Johnny Bond – Put the Country Back in Country Music / Fly Me, Try Me
952 – Reno & Harrell – Sweet Miss Sarah Jane / Truck Stop Boogie
953 –
954 – Arthur Prysock – Frisco Line / Today I Started Loving You Again
955 – Jack Ward – Honestly I Do / Falling For You
956 –
957 – Larry Sparks and the Lonesome Ramblers – Brand New Broken Heart / Kentucky Chimes
958 – Bailes Brothers – Jesus Hold My Hand / How Do You Talk To A Baby
959 – Pete Street – Here Comes My Baby / Can This Be the Trend
960 – Red Sovine – Go Hide John / Tear Stained Guitar
961 – Dale and Billy Joe – I'll Tell You Why / Something's Always Coming Between Us
962 – The Willis Brothers – Why Don't You Haul Off and Love Me / John Told Jack
963 – The Cumberlands – Sorrow Bound / No Way of Knowing
964 – Merle Kilgore – My Side of Life / A Different Kind of Pretty
965 – New Grass Revival – I Wish I Said (I Love You More Than One Time) / Great Balls of Fire
966 – Charlie Moore – Lorena Go Home / Your Letter
967 – Tommy Collins – Opal You Ask Me / Wildwood Flower
968 – The Family Jewels featuring Hal Rugg & Buddy Spicher – Chicken Gumbo / The Family Jewels featuring Buddy Spicher & Hal Rugg – Sweet Sauce
969 – Little Jimmy Dempsey – Strawberry Wine / Help Me Make It Through the Night
970 – George Avak – Little Pedro / I've Loved You All Over the World
971 – Dave Evans – Knoxville Court House Blues / Mommy and Daddy Can't Make It
972 – Jim Single – There's a Cold Wind Blowin' / Goodbye Love
973 – Charlie Monroe – I'm Going Away / Down In the Willow Garden
974 – New Grass Revival – Prince of Peace Part 1 / Prince of Peace Part 2
975 – Red Sovine – That's What You're Taken / Swing'Em High Swing'Em Lo
976 – Homer Bailes – Dust On the Bible / Lord of My Life
977 – Red Sovine – Take Time To Remember / Take Time To Remember
978 – Benny Barnes – Chillie Smith / Poor Man's Riches
979 – Little Jimmy Dickens – Dead Skunk (In the Middle of the Road) / Alabam
980 – II Generation – Let's / Raining In Nashville Tonight
981 –
982 – Ronnie Thompson – God Bless America / This Is Our Land
983 – Bailey Anderson – Don't Be Twisting Things / She'll Go Anywhere With You
984 –

Starday Albums – compiled by Nathan Gibson

When first starting to look for Starday LPs, I contacted Bob Ford, a fellow country music record collector in Massachusetts. He loaned me nearly fifty Starday albums that I listened to, took notes from, and returned. Much as I did with the singles, I then made it my mission to verify each and every Starday LP for spelling and title accuracy. In doing so, I found that many of the LPs were littered with text and it was often difficult to decipher the official title of the LP (for example, Lonnie "Pap" Wilson's album that states "*The Playboy Farmer*, Lonnie 'Pap' Wilson, *Jokes, Laffs, Songs and Gags About the Funny Side of Life*

RECORD LISTING

From NASHVILLE, TENNESSEE, The Musical Heart Of America
Country-Sacred-Bluegrass-Western-Old-Time INTERNATIONAL
PRESENTS

Various Starday LP covers (Courtesy of Nathan Gibson and Marc Bird)

or *How To Have Fun—Even If You're Married*"). Occasionally, the title on the cover spine differs from the title listed on the record label itself. In these instances, I have used my best judgment to discern the official title based on the album cover.

I wish I had room to include song titles, publishing information, mono/stereo details, and more, but space is limited. Hopefully there is enough here for collectors and fans to find out what material was released. Record numbers beginning with the number 8, 9, or 10 denote a release containing multiple LPs (usually a double pocket LP, though in some cases they are boxed sets).

SLP 101 – George Jones – *Grand Ole Opry's New Star*
SLP 102 – *Hillbilly Hit Parade, Vol. 1* – Various Artists
SLP 103 – *International Polka and Waltz Favorites for Dancing* – Various Artists
SLP 104 – *Banjo in the Hills* – Various Artists
SLP 105 – *Preachin', Prayin', Shoutin', and Singin'* – Various Artists

SLP 106 – The Stanley Brothers and the Clinch Mountain Boys – *Mountain Song Favorites*
SLP 107 – Carl Story and His Rambling Mountaineers – *America's Favorite Country Gospel Artist*
SLP 108 – Kirby Buchanan – *Songs of Faith and Inspiration*
SLP 109 – *Country Express* – Various Artists
SLP 110 – *Country Hit Parade* – Various Artists
SLP 111 – Bill Clifton and His Dixie Mountain Boys – *Mountain Folk Songs*
SLP 112 – Wally Fowler – *All Night Singing Concert*
SLP 113 – The Sunshine Boys – *The Word*
SLP 114 – *Fiddlin' Country Style* – Various Artists
SLP 115 – *The Bluegrass Special* – Various Artists
SLP 116 – *Old Time Religion, Country Style* – Various Artists
SLP 8-117 – *Country Music Spectacular* – Various Artists (2 LPs)
SLP 118 – Cowboy Copas – *All Time Country Music Great*
SLP 119 – Lonzo and Oscar – *America's Greatest Country Comedians*
SLP 120 – Marshall Pack – *Sacred Memories, Vol. 1*
SLP 121 – The Lewis Family – *Singin' Time Down South*
SLP 122 – The Stanley Brothers – *Sacred Songs From the Hills*
SLP 123 – *Y'all Come/Have a Country Christmas* – Various Artists
SLP 124 – Wayne Raney and the Raney Family – *16 Radio Gospel Favorites*
SLP 125 – George Jones – *The Crown Prince of Country Music*
SLP 126 – Jimmy Richardson – *Sweet with a Beat, Hammond Organ Melodies from Dixie Vol. 1*
SLP 127 – Carl Story and His Rambling Mountaineers – *Gospel Revival*
SLP 128 – *Nashville Saturday Night* – Various Artists
SLP 129 – The Sunshine Boys – *Golden Melodies*
SLP 130 – The Oak Ridge Quartet – *Master Showmen of Song*
SLP 131 – Benny Martin – *Country Music's Sensational Entertainer*
SLP 132 – Red Sovine – *The One and Only*
SLP 133 – Cowboy Copas – *Inspirational Songs by Cowboy Copas*
SLP 134 – Frankie Miller – *Country Music's Great New Star*
SLP 135 – Moon Mullican, The King of the Hillbilly Piano Players – *Playin' and Singin'*
SLP 9-136 – *Banjo Jamboree Spectacular* – Various Artists (2 LPs)
SLP 137 – Carl Story and his Rambling Mountaineers – *Everybody Will Be Happy*
SLP 138 – *Nashville Steel Guitar* – Various Artists
SLP 139 – A. L. Phipps Family – *The Most Requested Sacred Songs of the Carter Family*
SLP 8-140 – *More Country Music Spectacular* – Various Artists (2 LPs)
SLP 141 – Old Hickory Singers – *A Little Close Harmony from Dixie*
SLP 142 – Stringbean – *Old Time Banjo Pickin' and Singin'*
SLP 143 – *Country Music Samplers* – Various Artists
SLP 144 – Cowboy Copas – *Songs That Made Him Famous*
SLP 145 – Jimmy Richardson – *Jimmy Richardson and his Swinging Hammond Organ*
SLP 146 – Bill Clifton and His Dixie Mountain Boys – *Carter Family Memorial Album*
SLP 147 – Johnny Bond – *That Wild, Wicked but Wonderful West*
SLP 148 – The Duke of Paducah – *Button Shoes, Belly Laughs, and Monkey Business*
SLP 149 – The Jim Glaser Singers – *Old Time Christmas Singing*
SLP 150 – George Jones – *Sings His Greatest Hits*
SLP 151 – George Jones – *The Fabulous Country Music Sound of George Jones*

SLP 152 – Carl Story and His Rambling Mountaineers – *Get Religion*
SLP 153 – Lew Childre, The Boy from Alabam and His Friends – *Old Time Get-Together*
SLP 154 – Chubby Wise and the Rainbow Ranch Boys – *Tennessee Fiddler*
SLP 155 – The Lonesome Pine Fiddlers – *Lonesome Pine Fiddlers*
SLP 156 – The Sunshine Boys – *Golden Gospel Million Sellers*
SLP 157 – Cowboy Copas – *Opry Star Spotlight*
SLP 158 – Jim Glaser and the Americana Folk Trio – *Just Looking For a Home*
SLP 159 – Bill Clifton – *The Bluegrass Sound of Bill Clifton*
SLP 160 – Justin Tubb – *Star of the Grand Ole Opry*
SLP 161 – The Lewis Family – *Anniversary Celebration*
SLP 162 – Archie Campbell – *Make Friends*
SLP 163 – The Willis Brothers – *In Action*
SLP 9-164 – *The Country Music Hall of Fame* – Various Artists (2 LPs)
SLP 165 – Jimmie Williams and Red Ellis – *Holy Cry From the Hills*
SLP 166 – Sunshine Boys – *More Country Sing Along*
SLP 167 – Archie Campbell – *Bedtime Stories for Adults*
SLP 168 – *Tragic Songs of Death and Sorrow* – Various Artists
SLP 169 – *More Banjo In the Hills* – Various Artists
SLP 170 – *All Aboard! For the Railroad Special* – Various Artists
SLP 171 – Leon McAuliff and His Cimarron Boys – *Mister Western Swing*
SLP 172 – Buck Owens – *The Fabulous Country Music Sound*
SLP 173 – Arthur "Guitar Boogie" Smith and His Crackerjacks – *Mister Guitar*
SLP 174 – The Country Gentlemen – *Bluegrass at Carnegie Hall*
SLP 175 – Cowboy Copas – *Mister Country Music*
SLP 176 – *Tennessee Guitar* – Various Artists
SLP 177 – *Opry Time in Tennessee* – Various Artists
SLP 178 – *More Country Music Samplers* – Various Artists
SLP 179 – Stringbean – *More of That Rare Old Time Banjo Pickin' and Singin'*
SLP 180 – Pete Drake – *The Fabulous Steel Guitar Sound*
SLP 181 – *The Bluegrass Hall of Fame* – Various Artists
SLP 182 – Sam and Kirk McGee from Sunny Tennessee and the Crook Brothers – *Opry Old Timers*
SLP 183 – *Bluegrass Samplers* – Various Artists
SLP 8-184 – *The Hit Parade of American Country Music* – Various Artists (2 LPs)
SLP 185 – Hylo Brown – *Bluegrass Balladeer*
SLP 186 – Arthur Smith and the Crossroads Quartet – *The Fourth Man*
SLP 187 – Johnny Bond – *Live It Up and Laugh It Up with Johnny Bond and His Friends on Stage*
SLP 188 – "Little" Roy Wiggins – *Mister Steel Guitar Salutes Eddy Arnold*
SLP 189 – The Kentucky Travelers – *Bluegrass Banjo Ballads*
SLP 9-190 – *The Country Music Hall of Fame, Vol. 2* – Various Artists (2 LPs)
SLP 191 – Smiley Burnette – *Ole Frog*
SLP 192 – Bashful Brother Oswald – *Bashful Brother Oswald with His Banjo and Dobro*
SLP 193 – The Lewis Family – *Gospel Special*
SLP 194 – The Lonesome Pine Fiddlers – *Bluegrass*
SLP 195 – The A. L. Phipps Family – *Old Time Mountain Pickin' and Singin'*
SLP 196 – Dean Manuel with the Jim Reeves Blue Boys – *Town and Country Piano*
SLP 197 – Red Sovine – *The Golden Country Ballads of the 60's*

SLP 198 – Justin Tubb – *The Modern Country Music Sound*
SLP 199 – Frankie Miller – *The True Country Style*
SLP 200 – Ernest V. Stoneman and the Stoneman Family – *Bluegrass Champs*
SLP 201 – The Stanley Brothers and the Clinch Mountain Boys – *The Mountain Music Sound*
SLP 202 – Fiddlin' Arthur Smith and the Dixieliners – *Rare Old Time Fiddle Tunes*
SLP 203 – Red Ellis – *The Sacred Sound of Bluegrass Music*
SLP 204 – Hylo Brown and the Timberliners – *Bluegrass Goes To College*
SLP 205 – The Blue Sky Boys, Bill and Earl Bolick – *Treasury of Rare Song Gems from the Past*
SLP 206 – Lulu Belle and Scotty – *The Sweethearts of Country Music*
SLP 207 – *Prisoners Songs* – Various Artists
SLP 208 – Cowboy Copas – *Country Music Entertainer #1*
SLP 209 – *Fiddler's Hall of Fame* – Various Artists
SLP 210 – Tommy Hill's Nashville String Band – *The Swingin' Sound of Modern Country Music with Percussion*
SLP 211 – Buddy Starcher – *Buddy Starcher and His Mountain Guitar*
SLP 212 – Cowboy Copas – *Beyond the Sunset*
SLP 213 – Bill Clifton – *Soldier, Sing Me a Song*
SLP 214 – Alex Campbell and Olabelle and the New River Boys – *Alex Campbell and Olabelle and the New River Boys*
SLP 215 – Stringbean and His Banjo – *A Salute to Dave Macon*
SLP 216 – Arthur "Guitar Boogie" Smith with His Crackerjacks – *Arthur "Guitar Boogie" Smith Goes To Town*
SLP 217 – Lonnie "Pap" Wilson – *The Playboy Farmer*
SLP 218 – *Spotlight on Country Music* – Various Artists
SLP 219 – Carl Story – *Mighty Close To Heaven*
SLP 220 – Hylo Brown and the Lonesome Pine Fiddlers – *Hylo Brown Meets the Lonesome Pine Fiddlers*
SLP 221 – *Fire On the Strings* – Various Artists
SLP 222 – The Lonesome Pine Fiddlers – *More Bluegrass!*
SLP 223 – Archie Campbell – *"The Joker" Is Wild*
SLP 224 – Cousin Minnie Pearl – *Howdee!*
SLP 225 – Buddy Meredith – *Sing Me a Heart Song*
SLP 226 – Gene Martin – *Country and Western Confidential, a Backstage Expose*
SLP 227 – Johnny Bond – *Songs That Made Him Famous*
SLP 228 – Robert Lunn with Jug and Washboard Band – *The Original Talking Blues Man*
SLP 229 – The Willis Brothers (Oklahoma Wranglers) – *The Code of the West*
SLP 230 – Shot Jackson – *The Singing Strings of Steel Guitar and Dobro*
SLP 231 – Leon Payne – *A Living Legend of Country Music*
SLP 232 – *Bluegrass Spectacular* – Various Artists
SLP 233 – *The Steel Guitar Hall of Fame* – Various Artists
SLP 234 – Cowboy Copas – *The Unforgettable Cowboy Copas*
SLP 235 – Curly Fox and Texas Ruby – *Curly Fox and Texas Ruby*
SLP 236 – Leon Payne, the Country Music Minstrel – *Americana, Rare Ballads and Tall Tales*
SLP 237 – *Cavalcade of Country Comedy and Rural Humor* – Various Artists
SLP 238 – The Lewis Family – *Sing Me a Gospel Song*

SLP 239 – *Bright Lights and Honky Tonks* – Various Artists
SLP 240 – Jimmie Skinner – *The Kentucky Colonel*
SLP 241 – Arthur "Guitar Boogie" Smith – *Arthur "Guitar Boogie" Smith in Person*
SLP 9-242 – *Grand Ole Opry Spectacular* – Various Artists (2 LPs)
SLP 243 – Arthur "Guitar Boogie" Smith – *Blue Guitar*
SLP 244 – Lonzo and Oscar – *Country Music Time*
SLP 8-245 – *Country and Western Golden Hit Parade* – Various Artists (2 LPs)
SLP 246 – The Masters Family – *The Gloryland March*
SLP 247 – Cowboy Copas – *Star of the Grand Ole Opry*
SLP 248 – The A. L. Phipps Family – *Echoes of the Carter Family*
SLP 249 – Hylo Brown – *Sing Me a Bluegrass Song*
SLP 250 – *Diesel Smoke, Dangerous Curves and Other Truck Driver Favorites* – Various Artists
SLP 251 – Merle Kilgore – *There's Gold in Them Thar Hills*
SLP 252 – The Lewis Family – *All Night Singing Convention*
SLP 253 – *Merry Christmas Country Style* – Various Artists
SLP 254 – Cecil Campbell and his Tennessee Ramblers – *Steel Guitar Jamboree*
SLP 255 – *The Wonderful World of Gospel & Sacred Music* – Various Artists
SLP 9-256 – *Country Music Hall of Fame, Volume 3* – Various Artists (2 LPs)
SLP 257 – The Blue Sky Boys, Bill and Earl Bolick – *Together Again!*
SLP 258 – Howard Vokes – *Tragedy and Disaster in Country Songs*
SLP 259 – "Little" Roy Wiggins – *The Fabulous Steel Guitar Artistry of "Little" Roy Wiggins*
SLP 260 – Stringbean – *Way Back In the Hills of Kentucky*
SLP 261 – *Slipping Around* – Various Artists
SLP 262 – Clyde Moody – *Songs That Made Him Famous*
SLP 263 – *Live . . . Direct From the Stage, Country Music U.S.A.* – Various Artists
SLP 264 – *Big "D" Jamboree* – Various Artists
SLP 265 – Jackie Phelps – *Golden Guitar Classics: The Ten Talented Fingers of Guitar Star*
SLP 266 – Arthur "Guitar Boogie" Smith – *Down Home with . . . Arthur "Guitar Boogie" Smith*
SLP 267 – Moon Mullican – *Mister Piano Man*
SLP 268 – Cowboy Copas and his Friends – *Cowboy Copas and his Friends*
SLP 269 – Blue Sky Boys – *Precious Moments*
SLP 270 – *The Wonderful World of Country* – Various Artists
SLP 271 – Bill Clifton – *Code of the Mountain*
SLP 272 – *Lost Love and Lonely Nights* – Various Artists
SLP 273 – Red Ellis and his Huron Valley Boys – *Old Time Religion Bluegrass Style*
SLP 274 – *Kroger Country Music Festival* – Various Artists
SLP 275 – E. V. Stoneman and Family – *The Great Old Timer at the Capitol*
SLP 276 – *Opry Stage Show Number One* – *Country Music Cannonball*
SLP 277 – *Unforgettable Instrumentals* – Various Artists
SLP 278 – Carl Story and his Rambling Mountaineers – *All Day Sacred Singing*
SLP 279 – Wayne Raney – *Don't Try To Be What You Ain't*
SLP 280 – Leon McAuliff – *Swinging West*
SLP 281 – Jerry Rivers, of Drifting Cowboy Fame – *Fantastic Fiddlin' and Tall Tales*
SLP 282 – Jimmie Skinner – *Let's Say Goodbye Like We Said Hello!*
SLP 283 – *Fingers On Fire* – Various Artists

SLP 284 – Pee Wee King and Redd Stewart and the New Golden West Cowboys – *Back Again!*
SLP 285 – Lulu Belle and Scotty – *Down Memory Lane*
SLP 286 – Joe and Rose Lee Maphis – *Mr. and Mrs. Country Music*
SLP 287 – The Southlan Trio – *Gospel Songs from Dixie*
SLP 288 – The Duke of Paducah – *At the Fair*
SLP 289 – The Lewis Family – *Singin' In My Soul*
SLP 290 – The Sunshine Boys – *He's Got the Whole World in His Hands*
SLP 291 – *Country Music Memorial Album* – Various Artists
SLP 292 – *Grassroots* – Various Artists
SLP 293 – *Steel Guitar and Dobro Spectacular* – Various Artists
SLP 294 – *The Greatest Fiddlers of Our Time* – Various Artists
SLP 9-295 – *Country Music Hall of Fame, Vol. 4* – Various Artists (2 LPs)
SLP 296 – *Bluegrass Hall of Fame, Vol. 2* – Various Artists
SLP 297 – *Wonderful Waltzes of Country Music* – Various Artists
SLP 298 – Johnny Bond – *Hot Rod Lincoln, Three Sheets in the Wind and Other New Favorites*
SLP 299 – *Deck of Cards* – Various Artists
SLP 300 – Wilf Carter (Montana Slim) – *The Living Legend of Cowboy, Rodeo and Yodelling Country Music*
SLP 301 – Wally Fowler – *More Wally Fowler's All Nite Singing Gospel*
SLP 302 – Dottie West – *The Country Girl Singing Sensation*
SLP 303 – *Preachin', Prayin', Singin'* – Various Artists
SLP 8-304 – *Country Music Who's Who* – Various Artists (2 LPs)
SLP 305 – Dean Manuel with the Jim Reeves Blue Boys – *The Late and Great*
SLP 306 – *Let's Hit the Road!! More Truck Driver Favorites to Keep the Big Rigs Rolling* – Various Artists
SLP 307 – *Y'all Come* – Various Artists
SLP 308 – *Gospel Hall of Fame* – Various Artists
SLP 309 – Leon McAuliff – *Swingin' Western Strings*
SLP 310 – Floyd Tillman – *Let's Make Memories*
SLP 311 – The Country Gentlemen – *Songs of the Pioneers*
SLP 312 – *Doin' My Time* – Various Artists
SLP 313 – *Country Girl Hall of Fame* – Various Artists
SLP 314 – Jimmy Richardson and His Swinging Hammond – *Big Beat Country Melodies*
SLP 315 – Carl Story and his Rambling Mountaineers – *Sacred Songs of Life and the Hereafter*
SLP 316 – Joe Maphis – *King of the Strings*
SLP 317 – Cowboy Copas – *The Legend Lives On*
SLP 318 – Roger Miller – *Wild Child, The Madcap Sensation of Country Music/The Country Side*
SLP 319 – Pete Drake – *The Amazing and Incredible Pete Drake*
SLP 320 – *Wonderful World of Country, Vol. 2* – Various Artists
SLP 321 – Arthur "Guitar Boogie" Smith – *Town and Country Guitar Hits*
SLP 322 – Joe Maphis, the King of the Strings – *Golden Gospel Guitar*
SLP 323 – Willis Brothers – *Give Me 40 Acres (To Turn This Rig Around)*
SLP 324 – Buck Owens – *The Fabulous Country Music Sound/Country Hit Maker #1*
SLP 325 – Jimmy Dean and Johnny Horton – *Bummin' Around*

SLP 326 – *Country Guitar Hall of Fame* – Various Artists
SLP 327 – *Country Music Festival, Vol. 2* – Various Artists
SLP 328 – Johnny and Jonie Mosby – *The New Sweethearts of Country Music*
SLP 329 – *Mom and Dad Songs* – Various Artists
SLP 10-330 – *Wonderful World of Country* – Various Artists (4 LP box)
SLP 331 – The Lewis Family – *The First Family of Gospel Song*
SLP 332 – Smokey Rogers – *Gone*
SLP 333 – Johnny Bond – *Ten Little Bottles*
SLP 334 – Justin Tubb – *The Best of Justin Tubb*
SLP 335 – George Jones – *George Jones*
SLP 336 – Kenny Roberts, America's King of the Yodelers – *Indian Love Call*
SLP 337 – *The Tall 12* – Various Artists
SLP 338 – *More Slipping Around Songs* – Various Artists
SLP 339 – Frankie Miller – *Blackland Farmer*
SLP 340 – *That Dobro Sound's Goin' 'Round* – Various Artists
SLP 341 – Red Sovine – *Little Rosa*
SLP 342 – Alex Campbell and Olabelle – *Travel On*
SLP 343 – *Hit Parade of Bluegrass Stars* – Various Artists
SLP 344 – George Jones – *Long Live King George*
SLP 345 – *Spectacular Instrumentals* – Various Artists
SLP 346 – Cowboy Copas, Patsy Cline and Hawkshaw Hawkins – *Gone, But Not Forgotten*
SLP 9-347 – Cowboy Copas – *The Cowboy Copas Story* (2 LPs)
SLP 348 – Carl Story and His Rambling Mountaineers – *There's Nothing on Earth That Heaven Can't Cure*
SLP 349 – Sunshine Boys – *Happy Home Up There*
SLP 350 – *Stars of the Steel Guitar* – Various Artists
SLP 351 – Lulu Belle and Scotty – *Sweethearts Still*
SLP 352 – Dottie West and Melba Montgomery – *Queens of Country Music*
SLP 353 – The Willis Brothers – *Road Stop—Juke Box Hits*
SLP 354 – Johnny Bond – *Famous Hot Rodders I Have Known*
SLP 9-355 – *The Glorious Sound of Gospel* – Various Artists
SLP 356 – The Oak Ridge Boys – *The Sensational Oak Ridge Boys from Nashville Tennessee*
SLP 357 – *That's Truckdrivin'* – Various Artists
SLP 10-358 – *The Wonderful World of Gospel and Sacred Music* – Various Artists (4 LP box)
SLP 359 – Pete Williams – *Sings All Time Country Hits*
SLP 9-360 – *Country Music Hall of Fame, Volume 5* – Various Artists (2 LPs)
SLP 361 – Charlie Monroe – *Charlie Monroe*
SLP 362 – *Country Music Festival, Vol. 3* – Various Artists
SLP 363 – Red Sovine – *Giddy-Up Go*
SLP 364 – The Lewis Family and Carl Story – *The Lewis Family Sings the Gospel with Carl Story*
SLP 365 – Lester Flatt, Earl Scruggs and Jim and Jesse – *Stars of the Grand Ole Opry*
SLP 8-366 – George Jones – *The George Jones Story* (2 LPs)
SLP 367 – Molly O'Day – *The Living Legend of Country Music*
SLP 368 – Johnny Bond – *The Man Who Comes Around*
SLP 369 – Willis Brothers – *The Wild Side of Life*
SLP 370 – *Family Gospel Album* – Various Artists

SLP 371 – Cowboy Copas – *Shake a Hand*
SLP 372 – Charlie Monroe with the Kentucky Pardners – *Charlie Monroe Sings Again*
SLP 373 – Joe Maphis – *Country Guitar Goes on the Jimmy Dean Show*
SLP 374 – *Country Music Goes To War* – Various Artists
SLP 375 – Bob Wills, Leon McAuliff and Tommy Duncan – *San Antonio Rose, Steel Guitar Rag*
SLP 376 – Patsy Montana – *Cowboy's Sweetheart*
SLP 377 – Archie Campbell – *Grand Ole Opry's Good Humor Man*
SLP 378 – Johnny Bond – *Bottles Up*
SLP 379 – T. Texas Tyler – *The Man with a Million Friends*
SLP 380 – Minnie Pearl – *America's Beloved*
SLP 381 – The Lewis Family – *The Lewis Family Album*
SLP 382 – Buddy Starcher – *History Repeats Itself*
SLP 383 – Red Sovine – *Town and Country Action*
SLP 384 – The Stanley Brothers – *Jacob's Vision*
SLP 9-385 – *Country Sweethearts* – Various Artists (2 LPs)
SLP 386 – *Thunder on the Road* – Various Artists
SLP 387 – Willis Brothers – *Going to Town*
SLP 388 – Johnny Bond – *The Branded Stock of Johnny Bond*
SLP 389 – Wilf Carter – *Montana Slim*
SLP 9-390 – *Country Music Hall of Fame, Vol. 6* – Various Artists (2 LPs)
SLP 391 – *The Tall 12, Vol. 2* – Various Artists
SLP 392 – "Little" Roy Wiggins – *18 All Time Hits*
SLP 393 – The Stoneman Family – *White Lightnin'*
SLP 394 – *Cream of the Country Crop* – Various Artists
SLP 395 – The Lewis Family – *Shall We Gather at the River*
SLP 396 – Red Sovine – *The Nashville Sound*
SLP 397 – Minnie Pearl – *The Country Music Story*
SLP 398 – Moon Mullican – *The Unforgettable Moon Mullican*
SLP 399 – *The Fabulous Sounds of Those Nashville Cats* – Various Artists
SLP 400 – George Morgan – *Candy Kisses*
SLP 401 – George Jones – *Songbook and Picture Album*
SLP 402 – Johnny Bond – *Ten Nights in a Barroom*
SLP 403 – The Willis Brothers – *"Bob" and Other Songs to Make the Jukebox Play*
SLP 404 – *The Man Behind the Wheel* – Various Artists
SLP 405 – Red Sovine – *I Didn't Jump the Fence*
SLP 406 – Kenny Roberts – *The Incredible Kenny Roberts*
SLP 407 – *Big Stars and Big Hits* – Various Artists
SLP 408 – The Lewis Family – *Time Is Moving On*
SLP 9-409 – *Country Music Hall of Fame, Vol. 7* – Various Artists (2 LPs)
SLP 410 – George Morgan – *Country Hits by Candlelight*
SLP 411 – Carl Story and his Rambling Mountaineers – *My Lord Keeps a Record*
SLP 412 – Guy Mitchell – *Traveling Shoes*
SLP 413 – George Morgan – *Steal Away*
SLP 414 – Red Sovine – *Phantom 309*
SLP 415 – Arthur "Guitar Boogie" Smith – *The Guitars of Arthur "Guitar Boogie" Smith*
SLP 416 – Johnny Bond – *Drink Up and Go Home!!*
SLP 417 – George Morgan – *Barbara*

SLP 9-418 – *Modern Country Hits of Today* – Various Artists (2 LPs)
SLP 419 – The Lewis Family – *All Day Singing and Dinner on the Ground*
SLP 420 – Red Sovine – *Tell Maude I Slipped*
SLP 421 – Wynn Stewart and Jan Howard – *Sing Their Hits*
SLP 422 – The Lewis Family – *Golden Gospel Banjo*
SLP 423 – *Songs and Sounds from the Bonnie and Clyde Era* – Various Artists
SLP 424 – Glen Campbell – *Country Soul*
SLP 425 – The Crossroads Quartet – *Prayer Changes Things*
SLP 426 – Snooky Lanson – *Nashville Now*
SLP 427 – Red Sovine – *Sunday with Red Sovine*
SLP 428 – The Willis Brothers – *Hey, Mr. Truck Driver!*
SLP 429 – Dolly Parton and George Jones – *Dolly Parton and George Jones*
SLP 9-430 – *Country Music Hall of Fame, Vol. 8* – Various Artists (2 LPs)
SLP 431 – Billy Golden – *Country Music's Golden Boy*
SLP 432 – Guy Mitchell – *Singin' Up a Storm*
SLP 433 – The Lewis Family – *Did You Ever Go Sailing*
SLP 434 – Kenny Roberts – *Country Music Singing Sensation*
SLP 435 – George Morgan – *Sounds of Goodbye*
SLP 436 – Red Sovine – *Classic Narrations*
SLP 437 – Glen Campbell – *Country Music Star No. 1*
SLP 438 – Carl Story – *Daddy Sang Bass*
SLP 439 – Tommy Hill's Nashville Cats – *Golden Country Melodies*
SLP 440 – George Jones – *The Golden Country Hits*
SLP 441 – Red Sovine – *Closing Time 'Til Dawn*
SLP 442 – The Willis Brothers – *Bummin' Around*
SLP 443 – Bobby Harden – *Nashville Sensation*
SLP 444 – Johnny Bond – *Best of Johnny Bond*
SLP 445 – Red Sovine – *Who Am I?*
SLP 446 – Buck Owens – *Sweethearts in Heaven*
SLP 447 – Carl Story – *Precious Memories*
SLP 448 – Lois Williams – *A Girl Named Sam*
SLP 9-449 – *Country Music Hall of Fame, Vol. 9* – Various Artists (2 LPs)
SLP 450 – The Lewis Family – *Golden Gospel Best*
SLP 9-451 – *Country Music Memorial* – Various Artists (2 LPs)
SLP 452 – Tom Perryman and the Stars and Guests of Hee Haw – *Country Music Laugh-Out*
SLP 453 – J. David Sloan – *Exciting Young J. David Sloan*
SLP 454 – *The Best of the Truck Driver Songs* – Various Artists
SLP 455 – Carl Story – *The Best of Carl Story*
SLP 456 – Johnny Bond – *Something Old, New, Patriotic and Blue*
SLP 457 – George Morgan – *The Best of George Morgan*
SLP 458 – Cowboy Copas – *The Best of Cowboy Copas*
SLP 459 – Red Sovine – *I Know You're Married, But I Love You Still*
SLP 460 – Macon's Mayor Ronnie Thompson – *Here I Am*
SLP 461 – The International Strings and the Nashville Cats – *The Wide World of Country Hits*
SLP 462 – Hank and Lewie Wickham – *Little Bit Late*
SLP 463 – Rose Maddox – *Rosie!*

SLP 464 –
SLP 465 – The Lewis Family – *The Best of the Lewis Family*
SLP 466 – The Willis Brothers – *The Best of the Willis Brothers*
SLP 467 –
SLP 9-468 – *Country Music Hall of Fame, Vol. 10* – Various Artists (2 LPs)
SLP 469 – Bob Wills, Tommy Duncan and Leon McAuliff – *The Bob Wills Story*
SLP 470 – Kenny Roberts – *Jealous Heart*
SLP 471 – Mel Tillis – *Stateside*
SLP 472 – Johnny Bond – *Here Come the Elephants*
SLP 473 – The Willis Brothers – *For the Good Times*
SLP 474 – Tommy Collins – *Callin'*
SLP 475 – Johnny Bush – *Here's Johnny Bush*
SLP 476 – The Bailes Brothers – *Gospel Reunion*
SLP 477 – *Best of Truck Driver Songs, Vol. 2* – Various Artists
SLP 478 – *Bluegrass Revue* – Various Artists
SLP 479 – Merle Kilgore – *Big Merle*
SLP 480 – Larry Sparks – *Ramblin' Bluegrass*
SLP 481 – Reno and Harrell – *Bluegrass on My Mind*
SLP 482 – New Grass Revival – *New Grass Revival*
SLP 483 – Jimmy Dempsey – *Back to the Hills*
SLP 484 – Charlie Monroe – *Tally Ho*
SLP 485 – Don Reno and Red Smiley – *Last Time Together*
SLP 486 –
SLP 487 –
SLP 488 – Carl Story – *Carl Story*
SLP 489 – J. D. Crowe and the New South – *J. D. Crowe and the New South*

Mercury-Starday Country Series Singles – compiled by Nathan Gibson

The Mercury-Starday Country Series listing was perhaps the most difficult to complete. Mercury released over 200 singles in 1957, though only fifty-five with the Starday imprint. The Starday imprint was reserved for country material, though several country records were released on Mercury without the Starday imprint. Conversely, several rockabilly records appeared under the Mercury-Starday banner. A few records that had been released on Starday in 1956 were released on Mercury in 1957, but not on Mercury-Starday. Further complicating matters, I found many examples of the same record released on both Mercury and Mercury-Starday (presumably second pressings and reissues of Mercury-Starday releases were issued on Mercury after 1958). Adding to the confusion, some records were released as 45s on Mercury, but on Mercury-Starday as 78s (e.g., the Diamonds' "The Stroll"). This was surely a pressing plant error. Still, deciphering which records correctly belonged in the series was a challenge.

    I spent several years diligently collecting each and every Mercury-Starday record. (Carl Story's "Family Reunion" on Mercury-Starday proved most elusive and magically appeared to me just prior to this book's publication.) I now believe I have compiled the definitive list (though I am still perplexed by Minnesota disc jockey Johnny "T" Talley promoting his otherwise seemingly nonexistent Mercury-Starday release of "Heartaches, Teardrops and Sorrows" b/w "That Feeling Called the Blues" in the August 1957 issue of *Rustic Rhythm*). Along my journey, several collectors generously scoured their collections for Mercury-Starday records and provided much useful information. Thanks belong to Andrew Brown, Larry Davis, Shane Hughes, Tom Armstrong, Pasi Koskela, and Darwin Lee Hill.

71029 – George Jones – Don't Stop the Music / Uh, Uh, No
71057 – Benny Barnes – Poor Old Me / Penalty
71061 – George Jones and Jeanette Hicks – Yearning / Cry, Cry (It's Good for You)
71063 – Leon Payne – Lumberjack / A Million To One
71064 – Stanley Brothers and the Clinch Mountain Boys – The Flood / I'm Lost, I'll Never Find My Way
71065 – Denver Duke and Jeffrey Null, the Hardin County Boys – A Million Tears / All Washed Up With You
71066 – James O'Gwynn – Who'll Be the Next One / Muleskinner Blues
71067 – Eddie Bond and the Stompers– They Say We're Too Young / You're Part Of Me
71081 – Charlie Walker – Dancing Mexican Boy / Gentle Love
71082 – Buck Ryan – The Robert E. Lee / Nervous Breakdown
71088 – Carl Story and his Rambling Mountaineers – Light At the River / Mocking Banjo
71089 – Bill Wimberly and his Country Rhythm Boys – Back Street / Missouri Drag
71090 – Jimmie Skinner – Born To Be Wild / No Fault of Mine
71096 – George Jones – Too Much Water / All I Want To Do
71097 – Curtis Gordon – Sittin' On Top / Out To Win Your Heart
71110 – The Carlisles – Wouldn't You Like To / Ladder of Love
71111 – Charlie Walker with the Four Pals – I'll Never Let It Show / Take My Hand (I'll Understand)
71112 – Sleepy LaBeff – All Alone / I'm Through
71113 – Tibby Edwards – Long Time Gone / I'd Come Running
71119 – Benny Barnes – Nickel's Worth of Dreams / Mine All Mine
71120 – Jimmy Dean – Losing Game / Happy Child
71121 – Curtis Gordon – Cry, Cry / Sixteen
71127 – James O'Gwynn – I Cry / Do You Miss Me
71130 – Bill Clifton and the Dixie Mountain Boys – Little White Washed Chimmey / Pal of Yesterday
71135 – Stanley Brothers and the Dixie Mountain Boys – The Cry From the Cross / Let Me Walk, Lord, By Your Side
71138 – Rudy Grayzell – Let's Get Wild / I Love You So (unissued)
71139 – Marksmen – You Hurt Me So / Don't Gamble With My Heart (unissued)
71141 – George Jones and Virginia Spurlock – Flame In My Heart / No, No, Never
71143 – Carl Story and his Rambling Mountaineers – Got A Lot To Tell My Jesus / Banjo On the Mountain
71153 – Eddie Bond – Hershey Bar / Lovin' You, Lovin' You
71163 – Jimmie Skinner – No Maybe In My Baby's Eyes / Hafta Do Something' 'Bout That
71172 – Jimmy Dean – Look On the Good Side / Do You Love Me
71176 – George Jones – Hearts In My Dream / Tall Tall Trees
71179 – Sleepy La Beff – All the Time / Lonely
71183 – Curtis Gordon – I Wouldn't / Please Baby Please
71185 – Clyde Beaver – Crying For My Baby / Man In the Glass
71188 – Benny Barnes – King for a Day / Your Old Standby
71192 – Jimmie Skinner – I Found My Girl In the USA / Carroll County Blues
71200 – Bill Clifton and the Dixie Mountain Boys – Mary Dear / Lonely Heart Blues
71202 – Johnny Mathis – Moonlight Magic / You Don't Care
71207 – Stanley Brothers and the Clinch Mountain Boys – Fling Ding / Loving You Too Well
71212 – Roger Miller – Poor Little John / My Pillow
71218 – Carl Story and his Rambling Mountaineers – Family Reunion / Banjolina

71219 – Jape Richardson and the Japetts – Beggar to a King / Crazy Blues
71224 – George Jones – Take the Devil Out Of Me / Cup of Loneliness
71225 – George Jones – New Baby for Christmas / Maybe Next Christmas
71229 – Jim Eanes & the Shenandoah Valley Boys – Two Hearts Are Better Than One / Settle Down
71231 – Dorothy and Jimmy Blakley – Demon In My Heart / Tender Words
71234 – James O'Gwynn – Two Little Hearts / You've Always Won
71237 – Eddie Bond – Love, Love, Love / Backslidin'
71240 – Jimmy Dean – Bumming Around / Nothing Can Stop My Love
71242 – The Diamonds – The Stroll / Land of Beauty (78 RPM only, 45s appear on Mercury label)
71256 – Jimmie Skinner – We've Got Things In Common / What Makes a Man Wander
71257 – George Jones – Eskimo Pie / Color of the Blues
71258 – Stanley Brothers and the Clinch Mountain Boys – Life of Sorrow (mis-labeled as If That's the Way You Feel) / I'd Rather Be Forgotten

Mercury-Starday Country Series Albums – Compiled by Nathan Gibson

They are few, but these LPs add an important element to the Mercury-Starday and Starday story and demonstrate Pierce's early affinity for album releases. One particular Mercury-Starday advertisement (in the *1958 Country and Western Jamboree Yearbook*) boasts of future Mercury-Starday LP releases by the Carlisles (*On Stage with the Carlisles*), Jerry Byrd (*Byrd's Best*), Lester Flatt and Earl Scruggs (*A Country Concert*), Louisiana Hayride Stars (*The Louisiana Hayride*), and the Stanley Brothers (*Pickin' and Singin'*). Each album was eventually pressed, but on Mercury only, as the Mercury-Starday deal had already expired by the time of these releases.

MG 20282 – *Hillbilly Hit Parade Volume I* – Various Artists
MG 20306 – George Jones – *Grand Ole Opry's New Star*
MG 20319 – Jimmy Dean – *Sings His Television Favorites*
MG 20323 – Carl Story and his Rambling Mountaineers – *Gospel Quartet Favorites*
MG 20328 – *Hillbilly Hit Parade Volume II* – Various Artists

Starday Country Juke Box Oldies 7000 Series – compiled by Nathan Gibson, with thanks to Frank Frantik

This is another short-lived, but important addition to the Starday story. I have collected and verified most of these records personally, but owe many thanks to Frank Frantik who had first compiled a nearly complete listing.

7000 – Cowboy Copas – Alabam / Goodbye Kisses
7001 – Cowboy Copas – New Filipino Baby / Signed, Sealed and Delivered
7002 – Moon Mullican – New Jole Blon / I'll Sail My Ship Alone
7003 – George Jones – Seasons of My Heart / Ragged But Right
7004 – Red Sovine – Little Rosa / Why Baby Why
7005 – Lonnie Irving – Pinball Machine / Tom O'Neal – Sleeper Cab Blues
7006 – Willis Brothers – Truck Driver's Queen / Bobby Sykes – Diesel Smoke, Dangerous Curves

7007 – Arthur "Guitar Boogie" Smith – Guitar Boogie Twist / Under the Double Eagle
7008 – Frankie Miller – Blackland Farmer / Too Hot To Handle
7009 – Jimmie Skinner – Dark Hollow / I Found My Girl in the U.S.A.
7010 – Buck Owens – Down On the Corner of Love / Sweethearts In Heaven
7011 – Hylo Brown – Cocaine Blues / The Willis Brothers – Tattooed Lady
7012 – June Stearns and Gene Martin – Slipping Around / Willis Brothers and Helen Carter – The Wild Side of Life
7013 – Eddie Wilson – Just One More / The Warm Red Wine
7014 – Red Sovine and June Stearns – A Dear John Letter / Eddie Wilson – Back Street Affair
7015 – Cowboy Copas – I Dreamed Of A Hillbilly Heaven / Tragic Romance
7016 – Pee Wee King and Redd Stewart – Bonaparte's Retreat / Slowpoke
7017 – Moon Mullican – Mona Lisa / Sweeter Than the Flowers
7018 – Arthur "Guitar Boogie" Smith – South / Memphis Blues
7019 – Helen Carter and Bobby Sykes – Release Me / Eddie Wilson – There Stands the Glass
7020 – George Jones – Wasted Words / Any Old Time
7021 – Johnny Bond – Barrel House Bessie / Hot Rod Lincoln
7022 – Hylo Brown – Truck Drivin' Man / Red Sovine – Six Days on the Road
7023 – Pee Wee King and Redd Stewart – The Tennessee Waltz / Clyde Moody – The Shenandoah Waltz
7024 – Benny Martin – Radar Blues / Lonnie Irving – Gooseball Brown
7025 – Floyd Tillman – I Love You So Much It Hurts Me / Leon McAuliff – Steel Guitar Rag
7026 –
7027 – Johnny Bond – Three Sheets in the Wind / Divorce Me C.O.D.
7028 – Kenny Roberts – Chime Bells / She Taught Me How to Yodel
7029 – Roger Miller – I Ain't Never / Under Your Spell Again
7030 – Patsy Cline – Walking After Midnight / Lovesick Blues
7031 – Johnny and Jonie Mosby – Makin' Believe / Dear Okie
7032 – Roger Miller – Country Girl / Jimmy Brown the Newsboy
7033 – Johnny Bond – Tennessee, Kentucky and Alabam / Glad Rags
7034 – Dottie West – Crazy / I Fall To Pieces
7035 – Hank Locklin – Let Me Be the One / Send Me the Pillow You Dream On
7036 – George Jones – Why Baby Why / You Gotta Be My Baby
7037 – Red Sovine – I'll Step Aside / He'll Have to Go
7038 – Roger Miller – The Tip of My Fingers / I Wish I Could Fall In Love Today

Nashville Singles – compiled by Nathan Gibson, with thanks to Dick Grant, Mike Smythe, Terry Gordon, Frank Frantik, and Ken Clee

Compiling this listing presented another major challenge, primarily due to the scarcity of many of these recordings. Fortunately, I had some luck. In what was perhaps my greatest record purchase on eBay, I bought a box simply listed as "Nashville records." Upon opening the poorly described box of vinyl, I uncovered over two hundred records on the Nashville label (score!). I must also thank Dick Grant, a major collector of the Nashville label, in addition to Mike Smythe, Terry Gordon, Frank Frantik, and Ken Clee, all of whom have contributed time and expertise to this listing. Though I was not able to visually verify every record (the contributors listed above sent me lists of their collections), I do believe this to be the most thorough attempt to date at completing the label's catalog. Again, several labels included misspelled names or song titles (for example, Delmer Sexton's name appears on some labels as Delmer Sexton and others as Delmar Sexton), and I have made every attempt to present them as they appeared on the original label.

5001 – Ray Pressley – Your New Love / You're a Part of Me
5002 – Ray King – Are You Living Just For Me / Show Her Lots of Gold
5003 – Whalen James – My Beautiful / My Blue Angel
5004 – Jerry Gray – Graduation Dance / Watching Cupid
5005 – Lowell Varney and the Rocky Mt. Pals – Corner of My Heart / Why I Love You
5006 – Dave Stewart – Yearning Heart / Thinking About You
5007 – Hal Parsons – Lost Love / Lonely Juke Box Love
5008 – Ray Arden – I'll Never Sleep Again / Send Me Back My Heart
5009 – Ken Clark – Truck Driving Joe / A Thousand Miles Ago
5010 – Jimmie Zack – My Get Up and Go / Lost John's Gone
5011 – Joe Hudgins – Around the Town / Crying My Heart Out
5012 – Jimmy Richardson and his Swinging Hammond Organ – Jambalaya / Coffee Expresso
5013 – Ben & Bill and the Arkansas Travelers – My One Mistake / Monkey See—Monkey Do
5014 – Bobby Hodge – Carolina Bound / You're Always Welcome (To Cry On My Shoulder)
5015 – Buddy Meredith – Time / Please Stay a Little While
5016 – Bobby Nelson – Your Letter / Blues Stay Away From Me
5017 – The Singing Cherokee – When You Walked Out On Me / Heartache to Me
5018 – Sammy Smith – Consolation In My Dreams / Your Helping Hand
5019 – Paul Wayne – More Than I Can Bear / Blues Have Got the Best of Me
5020 – Smiley Smith – I Found Out / House Upon the Hill
5021 – Eddie Jones – The Needle / Memories of You
5022 – Jimmy Simpson – Life Goes On "I Wonder Why" / A Year and A Day
5023 – Brownie Johnson – Your Heart of Stone / My Memories
5024 – Leon Hobson – Ball and Chain Blues / My Friend Took My Love Away
5025 – Doc Williams – Polka Dots and Polka Dreams / Oh My Happy Heart
5026 – Bill Luttrell and the Ozark Playboys – Sweet Heart of Mine / Splendid Ozarks
5027 – Jimmy Gately and Harold Morrison – Bee Sting / Ghost Town
5028 – Loyd Howell – Little Froggy Went A Courtin' / They Don't Know
5029 – Kenneth Cooper – Have You Seen My Baby / Thinking Of You
5030 – Kenny Hill – Don't Let My Glass Run Dry / True Love Is Hard To Find
5031 – Merlin Hill – 36-22-36 / Just the Way I Do
5032 – Lee Hood – Two Eyes, Two Arms, Two Lips / Doorway to Your Heart
5033 – Jimmy Richardson – Freeway / Stockade Roll
5034 – Johnny Moore – I Can't Tell My Heart a Lie / Jimmy Went A-Walking
5035 – Ray Pressley – Half a Love / Living, Learning, Trying To Forget
5036 – Bill Dudley – That's What Happened to Me Yesterday / Top Ten In Heaven
5037 – Buddy Wright with the Six Allen Sisters – Echoes of Love / Six Allen Sisters – Crying Over You
5038 – Billy Davis – I Think of You / Here Comes Rain
5039 – Max Williams – From Smiles to Tears / My Love Is Real

5040 – Jim Durdel – Bright Lights Uptown / You're Looking For An Angel
5041 – Delmar Sexton and the Rome County Boys – Afraid to Fall in Love / I'll Never Be Happy
5042 – Buddy Meredith – Haunted House / I May Fall Again
5043 – Buzzy Brant – Intermission / Valley of the Moon
5044 – Connie Rose – You're Going Away / I'll Cry Tomorrow
5045 – Jessie Bryant – Blow Four Winds / Turn Around Heart
5046 – Rusty Mitchell – I'm Losing Too / Hang Up the Phone
5047 – Johnny Moore – Country Boy / Be Honest With Me
5048 – Dick Miles – The Dream / Valhalla
5049 – Brownie Johnson – Just Pretending / Best Dressed Beggar (In Town)
5050 – Leon Hobson – Three Little Roses / I Can't Forget Loving You
5051 – Mike Miller and Jack Casey and the Stone Mountain Boys – Outer Space Blues / Love Me
5052 – Jimmy Gee – I Know How It Feels / Yes My Baby Wants Me
5053 – Eddy Jones – Reality Behind / I Heard the Children Crying
5054 – Hal Parsons – Night Life Baby / Blues Of the Night
5055 – Dale Henderson – Two Windows and a Door / There's A Whole Lot of Women (In This Old World)
5056 – Leo Busch – Star Fall / Fantasy
5057 – The Six Allen Sisters – Jilted Blues / Valley of Heartaches
5058 – Jim Durdel – Dreaming's A Lonesome Thing / Another's Kisses
5059 – Delmer Sexton – I've Never Done You Wrong / The Path of Life
5060 – Milt Myers – Lots of Luck / Blue Side of the World
5061 – Ross Trio – The Phone Keeps Ringing / Needy Needs
5062 – Howdy Kempf – The Way You Want To Live / Kinda Halfway Feel
5063 – Ersle Standridge – Satan's Call to Kruschev / The Story of the Orphan
5064 – Bill Dudley – Get Your Old Friend Off Your Mind / I'm Just Here To Get My Baby Out Of Jail
5065 – Max Williams – My Lips Are Lying / It's Plain To See
5066 – Jay Johnson with Earl Taylor and the Stoney Mt. Boys – Crazy Blues On My Mind / Crying Darling
5067 – Ozark Playboys – Don't Look At Me / Most Broken Heart
5068 – Mary Richey – While I Live In Misery / Tell Me Why
5069 – Faye Oliver – Honky Tonk Queen / I Wind Up With A Broken Heart
5070 – Kenneth Cooper – Isabelle / Dreaming—Dreaming
5071 – Johnny Moore – 15 Acres Of Peanut Land / Train Whistle
5072 – Dean Mathis – Stubborn Heart / Gotta Lot Of Love
5073 – Virgil Owen – I Thought I'd Know You / Just When It Starts To Get Night
5074 – Thomas Hardy – Thief of Love / Just Before the Heartache
5075 – Jimmy Gately and Harold Morrison – Death Row / True Love (Has Finally Come My Way)
5076 – Gavin Dycus – I Just Want To Be Left Lonely / Senorita Jones
5077 – Vicki Van Winkle – My Little Blue Eyes / There Goes My Heart
5078 – Bob England – Sweet Talk / I'm Gonna Laugh and Smile and Sing
5079 –
5080 – Slim Foster with Glaser Brothers – Robin With A Broken Wing / Legend of the Lost Creek Mine
5081 – Jim McCoy – If the Truth Is Gonna Hurt / That's What Makes the World Go Round

5082 – Dale Henderson – Take Care of What You've Found / Busy Busy Man
5083 – Gene Crockett with the Jamestown Boys – I Cried / The First Step
5084 – Jim Creer and the Mac-O-Chee Valley Folks – Wedding Band / Pretty Country Girl
5085 – Jimmy Simpson – Mr. Sun / Walking, Crying, Hurting Inside
5086 – Charlie Parker – Troubles / Missing Love
5087 – Norville Dollar – Settle Down and Love Me / Who'll Be Next
5088 – Ron Smith – All About Blues / Side Winder
5089 – Johnny Nace – Look, Don't Touch / Today Is Tomorrow
5090 – Buddy Starcher – Star 35 / Little Red Riding Hood
5091 – Leon Hobson – Heaven Sent Me Someone To Love / Love Is Like A River
5092 – Howdy Kempf – I'm Lonesome In My Heart / That's What You Tell Me
5093 – Jim Kandy – Between Your House and Mine / I Forgot To Love Her
5094 – Leo Busch – Lover Boy Tim / Watching the Rain Fall
5095 – Bill Douglas – Heartaches and Teardrops Go Together / When Each Day Ends
5096 – Gene Galimore – Battle of Murfreesboro / Easy Way To Go
5097 – Justice Brothers, Jim & Bill & the Cumberland Mtn. Boys – Dreamland / My Darlin's Gone
5098 – Bobby Pierce – 21 Years / To-Ra
5099 – Bob Williams – Thanks For the Offer / Breaking Up the Heartaches
5100 – Bob Berndt – Just Step Back / Big Chi
5101 – Jim Greer and the Mac-O-Chee Valley Boys – I Want the World To Know / In the Sky
5102 – Buddy Starcher – The Man Who Rode the Hog Around the World / A Little Girl's Letter To Mr. K
5103 – Dean Mathis – Unfaithful Sweetheart / Crazy But I'm In Love
5104 – Patty Koenig – Someone to Care / He Died For You
5105 – Johnny Moore – Traveling Salesman / Old Memories Of You
5106 – Marvin Jackson – It's Easy To Say / Sticky Fingers
5107 – The Reece Sisters (Marjorie – Georgia – Martha) – A Memory And A Broken Heart / Leave It Alone
5108 – Tommy Thompson "The Missouri Cowboy" – Whose Heart Are You Breaking / I Cry Myself To Sleep
5109 – Shorty Barnhill – Beautiful Carolinas / Waltz of the Mountains
5110 – The Travelers (vocal by Bill McManners) – Lips That Do the Talking / The Travelers (vocal by Ben Cooley) – Make Believe World
5111 – Dale Henderson – Vicious Vodka / Tomorrow's Blue
5112 – Gavin Dycus – Let's Forget It / Katie Malone
5113 – Lyle Collins and the Rebel-Aires (vocal Bill Risner) – Johnnycake Mountain / I'll Buy This Dream
5114 – Johnny Nace – Heartbreak Hall of Fame / Make A Date With Me
5115 – Jimmy Ginn – Tell Me, Sweetheart / Blue Days and Nights
5116 – Teddy & Jack – Directions To Lonely Street / She Let Me Down
5117 – Bill Johnson – Big Bill Johnson / Pitchin' Woo
5118 – Jimmy Starr – Blind Date / Mister Misery
5119 – Charles Everidge – Fickle Hearted Fool / Four Walls and a Window
5120 – Spero Lavis – Let Her Go / Lets Stop the Clock
5121 – Leo Busch – Lonely Little Teardrop / Hold Tight
5122 – Paul Johnson – Flirtin' / The World's Biggest Fool
5123 – The Ozark Playboys – Angel In the Hills / If I Said It Once

5124 – Ron Smith – Angel Dreams / Honi B
5125 – Junior Garner – Conscience / Go On and Live With the Devil
5126 – Dallas Shaw – Don't Stay Away Too Long / It's Just Not Like It Used To Be
5127 – Justice Brothers, Jim & Bill and the Cumberland Mt. Play Boys – Missing Mother of Ohio / Visions of Heaven
5128 – Hobo Jack – Old Man's Story / Kentucky Hobo
5129 – Ray King – I'm An Old Pipe Liner / Who Put the Blues In Your Heart
5130 – Ersle Standridge – I Can't Live Without You / Going Back To Opello
5131 – Virgil Owen – They Ask Me Why I Cry / Whatever You Think Best
5132 – Slim Foster with Glaser Brothers – A Love Like Yours / My Foolish Heart
5133 – Johnny Colmus – Sweet Mary Troy / Someone Like You
5134 – Ken Clark – Talk About Love / Ease My Mind
5135 – Bob Williams – How Will It End / Pretending
5136 – The Byrd Family – There's A Light At the River / The Purple Robe / God Put A Rainbow In the Clouds / Keep Your Eyes on Jesus
5137 – Marvin Jackson – Peek-A-Boo / Heart Of Mine
5138 – Lyle Collins & the Rebel-Aires – House of Memories / The Wall
5139 – Big Bill Johnson – Umm, Boy, You're My Baby / Wasted Lives
5140 – Bill Schaeffer – Dice Fever / Now You're Gone
5141 – Sally Marcum – Still In Love / Blue Telephone
5142 – Ralph Davis – Way Cross County / Pull the Middle Chain
5143 – Robert White and His Candy Mountain Boys – Huggin My Pillow / All Day Singing
5144 – Brausser Family – Just a Closer Walk With Thee / Angel Band / Life's Railway To Heaven / There's No Excuse
5145 – Skeeter Bonn and Shirley Starr – For Sale / Old Memories
5146 – Lowell Varney – Why Did You Leave Me / Twelve Toed John
5147 – Marvin Centers – Luring Lights / I Can't Drive You From My Mind
5148 – Bud Stack – Jealous Hearted / I Don't Want To Hurt You
5149 – Phillip Atkinson – The Loneliest Night of the Year / Gonna Take a Walk
5150 – Big Bill Johnson – Lonesome Daddy Blues / Alimony
5151 – Robert White and the Candy Mountain Boys – It's Hillbilly Christmas (Every Saturday) /Robert White and the Candy Mountain Boys vocal by Donnie Ray White - Picture In the Wallet
5152 – Gene Pierson – Breaking My Vow / Engineer Mountain
5153 – Wilf Conway – Thunder and Lightning / I'm Wondering Why
5154 – The Travelers (voc. by Ben Cooley) – Passions Over Conscience / Most Of the Time
5155 – The Brausser Family – His Light On Me / Ask, Ye Shall Receive / Gethsemane / Satisfied
5156 – Marlan Centers – Out In the Open / How All Alone Am I
5157 – Bud Stack – My Farewell To You / T.B. Blues
5158 –Casuals (vocal by Linda Burke) – My Darling / Casuals (vocal by Rick Towson) – It's Gonna Work Out Right
5159 – Teenie Chenault – I'm So Alone / It's A Big Old Heartache
5160 – Johnny Dee & the Continentals – A Tribute to President Kennedy / The Continentals & the Grand Prees – Dark Night
5161 – Paul Holt and His King Cotton Playboys – Three Fools / My World Is Turning Gray
5162 – Phillip Atkinson – I'd Rather Be A Has-Been / Have You Ever Loved Someone (That Didn't Love You)

5163 – Sally Marcum – No Fool Like An Old Fool / Round and Round
5164 –
5165 – Lowell Varney & Albert Parsley, tenor by Trenton Marcum – Don't Leave / Lowell Varney & Albert Parsley – Five String Rock
5166 – Jimmy Dee – The One I Love / Please Don't Go
5167 – Robertson Brothers & Eddie Gilmer – Why Do I Cry / Poison Love
5168 – Roy Campbell – As Close As Your Phone / Deep Inside
5169 – Trail Blazers (voc. by Kay & Sue) – Cowboy's Sweetheart / I'll Be All Smiles Tonight
5170 – Charles Poston – It Only Hurts Forever / Nature Boy
5171 – Delta Flames – How Bout It / The Ring
5172 – Leon Nail – Life Without You / I Saw the Warnin'
5173 – Tom Dixon "The Singing Sailor" – Oswego, New York / A True Sailor's World
5174 – The Byrd Family – That Heavenly Home / Happy Living / The Great Speckled Bird / Hide You In the Blood
5175 – Diplomats – Grab a Little Sunshine / I'll Take Care of Your Cares
5176 – Rodney Rains – You'll Want To Come Back Home / You've Been Away Too Long
5177 – Dick & Dewrell – Ring Telephone / I Keep Talking
5178 – Bill McCormack – Tavern Lights / D-I-V-O-R-C-E
5179 – Blue Ervin – Alaska Earthquake / Please
5180 – Mel Grubbs – Skid Row / This Old Road
5181 – Johnny Nace – I Think It's Time To Go / I Thought I Knew
5182 – Joyce Ridings – You've Got My Ring On Your Finger / I'm Still Single
5183 – Seventeens – Fannie Mae / I'm Not Talking
5184 – Gerrie Lynn – Every Time I Do Right / Lonely
5185 – Billy Hill – Losing My Memory / The Biggest Fool
5186 – Larry Good – I Don't Think You Love Me Anymore / Money Troubles
5187 – Everrett Freeman – Wait A Minute / A Big Heartache
5188 – Robert White – Old Fashioned Christian / If You Don't Know His Love / Blazing Sun / Our Lord's Spaceship
5189 – Tex Climer & Jay Earls – Truck Drivin' Buddies / Blues In the Glass
5190 – Johnny Rexx – Queen of Hearts / Don't Waste Your Tears Over Me
5191 – Sammy Hearn – Love Is Worth More Than Gold / Thief In the Night
5192 – Chuck Holt – Lonesome Me / Straving For Love
5193 – Lee Hood – I've Never Made A Hit / I'll Go To the Jumping Off Place With You
5194 –
5195 – Roy Campbell – Why Go On / You Went Out of Your Way
5196 – Christian Heirs Quartet – What A Wonderful Time / We're Going To Move / We've Got To See God For Ourself / I'm Moving Up Home Someday
5197 – Betty Hitchcock – Count On Me For That / Memories Of You
5198 – Walter "Tex" Dixon and the Country Boys – Ballad of John Rollin / Girl in the Blue Velvet Band
5199 – Jay P. Mayton – Two Little Drops of Water / My Heart's My Daily Reminder
5200 – Slim Anderson – Tavern Town / Let's Walk the Line
5201 – The RG's (Joe Robertson – Harold Robertson Eddie Gilmer) – Take This Picture / Right Or Wrong
5202 – Red Steed – I Still See Your Face / No One Will Ever Know
5203 – Johnny Rexx – I Wish I Knew (Please Tell Me) / I Don't Believe I'll Fall In Love Today
5204 – Sweet Eva Lena Chenault – Miss You All the Time / Hurts Don't Hurt Anymore

RECORD LISTING

5205 – Betty Hitchcock – Last Night / Bring Back My Treasures
5206 – Mel Grubbs – Loserville / Born To Ramble
5207 – Art Pettibone – Footsteps / Moonlight
5208 – Blue Ervin – Talk To Me, Baby / Gold Fever
5209 – Stan White – I'm the Talk Of the Town / Is It Too Late
5210 –Ritchey Brothers (Melvin & Galen) – Way Down In Mexico / Stay Away From My Baby
5211 – Tom Dixon – A Place In My Heart / Cold Grey Moon
5212 – Billy Hill – Merry Little Party / Hello Mr. World
5213 – Gerrie Lynn – Heed My Warning / I Love You More and More Everyday
5214 – Tex Climer & Jay Earls – Things Aren't Like They Used To Be / Cigarette—Glass of Wine
5215 – Smokey Rogers – I'll Be Glad When It's Over / Everything's Coming Home (To Me, But You)
5216 – Marshall Hannah – Wonderin' Bill / Marshall Hannah and Pearl Hannah – No More Heartaches
5217 – Earl Green – That's What Keeps Loneliness Away / My Old Used To Be
5218 – Ersle Standridge – Listening To the Jukebox / Mr. Frog Hair
5219 – Abbie Gaye with Ken & Mel – I've Got a Polecat By the Tail / Don't Spread the Word Around
5220 – The Discords – Wiggle—Wobble and Jerk / The Discords, vocal by James Billings – Two Teen Hearts
5221 – Larry Edwards – Making the Rounds / Yours and Mine
5222 – Sweet Eva Lena Chenault– He Came To Heal / We Can See
5223 – Sweet Eva Lena Chenault – Grandpa Thompson / Just For Days Gone By
5224 – Gene Stewart and the River Ranch Boys – Love Letters To Me / Walk Easy
5225 – Art Pettibone – Plug Me / Cumberland Mountains
5226 – Cecil Baysingers – That's What Makes the Jukebox Play / When the Burp Hits the Fan
5227 – Chet Good – High Living / I Keep Forgetting I Forgot
5228 – Bill Brownlee – Hangover From Love / Columbus
5229 – Jackie D. Parrish – No More Hurt, No More Heart / Sad Town
5230 – Rome Duke – When the !! Hits the Fan?? / You're Always Brand New
5231 – Alex Campbell and Olabelle and the New River Boys – I Can't Be Satisfied / You Don't Even Know
5232 –
5233 –
5234 – George Winn & the Blue Grass Partners – Thinking Of You / Life Of Solitude
5235 – Bill Pierce – Fool That I Am / Remind Me To Cry Tomorrow
5236 – Chris Val – A Better Way To Die / Does It Have To Be
5237 – Bill Thomas – Wanting and Loving You / Cash On the Barrel Head
5238 – Jack Lionell – Passing Fancy / Was She Worth It
5239 – Mary Lou Turner – The Frame Of Mind You're In / I Lost My Biggest Race
5240 – Johnny Nace – Too Many Tears / I Should Have Written A Song
5241 – Sarah R. James – Chee-Chee / I Won't Play
5242 – Carol Charkarian – Put Your Accent On Love / Lost In This World Of Love
5243 – Red Steed – You're the One / Talk To Me Lonesome Heart
5244 – Slim Anderson – I Think A Lot Of You / Once Upon A Time
5245 – Larry Edwards – I'll Never Cry Again / I Walk the Dark Streets

5246 – Jimmy Kish – I Dare To Dream / It's My Lazy Day
5247 – Little George Jones – Kiss Me Darling / I Need Someone
5248 – Arvee Kiser – This War Between Us / Heartache Following Me
5249 – Archie Poe – Back Streets / Juke Box Julie
5250 – Harry Sexton – I'm Making Love To A Stranger / Little White Cross On the Hill
5251 – Bobby Mack – Who Put the Blues In Your Heart / Indian Love Call
5252 – Art Pettibone – Moon Rocket / Fire Fire Fire
5253 – Whalen James – Weaver Of Dreams / Love Me Just A Little
5254 – Bobby Mack – Come Back To Me / Tell You What I'm Gonna Do
5255 – Pete Williams – You Left the Memories / Truck Driving Man
5256 – Sweet Eva Lena Chenault – Wings Of A Dove / Way Of Life Eternal
5257 – Sweet Eva Lena Chenault – I'll Step Out Of Your Way / I'm Sinful Cinderella
5258 – Ersle Standridge – I'm A Rambling Man / The Fate Of Tommy Smith
5259 – Chris Val – Standing Alone / Lights Were Down Dim
5260 – Pappy Tipton "Mr. Opry D.J." – I'm Writing A Song / I've Waited As Long As I Can
5261 – Ralph Loveday – First Thing In the Morning / More Love Than I Could Give Her
5262 – Louie Owens – Honey, You're Not Fooling Me / What Am I Doing
5263 – Gene Stewart – The Only One You Love Is You / It's A Big World
5264 – Rome Duke – Mayor Of A Lonely Town / Half As Bad
5265 – Gavin Dycus – Let's Forget It / I Just Want To Be Left Lonely
5266 –
5267 – Bill Thomas – A Heart That I Can't Touch / Down Down Down
5268 – Bill Pierce – Someone I Used To Know / Hate Those Blues
5269 – Bobby Parrish – A Pack of Cigarettes / Gold Class Ring
5270 – Sally Marcum – Each Time We Kiss / Bright Eyed and Bushy Tailed
5271 – Luke Gordon – Love's Fantasy / Threshold To Heaven
5272 – Marvin Dawson – Great Divide / Curtis Brewton – Love Sick Pair
5273 – "Lil" Richard and the Caprees – Uuh Baby / By My Side
5274 – Polly Hutt & Her Crackers – Why Buy the Cow / You'll Never Love Him (Like I Do)
5275 – Betty Hitchcock – Don't Let the Sun Go Down / You've Gone And Left Me Blues
5276 – Cecil Baysingers – That Same Door Let You In / Swing Till My Rope Breaks
5277 – Don E. Lewis – The Chaplin / Mail Call
5278 – Art Pettibone – T. Bone Spoons / Clouds In the Sky
5279 – Little George Jones – A Broken Heart Love Affair / The One I Lost
5280 – Doy Lewis – Each Night At Nine / You're All the Sunshine I Need
5281 – Margie Lee – I'll Set You Free / Honky Tonk Blues
5282 – Tommy Belger – Bikini Time / Dancing Girl
5283 – Jimmy Stutts and Sue Robbins – Not Enough Time Left / How Many More Fools (Will You Find)
5284 – Fred Thompson – Shadows Of the Past / Thunder and Lightning
5285 – Pete Harris – This Twisted Heart of Mine / 18 Big Old Wheels
5286 – Jackie D. Parrish – I Like To Hear George Jones Sing / How Do You Teach A Heart
5287 – Don Lewis – This World Tomorrow / Two Minutes Of Reminiscing (At 45 R.P.M.)
5288 – Shirley Foley – Everything Has Stopped / She Couldn't Love You (Like I Do)
5289 – Leroy & Hurdis, The Lake Brothers – Thanks For Sending Me Your Friend / Two Time Loser
5290 – Pat & Darrell Wykle – Lonely Again / Left Out
5291 – Texas Bill Strength – The Moment I Found You / Best Thing In Life Is Love

RECORD LISTING

5292 – Bob Cooley – Just A Dream / Sioux City Sue
5293 – Kay Stump – You Even Fooled Me / Your Time Is All Your Own
5294 – Jay Stump – Rock It On Down / Slipping Around
5295 – Jerry McKinnon – Can't Get No Worse / Living the Blues
5296 – Bob Porter – Thanks To Heaven / Hearts Break Like Glass
5297 –
5298 – Dick Barnes – A Step Away From Heaven / King of the Road
5299 – Johnny Bondz – I've Played Second Fiddle (For the Last Time) / Remmington Ride
5300 – Easter Brothers and the Green Valley Quartet – God Isn't Dead / They Know Of You and Me
5301 – Johnny Stiffey with the Ranch Hands – You Really Shook Me Up / That Old Feeling
5302 – The GT's – Farewell Faithless Farewell / Bad Girl
5303 – Brenda Bishop with the G.T.'s – It's All Over / Just Passing Through
5304 – Joei Jordon with the G.T.'s – The Waltz of the Wind / Two Hearts That Broke Away
5305 – Jim Keeney – Grand Ole Opry Stage / Jump From A Moving Train
5306 – Don Lewis – Bama's Tiny Giants / Could You Wear These Shoes
5307 – Rolling Joe Johnson – Fighting Men of the U.S.A. / One Long Burning Kiss
5308 – Archie Poe – Foolish Notions / Everything Gets Me Down
5309 – Bobby Parrish – I Wish / I Always Will
5310 – Valora Louise – Mommy, How Come Daddy Don't Live Here With Us / Going Out of Style
5311 – Rita Lovelace – In Love With You / Keep Your Cotton Pickin' Hands Off Of Me
5312 – Doy Lewis – My Heart Mustn't Know / Turn Around
5313 – Shorty Barnhill – Every Hour of the Day / Sympathy
5314 – Jimmy Kish – Connie Moore / That's What Makes A Heartache
5315 – Betty Hitchcock – Left Over Kisses / Memoryville
5316 – Dean Hetrick – The String That I Was Dangling On / Red Wood Tree
5317 – Bud Stack – Believe Me / Please Santa, Take My Toys To Viet Nam
5318 –
5319 – Madeliene Behrle – The Unknown Soldier / When Johnny Comes Marching Home Again
5320 – Ted Wilkins – Shoulder To Cry On / All Is Forgiven
5321 – Bob Porter – Bad News / Tiny Finger Prints On the Wall
5322 – Margie Lee – You Don't Follow Through / The Joke Is On You
5323 – Johnny Rexx – Earful of Tears / Six Days On the Road
5324 – Dale Mason – You Taught Her Honky Tonk Ways / If I Lose Your Love
5325 – Billy Thomas – Wandering Man / I Broke A Bottle On the Table
5326 – Dick Unteed – The Little Black Dog / When the Bright Lights Grow Dim
5327 – Bob Smart – Four Steps To Me / Sweet Memories
5328 – Jerry McKinnon – A Better Me / Mr. Heartache
5329 –
5330 – Charlie Maybee – Forever / She's Breaking My Heart
5331 – Al Dean – It's Me—I'm Home Again / It Looks Up
5332 – Tommy Belger – Gossip Of the Town / Believe Me
5333 – Larry Marney – All Is Forgiven / Losing Her By Loving You
5334 – The Kenetics – Jo Ann / Put Your Loving On Me
5335 – Dick Unteed – Walk Slowly Darling / Billy Richardson's Last Ride
5336 – Jan Black – What Would You Do / This Time Tomorrow

5337 – Dempsey Sims – Truckers Rhythm / Blues Tomorrow
5338 – Sally Marcum – I Want To Be With You / Ten Gallon Teardrops
5339 – Pat and Darrell – Not Even Friends / Back To Me
5340 – William Huston – Troubles / Daddy Please Fix My Swing
5341 –
5342 – Ersle Standridge and the Osborn Sisters – My Little Boy Rena / I'd Like To Have My Picture (Made With You)
5343 – Billy Thomas – I Still Care / Deep Dark Mountain
5344 – Randy Spangler – The Little Voice / I'll Never Stop Lovin' You
5345 – Art Pettibone – Travelling Spoon Man / Don't Write Me A Letter
5346 – Bob Smart – My Life, My Dreams / Found She Was Gone
5347 – Larry Cline – I Wonder / Nine Times Out Of Ten
5348 – Gil Rogers – Sitting On A Bar Stool / Story On A Jukebox
5349–5448 –
5449 – Bobby Tidwell – I Wonder (Who Lives Next Door) / The Worst Of You (Has Got the Best of Me)
5450 – Bill Kohlmeyer – This Lonely / Somebody New
5451 – Brock McCoy – If My Heart Could Talk / Say You're Mine
5452 – Rolling Joe Johnson – Pretty Eyes / The Best of Luck (To You)
5453 – Barney Hughes – I'm Walking Out Of Your World / Money Joe
5454 – Jim C. Stevens – A Scene From Life's Picture / Walkin' Talkin'
5455 – Walt and Betty Riddle – You Can Be Sure / Sunny Side Of Things
5456 – Bud Strack – I Forgot To Say Good-bye To You / All Night Long
5457 – William Huston – Deadly Poison / Condemned, Convicted, Good-by
5458 – Bob Porter – Throw In the Crying Towel / Trouble Rang My Bell
5459 – Doug LaValley – The Shadow Of A Man / A Bottle And A Broken Heart
5460 – Galen Dean – Change Your Ways Of Living / The End Will Justify the Means
5461 – Larry Marney – As Long As It's You / Top Of Nowhere
5462 – Johnny Rexx – Bells of Southern Bell / Take Good Care of Her
5463 – Billy Thomas – How Time Changes People / I Couldn't Figure Out
5464 – Art Pettibone – Key In the Door / Full Moon
5465 – Henri Conley – Suzie's World / I Gave You All the Love (A Good Girl Can)
5466 – Keith Dovanda – For All We Know / [?]
5467 – Berde & Danny Farris – Honky Tonk Mother and Dad / Where the Mountains Meet the Moon
5468 – Tex Larabey – Big Heart / Throw A Snowball For Me
5469 – Ersle Standridge – Petti Jean Mountain / Un-Trusting Hearts
5470 – Keith Kovanda – Who Can I Turn To / Cecelia
5471 – Barbara Sanders – The Heart of the Matter / Jumpin' Jack
5472 –
5473 – Tex Larabey – Music To Get Stoned To / From the Trunk of the Car
5474 – Dempsey Sims – Sentimental Tears / Blue Eyed Baby
5475 – Billy Thomas – For the Sake Of Me / Welcome Home My Boy
5476 – Cheryle Wagner – God's Rain / Plow Man
5477 – Al Hilman – Keep It A Secret / Dear Hearts and Gentle People
5478 – Jody Irvin – Baby Oh Baby / Our Wedding Day
5479 – Hoyt Scoggins, Roy Ledford and Ricky Woods – Returned Package From Vietnam / Bluegrass Theme #1

5480 – "Rollin" Joe Johnson – This Wall of Tears / Our Own Little World
5481 – Skeeter Osborne – Gonna Whistle Me A Tune / A Broken Heart Won't Ever Tell Lies
5482 – Lucky Moore – Trembling Hands / Lucky Moore & Wanda Moore – Lonely Spot
5483 – The Southern Mountain Boys – Wasted Tears / My Childhood Home
5484 – Arlene Murphy – Fool's Paradise / You're Nothing But A Wild Rose
5485 – Billy Kent – Think Drink / You're Free To Go
5486 – Slim Bonniger – Outside of Loneliness / Con Man
5487 – Betty Bee & Linda – Lookin' For the Gal That Stole My Man / Country Girl
5488 – Donald Earl – Joe Monroe, Tennessee Mt. Boys – Get Out and Push / Easy Pickin'
5489 – Chuck Baxter – Reach You / Tell Me
5490 – Bob Smart – Something Ain't Right / 10 P.M.
5491 – The Gospel-Ettes – You Shall Find Me / My Home In America
5492 – The Gospel-Ettes – The Light of the Lord / Great Mystery
5493 – Jody Irvin – This Heart Of Mine / Generation Gap
5494 – Skeeter Osborne – My Little Playmate / One Week To Live
5495 – Jimmy Lynch – If You Don't Believe I Love You / Loose Talk
5496 – Arnold McKinney – The Girl Dressed In Blue / Understand The Weakness In You
5497 – Chuck Baxter – I'll Try Not To Bother You Again / My Restless Heart
5498 – Curly Dan and Wilma Ann – A Visit Back Home / South On 23
5499 – Danny Goodman – Blue and Lonesome / If You Only Knew
5500 – Chuck Hess – Boomerang / New Orleans
5501 – Skeeter Osborne – Bug House / Jest Like A Duck
100 – Chuck Baxter – Harold's Super Service / You Gave Me A Mountain
101 – Eddie Olvera – Don't Be Angry / Today I Started Loving You Again

Nashville Albums – compiled by Nathan Gibson with thanks to Mike Callahan and Jeff Porterfield

I have been able to personally verify nearly every Nashville budget LP, though specific thanks go to Mike Callahan and Jeff Porterfield for posting their Nashville LP discography on their website, Both Sides Now Publications. Their website, bsnpubs.com, includes song titles for the Starday and Nashville LPs (in addition to many useful though unrelated discographies).

NLP 2001 – *Bluegrass Special* – Various Artists
NLP 2002 – Wayne Raney – *The Big 18*
NLP 2003 – *Old Time Religion* – Various Artists
NLP 2004 – Bill Clifton – *Mountain Bluegrass Songs*
NLP 2005 – *Peace in the Valley* – Various Artists
NLP 2006 – *Country Express* – Various Artists
NLP 2007 – Carl Story – *Rambling Mountaineers*
NLP 2008 – The Sunshine Boys – *Country Music Sing Along*
NLP 2009 – *Nashville Saturday Night* – Various Artists
NLP 2010 – Sunshine Boys – *America's No. 1 Quartet*
NLP 2011 – *Banjo In the Hills* – Various Artists
NLP 2012 – *The Stars and Hits of Country Music* – Various Artists
NLP 2013 – Cowboy Copas – *The Late and Great Cowboy Copas*
NLP 2014 – The Stanley Brothers – *Mountain Song Favorites*

NLP 2015 – *Fiddlin' Country Style* – Various Artists
NLP 2016 – The Lewis Family – *Singing Time Down South*
NLP 2017 – *Nashville Steel Guitar* – Various Artists
NLP 2018 – Bill Clifton – *Bluegrass in the American Tradition*
NLP 2019 – *Big Train Express* – Various Artists
NLP 2020 – The Lonesome Pine Fiddlers – *Kentucky Bluegrass*
NLP 2021 – *Country Guitar* – Various Artists
NLP 2022 – Tommy Hill – *The Swingin' Sound of Modern Music with Percussion*
NLP 2023 – Lonnie "Pap" Wilson – *Country Comedy*
NLP 2024 – Carl Story – *Everybody Will Be Happy*
NLP 2025 – Hylo Brown – *Bluegrass Goes to College*
NLP 2026 – Shot Jackson With Buddy Emmons – *Steel Guitar and Dobro Sounds*
NLP 2027 – Ernest Carter and the Hymn Trio – *I Met a Man*
NLP 2028 – *Country Music's Greatest Stars* – Various Artists
NLP 2029 – *Country Girl, Sing Me a Song!* – Various Artists
NLP 2030 – *Everyday I Have the Blues* – Various Artists
NLP 2031 – *Stars of the Grand Ole Opry* – Various Artists
NLP 2032 – *Four Kings of Country Music* – Various Artists
NLP 2033 – Red Sovine – *Giddy-Up Go*
NLP 2034 – *Truck Drivin' Man* – Various Artists
NLP 2035 – George Jones – *Why Baby Why*
NLP 2036 – Cowboy Copas – *Alabam*
NLP 2037 – The Stanley Brothers – *Carter and Ralph*
NLP 2038 – Bob Kames – *You Can't Be True Dear*
NLP 2039 – Johnny Bond – *Sick, Sober and Sorry*
NLP 2040 – The Willis Brothers – *Travelin' and Truck Driver Hits*
NLP 2041 – Dottie West – *I Fall to Pieces*
NLP 2042 – Pee Wee King and Redd Stewart – *Tennessee Waltz and Slowpoke*
NLP 2043 – Minnie Pearl – *Lookin' Fer a Feller*
NLP 2044 – Red Sovine – *Dear John Letter*
NLP 2045 – The Lewis Family – *The Lewis Family Takes You to a Gospel Sing-Out*
NLP 2046 – Roger Miller – *Amazing Roger Miller*
NLP 2047 – Red Sovine, Willis Brothers and Others – *There Stands the Glass*
NLP 2048 – *Top 10* – Various Artists
NLP 2049 – *Back Street Affair* – Various Artists
NLP 2050 – Cowboy Copas – *Signed, Sealed and Delivered*
NLP 2051 – *Swingin' Instrumental Hits From Nashville* – Various ArtistsNLP 2052 – *Truck Stop* – Various Artists
NLP 2053 – The Willis Brothers – *Y'all Come/Satisfied Mind*
NLP 2054 – Johnny Bond – *Three Sheets In the Wind*
NLP 2055 – *Steel Guitar Hall of Fame* – Various Artists
NLP 2056 – Red Sovine – *Anytime*
NLP 2057 – *Five Queens of Music* – Various Artists
NLP 2058 – *The Country Side of Bonnie and Clyde* – Various Artists
NLP 2059 – *Folsom Prison Blues* – Various Artists
NLP 2060 – Arthur "Guitar Boogie" Smith – *Guitar Boogie*
NLP 2061 – George Morgan – *Misty Blue*
NLP 2062 – The Lewis Family – *Gospel Singing Sensations From Dixie*

NLP 2063 – The Stonemans – *Stonemans!*
NLP 2064 – Archie Campbell – *The Many Talents of Archie Campbell*
NLP 2065 – Dave Dudley – *Greatest Hits: Six Days on the Road*
NLP 2066 – *Truck and Country* – Various Artists
NLP 2067 – Flatt and Scruggs, Jim and Jesse, the Stanley Brothers, Mac Wiseman – *I'll Still Write Your Name In the Sand*
NLP 2068 – Dolly Parton, Dottie West, Jan Howard, June Stearns – *Release Me*
NLP 2069 – George Jones – *Mountain Dew*
NLP 2070 – Hawkshaw Hawkins – *Everlasting Hits*
NLP 2071 – Reno and Smiley – *Emotions*
NLP 2072 – Homer and Jethro – *Best of Homer and Jethro*
NLP 2073 – Sunshine Boys – *Peace in the Valley*
NLP 2074 – Guy Mitchell – *Heartaches By the Number*
NLP 2075 – *Truck Drivers Queen* – Various Artists
NLP 2076 – George Jones – *Seasons of My Heart*
NLP 2077 – Cowboy Copas – *Filipino Baby*
NLP 2078 – The Stanley Brothers – *Sweeter Than the Flowers*
NLP 2079 – *Gee From Haw* – Various Artists
NLP 2080 – Moon Mullican – *I'll Sail My Ship Alone*
NLP 2081 – *Honky Tonk Angels* – Various Artists
NLP 2082 – Leroy Van Dyke – *Greatest Hits*
NLP 2083 – Red Sovine – *Ruby Don't Take Your Love to Town*
NLP 2084 – *Haul Off and Love Me* – Various Artists
NLP 2085 – *Four Kings of Country Music, Volume 2* – Various Artists
NLP 2086 – The Oak Ridge Boys – *A Higher Power*
NLP 2087 – Flatt and Scruggs – *Foggy Mountain Breakdown*
NLP 2088 – *Four Kings of Country Music, Volume 3* – Various Artists
NLP 2089 – *Country Hit Parade* – Various Artists
NLP 2090 – *Making Believe* – Various Artists
NLP 2091 – Joe Maphis and Jackie Phelps – *Nashville Guitars*
NLP 2092 – Joe South with Royal Nash – *You're the Reason*
NLP 2093 – George Jones – *Color of the Blues*
NLP 2094 – George Morgan – *Room Full of Roses*
NLP 2095 – Kenny Roberts – *I Never See Maggie Alone*
NLP 2096 – *Truck Stop Favorites* – Various Artists
NLP 2097 – Grandpa Jones – *15 Cents Is All I Got*
NLP 2098 – *Swingin' Doors* – Various Artists
NLP 2099 – *Almost Persuaded* – Various Artists
NLP 2100 – Stringbean – *Hee Haw Corn Shucker*
NLP 2101 – *Country Dynamite From Nashville* – Various Artists
NLP 2102 – *Bluegrass Festival* – Various Artists
NLP 2103 – George Jones – *The Window Up Above*
NLP 2104 – *Nashville Wives* – Various Artists
NLP 2105 – Red Sovine – *Little Rosa*
NLP 2106 – T. Texas Tyler – *Remember Me*
NLP 2107 – *Whole Lotta Shakin'* – Various Artists
NLP 2108 – Johnny Cash – *I Walk the Line*
NLP 2109 – *Harper Valley PTA* – Various Artists

NLP 2110 –
NLP 2111 –
NLP 2112 – The Stanley Brothers – *Rank Strangers*
NLP 2113 – *The Stars and Hits of Bluegrass* – Various Artists
NLP 2114 – *Opry Special, Various Top Stars* – Various Artists
NLP 2115 – *Dueling Banjos* – Various Artists

Dixie Rock 'n' Roll Series Singles – compiled by Nathan Gibson, with thanks to Terry Gordon

This is yet another short-lived but fascinating aspect of the Starday story. Scouring eBay and various record shops allowed me to complete this listing rather quickly. Dixie 2013 is the oddity and is not usually noted on similar lists of Dixie rock records. Though the music is straightforward pop and the label (yellow label with the cursive Dixie font) is most often associated with the *Hillbilly Hit Parade* series, this record numerically fits within the Dixie Rock Series. I also want to thank Terry Gordon for his fantastic Rockin' Country Style website, rcs.discography.com, which provided label scans and soundbites for many of these records.

2001 – Benny Joy – Spin the Bottle / Steady with Betty
2002 – Doug Bragg – Red Rover / Lovin' On My Mind
2003 – Gene Watson – I'll Always Love You / Life's Valley
2004 – Doug Bragg – Pretty Little Things / Jerry
2005 – Jimmie Lee and the Playboys – Three Little Wishes / Teen Age Love Song
2006 – Pat and Dee – Gee Whiz / Don't Tease Me
2007 – Orville Couch – Easy Does It / Let It Happen
2008 – Derrell Felts and the Confederates – Playmates / The Weepers
2009 – Ken Hammock with Tennessee Valley Gang – Blue Guitar Jump / Angel in Person
2010 – Bill Carroll – Feel So Good / In My Heart
2011 – Eddie Skelton – Keep It Swinging / Without You
2012 – Dee Johnson – Just Look, Don't Touch / One More Chance
2013 – The Populaires – Gloria from Peoria / Honey / Princess Poo-Poo-ly / Sweet Violets
2014 – Bill Goodwin – Your Lying Ways / Will You Still Love Me
2015 – Eddie Skelton and his Rhythmtones – Love You Too Much / Rebels Retreat
2016 – Mel Price – Little Dog Blues / Until
2017 – Cathy Kelley – Blues Hanging Round / Every Now and Then
2018 – Groove Joe Poovey – Ten Long Fingers / Thrill of Love
2019 – Art Ontario – It Must Be Me / Last Goodbye
2020 – Alden Holloway – Blast Off / Swinging the Rock
2021 – Hughey Bunch and the Bradley Farm Hands – South Wind / Cry Tomorrow
2022 – Dee Johnson – Back to School / I'm Your Guy
2023 – Jay Gallegher – Crazy Legs / Steady Flame
2024 – Larry Streeter – It's All Over Now / Old Love Letters
2025 – Eddie Skelton – Curly / Feelin' Blue
2026 – Bobby Mack – Who Put the Blues in Your Heart / Indian Love Call
2027 – Eddie Dee and the Sputniks – Back to the Hills / Journey to the Moon

Starday Custom Series (Dixie) Singles – Compiled by the *Hillbilly Researcher*, with thanks to Malcolm Chapman and additions by Nathan Gibson

The mysterious (and highly collected) Starday custom series is one of the most difficult series to complete (if it ever can be completed at all). Over seven hundred records were pressed between 1953 and 1970, but neither Pierce nor Daily kept a comprehensive list of clients who submitted recordings. Thus, it has been entirely up to collectors to contribute to this listing. What makes this series particularly difficult to compile is that many different labels were used (label choice was left to the artist's discretion). In this listing, I have listed the chosen label name in parenthesis after the song titles.

Initially, several releases appeared on the Starday label with a numbering system beginning in the 500s. However, the Starday main series releases eventually entered the 500s as well, thus confusing many record collectors. One way to distinguish between the custom series or main series (for Starday releases numbered in the 500s or 600s) is to look at the placement of the Starday logo. The custom releases utilizing the Starday label placed the logo at the top of the label, whereas the Starday main series (in the #500s and 600s) placed the logo at the bottom. Eventually, the Starday logo within the custom series was replaced with the Dixie label. Even so, not all Starday-related Dixie labels were part of the custom series. Dixie was also used on the *Hillbilly Hit Parade* series as well as the Dixie Rock series. There were also several Dixie records pressed in the 1950s and 60s that were entirely unrelated to Starday. Determining which series a particular Dixie record is a part of often requires attention to the release number (most Dixie releases numbered between 634 and 1200 were custom pressings).

In determining whether or not a particular record is part of the Starday custom service, several other issues arise. Small independent labels often utilized the Starday custom service before they went on to press their records elsewhere. For example, some releases on the Brite-Star or Peach labels are true Starday customs, but not all. Also, most of the custom pressings list a Starday-related publishing company on the label such as Starrite, Starday Music, Tronic, or Golden State. Many songs appearing on other labels, however, were published by these publishing companies and are not part of the custom service. Thus, when labels other than Starday or Dixie are used, it is best to look for clues within the dead wax (space between the grooves and the label). The earliest custom pressings were pressed by Coast Records, and therefore include the prefix PD in the dead wax. Later, when records were pressed at the Rite Pressing Plant in Cincinnati, the prefix CP was used. Several custom records pressed by the King Plant, also in Cincinnati, are denoted by the numbers 634 etched into the dead wax.

Other indicators exist, and this is in no way a comprehensive list of all the details that might determine a record's place in the list. It is, however, a start. For further information, I direct any and all interested parties to the greatest website I have ever found, Malcolm Chapman's Starday Custom Pressings site: malcychapman.blogspot.com. He provides not only information about every known record in the custom series but also label scans, artist details, and any other related information.

There are many people to thank for this list. First, I must again thank Al Turner, founder of the *Hillbilly Researcher*. Several years ago, the *Hillbilly Researcher* published a booklet documenting the custom series label from #501–850, and Sir Turner has graciously allowed me to reprint their research. After updating their information with my own, I stumbled across Malcolm Chapman's website noted above. Several contributors to his website had discovered many more custom records and Sir Chapman was very kind to allow those to be added to this list. In doing so, I would like to note and thank the many contributors to his website, especially Pascal Perrault, Dave Sax, Phillip J. Tricker, and Al Turner. In addition, contributor credits are due to Mike Smythe, Terry Gordon, Neil Scott, Ray Topping, Tapio Vaisanen, Reg Bartlett, Boz Boorer, Andrew Brown, John Burton, Stephane Chatain, Kevin Coffey, Neil Davies, Dougy Dean, Mitch Drumm, Jack Dumery, Richard Edginton, Jim Fox, Udo Frank, Dick Grant, Kent Heineman, Dave Howe, John Ingman, *Kicks* magazine, Cees Klop, Barney Koumis, Henri Laffont, Big Joe Louis, Lars Lundgren, Red Moore, Brian and Lindy Nevill, Jean Louis Otin, Michael Proost, Ian Saddler, Sho-Me Blowout, Mack Stevens, Tom Sims, Bill Smoker, Bob Solly, Patti Terando, and Ned Walters.

    Even though much work has been done to complete these listings, gaps in the listings remain and more work needs to be done. If you are able to fill in any of the remaining empty spaces, please contact me at ndgibson@indiana.edu. Your input would be much appreciated and could be included in future revised editions. I assume full responsibility for any errors found in the listings.

500 – Cotton Henry – Patent On My Heart / Jimmie O'Neal & the Oklahoma Hillbillies – Streamliner Boogie (Coast)
501 – Hoyt Scoggins & the Kingsmen Quartet – Jesus Still Heals / The Pathway Is Not Crowded (Coosa)
502 – Conway Gospel Chorus – Going Down the Hill / King Jesus Is My Captain (Gospel)
503 – Big Bob Dougherty & His Orchestra – Whale / Okey Pretty Baby (voc. by Lonnie Dougherty) (Cosmopolitan)
504 – Jack Hammons – Tomorrows Goodbyes / Substitute For Love (Coast)
505 – Buddy Livingston & His All Girl Band – Back When She Was Young / Write Me, Right Away (Savannah)
506 – Billie & Gordon Hamrick, "The Honey Hill Sweethearts" – He Is My Guide / He's Gonna Take His Children Out (Rangeland)
507 – Al Warwick – Rag Doll / You Are the Only One (California)
508 – Early Graham & his Musical Drifters – I Wish You'd Start Fooling Again / Stop Fooling My Heart (Texas)
509 – Jerry Hopkins & the Southern Playboys – Cuddle Up To Me / My Everlasting Love (Dart)
510 – Ray Mayo – Mended Heart / Who Winds Your Clock (S-Kay)
511 – Jerry and the String Trio – Lead Me to the Promise Land Day (voc. by Jerry and Steve) / Judgement Day (Johnson)
512 – Joe Bryant and the Mississippi Woodchoppers – Pulpwood Blues / A Man Ain't Nothing But A Woman's Slave (Mississippi)
513 – Buddy Livingston and His All Girl Band – Back When She Was Young / I Can't Love No One (Like I Love You) (Savannah)
514 – Beamon Forse – Rest Of My Life / You Better Go Now (Rodney)
515 – Al Meyer and His Pals – You're the Same Old Moon / Somebody Cares (Diamond)
516 – Curt and Faye Bartmess – Country Music In A Sacred Way / The Narrow Way (Evangelistic)
517 – Buddy Livingston and His All Girl Band – I Can't Help the Way I Feel / When You Stuck Your Tongue Out At Me (Savannah)
518 – Daniel James – Magic Wands and Wishing Wells / Through the Barroom Door (Starday)

519 – Jim Cunningham and the Missouri Wranglers – A Pain A Pill Won't Reach / Take Time To Cry (Starday)
520 – Howard Bramlett – Let's Take Our Children to Church / City On A Hill (Starday)
521 – Rev. Campbell and Wonder Boy – Old Ship of Zion / You Can't Hurry God (Hoyt's)
522 – Billie and Gordon Hamrick with the Low Country Gospel Band – Our Prayer / When I Feel the Spirit (Brother) I'm Gonna Shout (Starday)
523 – Red Mansel and His Hillbilly Boys – I've Crossed You Off My List / Broken, Fickle Heart (Starday)
524 – Frank Leviner – Keep Looking Up / Plan of Salvation (Carolina)
525 – Mrs. R. D. Jones – I Ain't Got Time / My Prayer for the One I Love (The Joneses)
526 – Ken Roper – Soft Spot In My Heart / That Same Old Lie (Driftwood)
527 – Don Payne – Kickaroo / The Game of Breaking Hearts (Starday)
528 – Wanda Ballman with Eeny, Meeny, Miney and Mo – Think It Over (Before You Cast Your Stone) / I'm Gonna Keep My Eye on You (Starday)
529 – Otis Parker – They Don't Have To Operate (They Just Pull the Zipper) / False Love Affair (New Star)
530 – The Musical-Aires – Hop–A–Long Sister Mary / Wildcat Boogie (Starday)
531 – Johnny Sutherland – We'll Have a Time, Yes Siree / I'm In Love (Starday)
532 – Clyde Beavers – I Won't Always Love You / My Baby Is Gone (Georgia)
533 – Roy Fisher and the Rhythm Riders – Just Suppose / I've Got A Feeling (Indiana)
534 – Carl Tanner and His Southern Pine Boys – Sweet Talking Baby / What Makes the Blues (Moonlight)
535 – Joe Gibson – Puttin' On the Dog / Oh Brother (Starday)
536 – Leo Ogletree – Crooked Dice / You Done Got Me (Starday)
537 – Francis Rodgers and Ray Lucas – Oh Gee, Oh Gosh, Oh Golly / Mrs. Lucy N. Penney – Jolly Old Fellows (Lucas)
538 – Tommy Castle – Wanderlust / I've Done More Accidentally (Starday)
539 – Roy Robinson – I Told It to Jesus / Little Romeo (Big State) [issued twice with different versions]
540 – Frank Evans and the Western Hayriders – I'm Different / Another Love Like You (Starday)
541 – Jack Morris – My Pony Wants To Go / Cooing the Wrong Pigeon (Starday)
542 – Hoyt Scoggins and the Saturday Nite Jamboree Boys – What's Gonna Happen To This Old World / Kneel Down With Jesus (Starday)
543 – Harold Smith – Listen to Me Baby / Waiting For Someone (Rondo)
544 – The Ransom Gospel Singers – I'll Tell It / I'll Make It Home Someday (Hoyt's)
545 – Don Redfield and the Sagedusters – I Can't Go Back / Montana Waltz (Sage)
546 – Walter Ponder Jr. – I Had a Chance / Carry On (Hoyt's)
547 – Mack King with the Western Hayriders – This Is Your Life / No Wings—No Halo (Starday)
548 – Tommie Tolleson and the Western Playboys from Palacios, Texas – Warm Spring Waltz / Think Of Me (Gulf Coast)
549 – Curley Money and the Rolling Ramblers – Playing the Game / Why Must I Cry (Rambler)
550 – Luke Gordon acc by C. Smith and the Tennessee Haymakers – Goin' Crazy / Married Life (L & C) [also issued as Starday 550]
551 – Monroe Johnson & his Rocky Mountain Boys – I Hope Tomorrow Never Comes / What Am I Going To Do (Mid-West)

552 – Lucky Wray – It's Music She Says / Sick And Tired (Starday)
553 – Alton Guyon and His Boogie Blues Boys – River Boat Blues / Leave My Baby Alone (Arkansas)
554 – Marty Licklider – Cold Hands, Warm Heart / Our Anniversary Day (Starday)
555 – Luke Gordon – Let This Kiss Bid You Goodbye / Baby's Gone (Starday)
556 – Oklahoma Melody Boys – Wasted / Your Heart and Mine (voc. by Pearl Ritter) (H & C)
557 – Lewis Family – Lights In the Valley / My Jesus Is the One (Sullivan)
558 – Lewis Family – Did You Do What the Lord Said To Do / Wait A Little Longer Please, Jesus (Sullivan)
559 – Don Owens and the Circle "O" Ranch Boys – Somethings You Cannot Change / Adios Novia (Starday)
560 – Jerry Hanson – Cry / I'm Doing All Right (Starday)
561 – Jimmy Johnson – Woman Love / All Dressed Up (Starday)
562 – King Sterling – Slippin' Out—Stealing In / Alone, Lonesome and Blue (Gibson)
563 – Hoyt Scoggins and the Saturday Nite Jamboree Boys – Why Did We Fall In Love / Tennessee Rock (Starday)
564 – Tex Dixon – Your Lovin' Lies / I'm Just Feeling Sorry for Myself (Starday)
565 – Luke Gordon and His Lonesome Drifters – Big New Dance / Just Doin' What's Right (Starday)
566 – Moviecraft Orchestra – I'd Like to Be a Baby Sitter b/w I'm Dolling You Up For Somebody Else (Moviecraft Enterprises)
567 – Frank Evans and His Top Notchers – Go On and Be Carefree / What Is It (That I'm Too Young To Know) (Starday)
568 – Carl Tanner and Ineva Buckins and the Southern Pine Boys – Together Me and You / We're In Love (Moonlight)
569 – "Cousin" Arnold and His Country Cousins – Be My Baby, Baby Doll / What Is Life To You (Starday)
570 – Arnold Parker and the Southernaires – People Laugh At a Fool / Find a New Woman (Starday)
571 – The Tom Harmon Trio (piano acc: Dan Garret) – I'd Like to Know / God's Miracles (Alabama Gospel)
572 – Jack Frost and His Band – There Is No Tomorrow / Crying My Heart Out (Big State)
573 – Lucky Chapman and the Ozark Mountain Boys – I've Waited So Long / Blue Grass (Maryland)
574 – Hodges Brothers – I'm Gonna Rock Some Too / Because I Love You So (Mississippi)
575 – Lucky Wray – What-cha Say Honey / Got Another Baby (Starday)
576 – Al Clauser and His Oklahoma Outlaws – Cloudy Love / Who's Fooling Who (H & C)
577 – Luke Gordon – Is It Wrong / What Can I Do (Starday)
578 – "Cousin Arnold" and His Country Cousins – Heart of Fantasy / Sweet Talking Daddy (Starday)
579 – Don Collins – Why Am I Lonely / Too Late To Be Sorry (Space)
580 – Mack Banks and His Drifting Troubadours – You're So Dumb / Be-Boppin' Daddy (Fame)
581 – Southern Spirituals – Since I Laid My Burdens Down / If I Leave (Beverly)
582 – Jimmy Blakley and Dorothy Blakley – No One But You / Jimmy Blakley – Standing In Line (For Your Love) (Starday)
583 – [Unknown artist] – I'll Fly Away With An Angel / Cherished By A Song [Unknown label]

584 – The Delmar Williams Singers – I Wanna Walk a Little Closer / The Gates Will Swing Wide (Del-Mar)
585 – The Delmar Williams Singers – My Journey Home / The Last Love Letter (Del-Mar)
586 – Tennessee George and the Pennsylvania Plowboys – Cry Baby / Butterball (Plow)
587 – Andy Doll, 6 Men and 16 Instruments – Honey Dew / Goodbye Mary Ann (Starday)
588 – Slim Coxx and His Cowboy Caravan – Mocking Bird Special / Lonely Nights (Coxx)
589 – Joe Brown and the Black Mt. Boys with Curly Sanders and the San-Tones – Midnight Rhythm / Fishing Fever (San)
590 – Curley Sanders – Why Did You Leave Me / Brand New Rock and Roll (Jamboree)
591 – Gene Sterling – Living a Lie / I Won't Be Back No More (Mecca)
592 – Roland R. A. Faulk – You'll Never Know / My Baby's Gone (Big State)
593 – The Northwest Troubadours – Hey Mr. Copper (Lucky)
594 – Dorothy Blakley – Piano Bells / Yodelin' Ivory Waltz (Starday)
595 – Jimmy Simpson and His Oilfield Playboys – Can I Come Home / Memories Of You (Big State)
596 – Truitt Forse – Chicken Bop / Doggone Dame (Starday)
597 – Leon Holmes and His Georgia Ramblers – She's My Baby / You're Not Mine At All (Peach)
598 – Gene Terry and His Kool Kats – The Woman I Love / Tip, Tap and Tell Me (Rock-It)
599 – Burt Hughart – Our Last Goodbye / Memories I Can't Forget (Hughart)
600 – Tom Harmon Trio – My Secret Affair / Get Away, Satan (Alabama Gospel)
601 – Frank Bowen & Dave Warren and the Ark. Valley Wranglers – A Broken Heart / Rock & Roll Blues (Cimmaron)
602 – Frank Evans and His Top Notchers – Barrel of Heartaches (And a Bucket of Tears) / If You Knew (Starday)
603 – Ken Patrick with Chet Tant on Steel Guitar – Snowflake / Do You Love Me (Trend)
604 – Rod Burton – Wedding Bells Are Ringing For the Bride / My New Sensation (Moviecraft)
605 – Gene Harrell – I Won't Be Back No More / Mumbles (Cowtown)
606 – Hoyt Scoggins and The Georgia Boys – What's the Price (To Set Me Free) / The Old Chain Gang (Starday)
607 – Don Owens and the Circle "O" Ranchboys – Last Chance / A Thief (In the Heart of a Fool) (Starday)
608 – Lucky Wray with Link and Doug Wray – Teenage Cutie / You're My Song (Starday)
609 – Buddy Shaw – Just Like A Fool / I Belong To You (Starday)
610 – Leon McCall – I Lose Again / If I Don't Change My Mind (Tarheel)
611 – [Unknown artist] – All I Do Is Cry Over You / One Dark Sunday Night [Unknown label]
612 – The Gospel Troubadours – Cry Aloud and Spare Not / Ananias (Maryland)
613 – Art Rogers with the Texas Top Hands – Our Anniversary / Ten Thousand Miles (Starday)
614 – The Campbell Trio with Jerry Tuttle – Satan Lost a Sinner / God Can Do Without Your Service (Van)
615 – Hoyt Sullivan – Hoyt Sullivan's Drug Products 1 and 2 / Hoyt Sullivan's Drug Products 3 and 4 [Unknown label]
616 – Cowboy Huff – No Two Timin' Me / What's Gonna Happen To Me (Huff)
617 – Cowboy Huff – Lover's Waltz / Patonia (Pride of the Plains) (Huff)
618 – Buddy Shaw – No More / The Breath of Life To Me (Starday)

619 – Marvin Jackson with the Battreal Boys – Honey, If You Love Me / World of Make Believe (Crestwood)
620 – Rene McCall and Her Candy Ranch Boys – We're Strangers Now / The Waltz In the Rain (Carolina)
621 – Bill & Bob – Falling Apart At the Seams / Bill Bolan and the Country Melody Boys – Country Music (Jamboree)
622 – Lucky Hill – Fickle Baby / It's Comin' Home to You (Starday)
623 – Bob Cole – Face to Face / You Lied (Jay)
624 – Tom Crook and The Rock and Roll Four – My Heart Don't Lie / Weekend Boogie (Dixie)
625 – Ernest Painter – No One But You / Whispering Heart (Coosa)
626 – Billie and Gordon Hamrick with the Low Country Gospel Band – Gonna See My Lord Someday / Jesus Is the Name (Starday)
627 – Bob and Cindy Dean – I'm Knocking On the Door (To Your Heart) / One Life to Live (Starday)
628 – Willie Nelson – No Place for Me / Lumberjack (Willie Nelson)
629 – The Relative Quartet – A Home for My Soul / Heavenly City (Faith)
630 – Darnell Miller – Waiting Game for Love / Gettin' Out Of the Woods (Dale)
631 – Ken Clark and His Merry Mountain Boys – Ho Ho! Love 'em Joe / Quit Fool (Mamma's Lookin') (Starday)
632 – Mac Odell – It Was Springtime (When I Met You) / When I Was Young (Kentucky)
633 – Trice Gardner – Tombigbee / Lover's Hill (Gulf)
634 – Zeke Wilson and the Prairie Playboys – My Heart Needs a Vacation / I've Just Said Goodbye (To the Only Girl I Love) (Robin)
635 – Jimmy Stewart and the Night Hawks – Dream World / Nuthin' But A Nuthin' (Night Hawk)
636 – Slim and Orna Ball – Mother's Prayers (Were Not In Vain) / When I Get Home (I'm Gonna Be Satisfied) (Old Dominion)
637 – Mel Price and His Santa Fe Rangers – I Miss You So / Midnight Whistle Blues (Starday)
638 – The Delmar Williams Singers – Lonely Tomorrow / I'm Not Angry Now (Del-Mar)
639 – Ralph Johnson and the Hillbilly Show Boys – Reality / Henpecked Daddy (Ralph Johnson)
640 – Ernie Nowlin and Blue Shadow Boys – Tally Ho / Tell Me Why (Missouri) (issued twice with different versions)
641 – Bob Varney and His Stoney Mt Playboys – I Hear You Calling / Stoney Mountain Boogie (Blue Grass)
642 – Buddy Shaw – Don't Sweep That Dirt On Me / Second Place (Starday)
643 – Carl Trantham and the Rythm All Stars – Where There's A Will (There's A Way) / After I Go Away (Lincoln)
644 – Marvin Jackson – Someday You'll Be Sorry / My Crying Heart (Crestwood)
645 – Frank Evans and His Top Notchers – Pull the Shades Down Ma / Would You Believe Me (Starday)
646 – Gene Ray – I Didn't Mean (To Fall In Love) / I Lost My Head (Cowtown)
647 –
648 –
649 – Nathan Abshire and his Pine Grove Boys – Boora Rhumba / Carolina Blues (Khoury's)

650 – Clarence Baker – Hear My Plea / Soon I'll Hear My Savior Calling (Starday)
651 – Harry Peppel and his Shenandoah Valley Rangers – No Baby No / Take a Letter, Mr. Moon (Cowtown)
652 – Little Jody Rainwater and the Jamboree Gang – I Broke My Heart Waltzing / The Man That Wrote Home Sweet Home (Never Was A Married Man) (Starday)
653 – Ramblin' Red Bailey – The Hardest Fall / You've Always Got A Frown (Peach)
654 – Blue Ridge Quartet – House of God / Footprint of Jesus / Tenderly He Watches Over Me / Where Shall I Be On That Judgement Day (Blue Ridge)
655 – Chandos McRill and the Perryville Melody Boys – Money Lovin' Woman / Little Bit Too Bashful (Stardust)
656 – Pete Hardin and the Peaches – Ho Bo's Heaven / I've Wasted My Love On You (Peach)
657 – Lou Walker – Rock and Roll (Tennessee Style) / I'll Always Be In Love With You (Starday)
658 – Rocking Martin – All Because Of You / Do You Still Love Me (Starday)
659 – Hoyt Scoggins with Curley Bigham Band – Waiting For an Answer / One Heart, One Love (Starday)
660 – Leon Holmes – Half A Chance / Lost Love (Starday)
661 – Harry Holungor – Baby / Tell Me (Starday)
662 – Orangie Ray Hubbard – Sweet Love / David Lundy – If I Had A Nickel For Every Time You're Untrue (Dixie)
663 – Bill Floyd, music by the Swingsters – Hey, Boy! / Heartbreak (Starday)
664 – Billy Match and the Starfires – I Want My Baby / Girl of Mine (Starfire)
665 – Herbie Shott – You'll Cry Tomorrow / Take a Tip from a Fool (Shott)
666 – Gene Harper and His Saddle Pals – Thank the Lord for the Rain / Jesus Is A Friend To Me (Diamond)
667 – Luke McDaniel – You're Still On My Mind / Homeward Mule (Venus)
668 – Larry Nolen and His Bandits – Blue River / King of the Ducktail Cats (Starday)
669 – Dave Brockman and the Twilight Ramblers – Foolish Pride / Feel Sorry For Me (Starday)
670 – Joyce Love with Curley Sanders and his Santones – Why Did You Leave Me / Peace of Mind (Starday)
671 – Lee Voorhies and His Ozark Country Boys – Load up My Blues / Hand In Hand (Stardust)
672 – Johnny Skiles with the Harmony Ranch Hands – The Twinkle In Your Eyes / Ghosts of my Lonely Past (Corvette)
673 – Billie and Gordon Hamrick with Red Farrell – Cruel Jealous Heart / Gypsy Waltz (Starday)
674 – Frank Evans and His Top Notchers – I've Got a Patent (On My Kinda Love) / Lonesome Love (Starday)
675 –
676 – Al Runyon – The Day Before the Night / Baby Please Come Home (Starday)
677 – Gene Ray – Rock and roll Fever / If I'd Been Asked / Achin' Heart / Love Proof (Cowtown)
678 – The Singing Wills Family – I Need the Lord / He'll Answer You (Starday)
679 – Bill Goodwin – So Wrong / I'll Stand In Line (Mystic)
680 – Slim Foster and His Cedar Valley Boys– Singin' Guitar / Lover (Cedar)
681 – Al Sims and the Alpine Two – Party / Girl Without A Heart (Listen)

682 –
683 – Kelly Brothers (Abner and Newt) – Flying Saucers / Hero (Starday)
684 – May Hawks – Talk A Little Louder / Forever and a Day (Starday)
685 – Gene Scarbrough – Wanted / Lonesome for Someone (Starday)
686 – Lloyd McCollough – Half My Fault / What Can I Tell Them (Starday)
687 – Jimmie Dale – Man Made Moon / For A Day (Farrall)
688 – Bob and Cindy Dean – Long Time Gone / Gone For Another (Starday)
689 – Bill Goodwin – Angel In Disguise / It Don't Cost A Dime To Dream (Mystic)
690 – Al Sims and the Alpine Two – Your Love Is A Prison / Little Red Caboose (Listen)
691 – Al Sims and the Alpine Two – Eskimo Sweetheart / Party (Listen)
692 – J. C. Sawyer – Goin' Steppin' / Howard Bingham and the Rockets – Baby Love (Dixie)
693 – Dale Anderson – You'll Never Know / Long Way to Go (Valley)
694 – Taylor Porter – It's Over Now / No More Lovin' You (Starday)
695 – Dayton Harp and his Dixieland Drifters – Man Crazy Woman (with Dot Anderson) / You're One In a Million (Star)
696 – Johnny Tooley – The King of Dreams / Looking Glass Heart (Starday)
697 – Jeanie Christie with Earl Durrance and his Blue Sky Ramblers – Flying High / Sunshine (Blue Sky)
698 – Plez Gary Mann – Cheer Me Up / I Want To Be True (Playboy)
699 – Bill Johnson and the Dabblers – Lonesome Daddy Blues / Umm Boy, You're My Baby (Starday)
700 – Harry Peppel and his Shenandoah Valley Rangers – One Night's Love / Oh My Aching Head (voc. by Tommy Donahue) / Thermostat Baby / Old Fashioned (voc. by Dick Dorn) (Cowtown)
700 – Tex Turner – Why Not Honey! (Starday)
701 – Lou Walker – Little Bitty Man / Cause I'm Losing You (Starday)
702 – Gene Ray – Indigo Blues / Learning the Mambo / Oklahoma Waltz / A Picture Of You (Cowtown)
702 – The Kool Toppers – Is That Exactly What You Wanna Do / 'Cause I Love You So (Beverly)
703 – Lewis Pruitt and the True Lads – I'm In a Daze / Pretty Baby (Peach)
704 – Fuzzy Whitener with Jerry Dykes and His Band – Why Do I Love You / Sugar Buggar (Starday)
705 – Leroy Martin and the Rebels – Keen Teen Baby / Upon This Day (Delta)
706 – Tony and Jackie Lamie with the Swing Kings – Wore To a Frazzle / Sunset Blues (Sunset)
707 – Ked Killen – The School Bus Tragedy / You'd Better Take Time (KYVA)
708 – Jimmie Dale – Darlin' / Baby Doll (Saber)
709 – Dappa Smith – A Teenage Boy / China Doll (Peach)
710 – Bill Goodwin – Second In Your Heart / Teenage Blues (Starday)
711 – Lawson Rudd with Tippecanoe Valley Boys – Country Town Girl / Blues On the Run (Starday)
712 – Jesse Stevens and Big Sandy Boys – Mama, Mama / No Bluebirds In the Sea (Bluegrass)
713 – Hank Rector – I'm Gonna Let You Go / My One Desire (Starlite)
714 – Alden Holloway and His Tri City Boys – Chiquita / Loving Is My Business (Starday)
715 – Bill & Ben and the Arkansas Travelers – My Blue Eyed Baby / The Sun Shines Brighter (Traveler)

716 – The Three Ramblers – Walkin' Talkin' Babydoll / If You Call That Love (Ozark)
717 – The Imperials – Steppin' Out / Am I the One (Jewel)
718 – Johnny Brown and the Plainsmen (voc. by Sammy) – Shame / My Little Darling (Big State)
719 – Frank Evans and His Top Notchers – The Ain't Got Blues / All My Dreams Are Gold (Starday)
720 – Dale Anderson and the Elliot Bros. – I Did My Part / I'll Always Love You (Valley)
721 – Olen Little – You Heavenly You / The World Belongs To Me (Peach)
722 – John Worthan – The Cats Were Jumpin' / I Wrote You a Letter (Peach)
723 – Bobby Mack – Crazy Heart / Waitin' For You to Call (B–Mac)
724 – Ted McPherson and the Dixie Land Ramblers – I'll Cry Tomorrow / You Were Laughing (Peach)
725 – Art Ontario – I'm Proud / Wiggle Walkin' Boogie (Illinois)
726 – Fred Scarboro with the String Masters – (I'll Always Love You) Till I Die / Hula Dance (Country)
727 – Hal Payne – You'll Miss Me Tomorrow / Honky Tonk Stomp (Starday)
728 – Ray Anderson – You Can't Break a Heart (That's Been Broken) / Cryin' a River (Starday)
729 – Bob Cundiff – Don't Look Back / I'm Coming Back (Bluegrass)
730 – Warren Robbe – My Chicken Pen / My Heart Disagrees (Bluegrass)
730 – Leon Holmes – Dreams Come True / Tears On My Pillow (Peach)
731 – The Lewis Family – Born In Bethlehem / He's Got the Whole World In His Hands / A Beautiful City / Paul and Silas (Starday)
732 – Jim Pierce – Don't Tell Me / I Tore Up Your Picture (Nomad)
733 – Joe Poovey and the Royal Dukes – Careful Baby / Move Around (Dixie)
734 – Don Wilmot & Babe Humphrey – Today's Special / How Lucky Can You Be (Mystic)
735 – The Franklin Brothers – Mr. Policeman / Oh, Laura (Blue Sky)
736 – Gilbert Headley – I Tried To Be Fair / I Love Only You (Hi-Lite)
737 – John and Margie Cook – Do I Have To Stay Alone (Volunteer)
738 – Enos Jim Austin – It Was All Her Fault / Salt Creek Blues (Volunteer)
739 – Ramon (Ray) Langley – I Hear It In the Bells / If You Just Knew (Hi-Lite)
740 – Arvel Lewis – Pine Mountain Boogie / I Knocked On Your Door (Bluegrass)
741 – Daniel Nix with the Compensation Boys – Just as Lonesome as Can Be / Compensation Blues (N & R)
742 – Betty Parker with Eddie Jackson and His Swingsters – Couldn't See / Love Is Even Colder (Elm)
743 – Dick Fawcett – Talking Thru Your Hat / My Boyhood Days Back Home (Tex-Tan)
744 – The Green Brothers Quartet – Judge the Tree / Tell the News (Beverly)
745 – Dean Evans – One Boy, One Girl / Unfinished Castle (Hobo)
746 – Virgie Fossett – The Gypsy's Mistake / City Sidewalk Sale (Fern)
747 – Ray Guyce and the Lonesome Valley Boys – Please Don't Set Me Free / Ray Guyce and Little Jo with the Lonesome Valley Boys – Lonesome Guitar (Brite Star)
748 – Pete Hardin – Love Me Or Leave Me / Baby Be My Chickadee (Peach)
749 –
750 – Ernest and Agnes Joines – Falling In Love Again / Brown Eyes and Brown Hair (Rockland)
751 – Jerry Cox with the Cavaliers – Debbie Jean / Sherry (Frantic)
752 – Jimmy Wert and the Four Squirts – Please Believe Me / Bingo Blues (Skyline)

753 – Polly Feazel – I Love Everything About You / Settle Down (Ge-Mo)
754 – Ray Strong – You're Gonna Reap What You Sow / Love Shadows (Rocket)
755 – Mike Fernandez with the Del Royal's Orch. – A–Bomb Bop / Brake Jake (Raymond's)
756 – Danial Nix with the Compensation Boys and Girl – I Love You / Unlucky Man (N & R)
757 – Johnny Nelson – Alvin at the Crawdad Hole (with the Fairlanes) / I'd Rather Lose You (Up Town)
758 – Lyle Keefer– A Fool Doesn't Know / Come Back To Me (Lincoln)
759 – Harry Hanson – Golden Anniversary / Just Remember (Empire)
760 – Ricky Marlow – Gypsy Love / She's Gone (Pat)
761 – Wallace Lane – Falsely Accused / Please Come Back To Me Darling (Monticello)
762 – Bill Perry and Page Ross with the Melody Boys – Gone Away Forever / Unchanging Love (Bluegrass)
763 – Little Brenda Holly with Ray Guyce and His Lonesome Valley Boys – Lonesome Music / I Don't Know (Brite Star)
764 – Gary Link and the Rock-a-Fellas – Don't You Know / Rhythm Rock (Al Vic)
765 – Little Brenda Holly and Ray Guyce and the Lonesome Valley Boys – Yankee Can't Go Home / A Wedding Ring, A Broken Heart (Brite Star)
766 – Ray Guyce and the Lonesome Valley Boys – Slippin' Round On Me (Brite Star)
766 – Carl Brandenburg – Teardrops In My Eyes (Ozark)
767 – Juanita Smith with the Vanguards – Sometimes I Wonder / Conversational Walk (Vanguard)
768 – Mickey Nix – Do You Have To Go / Steady Love (Ge-Mo)
769 – Allen Segura with Shorty Fitch and the Rhythm Rockers – My Suzie Q / You Played Me for a Fool (Rome)
770 – Ray Williams and the Westerners – Four Walls, A Table and a Bottle of Wine / If I Knew All the Answers (De-Ada)
771 – Henry McPeak – Too Much Pride / I Feel Like Yelling (H G)
772 – James Gallagher – Are You the One / Ford and Shaker (B & G)
773 – Blankenship Brothers – Tears I Cried For You / Mary (Bluegrass)
774 –
775 – Virgie Fossett – I'm a Pistol Packin' Mama / My Heart Has Fallen (Fern)
776 – Don Burford – I'm Guilty / I Guess I'll Be Blue (Fern)
777 – Jeff Daniels – Switch Blade Sam / You're Still On My Mind (Big Howdy)
778 – The Weems Brothers and Billy Still – He'll Understand / Don't Turn God Away (Big Howdy)
779 – Shorty Barnhill and His Country Mountaineers – Beautiful Carolinas / I'm a Sad Sack (Inland Empire)
780 – W. F. James, Jr. – Where There's a Will There's a Way / My Teddy Bear (Faith)
781 – Jim Solley and the Lubocs – Debbie Darling / Night Train (Deb)
782 – Miss Jerry – That Don't Make Me a Bad Girl (Love)
782 – B. J. Johnson – Crying In Your Sleep / Wise Eyes (Big Howdy)
783 –
784 – Tim Johnson – Yes, Indeed / A Memory of Mother (Leo)
785 – Vernon Price – Lookin' Seekin' Searchin' (Love)
786 – Bob Kinney and the Sidekicks – The Girls I Left Behind / The Fool Who Walked Away (Barefoot)
787 – The Beck Brothers – Screamin' Mamie / I'll Love You for a Lifetime (Mid West)

788 –

789 – Horace Goodwin and the Etowah Valley Boys – I Just Dropped By (To Say Hello) / Here's My Heart (Etowah)

790 – Floyd Arthurs – You're Leaving Me for Good / Waitress (R.V. F.)

791 – Percy Welch and His House Rockers – Nursery Rhyme Rock / Back Door Man (Fran)

792 – Dickie Dameron – Gonna Have a Party / Rockin' Baby (Laurel)

793 – (National)

794 –

795 – Leon Kelly and the Rhythm Rockers – You Put My Heart in Orbit / Rockaway (Space)

796 – Junior Gravley with the Rock-A-Tones – You Lied to Me Honey / Take My Hand (Vel-A-Tone)

797 – Little Ernie Lee Joines with the Lundy Brothers – My Lord Is Near Me / Ernest and Agnes Joines with the Lundy Brothers – Grave upon the Hillside (Rockland)

798 – Bill Johnson – Judas Betrayed Jesus / My Daddy Is a Drunkard (Everglade)

799–C – The Songsters – My Little Angel Ruth / My Whole Family (Vicksburg)

799–D – The Songsters – You Have Been My Queen For Fifty Years / Sleep In Peace My Dear Sweet Girl (Vicksburg)

800 – The Songsters – Be Kind to Everybody / Historic Red Carpet, Vicksburg, Mississippi (Vicksburg)

801 – Bill Loop with His Seneca Indian Boys – Snowflakes (Reed)

802 – Bill Loop with His Seneca Indian Boys – The Wrong Way to Love / My Foolish Heart (Seneca)

803 – Bill Willis – Going Down to Sal's House (with Goldie Norris) / Poor Man (Dixie)

804 – Vern Terry – Miss You / Someone New (Athena)

805 – Chandos McRill and the Excellons – Poor Me / The Toddle (Stardust)

806 – Al Parsley – Country Courting / I Wonder Why I Can't Forget (Dixie)

807 – Clay Goodin – Make Me A Charm / Shadow Eyes (Dixie)

808 – Merle Kilgore – Jimmie Brings Sunshine / Dear Mama (J-I-M)

809 – Jannoice Wilson – What Have You Done to My Heart / Then Everything's Alright (Dixie)

810 – Hank Morrison and His Rambling Cowboys – Just To Wink My Eyes At You / To Share My Name (Dixie)

811 – Warren Robbe – If I Had My Dreams to Build Over / Single Man (Mystic)

812 – Hal Morgan – Gotta Great Big Date (Reed)

813 – Ira Leonard and His Rockin' Riffs – My Old Rocking Chair / I'm Knocking On Your Door (Drum Beat)

814 – Tommy Nelson and Band – Honey Moon Blues / Hobo Bop (Dixie)

815 – Jimmy Dane and His Great Danes – Tattle Tale / Please Have Mercy (Marv)

816 – Blankenship Brothers with the Sundown Playboys – Too Late / Lonesome Old Jail (Bluegrass)

817 – Horace Goodwin and the Etowah Valley Boys – The Georgia Two Step / Country Jitterbug (Etowah)

818 – June Draper with the Blue Ridge Mountain Boys – I've Lost You / Happy Birthday In Heaven (Country)

819 – Ray Hudson and the Western Rhythmaires – The Blues Walked Away / Mine For One Night (Dixie)

820 – Johnny Ray Harris – When a New Love's Born, Does an Old Love Die / Tired of Crawling, Gonna Start to Run (Ray)

RECORD LISTING

821 – Lovell Hall and the Country Singers Quartet – Light at the River / Record of Life (Spiritual)
822 – Dick Fawcett – That Smooth and Easy Waltz (with the T. Vanek Orch.) / Another Chance Is All We Need (Tex–Tan)
823 – Art Buchanan with the Pioneers – Queen from Bowling Green / Wonder Why (Dixie)
824 – Jimmie Pearson and the Melody Boys – Nobody Cares (with Jerry Hutchinson) / I'm Not Sure (Dixie)
825 – Bill Willis – Boogie Woogie All Night / Where Is My Baby (Dixie)
826 – Janet Terry and Her Arkansas Ramblers – Your Two Timing Heart / The Lips I Once Knew (Dixie)
827 – Lonnie Irving – Pinball / I Got Blues on My Mind (Lonnie Irving)
828 – Johnny and Evert "Gospel Singers" – My Mansion / Waiting / When the Trumpet Blows / In His Arms (Johnny and Evert)
829 – Buckskin Smith – New Fashioned Sweetheart / Out In Old Knobnoster / Black Eyed Suzie / Amen, Brother Ben, Amen (Buckskin)
830 –
831 – Bobby Peters and His Cass County Ramblers – Since You Left Me This Morning / Lonesome Street (Country)
832 – The Hi-Tombs – Sweet Rockin' Mama / Weeping Willow Rock (Cannon)
833 – Malcolm Nash with Putman County Play Boys – I Guess I'm Wise / Pretty Sally (Dixie)
834 – The Coffey Family – They're Building On Sand / I See Jesus (Scott)
835 – The Sunshine Melody Boys – The Saviour Is Calling / Walking On a Highway (Faith)
836 – Pete Peters and the Rhythmmakers – Rockin' N' My Sweet Baby's Arms / Dizzy (Dixie)
837 –
838 – Johnny Clayton – Man Alone / Never Again (Will Love Knock On My Door) (Dixie)
838 – Eddie Reynolds – I'm Missing You / What Was It (Dixie)
839 –
840 – Red Moore and His Rhythm Drifters – I'll Miss You When You're Gone / Crawdad Song (Red)
841 – Gene Mills – Yodlin Chime Bells / Nickels Worth of Dreams (Dixie)
842 –
843 – The Love Brothers – Baby, I'll Never Let You Go / One Time Love Affair (By-Love)
844 –
845 – Bill Willis – Boogie Woogie On a Saturday Night / Where Is My Baby (Dixie)
846 – Hoyt and Jo Webb – Richer Than a Millionaire / Don't Wake Me, I'm Dreaming (Dixie)
847 – Jon Hess – Ballad of Love / Two Timin' Fool (Dixie)
848 – The Rogers Brothers and the Tennessee Partners – I Don't Worry About You Anymore / Lost Creek Breakdown (Dixie)
849 – Romeo Sullivan and the Serenaders – Haunting Rhythm / What Will I Tell Our Friends When They Call (Top Knotch)
850 – Bob Weller acc. by Will Coffman and the Night Riders – Devil's Heart / Heartaches and Gloom (Dixie)
851 – Henry McPeak – I Overheard You Talking (with Bobby Horton) / When You Kissed Me (H G)

852 – The Cutups – She Has Gone / Double Date (JIM)
853 – Ray Bell and the Dixie Rhythm Ramblers – Yodelin' Echo Hills / Yodelin Catfish Blues (Friendly)
854 –
855 – Brooks Orrick and His Harmonica – The Fox Chase / Mamma Blues (Dixie)
856 – Singing Tex Gawryluk – I Love No One / I've Shed a Million Tears (Big State)
857 –
858 – Junne Miller – Think of Me / How Bad Can Bad Luck Be (Carvel)
859 – The Songsters – The Mighty Sprague / Thank God for Our Ladies / Georgene / Soldier Boy and the Radio Man (Dixie)
860 – Johnny Cale Quintette – The Purple Onion / Troubles, Troubles, Troubles (Chan)
861 –
862 – Dee Johnson – Back In Your Arms Again / You're Number One (Dixie)
863 –
864 – Davis Brothers (Herby and J. C.) – When the Family Was Young / More In the Man (Dixie)
865 – E. P. Williams and the Tucker Junction Boys – The Mystery of Lady–Be–Good / Dream of Love (Dixie)
866 – Bob Kinney – Queen of Broken Hearts / I Knew You Then / It'll Never Be the Same / First Or Last (Barefoot)
867 – Dottie Swan – You Blotted My Happy School Days / Blue News (Dixie)
868 – 5 Sable Sisters – Little Wee Lady / Hope Chest (Dixie)
869 – Larry Hollis – Oil Field Rock and Roll / Pat Becker – Baby I'm Lonesome (Seminole)
870 – Blankenship Brothers – The Story (The World Will Never Know) / You Went and Broke My Heart (Bluegrass)
871 – Carl Davis with Rhythm Ranch Boys – Searching For the Way (Back to Your Heart) / Backward or On (Dixie)
872 –
873 – Williams Brothers – Ali-Baba / Watcha Gonna Do Now (Dixie)
874 –
875 – Bobby Fenster and Orchestra – Chapel In the Valley / Midnight Mountain (Dixie)
876 –
877 – Lyle Keefer – Seventeen and Twenty / Hand Full of Love (Dixie)
878 – Arkansas Travelers – You Ask Me / Just One More (Traveler)
879 – John Snell – Sweet Passion (Of Your Love) / Tonight Is the Night (Art)
880 – Renaud Veluzat – Purty Lit'l / Race Track Boogie (Dixie)
881 – Bobby Kriss – Runaway Heart / Silence Baby (Action)
882 – Archie Day and His Rhythm Masters – A Mother Not Wanted / I Don't Want A Two Timing Love (Voc. by Jack Mahady) (Dixie)
883 – Beck Brothers – Just Like You / Big Rocker (Mid West)
884 –
885 – The Goad Sisters – Cabin On the Hill / The Return of the Prodigal (Swan)
886 – Connie Dycus – I Could Shoot Myself / Lying All the Time (Dixie)
887 – Mel Price and His Santa Fe Rangers – Jailed / I'm In Love With a Geisha Girl (Dixie)
888 – Charlotte Harden, The Little Ozark Sweetheart – I Hate Me (For Loving You) / Can't Get Enough (Of Loving You Baby) (Dixie)
889 – Jack Hanna – Brady and Dunky / Old Blue (Dixie)
890 – The Gentry Brothers – Swanky / Swooney (Dixie)

891 – Eddy Reynolds – Please Mr. Moon / Teen Lover (Dixie)
892 – Winston Shelton – When Sunday Comes Again / Mom Knows What's Best (Dixie)
893 – Lloyd Shoebottom, The Singing Country Boy – Waiting In the Little Country Church / Ice and Snow (Dixie)
894 – Dale Anderson – Before This Day Ends / I Can't Stay Home (Valley)
895 – Danny Brockman – Big Big Man / Jealous Dreams (Dixie)
896 – Delmer Sexton and the Rone County Boys – I Will Not Be Denied / Looking For an Old Fashioned Church (Blue Jay)
897 – Obie Benton and the Highlanders – I Just Walked Away From Paradise / Too Young For Love (Rainbow)
898 – Billy Davis – Last Night I Dreamed / Tear Stained Pillow (Dixie)
899 – Elsie Warren "Lincoln Jamboree" – I Love My Jesus / Unwanted Heart (Jamboree)
900 – Jackie Durham – Lovely Girl / I'll Leave It Up To You (Dixie)
900 – Buddy Meredith and His Dokato Cowboys – So Long Goodbye / Moon Song (Dixie)
901 – The Humming Bees – Jesus Step Right In / My House (Humming Bee)
902 – Pat Spencer – Some Boy's Dad / A Newsboy On Christmas Eve
903 – The Cackle Sisters (Mary & Kathy) – Gee It's Lonesome Here Tonight / Call My Name (Markay)
904 – Cheri Robbins – Please Don't Call Me Lonesome / High School Love (Action)
905 – Buddy Wright – Just For Today / Lilly of the Field (Dixie)
906 – Elmer Bryant – Will I Be Ashamed Tomorrow / Gertie's Garter Broke (Dixie)
907 – Junior Garner with the Sangamon Boys – Mr. Satellite / Blind Date (Dixie)
908 – Howard Mayberry and the Sangamon Boys – Proof of Love / This Just Can't Be Puppy Love (Dixie)
909 – Queens of Joy Gospel Singers – Jesus Is a Way Maker / Lord I Prayed (Faith)
910 – Charlotte Harden, the Ozark Sweetheart – That's All Right With Me / Loving You Baby (Dixie)
911 – Bob Bedard – (I'm Proud and It's) Nice To Be With You / You Caused the Blues (Dixie)
912 – Parker Cunningham – Little Teardrops / Blow Whistle Blow (Dixie)
913 – Ken Lightner and the Hay Ryders – The Corner of Love / Am I Still the One (Dixie)
914 – Eddie Reynolds and His Band – Cowboy Hall of Fame / Wrangler (Dixie)
915 – The King Brothers and the Virginia Mountaineers – I Wonder / King Shuffle (Dixie)
916 – Missouri Walker and the Ozark Ramblers – Lonesome Guitar / Your Tears Are Too Late (Dixie)
917 – Bill Perry and Jim Boyne – You Have A Heart of Stone / My Sweetheart Just Told Me Goodbye (Bluegrass)
918 – Jerry Venable – Pretty Girls / Heartaches to Burn (Raven)
919 – Tommy Nelson and Band – Dangling On a String / Like Let's Get Out (Dixie)
920 – Ray Anderson – The Middle Cross / He'll Be There (Faith)
921 – Jay Bouington – Here Am I / Willard Vinson – Someone Just Like You (Dixie)
922 – Junior Garner – Vacation Love / If You Want It (My Love) (Dixie)
923 –
924 –
925 –
926 – Johnny Holloway – I'll Always Be the One to Cry / Tavern Lights (Dixie)
927 – Queens of Joy Gospel Singers – Getting Ready / I Need the Lord Everyday (Faith)

928 – Dallas and Della Stamper – Brother, That's Charity / Dallas Stamper and His Spiritual Rhythmette Boys – I'm Going to Heaven When I Die (Dixie)
929 –
930 – O. H. Perry with Jorris Hennessee, Jack Holland, Leonard Hayes – It's Wrong To Hurt You So / The McMinnville Rock (Reo)
931 – Carolina Gospelers and Annie Bell Harrison – Somebody Called My Name / In a Simple Country Church (voc. by Johnny Davis) (Faith)
932 –
933 – Ralph Collier – Heartaches of Love / You're Coming Back To Me (Blazon)
934 – Keith Anderson and the Ohio Valley Boys – Locked Up Again / Counting the Hours (Ran-Dell)
935 – Richmond Friendly Four – Lord, I've Been A Hard Working Pilgrim / He Will Go / He Knows the Way / Someday They'll Be No Tomorrow (Walton)
936 – Mildred and Dean Bailey and the East Tennessee Playboys – Lovers For Tonight / Piano and Banjo Polka (Dixie)
937 –
938 –
939 – Loyal Pritchard – Driftwood / The Bounce (Moonbow)
940 – Jorris Hennessee and the Round Up Boys – Jorris Boogie / The McMinnville Rock (Reo)
941 – Leonard Lloyd – I Know My Mother's Happy Up There / Weeping Willow, Why Do You Weep (Dixie)
942 –
943 –
944 – The Happytimers – The Happytime Song / The Happytimers – Oh Who Can Make A Flower / Tonya – Smiles / Janice – Clap Hands (D-D)
945 – Bobby Brown and the Country Music Makers – Stoney Mountain (Where I Lost My Love) / Blackwater (Blackwater)
946 – Charlotte Harden, the Ozark Sweetheart – Sorry / Alone With You (Dixie)
947 – Jerry Harrington – Knocking Again / Why (Dixie)
948 –
949 –
950 – Winston Shelton and the Country Gospel Singers – From Bethlehem to Calvary / Stop and Think / I'm Not A Poor Man / On the Hands of Old Jordon (Walton)
951 – Pudgie Parsons – I Can't Live My Life Without You / I Can't Let You Go (B. E. S.)
952 – Fred Williams – City of Love / Where the Sun Is Always Shining (Dixie)
953 – The Reece Sisters – Wings of a Dove / Known Only To Him / Let Your Light Shine / Stand By Me (Faith)
954 – Little Miss Katie piano acc. by Hazel Haile – Many Tears Ago / I Cannot Find My Way / Evening Prayer / Just For Old Times Sake / A Good Man Is Hard To Find / I'm Gonna Lock My Heart (And Throw Away the Key) (Dixie)
955 – Vic Thomas and the Stringdusters – A Fool In Love / I Wonder (Memory)
956 –
957 –
958 – The King Brothers and the Virginia Mountaineers – Angel / Big Daddy (Dixie)
959 –
960 –

961 – Dykes Brothers with Pap and the Young'uns – Heartaches / Life Ain't Worth Living (S S S)
962 –
963 –
964 – Robert White and His Candy Mountain Boys – Divorce Granted the Judge Said / Wish My Dream Had Been True (Glass City)
965 – Ray Wolfe – Birds of the Air / The Silver Chalice (Dixie)
966 – Ken Capehart – I'll Wait a Lifetime (with Janet Smith) / Sitting Here Thinking (Hart)
967 – The King Brothers and the Virginia Mountaineers – That Blue-Eyed Girl of Mine / A True Loving Woman (Dixie)
968 –
969 –
970 –
971 – Joe the Shaker and the Playboys – Yea, Pretty Baby / Darlin Be Mine (Glass City)
972 – J. R. White and the Stabrites – Little Lonely Heart / Rock-N-Roll Twist (Dixie)
973 –
974 – Pudgie Parsons – Where Do I Stand with You / Now I Know (You'll Never Be Mine) (BES)
975 – The Tornados – Tornado Twist / Riot (Tornado)
976 – The A. L. Phipps Family – Glad Reunion Day / Some Sweet Day / A Soul Winner for Jesus / When He Blessed My Soul / I Want to Love Him More / Happy Day (Faith)
977 – The A. L. Phipps Family – Keep On the Sunny Side / The Carter Family – In the Sweet Bye and Bye / The Carter Family – I'll Be Satisfied / The A. L. Phipps Family – Amazing Grace / The A. L. Phipps Family – Only Trust Him / The A. L. Phipps Family – Plenty of Room (Faith)
978 –
979 –
980 –
981 – Bill and Paul, the Bluegrass Travelers – Change Of Heart / Cumberland Valley Special / Doin' My Time / Blue Grass Hop (Dixie)
982 –
983 –
984 –
985 – Gary Kelley – Homework / A Kiss (Dixie)
986 –
987 – Jack Thomas with Bluegrass Band – What'll I Do / If You Keep Doing (The Way You're Doing Me) (Dixie)
988 – Jerry Hoover – Pat Malone / Are You In Love With Someone (Pancho)
989 – Tommy Scott – Rosebuds and You / Carmella (Katona)
990 – Harry Head with the Tommy Scott Band – All the Way / Talkin' To Myself (Katona)
991 –
992 –
993 –
994 –
995 – Ernest Stacey – Harlin Kazy – I Do (Harron)
996 –
997 – Davis Brothers – Just A Beginner / Hold To My Bible (Dixie)
998 –

999 – Clyde Lay and the Rocketeers – Rocketeer Beat / Well Good Then (Tobi)
1000 – Howard and the Darts – Lightning / Oh My Love (Dixie)
1001 –
1002 – Art Buchanan – I Can't Help It / Hi Yo Silver (Dixie)
1003 –
1004 –
1005 – Ray Miller, the One Man Band – One Man Band (One Man Band)
1006 –
1007 –
1008 – Bob Cundiff and the Country Boys – Come On In, Ole Heartache / Devil In an Angel's Disguise (Dixie)
1009 –
1010 –
1011 – Watson Mishoe with Kenny and the Klovers – Why Do You Keep Teasing / She Told a Lie (Dixie)
1012 – Les Waldroop acc. By Wade and Mickey – Got It Made (In the Shade) / Country Boy's Lament (Flop)
1013 – Hoot Roberts and the Night Hawks – My Used To Be / Hey Sheriff (Owl)
1014 –
1015 – Wick Craig – Autoharp Melody / Blue Memories / Dreamy / Smile Awhile (Dixie)
1016 –
1017 –
1018 –
1019 –
1020 –
1021 –
1022 –
1023 –
1024 –
1025 –
1026 – The Byrd Family – There's A Light At the River / The Purple Robe
1027 –
1028 –
1029 –
1030 –
1031 – The Hi–Spots – Julie / Teenagers (Dixie)
1032 – Jay Earles, Lex Climer and the Blue Valley Boys – Peaceful Valley / Our Minister's Hand (Faith)
1033 –
1034 –
1035 –
1036 – Denny Lee – Judy's Clown / Cooly Mooly (Owl)
1037 –
1038 –
1039 –
1040 – Fred Netherton and Wildwood Playboys – I Can't Get It Off My Mind / Love Avenue (Day)
1041 –

1042 – William F. James – Foreign Car Craze / Pinto Beans and Taters (Dixie)
1043 – Ray Hudson and the Western Rhythmaires – Here I Am—Drunk Again / Jackhammer (Dixie)
1044 –
1045 –
1046 – David Powell – Walk In Love With Jesus / Forty Years Ago (L R C Lamon)
1047 –
1048 – Marie Strong with Smokey Greene and his Green Mountain Boys – Windows of Steel / Who Is She? (Green Mountain)
1049 – The Roy Boys, Roy Dunn Vocalist, Roy McCabe Steel Accomp. – What They Say About You / Walking Streets (Dixie)
1050 – Tito Mambo with the Men of Chantz – Jungle Farm / The Men of Chantz – Slush (R.L.)
1051 –
1052 – Jack and Sammy Stone and the Drifting Playboys – Love, Love, Love / I'm Coming Home (Orbit)
1053 –
1054 – Ron Ouderkirk – Honky Tonks Downtown / In Love with an Angel (Sitation)
1055 – Ron Ouderkirk – My Kind of Woman / Steppin' Out (Sitation)
1056 – Frank Zolton with Town and Country Boys – Cats Eyes / You're Gone (Dixie)
1057 – Smokey Greene and his Green Mountain Boys – Wrong Side of the Street / Turn the Heat On, Baby (Green Mountain)
1058 – Tennessee Stephens Quartette, Livingston Tennessee – When He Calls I'll Fly Away / Way Down In My Soul (Overton Records)
1059 –
1060 – Bill Martin – Our Fathers In Washington / There Are Only Ten (Orbit)
1061 –
1062 –
1063 – Jessie Floyd – Hangover Blues / Satan's Wife (Dixie)
1064 –
1065 –
1066 –
1067 –
1068 – Guy Gardner and His Country Four – High Society / I'll Be Waiting (Dixie)
1069 – Dale Willis – You Let Me Down Fast / Audition To the Opry (with George Johnson) (Dixie)
1070 – Bob Jones – There Goes the Bride / I Want Cha Baby (Dixie)
1071 –
1072 – Arvil Meers – The Future I Hold / The Way You Want It (Dixie)
1073 – Blankenship Brothers – Heap Big Blues / Travelin' (Harron)
1074 – The Holidays – Concussion / Pearl Diver (Dixie)
1075 –
1076 – Homer Briarhopper and His Jamboree Boys – Chicken / What Does the Deep Sea Say (L R C Lamon)
1077 – Bobby Powell – Just Acting / No One Dear, But You (L R C Lamon)
1078 –
1079 –
1080 –
1081 –

1082 –
1083 – Ray and May Dixon – When I'd Yoo Hoo In the Valley To My Lulu In the Hills (Dixon)
1084 – Don Sowards and the Laurel Mountain Boys – Nellie Joe / I Love You, Yes I Do (Laurel)
1085 –
1086 –
1087 –
1088 –
1089 – Jerry Gray, music by the Southern Gentlemen – Hearts Breaking Up Over Love / I Can't Take You Back Again (Ozark)
1090 –
1091 – Jim Wheeler and the Country Playboys – Honky Tonk Sweetheart / Hughes Ramble (Gen-Nell)
1092 – Hank Beach and the Countrymen – I Got the Time / Set Up Another (Staff)
1093 –
1094 – Flat Top's Rabble Rousers, vocal Norm Childs – Loneliest Guy In Town / Rosa-Lee / Coverup / Talking In Your Sleep (Flat Top)
1095 – Gerene Ellen – My Heart Will Stand the Wear and Tear / Echo Of Our Love (Dixie)
1096 – Gerene Ellen and the Western Drifters – Sweet Memories / A Letter To My Heart (Dixie)
1096 – Pete Peters – Red Wing / Wig Walk (Dixie)
1096 – Royals, vocal Bob Bren – Back In Town / Without You (Adirondack)
1097 – Edmond Samons, Starr Orr and the Kentucky Mountain Boys – Book Of Life / Where Shall I Shelter My Sheep (B 4)
1098 – Pete Peters – Barbara Allen / Little Rosewood Casket / Red Wing (Dixie)
1099 –
1100 –
1101 –
1102 – Country Ramblers (vocals by Susie and Otis Glover, Jr. and Donnie New) – Walkin', Talkin', Cryin', Barely Beatin', Broken Heart / A Little Bitty Tear (Dixie)
1103 –
1104 – Curly Smith Band – Orange Blossom Baby / Crying Over You (Hull)
1105 –
1106 –
1107 – Dick Mosely and the Lonesome Drifters – Why Do You Bother Me / What Good Is Money (Moby-Dick)
1108 – Timothy Shelby – When the Stars Begin To Fall / Not My Will / Just A Rose Will Do / Without Him (TIM)
1109 – Evangelistic Gospel Singers – My Only Friend / Lonely Jesus (Rosser)
1110 –
1111 –
1112 – Jack Thomas with the Tomcats – Poor Boy Blues / Meanest Blues (Dixie)
1113 – Avon Don – Strange Man / Hey—Hey—Hey (Dixie)
1114 – Ivan Taylor and the Blue Strings – Brand New Life / Just Pickin' (Bucked-Lid)
1115 – Red Moore and His Rhythm Drifters – Poor Lonely Me / Key's In the Mailbox (Todd)
1116 – Louie Clark – Tired of Being Blue / Lonesome Truck Driver (Dixie)

1117 – Dick Mosely – Cry No More / Crazy Blues (Moby-Dick)
1118 –
1119 –
1120 –
1121 –
1122 –
1123 – Al Bain – Which Way'd They Go / Far Far Away (Green Mountain)
1124 –
1125 –
1126 – Ronnie Miller – Who Was It / Dang You Pride (Dixie)
1127 – Smokey Reed with the Freeloaders with Don Winkler – Country Yodel / Caberet Angel (Dixie)
1128 – Smokey Reed with the Freeloaders with Don Winkler – Why / Susan (Dixie)
1129 –
1130 –
1131 – Jim Ridings and the Alabama Buddies – You're Gonna Pay / My Baby Don't Want Me No More (Dixie)
1132 –
1133 – Hank Rector – Santa Be A Pal / A Picture of Christmas At Home (Starlite)
1134 –
1135 –
1136 –
1137 –
1138 –
1139 – The Sid White Singers – What Will I Leave Behind / My Lord Keeps A Record / Twilight Is Falling / How Great Thou Art (Faith)
1140 – J. P. Dunn – Blue Yodel Blues / Lonely Soldier's Sweetheart (Dixie)
1141 – Noal Dales and the Country Buddies – One Way Street to Heartbreak (Skyview)
1142 –
1143 –
1144 – J. P. Dunn – Long Time Ago / Kentucky Fandango (Dixie)
1145 – The Holidays – I Got News for You / I Want To Do It (Dixie)
1146 – The Penetrators – Guitar Boogie (Penstar)
1147 – Don Waynick and the Green Bullets – There She Goes / Telephone Boogie (Dixie)
1148 –
1149 – Kenny Ezell and the Night Trains – That Same Old Thing / Slowly (Trusty)
1150 –
1151 –
1152 –
1153 – Little Chuck Daniels – I Still Care / Night Shift (Dixie)
1154 – Teddy Redman – Nightime (Is A World of Torture) / What Is Forever (Dixie)
1155 – The Blue Ridge Boys – My Heart Seems To Think You're Still Mine (Star)
1156 – The Holidays Combo – Little Miss Hurt / Land of 1,000 Dances (Dixie)
1157 –
1158 –
1159 – The Butler Family – Well I Wouldn't Take Nothing For My Journey Now / Neither Do I Condemn Thee / When Jesus Opened Up the Door / Give God Your Heart (Dixie)
1160 –

1161 – Homer Monroe and the Country Drifters – Don't Tell Me You Love Me (Unless You Do)/ It's Many a Mile From Me to You (Silvia)
1162 –
1163 –
1164 –
1165 –
1166 –
1167 – Jimmie Lee and the Oak Valley Rangers – The Little Things You Do / Wicked Words (Dixie)
1168 –
1169 –
1170 – Little Chuck Daniels and the Big Boys – I've Got My Brand On You (Dixie)
1171 – Paul Mendenall – Someone Sweet To Love / Now My Baby's Gone (Star)
1172 – The Bellevue Gospel Quartet – I Have Somebody With Me / I'm Too Near Home / I'm Bound For That City / Then the Answer Came (B G Q)
1173 – George Waite – Don't Be Angry / Someone Before Me (Star)
1174 – The Bondsmen – Big Boy Pete / Honky Tonk (Star)
1175 – Joe Calloway and the Country Ramblers – Tiny Doll / Lonesome Road Blues (Delmarva)
1176 –
1177 – Curley Vines – Mr. Blue / Lies (Dixie)
1178 – The Sloane Brothers, Bradley, Milburn, Orbin and Vernon – Lonesome Dove / Who's Knocking At My Door (Dixie)
1179 –
1180 – Ronnie Seymour – Teardrops Are Falling / Don't Be Angry (Delmarva)
1181 –
1182 –
1183 –
1184 –
1185 – Curley Vines – If They Should Ask Me / Good Things (Dixie)
1186 – Johnny Hartin – I'll Be Brave / Just As a Friend (Dixie)

BIBLIOGRAPHY

CHAPTER 1. YOU ALL COME

The Starday Story—The House That Country Music Built relies extensively on personal interviews, the majority with Don Pierce. Other research materials for chapter 1 include scrapbooks and keepsakes kept by both Don Pierce and Patsy (Elshire) Astorga. Bud Daily, Pappy Daily's son, also contributed to my understanding of the label's early history and directed me to Bear Family's "D" label box set liner notes by Colin Escott. Joyce Kelley and Darlena Blackwell, daughters of Jack Starns Jr. and Neva Starns, were also highly informative and friendly. *Billboard's The World of Country Music* annual series (1964–70) was also of great assistance, with many articles written by both Daily and Pierce.

I owe a great debt of gratitude to Andrew Brown, who provided me with transcripts from his interviews with Arlie Duff, Freddie Frank, and Bobby Black made between 1996 and 2005. Poughkeepsie, New York, disc jockey Darwin Lee Hill was also kind enough to send me an interview he had made with Don Pierce that I helped arrange. The Duff family was also of great support. After winning an autographed photo of Arlie Duff on eBay, I was contacted by Duff's daughter, Becky Rippy, who had never seen that photo. I gave her the photo and in return she sent a copy of Duff's long-out-of-print autobiography, which provided valuable reading.

Perhaps the single most helpful written account of the early Starday period was written by Don Pierce himself. In 1990, at the request of his family, Pierce typed up fifty-six pages of life memories and titled it *Life and Times of Don Pierce: Family, Friends and Happenings*. On several occasions, when I asked about a particular topic, Pierce asked me to use the quote from his unpublished manuscript.

Other sources for this chapter include George Jones's autobiography, written with Tom Carter. Though Pierce lobbied hard for an extensive interview with Jones on my behalf, when it finally happened, we only had time for seven or eight questions. I used a few quotes from Jones's book to fill out the rest of his story. Also helpful was Martin Hawkins's insightful article chronicling the life of Pappy Daily, and Bill Millar's excellent interview with Eddie Noack for *New Kommotion*.

As I set out to write the story of a record label, I found books on Motown, Atlantic, Gennett, Sun, and Chess to be particularly useful. Those books, as well as others that have informed my understanding of country music, are included in the following notes.

Author interviews that helped shape this chapter were conducted with Don Pierce, Patsy (Elshire) Astorga, Darlena Blackwell, Bud Daily, Joyce Kelley, Sleepy LaBeef, and Becky Rippy.

"Blackie Crawford – Pride of the Southwest" (1953). *Cowboy Songs Magazine* 30 (December).
Brown, Andrew (2005). "On the Road with Blackie Crawford and the Western Cherokees: The Bobby Black Interview." Unpublished.

Cohodas, Nadine (2000). *Spinning Blues into Gold: The Chess Brothers and the Legendary Chess Records*. New York: St. Martin's.

Cooper, Daniel (1995). *Lefty Frizzell: The Honky-Tonk Life of Country Music's Greatest Singer*. New York: Little, Brown.

Daily, H. W. "Pappy" (1964). "Pappy Daily Speaks His Mind." *Billboard: The World of Country Music* (Nov. 14).

Duff, Arlie (1983). *Y'all Come*. Austin, TX: Eakin Press.

Early, Gerald (1995). *One Nation Under a Groove: Motown and American Culture*. Hopewell: Ecco Press.

Erlewine, Michael, Vladimir Bogdanov, Chris Woodstra, and Stephen Thomas Erlewine (1997). *All Music Guide to Country*. San Francisco: Miller Freeman.

Escott, Colin (1995). Liner notes to *The "D" Singles Vol. 1* (BCD 15832). Habergeon, Germany: Bear Family Records.

—— (1996). *Tattooed on Their Tongues: A Journey Through the Backrooms of American Music*. New York: Schirmer Books.

Hawkins, Martin (1976). "Martin Hawkins on the Starday Label, and "Pappy" Daily, Its Founder." *Country Music Review* (December). London, England: Concorde Distribution.

Jones, George, with Tom Carter (1997). *I Lived To Tell It All*. New York: Dell Publishing.

Kennedy, Rick (1999). *Jelly Roll, Bix, and Hoagy: Gennett Studios and the Birth of Recorded Jazz*. Bloomington: Indiana University Press.

Kinsbury, Paul (1998). *The Encyclopedia of Country Music*. New York: Oxford University Press.

Malone, Bill (1985). *Country Music USA*. Austin: University of Texas Press.

McNutt, Randy (1988). We Wanna Boogie: An Illustrated History of the American Rockabilly Movement. Hamilton: HHP Books.

Millar, Bill (1976). "Talk Back with Noack Pt. 1." *New Kommotion* vol. 2, no. 2 (Issue 12). Middlesex, England: Shazam Promotions.

—— (1976). "Talk Back with Noack Pt. 2." *New Commotion* vol. 2, no. 3 (Issue 13). Middlesex, England: Shazam Promotions.

"Pappy Daily" (1935). *Billboard* (12 October).

Pecknold, Diane (2007). *The Selling Sound: The Rise of the Country Music Industry*. Durham: Duke University Press.

Peterson, Richard A. (1997). *Creating Country Music: Fabricating Authenticity*. Chicago: University of Chicago Press.

Pierce, Don (1990). "Life and Times of Don Pierce: Family, Friends, and Happenings." Unpublished.

Starns, Jack (1952). "Behind the Scenes with Jack Starnes (Lefty Frizzell's Manager)." *Country Song Roundup* 20 (October).

Turner, Allan (2005). *Starday—The Early Years, Texas to Tennessee*. Middlesex, England: Hillbilly Researcher.

Whitburn, Joel (2002). *Top Country Singles 5th Edition 1944–2001*. Menomonee Falls, WI: Record Research.

CHAPTER 2. ROCK IT

Andrew Brown was a great help toward understanding the early Texas days of Starday. In addition to sharing some of the articles he has written about the Starday and Dixie labels, he also made several CDs for me so that I might hear some of the rare and hard to find, but still very important recordings. Stories by John Pugh and John Tottenham also provided insight into the colorful early days of Starday. While interviewing Rudy Grayzell about his rockabilly recordings, he directed me to the Rockabilly Hall of Fame website and suggested that I use one of his quotes from the Dan Davidson story. Though hesitant to use an Internet quote, I decided it would be okay since Rudy suggested it.

Unfortunately, the John Pugh article listed below was a photocopied version kept at the Country Music Hall of Fame library. Page numbers listed in the notes section correlate to the photocopied version of the story. Similarly, page numbers were not visible on my copies of the Bill Millar and Ray Topping story regarding Sonny Fisher nor John Tottenham's story about Rudy Grayzell.

Author interviews that helped shape this chapter were conducted with Don Pierce, Glenn Barber, Darlena Blackwell, Luke Gordon, Rudy Grayzell, George Jones, Joyce Kelley, James O' Gwynn, Arnold Parker, and Link Wray.

Allen, Bob (1984). *George Jones: The Saga of an American Singer*. Garden City, NY: Doubleday.
Brown, Andrew (2001). "45 RPM: The Legendary Starday and Dixie Labels." *Discoveries* (June).
—— (2005). "All Dressed Up, No Place to Go: Jimmy Johnson." *Taking Off* vol. 1, no. 1 (Spring).
Davidson, Dan (date unknown). "Rudy 'Tutti' Grayzell." Rockabilly Hall of Fame website: rockabillyhall.com/RudyGrayzell1.html, accessed 1-01-2006.
Gart, Galen (compiled 1990). *First Pressings: The History of Rhythm and Blues Vol. 4 (1954)*. Milford, NH: Big Nickel Publications.
Gillett, Charlie (1975). *Making Tracks: The History of Atlantic Records*. Herts, England: Panther Books.
Horstman, Dorothy (1975). *Sing Your Heart Out, Country Boy*. New York: E. P. Dutton.
Millar, Bill, and Ray Topping (1980). "Sonny Fisher—That Rockin' Daddy." *New Kommotion* 25. Middlesex, England: Shazam Promotions.
Pierce, Don (1954). "Attention: Professional Vocalists and Bandleaders Promotional Letter." Unpublished.
Pugh, John (1971). "Pappy Daily: A Legend in His Time." *Music City News* (January).
Tottenham, John (1996). "Rudy: Elvis Liked What He Saw and Offered the Performer the Job." *Sunday Oregonian* (Portland) (21 April).
Turner, Allan, and Philip J. Tricker (1997). *Starday Custom Series Part One, Issue #500–850*. Middlesex, England: Hillbilly Researcher.

CHAPTER 3. DON'T STOP THE MUSIC

Colin Escott's liner notes to George Jones's Mercury releases proved very beneficial, as was his brief summary of the Starday label in his book *Tattooed on Their Tongues*. Other liner notes that proved helpful were the many bluegrass texts written by Gary B. Reid.

Author interviews that helped shape this chapter were conducted with Don Pierce, Clyde Beavers, Eddie Bond, Bill Clifton, Jimmy Dean, D. Kilpatrick, George Jones, Sleepy LaBeef, James O'Gwynn, Shelby Singleton, and Helen Story.

Asbell, Bernie, and Joel Friedman (1956). "Mercury to Absorb Starday Diskery." *Billboard* (15 December).
Dean, Jimmy, and Donna Meade (2004). *Thirty Years of Sausage, Fifty Years of Ham*. New York: Berkley Publishing.
Escott, Colin (1994). "Don Pierce: Inside Starday Records." *Journal of Country Music* vol. 17, no. 1.
——— (1994). Liner notes to *George Jones: Cup of Loneliness: The Classic Mercury Years* (314-522-635-2). New York: Polygram Records.
Gutterman, Jimmy (1995). Liner notes to *Fifty Years of Country Music From Mercury* (D207043). New York: Polygram Records.
Hawkins, Martin (1976). "Introducing James O'Gwynn." *Country Music Review* (December). London, England: Concorde Distribution.
Olofsson, Claes, and Bo Berglind (1995). Liner notes to *Benny Barnes: The Rockin' Honky-Tonk Country Man* (CD 506007). Reftele, Sweden: Star Club Records.
Reid, Gary B. (1993). Liner notes to *The Stanley Brothers and the Clinch Mountain Boys: 1953-58 and 1959* (BCD 15681). Habergeon, Germany: Bear Family Records.
——— (1999). Liner notes to *Jim Eanes and the Shenandoah Valley Boys* (BCD 15934). Habergeon, Germany: Bear Family Records.
Rice, Tandy (1967). "Men Behind the Scenes, Pappy Daily and Don Pierce." *Country Song Roundup* vol. 19, no. 100 (June).
"Starday Moves to Nashville" (1957). *Billboard* (13 April).

CHAPTER 4. RANK STRANGER

Once again, Gary B. Reid's liner notes saved the day. I am also grateful for John Rumble's great work in the oral history department of the Country Music Hall of Fame. Rumble conducted three separate interviews with Don Pierce, in addition to two by Doug Green, all of which provide insight into Pierce's role in the music business. There is also a substantial interview with Tommy Hill, who passed away shortly after I began this project. Though Hill did not talk about his role with Starday at great length, the transcript does provide a great portrait of the man and his role in country music.

During my freshman year at Emerson, I was assigned to write a twenty-page research paper on the topic of my choice. I chose rockabilly music. A few days later (October 22, 1997), Link Wray came to Boston to share the bill with a local rockabilly band, the Racketeers. For some reason, Wray turned away all interview requests except mine. I was invited backstage, where Wray, his wife Olive, and I talked about music for more than an hour. Unfortunately I kept asking about rockabilly music; fortunately, Link and Olive were quite patient with me. Link guided me through his life story, even talking about his Starday records. How serendipitous that I would begin writing a book about Starday just a few short years later!

Other interviews that helped shape this chapter were conducted with Don Pierce, Chuck Chellman, Aubrey Holt, Orangie Ray Hubbard, Jesse McReynolds, Frankie Miller, Lattie Moore, Jim Quest, Eddie Skelton, and Roni Stoneman.

Ackerman, Paul (1960). "Pierce Spearheads Europe C&W Push." *Billboard* (29 February).
Allen, Bob (1977). "Starday Helped Pave the Way to Modern Marketing." *Music City News* (January).

——— (1978). "Sound-Alikes Records Are a Big Business." *Music City News* (June).
"Days of Starday and Don Pierce" (1963). *The Country Music Who's Who 1964*. Denver: Heather Publications.
"Don Pierce Named C&W Man of Year" (1959). *Billboard* (9 November).
"Don Pierce—Country Music's Man of the Year 1959" (1959). *Billboard* (October).
Escott, Colin (1993). Liner notes to *Tommy Hill: Get Ready Baby* (BCD 15709). Habergeon, Germany: Bear Family Records.
Jensen, Joli (1998). *Creating the Nashville Sound: Authenticity, Commercialization, and Country Music*. Nashville: Vanderbilt University Press.
Pierce, Don (1960). "Formation and Growth of a Record Company—Starday Records." *Disc Collector* (May).
Reid, Gary B. (1998). Liner notes to *Country Gentlemen: High Lonesome* (King 3510-2-2). Nashville: King Records.
——— (2003). Liner notes to *Buzz Busby: Goin' Home* (Starday SD-0123-2). Nashville: King Records.
Rosenberg, Neil (1993). *Bluegrass, A History*. Champaign: University of Illinois Press.
——— (1967). "From Sound to Style: The Emergence of Bluegrass." *Journal of American Folklore* vol. 80, no. 316 (April-June).
"Starday Gathering Fruit of Early Expansion Abroad" (1962). *The Music Reporter* vol. 7 no. 16 (10 November).
"Starday's Unique Concept: A Country Label Exclusively" (1963). *Billboard: The World of Country Music* (2 November).
"The Banjo: America's Own Musical Instrument" (1964). *The Country Music Who's Who 1965*. Denver: Heather Publications.
Welding, Pete (1962). "Starday: The Bluegrass Label." *Sing Out* vol. 12, no. 3 (Summer).

CHAPTER 5. SUNNY TENNESSEE

Fortunately, Pierce wrote several articles for various trade publications during this period. Though written to promote Starday's place in country music, they provide a glimpse into the many issues that concerned Pierce at the time.

Author interviews that helped shape this chapter were conducted with Don Pierce, Mike Copas, Charlie Dick, David Hearle, Loyd Howell, Eddy Irving, Merle Kilgore, Billy Linneman, Jack "Hoss" Linneman, Rose Lee Maphis, Suzanne Mathis, David McKinley, Joan Proctor, and Jim Quest.

"Another Country Music Success Story from Nashville, TN" (1963). *The Music Reporter* (2 March).
"Bluegrass Bounces Back Across the Nation" (1963). *Music Reporter* vol. 7, no. 32.
"Bluegrass—The Brightest, Freshest Sound" (1963). *Billboard: The World of Country Music* (2 November).
Dean, Dixie (1967). "Don Pierce: Mr. Record Man." *Music City News* (January).
Goldbey, Brian (1994). "Don Pierce—Mr. Starday." *Country Music People* vol. 25, no. 1 (Issue 289, January). London, England: Music Farm, Ltd.
"Nashville Music Firms Diversify" (1965). *Billboard: The World of Country Music* (30 October): Section 2.

"Pay Dirt for Sidemen: New Studios provide work bonanza for musicians" (1964). *Billboard: The World of Country Music* (14 November).

Pierce, Don (1961). Liner notes to *The Duke of Paducah—Button Shoes, Belly Laughs, and Monkey Business* (SLP 148). Nashville: Starday Records.

——— (1961). Personal letter to Loyd Howell. June 2, 1961. Unpublished.

——— (1963). "Bluegrass and the Banjo." *Country and Western Record Review* vol. 5, no. 9 (February). Kent, England: Southwood.

——— (1964). "Don Pierce Analyzes Spread of C&W Among European and Asian Audiences." *Billboard: The World of Country Music* (14 November).

——— (1964). "Superiority Via Specialization: Starday's Album Marketing Philosophy." *Billboard: The World of Country Music* (14 November).

Samuelson, Dave (2007). Liner notes to *Cowboy Copas: Settin' Flat On Ready* (BCD 16990). Habergen, Germany: Bear Family Records.

"Starday Keeps Pace with Country Music Growth" (1965). *Billboard: The World of Country Music* (30 October): Section 2.

CHAPTER 6. GIDDY-UP GO

One of my great eBay purchases (in September 2006) was a box of cassettes sold as "Custom Jingles of Nashville." Having no idea what would be on those tapes, I was surprised to hear Hank Snow, Red Sovine, Barbara Mandrell, Jan Howard, the Willis Brothers, and many others singing about beer, banks cars, chewing tobacco, soap, and even Fender guitars. Included in the box of tapes were checks made out to Pete Drake and signed by Vic Willis. I contacted the seller to obtain more information about the tapes. Turns out the seller had dozens of cashed checks from the company. With his help, I compiled a small list of some of the performers who recorded for Custom Jingles of Nashville, Inc., by listening to the jingles, talking with Don Pierce about the sessions, and referencing the signed checks.

Author interviews that helped shape this chapter were conducted with Don Pierce, Chuck Chellman, Merle Kilgore, Billy Linneman, Jack "Hoss" Linneman, David McKinley, Tim Ormond, Tandy Rice, John Rumble, and Glenn Sutton.

Daughtrey, Larry (1965). "The Man Who Went Giddy-Up." *Nashville Tennessean Sunday Magazine* (19 December).

Davis, Hank, and Colin Escott (1984). "Don Pierce: A Record Industry Pioneer." *Goldmine* vol. 10, iss. 8, no. 99 (11 May).

"Don Pierce and Starday Records" (1965). *Country Song Roundup* no. 87 (February).

"Hollywood Calls . . . Nashville Answers" (1967). *Billboard: The World of Country Music* (28 October).

Leadbitter, Mike (1973). "Money Is the Name of the Game." *Country Music Review* (July). London, England: Hanover Books.

"Majors Dominate Singles Field" (1964). *Billboard: The World of Country Music* (14 November).

"More Country Music Success at Starday in 1965" (1965). *The Country Music Who's Who 1966*. Denver: Heather Publications.

Pierce, Don (1959). "Let's Stick Together." *Country Music Who's Who 1960*. Cincinnati: Cardinal Enterprises

——— (1966). Letter to distributors. Unpublished.
——— (1967). "Country Music One Stop Service" (ad). *Billboard: The World of Country Music* (28 October).
"Starday's Country Music Record Club Spearheads Another Year of Expansion" (1964). *Country Music Who's Who 1965*. Denver: Heather Publications.

CHAPTER 7. A SATISFIED MIND

In preparing this chapter, I was fortunate to have been granted access to Don's office and Starday-related file cabinets. I was able to track down Starday LP sales information, Lin Broadcasting financial statements, personal correspondence with Pappy Daily, Tommy Hill, Hoss Linneman, Faron Young, Syd Nathan, Hal Neely, and many others. I was like a kid in a Necco shop. It was a truly remarkable adventure. When I finished raiding the office, Don mentioned to me that he had several more cabinets of Starday photos and papers at his home. I must have spent another ten hours digging through the boxes of Starday photos and Starday-related trinkets. Hopefully my digging has led to some worthwhile discoveries. I only wish there was enough space to include more of the hundreds of phenomenal photos I saw. Perhaps the University Press of Mississippi can whip up a second pressing at some point just for that purpose.

Author interviews that helped shape this chapter were conducted with Don Pierce, Betty Amos, Tillman Franks, David McKinley, Tom Perryman, Chuck Chellman, Kenny Roberts, and Howard Vokes.

Cason, Albert (1968). "Record Production Gross $8 Million." *Nashville Tennessean* (1 November).
Fox, John Hartley (2009). *King of the Queen City: The Story of King Records*. Urbana: University of Illinois Press.
Neely, Hal (1971). Private memo to Don Pierce. Unpublished.
Pierce, Don (1967). Letter to the editors. *Bluegrass Unlimited* vol. 1, no. 9 (March).
——— (1967). Letter to the editors. *Bluegrass Unlimited* vol. 1, no. 12 (June).
——— (1968). Letter to the editors. *Bluegrass Unlimited* vol. 2, no. 2 (June).
——— (1968). "Letter to Bill Vernon." *Bluegrass Unlimited* vol. 2, no. 7 (June).
Powell, Bob (1976). "Fond Memories of the Starday Label." *Country Music People* vol. 7, no. 8 (August). Kent, England: Country Music Press.
Rosenberg, Neil V. (1967). "Don Pierce: The Rise and Fall of Starday and the Perplexing Patriot Problem." *Bluegrass Unlimited* vol. 1, no. 11 (May).
Williams, Bill (1970). "Don Pierce Exits Starday." *Billboard* (8 August).

INDEX

Page numbers in **boldface** refer to illustrations.

Abramson, Herb, 25. *See also* Atlantic Records
ACA Recording Studios, 11, 13, 20, 23, 44
Ackerman, Willie, 109
Acorn Sisters, 102
Acuff, Roy, 27, 31, 37, 68, 123, 129, 130, 138. *See also* Smokey Mountain Gang
Adcock, Eddie, 87, **87**, 89
Adelman, Ben, 44, 88–89
Adkins, Hobo Jack, 72, 119
AFM (American Federation of Musicians), 24, 27, 59. *See also* Recording bans
Akeman, David. *See* Stringbean
"Alabam," 112–14, 129, 146
Allen, William Hoss, 164
Ames, Nikki, 127
Amos, Betty, 154–55, **154**
Amos, Jean, 155
Anderson, Vicki, 164
Annett, Milburn "Burney," 10, 22
Anthony, Chubby, 85
Apollo Records, 25
Armed Forces Radio Network, 105, 125
Arnold, Eddy, 111, 123, 135, 138, 143, 145
Atkins, Chet, 45, 54, 67, 122, 137–38; and the Nashville Sound, 82. *See also* RCA Victor
Atlantic Records, 24–25, 165
Austin, Leon, 164
Aycock, Earl, 66–67

Ballard, Hank, 162, 164
Barber, Glenn, 32, 40, 77, 96, 130
Barnes, Benny, 48, 61–64, **61**, 66, 72, 75–78, 92
BBC (London), 106

Beck, Jim, 3, 5–6
Bell, Lloyd, 70
Bennett, Henry, 96
Berman, Ike and Ben, 25
Bienstock, Freddy, 165–66
Big Bopper, 20, 38, 59–62, 74, 77
Big "D" Jamboree, 54, 62, 80
Biggar, Jimmy, 10, 21–22
Black, Bobby, 10, 19–20
"Black Land Farmer," 96–99
Blackwood Brothers, 99
Blake, Randy, 35, 66, 99–100, **100**, 103, 131
Blakley, Cliff, 40, 65
Blakley, Jimmy and Dorothy, 43, 64–66
"Blue," 155–56, 165
Blue Boys, 95, 123
Blue Sky Boys, 27, 151, 167
Bluegrass recordings, 70–74, 76, 83–92, 115, 119–21, 152–53, 155, 163, 167
BMI, 16–17, 27, 38–39, 77, 85–86, 113, 160, 169; as award, 20, 118, 149. *See also* Music Publishing
Bolick, Bill. *See* Blue Sky Boys
Bolick, Earl. *See* Blue Sky Boys
Bond, Eddie, 59, 68–69
Bond, Johnny, 122, 135, 149–50, **150**, 153, 163, 168
Boone, Claude, 70, **70**
Bordelon, Sinton "Corlue," 10
Bradley, Owen, 82. *See also* Decca Records; Quonset Hut
Brewer, Joe, 23
Brewster, Bud, 70, **70**
Brewster, Willie, 70, **70**
Brown, Andrew, 13, 19, 32
Brown, Charles, 18
Brown, Hylo, 121, 167
Brown, James, 161–65, **164**

257

INDEX

Browning, Bill, 92, 115
Browning, Bill Zekie, 81, **81**
Bryant, Russell Vernon "Hezzie," 47, 62, 96
Buchanan, Art, 82
Buchanan, Kirby, 100
Burnette, Smiley, 94, 122
Burns, Sonny, 21–23, **22**, 31–32, 37, 39, 76
Burroughs, Frank, 117
Busby, Buzz, 83, 88–89, **89**, 115, 167
Byrd, Bobby, 164

Caldwell, Eddie, 23
Campbell, Alex and Ola Belle, 151
Campbell, Archie, 49, 122
Campbell, Cecil, 123
Campbell, Glen, 20, 27, 138, 158–59, **159**
Capitol Records, 83, 129–31, 141, 158
Carlisles, 49, 62, 68, 75, 154
Carter, Wilf, 151
Carter Family, 29, 90
Caruthers, Earl, 47
Casey, Elizabeth, 131
Casey, Jack, 120
Cash, Johnny, 27, 34, 52, 58, 64, 67, 116, 132–33, 142
Casuals, 119
Cedarwood Music Publishing, 50, 112, 115, 146
Chambers, Les, 48, 65
Chance, Lightnin, 98
Chapman, Lucky, 43
Charles, Ray, 18, 140
Chelette, Mary Jo, 11–12, **12**, 21
Chellman, Chuck, 135, **135**, 160
Childre, Lew, 127
Choates, Harry, 47
Chudd, Lew, 17. *See also* Imperial Records
Clark, Ken, 83, 119
Clement, Governor Frank, 52, 115
Clements, Vassar, **86**, 87
Clifton, Bill, 72–74, **73**, 83, 89–91, 102, 121, 167
Cline, Patsy, 16, 127, 132, 142–43, 156
CMA (Country Music Association), 105–6, 137–39, 169
CMH Records, 126
CMRCA (Country Music Record Club of America), 130–31, 149, 162

Coast Recording Company pressings, 18, 33, 52, 227
Cochran, Eddie, 40
Coffeen, Selby, 98
Cole, Dorothy "Dot," 92, 94
Colley, Sarah Ophelia. *See* Pearl, Minnie
Collie, Biff, 21, 48
Collins, Lyle, 119
Collins, Lyn, 164
Collins, Tommy, 163
Columbia Records, 24, 43, 82–83, 107, 110, 129–30
Comedy recordings. *See* Rural humor recordings
Como, Perry, 42, 138
Concept albums, 142–43
Connie and Joe, 83, 115
Cooper, Myrtle Eleanor. *See* Lulu Belle and Scotty
Copas, Cathy, 112
Copas, Cowboy, 69, 104, 110–15, **111**, **114**, 127–28, 137, 146, 156, 162, 167
Country Gentlemen, 72, 83, 87–88, **87**, 90, 115, 120, 167
Country Juke Box Oldies Series, 132
Country Music Association. *See* CMA
Country Music Hall of Fame, 105, 167–68
Country Music Record Club of America. *See* CMRCA
Cousin Jody, 123
Cox, Jim, 87, **87**
Crawford, Blackie, 5, 7, 9–11, **11**, 13, 21–22, 59. *See also* Western Cherokees
Crawford, Bud, 10
Crawford, Fred, 48
Criss, Herman, 80–81, **81**
Crook Brothers, 127
Crooks, Tom, 80
Crosby, Bing, 19, 21
Crowe, J. D., 163
Custom Jingles of Nashville, 135–37
Custom pressings. *See* Dixie Records: as custom label

D Records, 60, 77
Daily, Bud, 7, 9, 153
Daily, Don, 153
Daily, Harold W. "Pappy," **8**, 13–18, 20,

27–30, 39, **48**, 51–52, 59–62, **61**, 74, 88, 168; association with 4 Star, 7–9, 16; departure from Starday, 75–78; on founding Starday, 9, 17; on managing George Jones, 29–35, 54–58, 75; as record producer, 23, 47–48, 68; on recording rockabilly, 34–36, 38, 41–42. *See also* D Records; Daily's Record Ranch
Daily's Record Ranch, 7, 25, 36
Daniels, Fred, 102
Davis, Cindy, 88. *See also* Adelman, Ben
Davis, Link, 23, 37–39, **37**, 47, 60, 62, 143
Day, Jimmy, 98
Dean, Jimmy, 49, 59, 67–68, 74–75, 82, 168
Decca Records, 19, 24, 82–83, 91, 129
Dee, Buddy, 40
Dempsey, Little Jimmy, 115
Dennis, Jimmy, 10, 21
Denny, Jim, 50, 93, 112, 146. *See also* Cedarwood Music Publishing
Dick, Charlie, 143
Dickens, "Little" Jimmy, 19, 37
Disc Jockey Convention, 48, 50–51, 105, 140, 149–50
Dixie Records: as custom label, 42–45, 64–66, 75, 79–82, 115–18, 120, 137, 142, 167; as *Hillbilly Hit Parade* series, 35, 65–67, 75, 80, 99, 103–4; as rock'n'roll 2000 series, 79–80, 118, 167
Doane, Clinton, 81, **81**
Doll, Andy, 43
Dolphin, John, 17–18, 25. *See also* Hollywood Records
Don and Earl, 102
Doss, Bob, 40
Drake, Pete, 98, 109, 123, 160, 164
Drumright, Joe. *See* Connie and Joe
Drusky, Roy, 28, 48, 78, 134
Dudley, Dave, 92, 115, 143
Duff, Arlie, 13–14, **14**, 19–21
Duffey, John, **87**, 88. *See also* Country Gentlemen
Duke, Denver, 92
Duke of Paducah, 121–22

Eanes, Jim, 72, 83, 102, 115, 117, 167
Echo chamber, 40, 110

Edwards, Darrell, 34
Edwards, Tibby, 68
Ellis, Bob, 104
Ellis, Curly, 104
Ellis, Red, 102, 121
Elshire, Patsy, 20–22, 28
Emerson, Bill, 88–89
Emerson, Lee, 140
Emery, Ralph, 112–13, 134
Emmons, Buddy, 98, 123
Ervin, Sid, 48
Escott, Colin, 15, 28, 53, 71, 74

Fairchild, Tommy, 101
Figure eight races, 134–35
Films, country music exploitation, 133–34
Fisher, Sonny, 36–38, 40
Flat Mountain Boys, 72, 83
Foley, Red, 13, 25, 27, 102, 146
Folkways Records, 88
Ford, Benjamin Francis "Whitey." *See* Duke of Paducah
Ford, Rocky Bill, 40
Forrester, Howdy, 123
4 Star Records, 7–9, 15–17, 24, 42, 66–67, 88, 96–97
Fowler, Wally, 49, 100–1
Fox, Curly, 127, 129
Frank, Freddie, 10, 21–22, 25
Franks, Tillman, 94, 129–30
Frisby, Lew, 32
Frizzell, Lefty, 3–5, **4**, 10, 31, 82; contract dispute, 5–7, 9
Frost, Murray "Jack," 18, 52, 63, 92
Fulson, Lowell, 18

Gabbard, Harley, 72
Gaddis, Rudy, 40
Garland, Hank "Sugarfoot," 98, 101, 109
Gately, Connie. *See* Connie and Joe
Gately, Jimmy, 120
Gatlin, Smitty, 101
Gay, Connie B., 67–68
"Giddy-up Go," 146–49, 152–53, 166
Gillet, Charlie, 25
Glover, Henry, 164
Gold Star Recording Studio, 20, 36, 39–40, 47, 54, 60, 62, 96

260 INDEX

Golden, Billy, 158
Golden Eagle Master Achievement Awards, 167–68
Gordon, Curtis, 58–59, 68, 74
Gordon, Luke, 44, 92, 120
Gospel and sacred recordings, 70–71, 99–105; as EP Series, 102–3
Grammy Award, 59, 102, 137, 156, 158
Grand Ole Opry, 50–52, 54, 72–75, 88, 93–96, 100, 105–6, 112, 121, 127, 133, 170
Grayzell, Rudy "Tutti," 40–41, **41**
Green, Irving B., 49–51, **51**, 57, 63, 68, 75. *See also* Mercury Records
Greer, Jim, 120
Gregg, Fred, 162–63
GT's, 119
Gunter, Sid "Hardrock," 102, 115
Gusto Records, 107, 166–67
Gutherie, Ansel, 104
Gutterman, Jimmy, 71

Haerle, Martin, 125–27, **125–26**, 130, 143
Harden, Bobby, 158
Harper, Herman, 101
Harrell, Bill, 83
Harris, Charlie, 62
Harris, Harold "Hal," 36, 46–47, **46**, 60, 62
Harrison, E. J. "Dutch," 138, **139**
Hawkins, Martin, 8, 23, 32, 45–46, 60, 62
Hayes, Joe "Red," 10–11, 21–22, 25–27, **26**, 47, 62, 140
Hayes, Kenneth "Little Red," 11, 21–22, 25, 47
Hayes, Leon, 11
Hayes, Linda, 17–18
Heap, Jimmy, 13
Hendon, R. D., 8, 28, 48
Henson, Buck, 23
Heppler, Bob, 10, 13, 21
Hicks, Jeanette, 20, 65
Hill, Tommy, 22, 94–98, **95**, **97**, 107–8, **108**, 123, **126**, 134–35, **135**, 146–49, **156**, 160, 166, 168; as producer, 108–10, 118–19, 136, 155, 163; as songwriter, 94, 146–48
Hill and Range Music Publishing, 6, 140, 165
Hi-Tombs, 115
Hodge, Bobby, 119

Holford, Bill, 11. *See also* ACA Recording Studios
Holly, Buddy, 48, 61, 82
Hollywood Records, 17–18, 25, 40, 52, 65, 77, 163–64
Holt, Aubrey, 72
Honky-tonk recordings, 23, 45–48, 92–94, 115, 167
Hopkins, Jerry, 43
Houston Hometown Jamboree, 19, 21–22, 31, 46–47
Howell, Loyd, 118–19, **118**
Hubbard, Orangie Ray, 80–82, **81**
Hunter, Ernie, 47, 62
Hunter, Pete, 53
Husky, Ferlin, 14, 133–34, 168
Husky, Roy "Junior," 98, 108–9, **108**
Hutt, Polly, 119

Imperial Records, 17, 24
Instrumental recordings, 122–24
Irving, Lonnie, 116–18, **117**, 142

Jackson, Alan, 59
Jackson, Marvin, 119
Jackson, Shot, 123, 143
James, Sonny, 57, 66, 157
Jericho, Jerry, 8, 21, 48
Jim and Jesse. *See* McReynolds, Jim and Jesse
Johnson, Big Bill, 120
Johnson, Jay, 120
Johnson, Jimmy, 44
Jones, George, 20–21, 29–35, **30**, **33**, 39, 47–48, **55**, 61–62, 64, 66–67, 72, 102, **114**, 134, 141, 154; with Sonny Burns, 23, 31–32; as Thumper Jones, 35, 51; on Mercury-Starday, 53–59, 74–78; on signing with Starday, 30
Jones, Thumper, 35, 51. *See also* Jones, George
Joy, Benny, 80
Jubilaires Quartet, 100
Juricek, Frank, 47
Justice Brothers, 120

Kane, Jack, 165
Kempf, Howdy, 119, 154

INDEX

Kenetics, 119
Kennedy, Jack, 96
Kentucky Travelers, 121
Kilgore, Merle, 99, 115–16, 163–64, 168
Kilpatrick, Walter David "D.," 49–52, 67–69, 71–73, 75
King, Pee Wee, 111, 138, 151
King, Sid. *See* Ervin, Sid
King Records, 16, 25, 83, 85, 111, 127, 161–67
Kingston, Jack, 92
Kirby, Beecher Ray. *See* Oswald, Bashful Brother
KLEE (Houston, TX), 23, 97
KNUZ (Houston, TX), 21, 23
KRIC (Beaumont, TX), 31, 60
KTRM (Beaumont, TX), 4, 20, 59–60
KTSA (San Antonio, TX), 94
KTXJ (Jasper, TX), 31
KWTO (Springfield, MO), 25
KYOK (Houston, TX), 46

LaBeef, Sleepy, 39–40, 65–67, 74, 134
LaBeff, Thomas. *See* LaBeef, Sleepy
Lamie, Tony and Jackie, 82
Lanson, Snooky, 157–58
Lauderdale, Jack, 18. *See also* Swingtime Records
Law, Don, 82. *See also* Columbia Records
Lee, Anna, 100
Lee, Judy, 155
Lefevres, 99
Lewis, Charles R. "Doc," 32, 47, 60, 62
Lewis Family, 83, 102, 121, 167
Lieber, Jerry, 165
Lin Broadcasting Company, 162–63, 165
Linneman, Billy, 109
Linneman, Jack "Hoss," 109–10, 142, 146–47, 160, 163
Locklin, Hank, 7–8, 21, 132
Lonesome Pine Fiddlers, 20, 121
Long, Joey, 37
Long play albums, 124–27, 142–43
Lonzo and Oscar, 93–94, 122, 133
Lord, Bobby, 138–39, **139**
Louisiana Hayride, 46–48, 63, 99, 129–30
Lubinsky, Herman, 25, 77. *See also* Savoy Records

Lulu Belle and Scotty, 151
Lundy, David, 80
Lunn, Robert, 127, 129
Lunsford, Mike, 166
Lunsford, Ray, 69
Luttrell, Bill, 120
Lyle, Rudy, 158
Lyons, Marie "Queenie," 164
Lytle, Moe, 166–67. *See also* Gusto Records

Mack, Bill, 40, 155–56
Maddox, Rose, 15–16, 163
Maddox Brothers and Rose, 15–16
Malone, Bill C., 73
Manhattans, 164
Manuel, Dean, 98, 109, 123, 128
Maphis, Joe, 20, 40, 151, 153
Maphis, Rose Lee, 151
Marais, Dee, 62–63
Marburg, William August. *See* Clifton, Bill
Martin, Benny, 123, 129–30
Martin, Gene, 122–23
Martin, Grady, 45, 98, 112, 138
Martin, Jimmy, 69, 74, 166
Mathis, "Country" Johnny, 64–66, 77
Mathis, Suzanne, 143
Mayfield, Chuck, 48
Mays, Earl. *See* Don and Earl
McAuliffe, Leon, 123
McCall, Bill, 7–9, 15–17, 66. *See also* 4 Star Records
McCoy, Herman, 10
McDuff, Eddie, 154
McGee, Kirk, 127
McGee, Sam, 127
McHan, Don, 86–87, **86**
McKinley, David, 110, 136
McReynolds, Jim and Jesse, 83, 86–88, **86**, 90, 167
Melody Quartet, 100
Mercury Records, 18, 49–52, 63, 74–75, 78, 83, 129
Mercury-Starday Country Series: dismantling of, 74–75; formation of, 50–52
Meredith, Buddy, 119
MGM Records, 82–83

262 INDEX

Millar, Bill, 23, 36
Miller, Darnell, 92
Miller, Frankie, 23, 96–99, **97**, 110, 130, 153, 167
Miller, Mike, 119–20
Miller, Norman, 96
Miller, Roger, 58–59, **58**, 68, 74, 141–42, 167
Millhouse, Frog. *See* Burnette, Smiley
Mitchell, Guy, 158
Monroe, Bill, 20, 70–72, 74, 83–84, 89–91, 129
Monroe, Charlie, 151
Montana, Patsy, 151
Montana Slim. *See* Carter, Wilf
Moody, Clyde, 36, 151
Moore, Charlie, 83, 102, 104–5
Moore, Lattie, 92
Moore, Red, 115
Morgan, Billie, 93
Morgan, George, 35, 135, 156–57, **157**
Morrison, Harold, 120
Mosley, Charles, 135
Mullican, Moon, 114–15, 134, 162
Mullins, Lonnie, 115
Music City Pro-Celebrity Golf Tournament, 133, 137–39
Music Publishing, 16–17, 29–30, 42–43, 50, 74, 76, 88, 98, 106, 119, 139–40, 165. *See also* BMI; Starday Music publishing; Starrite publishing
Music Row, 53, 127

Nace, Johnny, 119
Nallie, Luther, 10
Napier, Bill, 85, 105
Nashville Records, 163; as albums, 90, 131–32, 142, 153; as singles, 118–20, 131, 142
Nashville Sound, the, 82–83
Nathan, Syd, 16, 30, 83, 161. *See also* King Records
Neely, Hal, 116, 137, 157, **157**, 159, 162–66
Nelson, Ken, 82–83. *See also* Capitol Records
Nelson, Tommy, 115
Nelson, Willie, 64–65; label scan, 64
Nettles, Bill, 48
Neva's Managing and Booking Agency, 3–4, 9, 13

New Grass Revival, 163
Newman, Jack, 48
Newman, Jimmy C., 34, 54, 138
Newton, Don, 62
Noack, Eddie, 8, 23, 40, 48, 60, 65, 76–77
Null, Jeffrey, 92

Oak Ridge Boys, 27, 100–2
Oak Ridge Quartet. *See* Oak Ridge Boys
Ogletree, Lee, 44
O'Gwynn, James, 8, 47–48, 65–66, 75–76, 78
Old Hickory Singers, 127
O'Neal, Tom, 115
Ormond, Ron, 133–34
Ormond, Tim, 133
Osborne, Jimmie, 19
Oswald, Bashful Brother, 52, 123
Owens, Buck, 20, 98–99, 132, 140–41
Owens, Ruby. *See* Texas Ruby
Ozark Playboys, 120

Page, Ronnie, 101
Paradise, Lucille, 131
Park, Ray. *See* Vern and Ray
Parker, Arnold, 43–44, **43**
Parsons, Bill, 115
Payne, Hal, 82
Payne, Leon, 25, 35–36, 64–66, 137, 151
Pearl, Minnie, 13, 20, 122, 130, 133–34, 138, 148–49, **148**
Peer, Ralph, 29–30
Perryman, Tom, 160
Petty, Al, 25
Phelps, Jackie, 123
Phillips, Sam, 25, 34, 40, 50. *See also* Sun Records
Pierce, Don, **viii**, **xvi**, 48, **51**, **61**, **95**, **104**, **126**, **139**, **168**, **170**; on clash with Starns, 28; on founding Starday, 17–19; as with 4 Star, 8–9, 14–17; international marketing, 91, 105–6; life after Starday, 167–70; on marketing innovations, 105, 124–27, 130–39; on moving Starday to Nashville, 51–52; as record producer, 15, 54–55; sale of Starday, 160–63, 169; split with Pappy Daily, 75–78. *See also* Hollywood Records

Pierce, Webb, 8–9, 16, 33
Plastic Products pressings, 28, 52
Platters, 18, 49, 63, 74
Political Campaign Songs, 115–16
Poovey, "Groovey" Joe, 80, 82
Poteet, Theron, 23
Potter, "Cowboy" Bill, 20
Presley, Elvis, 34–37, 40–41, 49–50, 66, 82, 158, 164
Proctor, Joan, 143
Prophet, Orval, 154
Prysock, Arthur, 164
Pugh, John, 34, 47

Quest, Dan, 127, 143
Quinn, Bill, 23. *See also* Gold Star Recording Studio
Quonset Hut, 54, 77, 94, 97–99, **97**, 107

Rainbow Ranch Boys, 123
Raney, Wayne, 102–4, **104**, 152, 162
Rapp, Barney, 81, **81**
RCA Victor, 29, 82–83, 107, 110, 129–30
Recording bans, 24, 27
Recording contracts, 5–6, 9, 84
Reed, Ola Belle. *See* Campbell, Alex and Ola Belle
Reedy, John, 83, 102
Reeves, Jim, 12, 82, 123, 128. *See also* Blue Boys
Reid, Bill, 83, 102
Reid, Gary B., 72
Reid, Mary, 83, 102
Remington, Herb, 32, 47, 62
Reo Palm Isle, 5, 10
Rhodes, Jack, 25–26
Richardson, J. P. *See* Big Bopper
Richardson, Jimmy, 119
Richmond, Ace, 102
Riddle, George, 154
Riddle, Jimmie, 123, 136
Rimes, LeAnn, 156
Rite pressings, 227
Ritter, Tex, 132–33, 147, 149–50, **150**
Rivers, Jerry, 123, 136
Roberts, Kenny, 154–56, **156**, 163, 165, 169–70
Robinson, Jimmy, 96

Rockabilly recordings, 34–42, 49–50, 74, 79–82, 115, 119, 167
Rogers, Rock, 36. *See also* Payne, Leon
Rogers, Smokey, 119, 151
Roland, Adrian, 154
ROPE (Reunion of Professional Entertainers), 167–68
Rosenberg, Neil, 152–53
Royal Plastics pressings, 111, 127, 161, 227
Rural humor recordings, 93, 121–22, 148–49
Russell, Roy, 117
Ryan, Buck, 68

Satherley, Art, 3, 5–6
"Satisfied Mind, A," 25–29, 76, 140, 163, 170
Savoy Records, 25, 77
Schaible, Eddie. *See* Wilson, Eddie
Schucher, Herb, 126, **126**
Schwartz Brothers, 91
Scoggins, Hoyt, 43, 83, 102
Scoggins, Tyrone, 83
Scott, Buddy, 164
Sepolio, Tony, 32
Sexton, Delmer, 120
Sharp, Harold, 47
Sheet music, 5, 19, 29
Shelton, Allen, 117
Shepard, Jean, 25, 27–28, 145, 154
Shepard, Roy, 102
Shivers, Robert, 10
Shook, Jerry, 109
Shumate, Lewis, 92
Simpson, Jimmy, 43, 115, 119
Singer, Hal, 164
Singleton, Margie, 63–64, 77, 93
Singleton, Shelby, 63–64, 75, 78, 116
Sisk, Duck, 104
"Sixteen Chicks," 38–39
Skelton, Eddie, 80
Skinner, Jimmie, 23, 50, 69–70, 74–75, 78, 85, 91–92, 151–52, 166
Sloan, J. David, 158
Smith, Arthur "Guitar Boogie," 123–24, 153
Smith, Barney, 92
Smith, Bobby, 164
Smith, Carl, 36, 67, 168
Smith, Fiddlin' Arthur, 123–24, 127, 134

Smith, Hank, 51. *See also* Jones, George: as Thumper Jones
Smith, Jerry, 109
Smith, Tiny, 47
Smith, Vernon, 92
Smokey Mountain Boys, 123
Snoddy, Glenn, 107
Snow, Hank, 35, 60, 66–67, 123, 136. *See also* Rainbow Ranch Boys
Soundalike recordings, 35. *See also* Dixie Records: as *Hillbilly Hit Parade* series
Southlan Trio, 92, 102, 121
Sovine, Red, 27, 33–34, 62, 110, 136, 145–48, **145**, **148**, 156, 163, 165–66, 168
Sparks, Larry, 163
Spurling, Charles, 164
Square Dance Series, 75
Stanley, Carter. *See* Stanley Brothers
Stanley, Ralph. *See* Stanley Brothers
Stanley Brothers, 49, 71–73, 75, 83–85, **84**, 90–91, 99, 102, 105, 121, 167
Starcher, Buddy, 119, 123
Starday Music publishing, 76, 140, 162
Starday Sound Studios, **53**, 85, 95–96, **95**, 101, 107–10, **108**, 118–19, 122, 131, 136–37, **145**, 149, 156, **156–57**, 162–64
Starday-King Records, 116, 163–65, 167
Starnes, Bill, 13, 29
Starnes Kelley, Joyce, 9, 28
Starns, Jack, Jr., 3–7, **6**, 9, 13–14, 21, 25, 36–37; as club owner, 5, 10; contract dispute, 5–7, 9; departure from Starday, 27–29; on founding Starday, 9, 17; home studio, 20, 30, 39, 54
Starns Dupree, Neva, 3–4, 9–10, **10**, 13, 21; as club owner, 3, 5, 9, 13–14; departure from Starday, 28. *See also* Neva's Managing and Booking Agency
Starrite publishing, 17, 19, 23, 30, 38–39, 74, 76
Statesmen, 99
Stearns, June, 123
Steele, Bob, 115
Sterling, King, 43
Stewart, Redd, 151
Stoller, Mike, 165
Stoneman, Ernest V., and the Stoneman Family, 85, 121
Stoneman, Roni, 85
Stoneman, Scotty, 85, 88–89
Story, Carl, 49, 67, 70–71, **70**, 75, 83, 87, 102–3, 121, 166
Story, John, 107–8, 137
Stover, Smokey, 21, 48
Strevel, Burl, 102
Stringbean, 127, 167
Stripling, Chick, 86, **86**
Stubbs, Eddie, 89
Studio musicians: in Houston, 46–47, 62; in Nashville, 98, 109, 135–36
Sullivan, John. *See* Lonzo and Oscar
Sullivan, Phil, 93–94
Sullivan, Rollin. *See* Lonzo and Oscar
Sulphur Dell Speedways. *See* Figure eight races
Summey, Clell. *See* Cousin Jody
Sun Records, 25, 34, 37, 40, 50
Sunshine Boys, 20, 99–102, **101**, 104
"Sweet Love," 80–81
Swingtime Records, 18, 77

Taft-Hartley Labor Act, 27. *See also* Recording bans
"Tall Tall Trees," 59, 163, 165
Talmadge, Art, 51, 63, 74
Taylor, Earl, 120
"10 Little Bottles," 149–50, 152
Tennessee Recording and Publishing, 165–66
Terry, Gene, 44
Texas Ruby, 127–28
Thompson, Bobby, 70, 86–87, **86**
Tillis, Mel, 166
Tillman, Floyd, 151
Tipton, Riley, 80
Tomlin, Terry, 127
"Too Hot to Handle," 23
Topping, Ray, 36
Truck driving music, 115, 117–18, 142–49, 155, 157
Tubb, Ernest, 36–37, 66, 69, 72, 138, 154–55
Tubb, Justin, 59, 151
Tyler, T. Texas, 15–16, 65, 146, 151, 153

Upchurch Family, 102

INDEX

Vanity pressings. *See* Dixie Records: as custom label
Varney, Lowell, 120
Vern and Ray, 83
Vokes, Howard, 151

Wagoner, Porter, 20, 25, 27, 66, 138, 168, **168**
Walker, Charlie, 40, 74, 138
Wallace, Ed, 102
Wallace, Gerald, 102
Waller, Charlie, 88–89, **87**. *See also* Country Gentlemen
Watts, Slim, 20
Wayne, Paul, 119
WBAL (Baltimore, MD), 90
WBBL (Louisville, KY), 80
WCKY (Cincinnati, OH), 103
WCYB (Bristol, TN), 71
Weakley, Harold, 109
Wells, Kitty, 36, 52, 72, 94
WENO (Nashville, TN), 147
West, Dottie, 136–37, **136**, 141, 157
Western Cherokees, 5, 7, 9–10, 13, 59, 95; on backing "You All Come," 19–20; on group structure, 21–22
Wharton, Glendle "Pee Wee," 10
WHAS (Louisville, KY), 161
WHBB (Belton, SC), 104
Wheeler, Onie, 154
White, Robert, 120
Whitney, Boyd, 4
Whitney, Marva, 164
"Why Baby Why," 31–34, 48, 57, 76, 146
Wiggins, Little Roy, 123, 135
Willet, Slim, 42, 94
Williams, Don. *See* Don and Earl
Williams, Hank, Sr., 3, 31, 35, 45–46, 69, 95, 97, 123, 128, 143–45
Williams, Jimmy, 102, 121
Williams, Pete, 119
Williams, Vern. *See* Vern and Ray
Willis, Charles "Skeeter," 143–44. *See also* Willis Brothers
Willis, James "Guy," 143–44. *See also* Willis Brothers
Willis, John "Vic," 135–36, 140, 143–45. *See also* Willis Brothers
Willis Brothers, 20, 49, 134, 136, 143–45, **144**
Wilson, Eddie, 140
Wilson, Lonnie "Pap," 122
Wimberly, Bill, 68
Winn, George, 120
Wise, Fiddlin' Chubby, 123
Wiseman, Scott. *See* Lulu Belle and Scotty
WJJD (Chicago, IL), 35, 66, 99
WLAC (Nashville, TN), 110
WLW (Cincinnati, OH), 100, 111
WNOX (Knoxville, TN), 111, 129
Wray, Doug, 44–45
Wray, Link, 44–45
Wray, Lucky, 44–45
Wright Brothers, 83
WSM (Nashville, TN), 53, 106, 112–13, 123, 138, 161
WSPA (Spartanburg, SC), 104
Wynn, "Little" Willie, 101

XERF (Del Rio, TX), 35
XERL (Del Rio, TX), 66

"Y'all Come." *See* "You All Come"
York, William, 85–86. *See also* Pierce, Don
"You All Come," 13–14, 18–20, 25, 29, 76
Young, Faron, 20, 23, 27, 59, 64–65, 78, 133–34, 136, 168
Young, Nelson, 81, **81**

www.ingramcontent.com/pod-product-compliance
Lightning Source LLC
Chambersburg PA
CBHW021836220426
43663CB00005B/269